FORECLOSURE PREVENTION COUNSELING

Preserving the American Dream

NATIONAL CONSUMER LAW CENTER PUBLICATIONS

BOOKS FOR COUNSELORS AND CONSUMERS

Foreclosure Prevention Counseling
Stop Predatory Lending
Bankruptcy Basics
NCLC Guide to Surviving Debt
NCLC Guide to The Rights of Utility Consumers
NCLC Guide to Consumer Rights for Domestic Violence Survivors
NCLC Guide to Mobile Homes
Return to Sender: Getting a Refund or Replacement for Your Lemon Car

LEGAL PRACTICE MANUALS

Debtor Rights Library

Consumer Bankruptcy Law and Practice
Fair Debt Collection
Foreclosures
Repossessions
Student Loan Law
Access to Utility Service

Credit and Banking Library

Truth in Lending
Fair Credit Reporting
Consumer Banking and Payments Law
The Cost of Credit
Credit Discrimination

Consumer Litigation Library

Consumer Arbitration Agreements
Consumer Class Actions
Consumer Law Pleadings

Deception and Warranties Library

Unfair and Deceptive Acts and Practices
Automobile Fraud
Consumer Warranty Law

Also for Lawyers

NCLC REPORTS Newsletter
Consumer Law in a Box CD-Rom
The Practice of Consumer Law

For information on all NCLC titles visit:
www.consumerlaw.org

FORECLOSURE PREVENTION COUNSELING

Preserving the American Dream

Elizabeth Renuart

Odette Williamson

Mark Benson

With Contributing Authors
Alys Cohen, Charlie Harak, Deanne Loonin,
John Rao, Diane Thompson, Steve Tripoli,
Tara Twomey, Chi Chi Wu

National Consumer Law Center

The National Consumer Law Center (NCLC), a nonprofit corporation founded in 1969, assists consumers, counselors, advocates, and public policy makers nationwide who use the powerful and complex tools of consumer law to ensure justice and fair treatment for all, particularly those whose poverty renders them powerless to demand accountability from the economic marketplace. For more information, go to www.consumerlaw.org.

Order NCLC Publications securely on-line at www.consumerlaw.org, or contact Publications Department, National Consumer Law Center, 77 Summer Street, Boston, MA 02110, (617) 542-9595, FAX: (617) 542-8028, e-mail: publications@nclc.org.

NCLC Training and Conferences are posted at www.consumerlaw.org. NCLC participates in numerous national, regional, and local consumer law trainings. Its annual fall conference is a forum for consumer rights attorneys and others to share insights into common problems and explore novel and tested approaches that promote consumer justice in the marketplace.

Comments and Corrections can be sent to the above address to the attention of the Editorial Department or e-mail consumerlaw@nclc.org.

About the Authors

Elizabeth Renuart is an NCLC staff attorney focusing on home ownership issues, Truth in Lending, consumer credit, and predatory lending. She is author of *Stop Predatory Lending* (2002), co-author of *Truth in Lending* (5th ed. 2003), *The Cost of Credit* (3d ed. 2005), and the editor of NCLC REPORTS, *Consumer Credit & Usury Edition*. Prior to joining NCLC, she was the managing attorney of a legal services office in Baltimore, Maryland, where she litigated cases involving mortgage lending, Truth in Lending, usury, deceptive practices, and fraud. She has been a legal services attorney for over twenty-five years.

Odette Williamson is an NCLC staff attorney with a focus on sustainable homeownership, consumer credit and foreclosure prevention and is co-author of *Foreclosures* (2005). She formerly was an assistant attorney general with the Consumer Protection Division of the Massachusetts Attorney General's Office.

Mark Benson has been a consultant to NCLC for ten years, coordinating and conducting foreclosure prevention training. He was also head of the Housing Counseling Division of St. Ambrose Housing Aid Center in Maryland. He is a past president of both the National Shared Housing Resource Center and the Maryland Center for Community Development.

The Contributing Authors are: Alys Cohen, Charlie Harak, Deanne Loonin, John Rao, Diane Thompson, Steve Tripoli, Tara Twomey, Chi Chi Wu.

Acknowledgments

This volume is derived from training materials for housing counselors that NCLC wrote in 2006, entitled *Preserving the American Dream: Foreclosure Prevention for FHA-Insured and Other Mortgage Loans*. We want to thank Carolyn Carter and Jonathan Sheldon for converting these training materials into book form; Denise Lisio for editorial supervision; Nathan Day for editorial assistance; Julie Gallagher for design and typesetting; Lightbourne Images for cover design; Shannon Halbrook and Svetlana Ladan for CD-Rom design; and Mary McLean for indexing. Also thanks to Annie St. John and Ariel Patterson for research; and to Rich Dubois for helping to shepherd this project along. Financial support for the training materials was received from the United States Department of Housing and Urban Development, but the views expressed herein are solely those of the National Consumer Law Center. Finally, we want to especially thank Gary Klein who first developed a project at NCLC to encourage mortgage workouts and who was a principal author of NCLC's first materials in this area.

Contents

PART IV
Advanced Topics

PART
I

Getting Started

CHAPTER 1

The Foreclosure Process

Who Should Use This Book. This book is designed for those counseling homeowners threatened with foreclosure, whether they are housing counselors or any other type of counselor. This handbook is also appropriate for attorneys who seek to help clients establish workout plans with lenders, but attorneys should also utilize NCLC's *Foreclosures*, a more detailed legal practice manual examining foreclosure defenses and challenges to mortgage servicing abuses. Homeowners may also find this volume helpful, but they should be cautioned that this is not a self-help manual and it is geared to those with some familiarity with lending and mortgage issues.

This handbook focuses on workout options for home mortgages. While it touches on other strategies to respond to non-mortgage debt, other NCLC books may be more appropriate to help consumers with more general debt problems. The *NCLC Guide to Surviving Debt* covers all types of problems faced by families in financial distress: debt collection; collection lawsuits; evictions; student loan garnishments; car repossessions; credit reporting problems; credit card debt; which debts to pay first; income tax collections; credit counseling; and much more.

The *NCLC Guide to the Rights of Utility Consumers* focuses on utility terminations, unaffordable utility bills, and ways to reduce utility payments. The *NCLC Guide to Consumer Rights for Domestic Violence Survivors* focuses on the unique debt and other consumer issues that survivors face. NCLC's *Stop Predatory Lending* is another related volume that examines various forms of abusive lending, both in the mortgage and the non-mortgage context.

How This Book Is Organized. This handbook consists of four parts, appendices, and a CD-Rom. Part I, Getting Started, examines a number of preliminary issues. Chapter 1 is an introduction to the foreclosure process and the counselor's role. Chapter 2 lays out fourteen steps to foreclosure prevention. Chapter 3 examines the abusive side of mortgage lending, to help counselors inform homeowners about the pitfalls to avoid and also to help counselors recognize illegal loan transactions that should be referred to an attorney. Chapter 4 lays out a number of steps that the homeowner can take to reduce payments on non-mortgage debt and to otherwise improve the family's financial picture to make a mortgage loan workout more feasible.

Part II analyzes the workout process in detail. Chapter 5 is an overview, examining the mechanics of arranging a workout, irrespective of the type of loan. The next three chapters of Part II detail workout options for particular types of loans. Chapter 6 covers loans purchased by Fannie Mae and Freddie Mac, and also examines subprime loans. Chapter 7 focuses on FHA-insured loans, and Chapter 8 considers VA-guaranteed loans and loans extended by or guaranteed by the Rural Housing Service. Finally, Chapter 9 considers the tax and credit rating implications of a workout.

Part III takes a more aggressive stance regarding pending foreclosure, in effect challenging the lender's right to seize the home. Chapter 10 examines various legal defenses the homeowner may have to a threatened foreclosure. Chapter 11 surveys the homeowner's right to use bankruptcy to stop a threatened foreclosure. Chapter 12 details situations where the homeowner should dispute the amount owed on the mortgage and thus whether in fact there is a default. Chapter 13 considers homeowner options after the foreclosure sale, including steps that can be taken to recover the home.

Part IV is devoted to advanced topics, issues that a more experienced counselor may want to review, but which are not essential to someone just learning how to work with distressed homeowners. Chapter 14 reviews the securitization process for home mortgages and the role of MERS in the foreclosure process. Chapter 15 is a brief guide to how to dispute information in the consumer's credit report, and also other laws that provide special consumer rights to dispute certain debts and charges.

The Appendices provide much useful information for the counselor, including a bibliography, helpful websites, a glossary, a special glossary of servicing terms, and an index. Appendix A provides various forms and checklists that are essential to foreclosure prevention counseling: a foreclosure prevention intake form; a foreclosure prevention counseling checklist; an authorization to release information form; a request for information from loan servicer; a sample qualified written request; and a homeowner's checklist for avoiding foreclosure. Appendix B provides a guide to shopping for a credit card. Appendix C contains information on the Earned Income Tax Credit.

Appendix D contains sample loan and other documents. Appendix E is a summary of state foreclosure laws and Appendix F is a summary of state real estate tax abatement laws. Appendix G contains an answer sheet for the questions asked the reader at the end of Chapter 3.

The CD-Rom accompanying this handbook contains the appendix materials and much more. A listing of the CD-Rom contents and how to use the CD-Rom is detailed at the end of this book.

INCREASING PREVALENCE OF FORECLOSURES

Foreclosures today are much more prevalent than they were a generation before. From 1980 to 2006 the per capita rate of homeownership has increased 5.2%, while the number of foreclosures (prime and subprime combined) per residential mortgage has increased over 155%! The actual number of foreclosures a year will vary each year depending on economic conditions and other factors. But in recent years, the number of annual foreclosures have always been well over half a million, and in some years much more than that.

There are many causes for the increase in foreclosures. One is the growing number of two income families. Statistically, a family with two incomes is at a greater risk of foreclosure. Because mortgage payments rely on the income of both incomes, there is a much greater chance that something will disrupt this income flow. If either of two wage-earners loses a job or becomes sick, the income may be lowered dramatically. If a child or other relative is seriously sick, there may not be an alternative but for a wage earner to leave work and care for the child. Divorce can have catastrophic results. Another cause for the increase in foreclosures

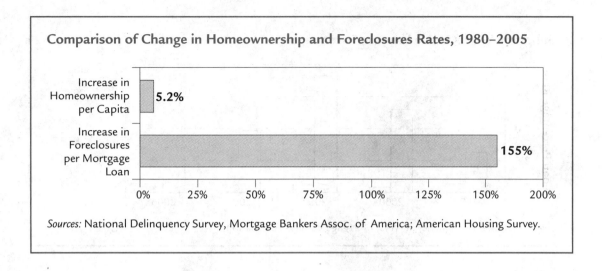

is health care. Spiraling medical costs and increases in the numbers of Americans without health insurance adds to the instability of the average American family's finances.

Foreclosures are also on the rise as the result of the increasing indebtedness of the average homeowner. Home prices have been rising faster than inflation, and homeowners have been taking out larger and larger mortgages to purchase them. In addition, lenders have been aggressively offering home equity lending as a means for consumers to borrow. The tax code which makes mortgage interest deductible is an incentive to borrow against the home. As shown by the next chart, mortgage debt is growing much faster than home equity. In 1989, total home-secured debt was at about 45% of the value of all homes, but in 2004 that had increased to almost 60%. Looked at in another way, while homeowner equity increased 16.7% from 1989 to 2004, home-secured debt increased 102.6%.

Mortgage debt to income ratios are also higher today than they were a decade or two ago, as are the costs of homes, even adjusted for inflation, particularly in certain communities. In addition, the amount of non-mortgage debt held by the typical American family has skyrocketed.

There has also been an enormous growth in subprime mortgage lending, and those mortgages have much, much higher foreclosure rates—over ten times the rate of prime loans

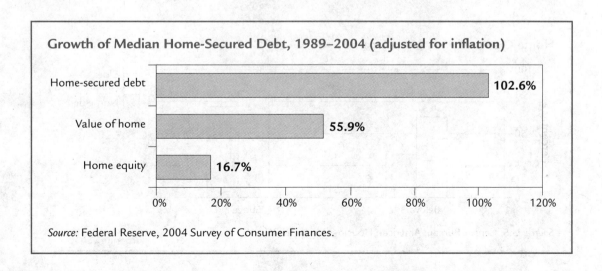

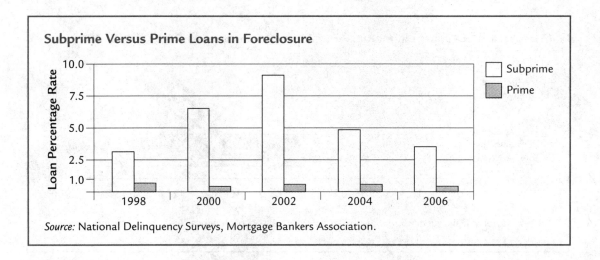

Subprime Versus Prime Loans in Foreclosure

Source: National Delinquency Surveys, Mortgage Bankers Association.

on average. Lenders in recent years also have been aggressively offering adjustable rate mortgages, sometimes with low teaser rates that rise dramatically over time.

In addition, increases in predatory lending affect foreclosure rates. There are cases where brokers and loan originators arrange mortgage loans to those who they know cannot afford to repay them. The broker or originator still gets paid, and in any event the home's value may protect the lender when the inevitable foreclosure occurs. In property flipping schemes and cases involving appraisal fraud, brokers, realtors, and others may have incentives to push homeowners into unaffordable mortgages even if the eventual mortgage holder loses money upon foreclosure.

Predatory loans may particularly target elders, who have built up equity over the years, but who may lack financial sophistication to review loan terms. Elders also are likely to be on fixed incomes after retirement, with few options to deal with unexpected expenses. Elders are more likely to own homes than non-elders, and this is most marked among those below the federal poverty level. Homeownership rates among elders below the federal poverty line are almost double that of non-elders below the poverty line.

The mortgage lending business has also changed. It is no longer predominated by local savings banks servicing loans that they originate. Instead, those originating the loan will quickly divest themselves of any servicing responsibility. There is also increasing concentration in the servicing market. Rather than a local bank, the servicer is more and more likely to

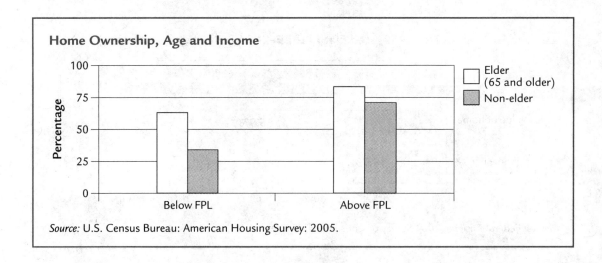

Home Ownership, Age and Income

Source: U.S. Census Bureau: American Housing Survey: 2005.

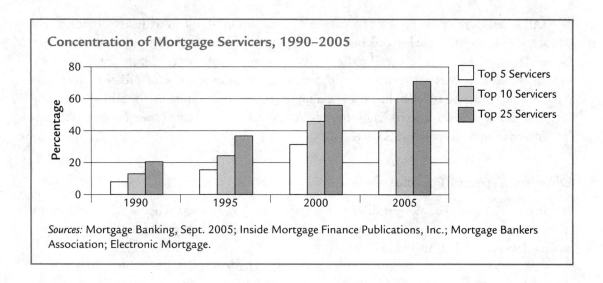

be a corporation with a national scope. As the chart above indicates, the top ten servicers now handle most mortgage servicing, while in 1990 they only handled 13%.

Changes in servicer concentration has happened at the same time as changes in collection tactics in the mortgage industry. Deregulation of the lending industry has also meant less government supervision not only over interest rates, but over every other aspect of the loan transaction.

UNDERSTANDING THE FORECLOSURE PROCESS

What Is Foreclosure?

Foreclosure occurs when real property is sold to satisfy an unpaid debt. The debt is often a home mortgage, but foreclosure can happen because of other liens, too. Tax liens, mechanics' liens, and other debts can lead to foreclosure of the home.

Foreclosure—the process by which the home is sold—is governed by state law. Advocates and counselors must be aware of the laws governing the process in their states. A summary of the foreclosure laws in each state is found at Appendix E, below.

The foreclosure process may also be limited by the terms of the note and mortgage or requirements of the mortgage insurer. FHA, VA, Freddie Mac, and Fannie Mae all impose additional requirements as to the foreclosure of homes where they insure the mortgage.

Prerequisites to Foreclosure

In order for there to be a foreclosure, there must first be a default. Generally, this default is a failure to make current payments on the mortgage, but it could also be selling the property without permission or failing to pay current taxes, for example. The note and mortgage will set out what constitutes a default and list the lender's remedies.

If required under the terms of the mortgage or deed of trust, the servicer will send the borrower a notice of default that permits the homeowner to become current by paying all amounts due. This right also exists under the laws of some states. If the homeowner does not "cure" the default, the servicer or the foreclosing attorney usually sends an "acceleration" letter. This letter tells the homeowner that the *entire* balance is now due and owing, not just the arrearage.

All states permit the borrower a period of time after default in which to "redeem" the property. This requires paying off the loan in full, plus any accrued costs—past-due interest, lawyers' fees, or monies advanced by the lender to cover escrow shortfalls are some common examples. Most homeowners who are in financial difficulty cannot afford the lump-sum payment necessary to redeem, but may be able to redeem by refinancing or selling the property. Usually borrowers have the right to redeem the property up until the sale date, but state law governs the final redemption date.

Different Types of Foreclosure

If reinstatement or redemption does not occur, state law dictates whether the foreclosure must happen through a judicial or a non-judicial process. A description of each state's foreclosure law is found at Appendix E, below.

Two states, Connecticut and Vermont, permit strict foreclosure, which requires a court order but transfers title to the lender without a sale. The results of strict foreclosure can be grossly unfair to borrowers when the property is worth more than the amount of the debt. The foreclosing lender gets title without regard to the amount owed. The borrowers lose all of their equity and the lender gets a windfall.

Four states (Maine, Massachusetts, New Hampshire, and Rhode Island) permit lenders to combine a power of sale foreclosure with the right to foreclose by entry and possession. This means that the lender physically enters onto the property and takes possession. Some limitations on this process may make it less inviting to lenders. For example, in Massachusetts, a lender must also conduct a foreclosure sale but provide the homeowner with three years to redeem the property, thus tying up clear title for a significant period of time.

Judicial Foreclosure

All states permit judicial foreclosure. However, in just under half of the states, mortgages or deeds of trust must always be foreclosed judicially. In a state where the judicial process is not required, a lender may choose to use judicial foreclosure for various reasons, including to clear title problems or to obtain a deficiency judgment. If the mortgage lacks a power of sale clause, the lender must foreclose judicially. A judicial foreclosure usually takes longer than a non-judicial foreclosure, ranging from six months to two years.

Typically, a judicial foreclosure goes through the following steps after default:

- Filing of a complaint;
- Service of the complaint upon the homeowner;
- A hearing on the sufficiency of complaint (if the borrower does not appear or is unrepresented, this hearing will usually be cursory, and there may not be any hearing at all if the homeowner does not file a written answer to the complaint);
- A date set for redemption;
- A date set for sale;
- The sale, usually conducted by a public officer appointed by the court; and
- Confirmation of the sale.

In most cases, the borrower may remain in the home through the confirmation of sale, or even longer, according to state law.

During this process, before the sale date, the homeowner has a right to enter an appearance and contest the foreclosure. The borrower can defend the foreclosure either because there are problems with the procedure the lender used (a notice was not served correctly, for example) or because there is a substantive defense to the mortgage. Substantive defenses include the fact that the borrower is current or that the lender violated state or federal law in making the loan.

At the time of filing the complaint, the foreclosing lawyer in some states will also file a "*lis pendens*" with the county recorder's office. This provides notice of the foreclosure and is one source for foreclosure rescue scammers to identify homeowners in foreclosure.

Non-Judicial Foreclosure

In over half of the states and the District of Columbia, foreclosing lenders may sell the property without court action. They may do this only if the mortgage or deed of trust contains a power of sale clause. A power of sale clause allows the mortgagee, after notice of default to the borrower, to sell the property without first going to court. The actual notice given must comply with both the mortgage and state law. Some states require further notices after sale.

The steps after default in a non-judicial foreclosure are as follows:

- Notice of default;
- Notice of sale;
- Foreclosure sale.

Non-judicial foreclosure can proceed quickly and take from as little as one month to one year to complete. If the borrower wishes to challenge or stop the foreclosure, the borrower must file either bankruptcy or a suit for an injunction.

Eviction of the Homeowner

After the foreclosure sale, confirmation of the sale, or expiration of the redemption period (whichever is latest), the borrower loses all legal interest in the home. Some states provide for a period after the confirmation that the homeowner may remain in the home. Whether a separate action is required to evict the homeowner is dependent on state law. Most non-judicial states require a separate eviction action to be brought. This may or may not happen in the regular eviction court where tenants are also evicted, depending on state law. Some judicial foreclosure states permit an order of possession to be entered in the foreclosure proceeding. The order may then be enforced by the sheriff without further court proceedings, providing the occupant was named in the foreclosure action.

Consequences of Foreclosure

No one wins in a foreclosure. For the homeowner, the consequences are most obvious. The homeowner loses the home, and may have difficulty finding alternative living arrangements. The homeowner's new living situation may mean loss of easy access to friends, former neighbors, work, and other established relationships. Elders in particular may be forced into restricted living environments. The homeowner is also likely to lose any equity in the home, and may even owe a deficiency. The homeowner's credit rating will be severely damaged. Moving expenses can be considerable, and personal property may be left behind, lost, or damaged in the move.

Stress on the family will be immense. Others living in the house will also lose their shelter, and will often need to pay more for new housing. There can even be unexpected negative tax consequences, as described below in Chapter 9.

The mortgage holder will often be a loser as well. Overall, mortgage holders do not get all their money back after foreclosure. The mortgage holder will often sell the home for much less than it is worth and for less than the amount owed on the mortgage. It may be difficult or impossible to collect any deficiency. Various expenses may never be recouped. And of course the mortgage holder was expecting to make a profit from an ongoing stream of mortgage payments, which never materialize. The mortgage holder has also lost a customer, someone who might have taken out additional loans in the future or have purchased other products or services from the lender.

A rash of foreclosures can also have a negative impact on a whole community. The foreclosed houses can end up abandoned, and property can deteriorate. There is an increased potential for vandalism and crime. Property values for the whole neighborhood can drop, and with that a reduction in the locality's tax base. Neighbors will be lost, and with that a loss of community cohesiveness.

The Workout As an Alternative to Foreclosure

For most homeowners, the most effective way to stave off foreclosure is to enter into a workout agreement with the mortgage holder, so that the loan terms are reworked in a way that the consumer can afford to make both the past-due and future payments. This may involve paying out past-due amounts over time, a change in the length of the mortgage, a change in the interest rate, or even a change in the type of mortgage.

Much of this handbook is dedicated to examining the homeowner's workout options. The homeowner's ability to enter into a workout may depend on who owns the mortgage, who services the mortgage for the owner, and who insures the mortgage. For example, Chapter 4 examines workout options for mortgages insured by the Federal Housing Administration (FHA). Chapter 5 looks at those options for mortgages insured by the U.S. Department of Veterans Affairs (VA) and the Rural Housing Service (RHS), or for mortgages purchased by Fannie Mae or Freddie Mac. No matter who owns or insures a loan, including a private mortgage insurance company, the homeowner in most cases will begin the workout process with the entity servicing the mortgage. Servicers are examined in Chapters 5, 14, below.

Another key to a workout solution in a threatened foreclosure is to determine what payments the homeowner can realistically make under a workout plan. This will involve not only establishing a budget for the homeowner, but also determining if there are practical ways that the homeowner can increase income and reduce expenses. These strategies are outlined below in Chapter 3 and at a more advanced level in Chapter 12.

THE ROLE OF THE COUNSELOR

In many communities, housing counselors play an important role bridging the worlds of the homeowner, community, lender, and insurer. Sometimes, the interests of each of these parties are not the same and the counselor's role is made even more complicated. The following suggestions are among the issues to consider when serving as a housing counselor working with homeowners who are behind on their mortgages:

Understand the Counselor's Role. In general, the counselor's role is to provide all the information that homeowners need to make informed choices concerning their homes.

Be Fully Informed on All Options. This body of knowledge continues to evolve as lenders, insurers, and the secondary market amend practices in response to changing conditions. The counselor should be in a position to receive new information as it becomes available. Not being fully informed as a counselor is a grave disservice to the homeowner and prevents full examination of all of the options. Giving out anything less than all of the information could be considered "steering" or even negligence.

Admit Any Limitations. It is the responsible thing to admit any limitation in knowledge to the homeowner and offer to find out the information.

Educate, Do Not Advise. Unless the counselor is an attorney, any advice the counselor gives could be considered the unlicensed practice of law. Counselors should be especially careful when talking to homeowners about issues that involve legal rights.

Disclose Any Bias the Counselor May Have. It is fine for the counselor to have a bias as long as the homeowner understands why the counselor feels that way. For example, the counselor may believe it is a lost cause to submit a partial claim request to ABC Mortgage Corp. because they have never approved one. The homeowner may still choose that option.

Disclose Personal Limitations. If the homeowner wants the counselor to do something which goes beyond the counselor's limits of propriety, the counselor should decline to do it and explain why. The counselor should give the homeowner a referral, if possible, where the homeowners can pursue their choice.

Disclose Any Fee Related to the Counseling Session. If the homeowner is expected to pay anything for the counselor's services, that should be disclosed before the appointment is finalized. Agencies which receive HUD counseling funds are prohibited from charging HUD homeowners for counseling. It is appropriate to explain what funding sources are making this counseling session available to the homeowner. It is not ethical counseling to push for a certain outcome because a funder demands that result without disclosing that bias.

Confidentiality. The information given to the counselor by the homeowner is of a highly personal nature and should not be shared with anyone without the homeowner's consent.

CHAPTER 2

Fourteen Steps to Foreclosure Prevention

This chapter provides a fourteen step checklist for foreclosure prevention counseling. It does not include every issue that might come up in a particular case, nor will every step be necessary in every case. Each case will have different issues that must be treated on an individual basis. More detail on these fourteen steps and other aspects of foreclosure prevention counseling is found in the later chapters.

Step 1: Understand the homeowner's objectives and needs. Homeowners seek foreclosure counseling for many different reasons. Counselors should provide help consistent with the homeowner's needs. For example, a homeowner who wants help proving to a lender that she has made a particular payment that the lender claims not to have received needs a different type of counseling than someone who wants to put a foreclosure avoidance plan in place.

In determining whether the homeowner's objective is realistic, the counselor should not make snap decisions, but should reserve judgment until obtaining a complete understanding of the homeowner's financial situation. Even where the homeowner's objective is clearly unobtainable, an investigation of the homeowner's financial situation will help the counselor to suggest alternative housing and other resources that might be available.

In addition, homeowners in default on their mortgage loans are often behind on other bills, and may be receiving many calls and letters from debt collectors. These aggressive debt collection tactics may be a distraction that prevents the homeowners from focusing on the task at hand—curing the mortgage delinquency. In this situation, the counselor might first help the homeowner stop the debt collectors' dunning notices and telephone calls. Detailed information on how to deal with debt collectors is set out in the *NCLC Guide to Surviving Debt*. Chapter 4, below, also provides information on dealing with the homeowner's other bills.

Step 2: Determine any time constraints in the case. At the outset, identify any deadlines that the homeowner faces, especially any foreclosure sale date, and tell the homeowner to contact the counselor *immediately* upon receipt of any notices related to foreclosure. A completed foreclosure sale typically will terminate a homeowner's ability to put a foreclosure alternative in place. If the homeowner is unaware of a foreclosure sale date, the counselor should find out if one has been set, usually from the entity servicing the mortgage loan or by the servicer's attorney. The servicer may be the originating lender, the lender holding the loan, or a completely different party.

The homeowner usually knows who is servicing the loan, because the homeowner makes mortgage payments to that entity and that entity will be sending the homeowner delinquency notices. The lender holding the mortgage and an attorney representing the homeowner are other possible sources as to the identity of the servicer. (Obtaining the name of the servicer from "MERS" is also discussed in Chapter 14, below.)

Step 3: Establish the reasons for the default and prepare a hardship letter. Explore and document the reasons for the default. This will help prepare a hardship letter and will provide some clue as to the economic problems that need to be resolved to restore stability and prevent foreclosure. In drafting a hardship letter to the party to whom mortgage payments are sent, use the homeowner's own words, whenever possible, and have the homeowners sign and date it.

Step 4: Prepare a *current* budget. The heart of the counseling process is to determine the amount of money that the homeowner will have available on a monthly basis to devote to mortgage payments. Both income and expenses must be evaluated. The goal is to help the homeowner establish a budget that maximizes the amount available to make mortgage payments but is realistic given the homeowner's situation.

The first step in this process is to establish the homeowner's *current* income and expenses as realistically as possible. This step will also help determine whether realistic and appropriate choices are being made and whether there are ways to increase income or reduce expenses that will free up additional money for ongoing mortgage payments. To determine current income and expenses, use worksheets to make the necessary calculations. A sample worksheet is found in Appendix A, below, and on the CD-Rom accompanying this handbook. In evaluating the expenses, the counselor should make sure that the homeowner is not *understating* some expenses, such as food costs. If so, the plan may fail if the expenses are not realistic.

Step 5: Consider ways to increase the homeowner's income or available cash. Determine if there are ways to increase the amount of income or other assets that the homeowner can devote to mortgage payments, including the following:

- Does the homeowner qualify for public assistance, food stamps, or medical benefits that she is not taking advantage of?
- Does the homeowner have assets other than the home that can be sold to generate money to contribute to a foreclosure avoidance plan on the mortgage? Some examples may be life insurance policies, unnecessary automobiles, boats, vacation homes, valuable collectibles, retirement benefits that go beyond legitimate needs, stocks, bonds, etc. The homeowner may have to make difficult choices in this area.
- Does the homeowner have a realistic possibility of increasing employment income in the short term, based on job prospects, return from disability leave, or the ability to take on a second job or overtime hours? If the homeowner has realistic possibilities and needs some time to see if they can be realized, this may be a basis to request forbearance from the mortgage holder to delay foreclosure.
- Does the homeowner have a realistic possibility of a lump-sum award from Social Security, workers' compensation, or a lawsuit? Does she have a right to a tax refund that will not be offset by a tax intercept (e.g., for child support)? If so, this can be treated as an asset that can be used to deal with the default.
- Is there a relative who is willing to help out? If so, what can be done to formalize the arrangement in order to make the income from the relative something that the

homeowner and mortgage holder can reasonably rely on in making a strategy for a foreclosure avoidance plan?

■ For multi-family properties, is there a way to create or increase rental income? If the problem is nonpayment by a tenant, can something be worked out on a cooperative basis with the tenant? If not, can eviction and a replacement tenant be managed quickly? If the problem is that the income producing unit is not rented, is there a way to assist in getting the property rented soon? If repairs are necessary, is there assistance available to help get those done?

Step 6: Consider ways to reduce the homeowner's other financial obligations. There are two reasons to address the homeowner's other obligations. Reducing the amount owed will free up more money to contribute to a foreclosure avoidance plan. Just as importantly, default in some of these other obligations may threaten the homeowner's ability to stay in the home. Each type of expense must be addressed individually.

Other Mortgages
Preventing foreclosure by the first mortgage holder will be an empty gesture if another mortgage lender has the right to foreclose. Therefore, a plan must be worked out to deal with second mortgage payments. If it is a high rate or other abusive mortgage, sometimes a legal defense can wipe out the debt entirely or reduce it significantly. In that case, the homeowner should be referred to an attorney with experience in consumer law. At the same time, a plan must be made for the legitimate amount of the debt that covers both current payments and any default.

Property Taxes, and Tax and Water Liens
If the taxes are collected as part of the escrow, they will most likely be paid by the servicer, even if the homeowner is in default. These amounts will be part of the arrears. However, if the taxes are not collected and paid through escrow, they have to be dealt with as an item in the homeowner's budget. If they are not paid, a lien will result, and it is even possible that the taxing authority will seek to foreclose.

Most taxing authorities have special programs for people who can afford to pay a debt in installments. Available exemptions and deferrals also should be examined to determine if the tax bill can be lowered. Depending on the locality, these may include residential exemptions, elder and disability exemptions, veteran exemptions, and hardship deferrals. Various property tax abatement rights are set out by state in Appendix F, below. If property is over-assessed, another approach is to challenge this assessment, although this may require that the taxes first be up to date.

Failure to pay water and sewer bills also can result in a lien on the property, and that lien will be a default under the mortgage. Water conservation may be useful, as discussed below in connection with other utility bills.

Property Insurance
The servicer may or may not be collecting the homeowner's insurance premium as part of the escrow. In either case, available reductions should be explored with the homeowner's insurance agent. The property should be insured for the value of the dwelling rather than for the full value of the property, because the land itself cannot burn down.

Homeowners should also be aware that if the insurance is not paid and therefore canceled, or if the lender does not have proof of coverage, the lender will get a new insurance policy that usually protects only its interest. This insurance is called "force placed insurance" and it may be three or four times more expensive than regular policies. The lender may add its cost to the mortgage payment or demand a lump-sum payment. Homeowners should provide lenders with proof of coverage or obtain coverage on their own.

Private Mortgage Insurance

When the homeowner's original down payment is less than twenty percent of the purchase price, lenders often require private mortgage insurance (PMI), that protects the lender in case of default, and that the homeowner pays for in each month's mortgage payment. The federal Homeowner's Protection Act of 1998 requires PMI to be canceled automatically or at the homeowner's request when the amount of equity in the home reaches a certain level. Homeowners having trouble making their mortgage payments will always benefit by eliminating this insurance. More information about private mortgage insurance can be found in Chapter 5, below.

Other Liens

Other creditors may have liens on the property as a result of a court judgment. This may make them more aggressive about collection because they can "execute" (foreclose) on their liens if they are not paid. A plan should be worked out to deal with these creditors, but not at the expense of payments on the first mortgage. Judgment liens can be treated as a lower priority because these creditors in most cases prefer to sit and wait for the property to be sold and their liens to be paid from the proceeds. They do so to avoid incurring the costs of selling the property on their liens. (Note that this dynamic may be different in some areas, where there is more of a tradition of holding sales of property based on judgments.) In addition, in some cases a home with not a lot of equity may be fully protected under a state homestead exemption from seizure because of a court judgment.

Utilities

It is important to address utility payments not only because of their financial drain on the homeowner, but because termination of electricity or gas could make the home uninhabitable. Ways of addressing utility bills and terminations are explored in more detail in Chapter 4, below, and in much more detail in the *NCLC Guide to the Rights of Utility Consumers.* But in a nutshell:

- Check the availability for lower income homeowners of government assistance with heating or cooling costs through LIHEAP (Low Income Home Energy Assistance Payments). Applications should be made through the local energy assistance agency.
- Determine if a low income homeowner qualifies for a rate discount with the utility company. Applications should be made directly to the utility company.
- Consider energy conservation options as a means to reduce bills on a forward going basis, including applying for a home energy audit from the local utility companies or weatherization benefits through the local energy assistance agency.
- For dealing with past bills, the homeowner should ask the utility company to let her pay off the debt in installments. The agreements should be for the longest possible term and should minimize the required initial lump sum.
- Determine if state law prevents shut off during certain months, or for elder homeowners or those with significant medical problems. If the homeowner qualifies, past bills can be treated as a slightly lower priority.

Home Repair Needs

There is no point to protecting a home that is uninhabitable because the homeowner cannot afford basic repairs. The mortgage holder may be willing to consider paying for some home repair costs if they are essential to preserving the collateral. Alternatively, home repair grant programs and other assistance should be evaluated. Home equity loans should be treated as a last resort since they will increase the burden on the homeowner to make monthly payments to retain the home.

Credit Card Bills, Medical Bills, and Other Unsecured Debts
Failing to pay credit card bills, medical debts, and other unsecured debts can have a negative effect on the homeowner's credit rating. However, if the homeowner's credit rating already shows a mortgage default or a threatened foreclosure, failure to pay these unsecured debts probably will not make it worse. Nonetheless, no money should be paid on these debts (not even minimum payments) ahead of the mortgage payments, since these types of creditors cannot foreclose on the property except in very rare circumstances. These homeowners may want to contact theses creditors and explain that they are unable to pay at the moment but will start paying as soon as they can. Only if there is money left over after a foreclosure avoidance plan is implemented should that money be devoted to pay on these debts. Additional information regarding credit card bills and other unsecured debt is included in Chapter 4, below, and can be found in even more detail in the *NCLC Guide to Surviving Debt*.

Student Loans
Student loans are a special case of unsecured debt since non-payment can result in seizure of the homeowner's tax refunds and certain other government benefits, and to partial seizure of the homeowner's wages. On government student loans, the monthly payments can almost always be reduced. Homeowners should call their student loan agency and insist on "a reasonable and affordable payment agreement" or consider a loan consolidation. Additional information regarding student loans is included in Chapter 4, below, and can be found in even more detail in the *NCLC Guide to Surviving Debt*.

Other Expenses
Each and every other expense should be evaluated to see if it can be realistically reduced or eliminated. In some cases the homeowner may be faced with tough choices, such as eliminating a $50 per month smoking habit in order to make that money available for a foreclosure avoidance proposal. Obviously, the counselor can make suggestions. Final choices need to be left up to the homeowners.

Step 7: Ask the homeowner to start putting money aside to commit to the foreclosure avoidance plan. Once a realistic budget is reached and it is clear how much is available each month to commit to the mortgage, if the homeowner wants to try to keep her property, have her begin to put money aside each month (possibly in a special savings account) to commit to a foreclosure avoidance plan. Having a lump sum available will make the plan easier and will demonstrate the homeowner's commitment and ability to follow through. Additionally, it helps gauge whether or not the budget is realistic. If no plan is possible, then the money can be used to arrange alternative housing.

Step 8: Get exact totals on the amount of current mortgage payments, the arrears, and the balance due on the mortgage. A prerequisite to evaluating the homeowner's options is a complete understanding of the current mortgage situation, including the amount of current payments, the amount of the arrears, and the total due on the mortgage. This information must be obtained from the lender or servicer, who will typically require the homeowner to sign an Authorization to Release Loan Information before they will provide any information to the counselor. A sample release is included in Appendix A, below, and is on the CD-Rom accompanying this handbook.

      The mortgage information obtained should be reviewed with the homeowner to determine if there are discrepancies, lost payments, or other errors. In addition, there are other reasons to examine each of these numbers, as described below:

Current Mortgage Payments

An initial evaluation must be undertaken to determine whether the homeowner can afford her current monthly payments on an ongoing basis. The monthly payment should be broken down into "P.I.T.I.," that is, the principal and interest are separated from the taxes and insurance. The taxes and insurance are also called the "escrow" charge. Not all loans include an escrow payment. Remember that taxes and insurance must be paid, whether through escrow or by the homeowner directly, and those amounts must be included in evaluating what the homeowner can afford to pay in the future. When determining the amount of money that homeowner has available to pay the mortgage and escrow, it is useful to calculate the monthly expenses without the mortgage and escrow. Then the counselor can subtract the expenses from the monthly income, to determine the amount available for the mortgage and escrow payment. If the escrow payment is subtracted, the amount that is left represents what the homeowner can afford to pay on the mortgage.

The Arrears

The arrears are the total of all missed payments, plus any foreclosure fees and costs that have come due. For example, if the homeowner with a $1,000 monthly payment are five months behind, she owes $5,000 in back payments, plus any money *actually expended* by the mortgage holder or servicer for foreclosure-related fees and costs. This may include attorney fees, court costs, inspection fees, reappraisal fees, and other similar charges. One issue in some cases is whether these fees and costs have actually been expended. For example, early in the foreclosure process, the servicer may have sent a retainer fee to an attorney. If a foreclosure avoidance plan goes forward, the attorney will not have done all of the contemplated work and the servicer will be entitled to a refund. That refund should be credited to the homeowner's account.

The Total Amount Due on the Mortgage

The total amount due on the mortgage will usually include: (1) the outstanding principal balance; (2) unpaid interest; (3) the unpaid escrow balance (if there is an escrow account); (4) foreclosure attorney fees; and (5) other foreclosure costs. Late charges may also be included. Generally, if a foreclosure avoidance plan is possible, late fees may be waived by the servicer if a request is made.

Note: The total amount due on the mortgage *cannot* be obtained by adding the arrears to the outstanding principal balance because the arrears includes some unpaid principal. If the two numbers were added, that amount of principal would be double counted.

Do not forget to consider payments that will come due between when a proposal is made and the plan is finalized. A foreclosure avoidance plan will not be implemented instantaneously.

Step 9: Work with the homeowner to make realistic choices. Once the budget is complete, and the amount of the delinquency established, the counselor should sit down with the homeowner again to review whether her objectives are consistent with her available resources. It is very important to help the homeowner make realistic choices from among the available alternatives. For example, some homeowners will not want to keep the property, but would nevertheless like to avoid foreclosure because of the credit reporting implications. Others will want to keep the property at all costs, including making choices that, to others, would appear to be unacceptable sacrifices. Although the counselor's role is not to provide substitute judgment for the homeowner, the counselor may need to point out unrealistic or inappropriate expectations.

Review with the homeowner the workout options available from the mortgage holder, to determine whether the homeowner can resolve her default. It is important that the proposed resolution be realistic from the homeowner's perspective because a failed workout will only leave the homeowner in a worse position. If no proposal is possible, or if the homeowners have other objectives, other strategies should be explored. No matter which strategy is chosen, the homeowner should understand the pros and cons of each available option.

The counselor should help the homeowner understand the various options and should work to obtain a result that is as consistent as possible with what the homeowner wants. In extreme circumstances, the counselor may need to withdraw from the case. This may occur if the homeowner proposes to make misrepresentations to the mortgage holder or if she will not bring her expectations into line with the possible outcomes. If that choice becomes necessary, a full written explanation of the reasons for withdrawal is essential.

Step 10: Fill out the budget papers and obtain necessary documentation of income and expenses. If a foreclosure avoidance plan is possible and desired, fill out the necessary budget forms and obtain verification of income and expenses. Income verification can be in the form of tax returns, benefit award letters, or other proof appropriate to that type of income. Expense verification needs are usually flexible, but it is helpful to have copies of bills.

Step 11: Request a delay of the foreclosure sale to give enough time to put a workout plan in place. The counselor's most important request of a servicer may be for a delay of the foreclosure sale process long enough to make a workout application. If there is no sale date, or if it is a good way off when workout negotiations begin, it is still important nevertheless to keep an eye on the sale process. It is not unheard of for a property to be sold without notice to a counselor while a workout application is pending.

Delaying a foreclosure sale date is critical for several reasons. A completed foreclosure sale will generally cut off all workout possibilities. In addition, as the foreclosure process moves forward, the mortgage holder continues to incur costs that will eventually have to be reimbursed by the borrower. These costs increase the amount the borrower must raise to cure the delinquency, and efforts should be made to keep costs to a minimum. For example, getting the mortgage holder to agree to wait thirty days before referring the case to a foreclosure attorney may significantly reduce attorney fees the homeowner must pay.

A request for delay is more likely to be granted when preliminary information is provided about the homeowner's potential to make a reasonable workout proposal. For example, if a homeowner has recently returned to work, documentation of employment would almost always justify postponing a sale. Similarly, an offer of partial payment may help obtain several months' delay. Mortgage holders have different approaches to handling requests for delay.

Definitely avoid leaving the decision to grant a delay in the mortgage holder's hands up to the very last minute. The risk is that the counselor and the homeowner will assume that the application is being acted upon and will lose the opportunity to pursue other strategies prior to sale. When a timely request is made, agreements to delay should be granted at least seven days before the foreclosure sale date if the mortgage holder is considering a workout proposal in good faith.

When an agreement to delay a sale is reached, it is essential to reduce it to writing. In most cases, a confirming letter should be sufficient unless the sale will be a court-supervised process, and the lender has already initiated this court process. In that case, the court's procedures as to obtaining a delay must be followed. If the homeowner is represented by an attorney, ask the attorney to obtain the delay with the court. Otherwise, either make sure you see a copy of a request the servicer files with the court, or make sure the homeowner files such a request with the court.

Step 12: Determine which of the available workout options is appropriate given the homeowner's goals and resources. Lenders may make available a number of workout options, and those options vary depending on who owns the mortgage loan and whether a government agency insures it. Later in this handbook, Chapter 5 discusses workouts generally, and Chapter 6 details workout options offered when Fannie Mae or Freddie Mac purchase a mortgage loan. Chapter 7 examines options where a mortgage loan is insured by the Federal Housing Administration (FHA), and Chapter 8 discusses options where the loan is guaranteed by the U.S. Department of Veterans Affairs (VA) or where the Rural Home Service (RHS) owns or guarantees the loan. A foreclosure avoidance plan may also be available for other types of loans as well, but these options will be unique to the particular lender and type of loan.

The counselor must identify the type of loan at issue, and determine what workout options are available for that particular loan. The counselor should then recommend a solution that is acceptable to both the lender and homeowner, and that is financially viable for the homeowner. It generally makes sense first to consider options that are designed to help the homeowner retain her home. Only if these options are infeasible will the homeowner want to consider options that involve giving up the home. Foreclosure avoidance plans are briefly summarized below, but more details on these plans for specific types of loans are found in Chapters 5–8, below.

Repayment Plan

A repayment plan involves curing a default by making regular monthly mortgage payments as they are due, together with partial monthly payments on the arrears (including fees and costs). A typical agreement might call for making one-and-a-quarter monthly payments until the default is resolved. Homeowners most likely to benefit from this type of payment agreement are those who have experienced temporary financial difficulties that are now resolved. The homeowner needs to have some excess income in her budget to commit to the mortgage beyond the regular monthly payment.

A short-term repayment plan allows a homeowner to repay the arrears over a three- to six-month period. These repayment plans are typically informal and servicers verbally approve the plan. Until recently, most mortgage holders limited repayment plans to no more than one year for reinstatement. Agreements up to twenty-four months are now common, though these longer term arrangements may be referred to as forbearance plans and a written agreement is usually required. Time periods of thirty-six and even forty-eight months are also possible; the servicer, however, must generally get special approval from the mortgage holder.

Forbearance

Under a forbearance plan, monthly payments are temporarily reduced or suspended. Typically, the homeowner must begin paying at least the full amount of the monthly mortgage payment due under the mortgage at the end of the period of reduced or suspended payments, plus extra to pay down the accumulated arrears.

Modification

The intent of a modification is to eliminate the arrearage and reduce monthly mortgage payments for homeowners who have recovered from financial distress but whose net income has been reduced to a level lower than it was before the default, such that they can no longer afford the original loan. Mortgage holders may agree to the following types of permanent changes in terms of the loan:

- *Reduction of the Interest Rate.* The most common scenario for a permanent interest rate reduction is when the interest rate on the loan is above the current market rate. The mortgage holder may also consider converting a variable rate loan to a fixed rate loan.
- *Extension of the Loan Payment Period.* Extending the loan repayment period helps homeowners by allowing them to repay the principal over a longer term, thereby reducing the monthly payment. Homeowners should resist extending their loan term beyond 30 years. Forty year terms are more common these days and servicers may suggest this option. However, the homeowner should consider that accumulation of equity in the home will take even longer if the term is 40 years because the total interest cost rises.
- *Reamortization with Capitalization of Arrears.* With capitalization, the missed payments are added to the principal and spread out over the remaining balance of the loan. This cancels the arrears. The loan is then reamortized, which means payments are recalculated using the existing interest rate and new principal balance. Payments will go up slightly. Reamortization is generally combined with other permanent modifications to the interest rate or term of the loan. If reamortization is combined with an interest rate reduction, an extension of the period of the loan, or a cancellation of principal, payments can be significantly reduced.
- *Reduction of the Principal Balance.* Reduction of the principal balance may be available when the loan amount is more than the value of the property due to depreciation for reasons beyond the borrower's control. The mortgage holder may agree to reduce the principal when it recognizes that its best potential result in foreclosure is to obtain the current value of the property minus the costs of foreclosure and disposition. A permanent reduction of the principal also may be available as a negotiated result in litigation. Once the principal is reduced, if the loan is reamortized, payments should be lower. Some mortgage holders are willing to think about reductions in principal to the value of the property only if they are allowed to keep deferred junior mortgages in the amount of the principal reduction. This protects the mortgage holder in the event that the property value later goes up. The deferred junior mortgage typically would not require payment except on transfer of the property. The homeowner should be made aware of the potential difficulties that a deferred junior mortgage creates for home equity borrowing.

Short Sales/Preforeclosure Sales

A short sale is a sale of property for less than the amount due on the mortgage in order to avoid foreclosure. Some homeowners prefer a short sale to foreclosure because the consequences to a credit record are less dramatic. As part of the process, the lender should agree to waive any deficiency. The mortgage holder will generally review each proposed short sale on its merits and will consider agreeing to postpone the foreclosure if there is a buyer willing to sign a purchase and sale agreement. Generally, a price that is very close to the appraised value must be obtained. This price is likely to be higher than the amount the mortgage holder will receive if the mortgage is foreclosed. Mortgage holders usually will not agree to short sales involving family members or others with close personal relationships to the homeowners. (This prevents below market price deals that do not get a fair return to the mortgage holder.)

Sometimes, homeowners will have equity in their property and will need time to sell the property at fair market value to avoid loss of equity in the foreclosure process. Mortgage holders can often be persuaded to consider postponing a foreclosure if the value is high enough to protect their interest during a sale process.

For any sale, the homeowners will have to list the property for sale and engage in other good faith efforts to sell the property. Where appropriate, this should happen as soon as possible in the counseling process, especially in states where the time line for foreclosures is short. Since not all foreclosure avoidance plans involving retention of the home will be accepted, listing the property for sale may be a good idea in almost every case as a back up strategy.

Deed in Lieu of Foreclosure

A deed in lieu of foreclosure is a transfer of property to the mortgage holder to satisfy the mortgage. A deed in lieu of foreclosure is only possible when there are no junior liens on the property, because it will not clear the title of other liens. A deed in lieu of foreclosure might be considered the best choice by homeowners who wish to move on with their lives as smoothly as possible. The mortgage holder may or may not agree to accept it. Lenders will often require the homeowner to attempt to sell the home before agreeing to a deed in lieu.

A deed in lieu should not be pursued unless the mortgage holder will agree to provide a reasonable amount of time for the homeowners to find alternate housing. Sometimes, on request, the mortgage holder will agree to make a small payment to homeowners in consideration of their moving out of the property in a timely way. The mortgage holder should also formally agree to waive in writing any further collection efforts, including collection of a mortgage deficiency. Finally, if a deed in lieu is offered, the mortgage holder should be asked to inform the appropriate credit reporting companies, since this may make it slightly easier for homeowners to obtain new credit. Homeowners should understand, however, that a deed in lieu will not entirely fix their credit report.

Assumptions

Some mortgages can be assumed (taken over) by a third party. When a mortgage is assumable the property can be transferred, and the person to whom it is transferred can pick up the payments on the mortgage. If payments were behind when the mortgage was assumed, absent a workout agreement, the person assuming the mortgage will be in default and subject to the same collection activity as the transferring homeowner. The advantage may be that the assuming party is in a better position to deal with the default than the original homeowner.

A mortgage is always assumable if the contract documents say it is or, in most states, if the documents are silent on this issue. Other loan contracts contain a "due on sale" provision, a clause specifying that transfer of the property accelerates the full loan balance. However, there are a number of situations in which assumption can take place despite attempts by the mortgage holder to enforce a due-on-sale provision. For example, mortgage holders generally cannot block a transfer from parent to child. Additionally, mortgage holders will sometimes agree to otherwise impermissible assumptions so that they can start getting payments from someone. If so, this agreement must be in writing.

After a mortgage assumption, the former homeowner generally remains personally liable on the loan note. Of course, the lender can release the borrower from this obligation, but rarely will do so unless there is a financial incentive to do so, or the borrower can demonstrate some type of extreme hardship.

Other Workout Options

Other workout options may be available. For example, a temporary interest rate reduction could be proposed to make payments more affordable in the short term. Missed payments could be "recast," which involves canceling missed payments and adding the obligation to make those payments to the end of the loan term. The loan is then reamortized. Counselors should contact the mortgage holder or servicer before making proposals along these lines. Recasting is generally available for retroactive (already missed) payments rather than for payments due in the future. Because of changes in mortgage accounting practices, most large institutional lenders (including Fannie Mae and Freddie Mac) no longer consider recasting. When it remains available, the mortgage holder is usually unwilling to recast more than six monthly payments.

Step 13: Review other options not requiring the lender's consent. Even when the goal is to develop a workout procedure between the mortgage holder and homeowners, homeowners should be informed that they may have other options.

Bankruptcy

Bankruptcy can be an effective way for homeowners to keep their home when faced with foreclosure. A chapter 13 bankruptcy allows homeowners to reorganize their debt and pay it back according to a plan that they develop and is then approved by the bankruptcy court. This is most useful for homeowners who have experienced a temporary decrease in income, but can now afford to resume monthly payments while paying the arrears over time. The counselor should emphasize to the homeowner that, in addition to the payments on the delinquency, the homeowner must recommence paying their regular mortgage payment plus, in most cases, something to their unsecured creditors. Homeowners should understand that bankruptcy can be pursued regardless of the outcome of workout discussions. In 2005, the federal Bankruptcy Code was overhauled. While the new law has made the process more complicated, the basic right to file bankruptcy and most of the benefits derived from it remain unchanged for most consumers when filing chapter 13 cases. If the homeowner wants to pursue bankruptcy, she should consult a bankruptcy attorney. Bankruptcy is discussed in Chapter 11, below, and in even more detail in the *NCLC Guide to Surviving Debt*.

Litigation

If the homeowner believes that there has been an error, this should be brought to the mortgage holder's attention. If the mortgage holder refuses to correct the error, then it may be appropriate for the homeowner to consider litigation. Another situation where litigation may be appropriate is where the loan appears to have been abusive. For example, if a second mortgage was made in connection with home improvements that were not completed properly or in some cases involving very high interest rates or other abusive terms, legal defenses may be available. As with the bankruptcy option, homeowners wishing to pursue litigation should contact an attorney. More details are found in Chapters 3 and 12 of this handbook.

Staying Until Eviction

If the homeowner does not want to keep the home and is unable to afford the home under any potential circumstances, it may be best to prepare to move. This option works best for homeowners who are not concerned about a negative credit rating or whose credit rating is already poor. It can also be the best strategy when a deed in lieu does not work because of other liens on the property. Some homeowners favor this choice in order to avoid continued headaches associated with homeownership. The homeowner has the right to stay in the property until an actual eviction occurs. It may be preferable to stay in the home until then to protect it from the vandalism that may occur if the house is obviously vacant. In addition, it gives the homeowner the maximum time to get her affairs in order and plan her move.

Counsel the Homeowner About Foreclosure Related Scams

There are many consumer abuses aimed at homeowners in financial distress. Counselors should not forget to warn their homeowners to avoid scams such as sale/leaseback arrangements, hard money lenders, and bankruptcy petition preparation mills. Additional information regarding these scams can be found in Chapters 3 and 4, below.

Step 14: Making the proposal and meeting documentation requirements, and what to do if the proposal is rejected. Proposals can be made to the mortgage holder or the servicer, and the counselor should find out the mortgage holder's preference. Documentation that is routinely required (such as income verification) should be submitted with the application. Other documents, such as a broker's opinions of value (similar to an appraisal), may be required and should be supplied on request.

Some cases will involve negotiation to arrive at terms that the homeowner can accept. A counselor assisting with a foreclosure avoidance plan should make sure that the strategy is in place well before the foreclosure sale date. If a proposal is rejected, this may leave the homeowner with other options.

If an agreement is reached, the mortgage holder or servicer will need to draw up the necessary forms to finalize the workout. Counselors should work with the homeowner and the servicer to make sure the forms accurately reflect the workout terms and that they are signed and promptly returned. Homeowners should resist signing a workout agreement that waives their rights to sue on claims and defenses they may now have or may have in the future against either the mortgage lender, holder, or servicer.

If a proposal is rejected, determine whether the proposal can be modified in order to meet the needs of the homeowner and the mortgage holder. If the proposal is rejected unreasonably or if no action is taken in a timely manner, consider seeking help from a supervisor in the mortgage holder's loss mitigation department.

CHAPTER 3

Recognizing the Abusive Side of Mortgage Lending

WHY COUNSELORS SHOULD BE CONCERNED ABOUT MORTGAGE LENDING ABUSES

Homeownership counselors will inevitably see some homeowners who have fallen prey to abusive lenders. The abusive nature of the loan, rather than financial problems on the part of the homeowner, may be the main reason the homeowner is facing foreclosure. Some lenders make mortgage loans knowing that the homeowner will not be able to make the payments and will lose the home.

Counselors should be alert to signs of abusive mortgage lending because normal foreclosure prevention techniques may be insufficient for these homeowners. If the homeowner was victimized by a predatory lender, the loan may simply be unaffordable. More drastic measures, such as bankruptcy or a lawsuit, may be necessary to save the home. Ideally, the counselor, the homeowner, and an attorney can work as a team. If the attorney is able to wring concessions from the foreclosing creditor or monetary settlements from the responsible parties, then the counselor can help put together an affordable plan.

Another reason to be alert to signs of these abuses is that arranging for the homeowner to repay an abusive loan means that predatory lending remains profitable. If the homeowner takes a strong stand and demands justice, it is less likely that others will be victimized.

This chapter describes several common abuses in the mortgage market and steps counselors can take when dealing with them. It concludes with a case study that illustrates a number of red flags of predatory mortgage lending. The inventiveness of scam artists is unlimited, however, so counselors should be alert to new abuses as well.

PROPERTY FLIPPING

What Is Property Flipping

Property flipping scams typically involve speculators who buy dilapidated residential properties at low prices and resell them at huge markups to unsophisticated (and often first-time) home buyers. Buyers are often persuaded to enter into purchase agreements only after the seller has promised to make significant repairs to the property. When the closing date arrives, however, the seller has made few, if any, of the repairs. Buyers may then be threatened with the loss of their earnest money deposit and the loss of an "opportunity" to be a homeowner if they do not complete the transaction. The end result is that the buyer has purchased property in questionable condition and is saddled with a loan that exceeds the fair market value of the property. The loan payments may also be higher than the consumer can afford.

Warning Signs of Property Flipping

Buying a home at a low price and selling it, within a short time period, at a much higher price is not in itself illegal. However, property-flipping schemes generally involve some type of fraud or other misconduct. The following are the most common warning signs that a homeowner may have been scammed.

- The sale price significantly exceeded fair market value.
- Promised repairs were not completed.
- The seller used high-pressure tactics, such as threats that the buyer would lose her earnest money deposit.
- The seller owned the property for less than six months.
- The mortgage loan was unaffordable.

Inflated Appraisals. An inflated appraisal is often the linchpin of property flipping scams. Inflated values are typically achieved by misrepresenting the condition of the property or by using comparable sales that are not really comparable (e.g., using sale prices of other "flipped" properties). Appraisals for loans insured by the FHA are commonly inflated by 30–50% and appraisals in sub-prime transactions may be inflated by up to 300%. It is important to obtain copies of any appraisals that were used as part of the underwriting process when the homeowner took out his or her loan. Public tax records may also give some indication of actual value. If resources are available, obtaining a current appraisal or broker's price opinion is extremely useful.

Incomplete or Shoddy Repairs. Incomplete or shoddy repair work is also a hallmark of property flipping. Often, the seller or real estate agent will assure the buyer that the home will be completely rehabilitated or that certain repairs will be made. The reality, however, is that few or no significant repairs are ever made. Frequently, the seller may perform cosmetic repairs to hide more serious structural damage. For example, a fresh coat of paint and a drop ceiling may have been used to conceal significant roof damage. In other situations, incomplete repairs or poor workmanship may not be discovered until months after the sale. A leaky roof may not be apparent until after the first rain and a nonfunctioning furnace may not be noticed until the weather turns cold.

It is important to document what the homeowner was told regarding repairs to the property and by whom. In addition, it is a good idea to check the local public records for building permit information. Most cities and towns require building permits for any significant home rehabilitation. Property flippers may skip the permitting process altogether or may obtain a permit which designates work different from what the buyer was promised. It is important to get an estimate for any needed repairs from a reliable contractor.

Pressure Tactics. Home buyers often are subjected to a variety of pressure sales tactics. During the initial contact with the potential home buyer, the seller or real estate agent focuses on building a trusting relationship. They appear friendly, accommodating, and understanding of the prospective buyer's needs. After the relationship has been established, however, these players may use a variety of pressure sales tactics to close the deal.

- "Act now." Frequently, the sales representative will convey a sense of urgency to the transaction or a need for the buyer to act immediately. Comments such as "if you don't sign the paperwork today, the house will be gone" are not uncommon.
- "Lost opportunity." Scammers often convince victims that the offered deal may be the buyer's only opportunity to share in the "American Dream." Using the "act now" rhetoric described above, property flippers exploit this idea from the outset of the transaction. Emphasis on the lost homeownership opportunity may also come into play if the buyer expresses doubt about completing the transaction, about the condition of the property, or about the terms of the financing.
- "You can't back out now." Unsophisticated homeowners typically do not fully understand the legal documents they are instructed to sign. As a result, property flippers may assert that the buyer cannot back out of the transaction after signing "papers." Other buyers may be threatened with the loss of their earnest money deposit. Such threats are often effective in getting the buyers to complete the transactions. Even though deposits in these transactions may be relatively low compared to industry standards, such deposits often represent the buyer's entire savings.
- "You don't need a lawyer or an inspector." Routinely, buyers are told that they do not need a lawyer or an inspector because everything will be taken care of. Based on the trusting relationship developed in the initial contact and the additional costs that the buyer would have to pay, many buyers forego hiring their own professionals. Instead, a lawyer is "supplied" by the real estate agent or the lender. In most cases, the lawyer provided does not bother to explain the transaction or the loan documents to the buyer.

The Flip. A short ownership period for the seller in the transaction is a certain warning sign of a property-flipping scheme. The nature of the transaction is that the seller purchases property at a low price and within a short time sells the property at a much higher price. Sellers typically do not hold property for more than six months, and in many cases, the property may be "flipped" within 90 days.

In an attempt to curb the increasing number of property-flipping schemes, the Federal Housing Administration (FHA) has recently implemented guidelines for FHA-insured mortgages. The final rule requires that:

(1) any resale of a property may not occur fewer than 90 days from the last sale to be eligible for FHA financing;

(2) for resales that occur between 91–180 days where the new sales price exceeds the previous sale price by 100%, the FHA will require additional documentation validating the property's value.[1]

In evaluating the homeowner's situation, it is useful to know whether the mortgage loan is FHA-insured, and thus covered by the regulation. It is also important to determine when the seller purchased the property. This can usually be figured out by checking local public property records.

Unaffordable Loan. Loan originators and mortgage brokers can make a significant profit on property flipping transactions. As a result, lenders and brokers may also be active participants in these scams. They may engage in fraudulent conduct in documenting and underwriting the loan or may have knowledge of falsified credit applications and down payment information.

It is also common in property flipping schemes for brokers and/or lenders to misrepresent or fail to disclose certain terms of the loan. For example, buyers may be told that they will have an affordable mortgage payment of $500 a month. At the time of closing, however, the payment is $750 per month. The pressure tactics described above are then used to coerce the buyer into completing the transaction. Alternatively, the initial payment may in fact be $500 per month, but the broker and/or lender has failed to disclose that the loan is an adjustable rate mortgage. At the first change date, which may be as soon as thirty days after closing, the payment can increase significantly and become unaffordable for the homeowner. The lender also may fail to tell the buyer that the payment does not include the escrow for taxes and insurance.

Legal Challenges

These cases often include a variety of players and potential defendants, e.g., seller, real estate agent, building contractor, appraiser, seller's attorney, home inspector, and lender. A variety of legal claims can be raised against these parties, including fraud, civil conspiracy, negligent misrepresentation, aiding and abetting, unfair and deceptive practices, breach of fiduciary duty, licensing violations, Racketeer Influenced and Corrupt Organizations Act (RICO), and the federal False Claims Act (where a false insurance claim is submitted to the FHA).

Referrals

Homeowners harmed by property flipping should consult a lawyer as soon as possible. Legal services offices exist in all major cities and serve all rural regions of the country. Referrals can be made to those offices for low-income clients. To locate private consumer attorneys, see the website for the National Association of Consumer Advocates at www.naca.net and click on "Find a Lawyer."

You may also suggest that the homeowner file a complaint with your state Attorney General and/or Consumer Protection Office. If any of the participants to the scam are licensed, the homeowner also can file a complaint with the appropriate licensing agency.

INTEREST-ONLY AND OPTION ARM MORTGAGE LOANS

General

Many lenders are now offering novel types of mortgage products. These carry more risk than traditional mortgages and are appropriate only for a small subset of borrowers. Unfortunately, lenders have made these non-traditional loans to many borrowers for whom they are not appropriate. And, even if one of these non-traditional loans appeared to be appropriate for a borrower at the time it was made, since they are so risky the borrower may face foreclosure after even a minor financial setback.

These novel mortgage products take many forms. The most common are interest-only ARMs and option ARMs.

Interest-Only Adjustable Rate Mortgages (Interest-Only or IO ARMs)

With an interest-only ARM, the interest rate fluctuates like a traditional adjustable rate mortgage, so the consumer's monthly payment can increase significantly. In addition, for a specified number of years (e.g., three or five years), the homeowner is required only to pay interest on the loan. During this period, the homeowner pays nothing toward principal, so the principal does not go down at all. When the interest-only period is over, the homeowner's payment increases to cover both interest and principal. This can mean that the payment rises significantly and can even double or triple. If the homeowner's income has not increased enough to cover this payment shock, the homeowner will have to sell the home, refinance, or face foreclosure.

The advantage to an interest-only ARM, according to lenders, is that if the value of the house goes up the homeowner will have gained equity in the home even without having paid down the principal. The homeowner can then sell the home, and use the equity to buy another home with a less risky mortgage. However, whether the market will go up that much is very speculative. If the market does not go up, the homeowner will have an unaffordable payment and little or no equity in the home. Lenders may market these loans in regions where the cost of real estate is high and to homeowners who cannot otherwise afford the higher principal and interest monthly payments. This is a recipe for disaster once the full payment amount kicks in.

Here is an example of the sticker shock that a homeowner can experience with a $180,000 ARM that has an initial 5-year interest-only period and an initial interest rate of 6.6%:

- Monthly payment for the first five years is **$990 (payment covers interest only).**
- Monthly payment after 5 years when payments include both principal and interest is **$1,227 (payment covers principal and interest), an increase of $222.**
- If the interest rate also adjusts upward to 7.6%, the monthly payment after 5 years is **$1,462 (payment covers principal and interest), an increase of $457.**

Option Adjustable Rate Mortgages (Option ARMs)

With an option ARM, the interest rate is adjustable like a traditional adjustable rate mortgage. In addition, the homeowner can choose among several payment amounts each month. For example, the homeowner may be allowed to choose: (1) a payment amount that covers just the interest; (2) a payment that does not even cover the interest, so that the principal owed actually *increases*; (3) a payment that includes both interest and enough principal to pay off the loan in 30 years; and (4) a payment that includes interest and enough principal to pay off the loan in 15 years. The first and second options may be available to the borrower only for a certain period of time, after which the payment is recalculated. Choosing the first or second option may also result in a balloon payment being owed at the end of the loan term.

The risk that an option ARM creates is that, if the borrower chooses one of the lower payment options, the home may become unaffordable. The payment shock when the payment is recalculated may be more than the borrower can afford. In the meantime, if the borrower has made payments that do not even cover the interest, the borrower's equity in the home may have decreased, making it harder to refinance. (The increase in the principal may be offset by an increase in the value of the home, but this depends on what is happening with the real estate market.) The borrower may also be unable to afford any balloon payment that becomes due at the end of the loan term.

Here is an example of what these payment options can cost using a $180,000 loan with an interest rate of 1.25% in the first month, 6.4% for months 2 through 60, and adjustable after that. This and the previous example are based on a chart published by the Federal Reserve Board at 71 Fed. Reg. 58672 (Oct. 4, 2006).

- Minimum monthly payment for the first five years: **$600 (payment does not even cover interest).**
- Balance owed after 5 years of making minimum monthly payment: **$197,945.**
- Monthly payment required after 5 years if interest rates do not increase: **$1,324 (payment covers principal and interest), an increase of $724.**
- Monthly payment required after 5 years if interest rate increases 2%: **$1,581 (payment covers principal and interest), an increase of $981.**

To pay off this loan in equal payments over 30 years, the monthly payment would be $1,078 (assuming no increase in interest rates).

Tips for Counselors

1. When counseling a homeowner who is facing foreclosure on an interest-only ARM or an option ARM, remember that the monthly payment may change dramatically in the future. When devising a plan to avoid foreclosure, you should make sure you know whether the payment amount is scheduled for recalculation. If it is, the homeowner may need to budget a larger amount.

2. If you are negotiating a workout on an interest-only ARM or an option ARM, consider asking the lender to recast the loan to avoid terms that will be troublesome in the future. For example, the lender may be willing to modify the terms to eliminate the option payments, capitalize the arrears, and extend the term. For example, consider asking the lender to extend the loan term so that the borrower will not face a large balloon payment.

3. If a homeowner is considering an interest-only ARM or an option ARM as a way of refinancing a mortgage to avoid default, the borrower must understand the risks involved. You or the borrower should find out from the lender what the maximum monthly payment will be if the adjustable interest rate rises to the maximum. It is necessary to find out the maximum monthly payment amount for *each stage* of an interest-only loan, i.e., not just the initial period when the borrower's payment only covers interest, but also the second stage when the payment covers principal as well. Likewise, for an option ARM, the counselor should get an analysis of the payment amounts and the effect on the principal, both short-term and long-term, for each payment option. *Lending laws currently do not require lenders to give this information to borrowers,* so the counselor will have to make a special request for it.

4. A borrower should not enter into an interest-only ARM or an option ARM without:

   - A full understanding of the potential increases in the monthly payment amount.
   - A full understanding of the effect of the monthly payment amount on the principal owed and the accumulation of equity in the home.
   - A realistic plan for dealing with the payment shocks built into the mortgage.

FORECLOSURE RESCUE SCAMS

General

A growing scam that disproportionately targets homeowners in financial distress can, and often does, literally cost them the homes they have lived in for years and worked hard to obtain. It is called a foreclosure "rescue" scam, and in no sense is it a genuine rescue; in fact it is usually quite the opposite.

Foreclosure "rescue" scams target those who have fallen behind on their mortgage payments. In this scam, a con artist who promises to help consumers save their home is actually intent on stealing the home—often a family's most precious asset—or most of its accumulated equity.

Some homeowners will be facing foreclosure because of a foreclosure rescue scam. The "rescuer" may be the foreclosing creditor, although this scenario is uncommon. Usually, the rescuer acquires title to the property, not just a mortgage on the property, and then proceeds by way of eviction rather than foreclosure to remove the (former) homeowner. Other times, the rescuer acquires title to the home but does not pay off the original mortgage. Then the original lender may be foreclosing. It is important to recognize the red flags of a foreclosure rescue scam so that these cases can be given special treatment.

"Rescuers" are also likely to be soliciting the homeowner while you are trying to put together a workout. It is important to alert homeowners about these scams so that they know to avoid them.

What Are Foreclosure "Rescue" Scams?

Foreclosure rescue scams most often appear in one of three varieties:

Phantom Help Scams. The first might be called "phantom help," where the "rescuer" charges outrageous fees either for light-duty phone calls and paperwork the homeowner could have easily performed, or makes a promise of additional representation that never occurs. In either event, the homeowner is usually left without enough assistance to save the home and with little or no time left to prevent the loss of the home or seek other assistance. The "rescuer" essentially takes the fees and abandons the homeowner to a fate that may have been prevented with better intervention and assistance.

False Bailouts. A second variety of the scam is the "bailout" that never quite works. This scenario includes various schemes under which the homeowner surrenders title to the house in the belief that she is entering a deal where she will be able to remain as a renter, and then repurchase the house over the next few years. This is also known as a "lease/buyback scheme." Homeowners are sometimes told that surrendering title is necessary so that someone with a better credit rating can secure new financing to prevent the loss of the home. But the terms of these deals are invariably so onerous that the buyback becomes impossible, the homeowner permanently loses possession, and the "rescuer" walks off with all or most of the home's equity.

Bait and Switch. The third variety is a bait and switch where the homeowner *does not realize* he or she is surrendering ownership of the house in exchange for a "rescue." Many homeowners later insist that they believed they were signing documents for a new loan to make the mortgage current. Many also say they had made it quite clear they had no intention of selling or giving up their home to anyone. It is important to note that substantial numbers of this third type of scenario involve fraud and forgeries of deeds. In many cases, the home is transferred for a small fraction of its actual value.

Typical Tactics Employed by "Rescue" Scammers

The "rescuer" starts by identifying distressed homeowners through public foreclosure notices in newspapers or at government offices. These records are more readily accessible than in the past because they are computerized and private firms now compile and sell the lists. The homeowner has not been foreclosed on yet, but is merely threatened with foreclosure after falling behind on mortgage payments.

The "rescuer" then contacts the homeowner by phone, personal visit, card or flyer left at the door, or advertises. The initial contact typically revolves around a simple message such as "Stop foreclosure with just one phone call," "I'd like to $ buy $ your house," "You have options," or "Do you need instant debt relief and CASH?" This contact also frequently contains a "time is of the essence" theme, adding a note of urgency to what is already a stressful situation.

Initial meetings stress the promise of a "fresh start"—likely what a frightened homeowner most wants to hear—and often feature written or recorded "testimonials" from other homeowners the "rescue" scammer supposedly saved. What is glossed over is that the rescuer's help often comes at a very steep price and is usually either ineffective or affirmatively harmful. Homeowners are also frequently instructed to cease all contact with lawyers or the mortgage lender and let the "rescuer" handle all negotiations. This devious tactic simultaneously cuts off access to possible refinancing options while running out the clock on ways to prevent the foreclosure.

Once it is too late to save the home, the property is either taken by the "rescuer" or, having been drained of substantial equity through the "rescuer's" imposition of heavy fees and other charges, simply lost to foreclosure. After things fall apart, many homeowners suffer the added stress and indignity of being evicted by their "rescuer" from the home they once owned.

Legal Challenges to Foreclosure Rescue Scams

Homeowners who have been victimized by foreclosure scammers have a number of legal options. What follows is a brief summary of some legal options advocates can use to challenge foreclosure rescue scams. These claims may be complex; please consult the additional resources listed at the end of this discussion.

State Laws Governing Foreclosure Assistance. Several states have enacted laws targeting foreclosure scam activities, including California, Florida, Georgia, Illinois, Maryland, Michigan, Minnesota, Missouri, New York, Rhode Island, and Washington.[2] State laws differ dramatically in scope and strength. The common thread among them is that they contain a right to cancel the transaction for a limited time period. However, several exceptions—those for attorneys, accountants, real estate licensees, consumer finance lenders, mortgage brokers, and others—diminish some statutes' protections considerably.

State Unfair and Deceptive Acts and Practices Laws. Many of the misrepresentations and abusive practices of foreclosure scammers can be challenged under state unfair and deceptive acts and practices (UDAP) laws. If a state's UDAP statute covers the type of transaction or the parties involved, advocates may bring UDAP claims. Be aware, however, that some state UDAP laws exclude certain types of transactions such as real estate transactions, or certain professions such as attorneys or realtors.

The Truth in Lending Act (TILA). A sale/leaseback type of foreclosure rescue scam may be a thinly disguised loan, subject to Truth in Lending rescission rights.

Fraud, Conspiracy and Other Laws. The homeowner may also have claims for fraud, usury, conspiracy, unconscionability, breach of fiduciary duty, equitable mortgage, and breach of contract. Other laws, including state credit repair statutes, may apply if the perpetrators promise to obtain a loan or improve the homeowner's credit. State home solicitation laws and telemarketing laws may also apply depending on how the transaction was solicited and consummated.

Counseling Issues

1. You should educate homeowners who have fallen behind on their payments that they should proceed with extreme caution if an individual or company:

   ■ Calls itself a "mortgage consultant," "foreclosure service," or something similar.
   ■ Contacts or advertises to people whose homes are listed for foreclosure, including anyone who sends flyers or solicits door-to-door or by phone.
   ■ Collects a fee before providing services.
   ■ Tells the consumer to make home mortgage payments directly to the individual or company (and not the mortgage lender).
   ■ Tells the consumer to transfer the property deed or title to the individual or company.

   Contrary to advice given by many scammers, homeowners in trouble SHOULD stay in touch with their mortgage company. Homeowners should contact the mortgage company or a lawyer first when in trouble. There are many ways to prevent the loss of a home or at least to walk away with all or most of its accumulated equity if all else fails and the homeowner is forced to sell.
   The box on page 35 contains advice for homeowners in financial distress to help them avoid various scams.

2. If you spot red flags of a foreclosure rescue scam, you should interview the homeowner carefully and consider making a referral to an attorney (see page 34). Some of the red flags are:
   ■ Indications that title to the home is no longer in the homeowner's name;
   ■ Confusion on the part of the homeowner as to who the current mortgage lender is;
   ■ The filing of an eviction action against the homeowner, when normally you would expect a foreclosure;
   ■ Transfer of the home to a living trust for the homeowner (a technique used by one type of foreclosure rescue scam).

Information and Referrals

For More Information: For more information on foreclosure "rescue" scams and how to avoid them please see NCLC's report *Dreams Foreclosed: The Rampant Theft of Americans' Homes*

Through Equity-Stripping Foreclosure "Rescue" Scams. You can find it on NCLC's website at: www.consumerlaw.org/news/ForeclosureReportFinal.pdf.

Referrals: Legal services offices exist in all major cities and serve all rural regions of the country. Referrals may be made to those offices for low-income clients. To locate private consumer attorneys, see the website for the National Association of Consumer Advocates at www.naca.net and click on "Find a Lawyer." Clients looking for a bankruptcy attorney may wish to consult the website of the National Association of Consumer Bankruptcy Attorneys, www.nacba.org, which lists its members.

You may also suggest that the homeowner file a complaint with your state Attorney General and/or Consumer Protection Office.

OTHER FORECLOSURE RELATED SCAMS THAT HOMEOWNERS SHOULD AVOID

Credit Repair Companies

These companies often promise to erase bad credit or accurate (but harmful) information on a consumer's credit report. They generally cannot deliver what they promise. A consumer can do the same or a better job of cleaning up a credit report at no cost, just by following the advice in *NCLC Guide to Surviving Debt.*

For-Profit Bankruptcy Counseling or Preparation Companies

For-profit bankruptcy counseling is rarely a good idea. Unfortunately, there are many people who offer counseling to consumers with debt problems in order to rip them off.

In addition, various types of non-attorney operations have sprung up which purport to offer consumers assistance in filing bankruptcy cases. Typically dubbed "typing services," "document preparation services," "independent paralegal," or "*notarios*," these entities advertise that they can prevent foreclosures without the necessity of an attorney.

Generally, these operations are downright fraudulent, making promises which they cannot hope to keep and extracting fees which far exceed the value of the work performed. Consumers are sent to file bankruptcy petitions with papers that are inadequate or defective, leading to a quick dismissal or, at best, a bankruptcy case that does not give the consumer all of the relief to which she is entitled. In the worst cases, the consumer is not aware that a bankruptcy has been filed and her signature is forged.

Solicitations to Refinance After the Foreclosure Has Been Filed

As one might suspect, the terms of any refinancing that a homeowner might obtain *after* a foreclosure has started are likely to be onerous and very expensive. A refinance at this stage, unless made under a special program offered to victims of predatory loans, will provide only temporary relief, steal more of the homeowner's equity, and lead to another foreclosure in a relatively short time. The Refinancing Dos and Don'ts discussed on pages 71–73, below, should be consulted before counseling a homeowner who is considering this "solution."

Some Major DON'Ts for Homeowners in Financial Distress

Do not panic. Get information on the foreclosure process in your state; find out how much time you have to resolve your problems short of losing your home. Make sure you understand all the deadlines for responding to court documents, documents from lenders, and other important papers. Be sure that you know the point at which you can lose the legal right to own your home.

Ask a lawyer to review any contract you are asked to sign. Make sure this is an attorney that you have chosen, without any help from the person who wants you to sign the contract. If the other party will not give you an advance copy of the contract, or discourages you from consulting your own attorney, it is a sign that he or she has something to hide. See page 34, above, for suggestions about finding a lawyer.

Never sign a contract under pressure. Take your time to review the paperwork thoroughly, preferably with a lawyer who is representing your interest.

Do not sign away ownership of your property (often referred to as a "quit claim deed") to anyone without advice from your lawyer. Be suspicious of offers to take over ownership of your home as part of a deal that will allow you to lease it and then buy it back after two or three years; experience shows that the buy-back is often extremely expensive or otherwise out of reach, so in reality you either never get your home back or, if you do, you have paid an outrageous amount to recover it.

Do not pay your mortgage payments to someone other than your lender even if he or she promises to pass the payments on to the mortgage company.

If you find you cannot pay your mortgage do not ignore warning letters from your mortgage lender. Call your lender, housing counselor, or a lawyer for help.

Beware of any home sale contract where you are not formally released from liability for your mortgage. Surprisingly, some people lose their home but still wind up owing on the mortgage! Make sure you know what rights you are giving up in any contract and that you agree to give them up.

Never make a verbal agreement. Get all promises in writing and get copies of the agreement.

Do not sign anything containing blank lines or spaces. Information can be added later without your permission.

Do not fall for promises like these, often used to lure homeowners into deals that will cost them a lot more than they will "save":

- "We will save your credit."
- "We will pay your first two months' rent or payments in your new place."
- "You will get several thousand dollars in cash back that you can use any way you want."
- "If you sign the house over to us the foreclosure will be recorded against us, not you."
- "We will buy your house 'as is.' "
- "We guarantee we will find you a buyer in seven (or 14) days."
- "We will help you file bankruptcy to stop this foreclosure."[3]
- "It may cost you thousands more if your property is sold at public auction."
- "We will give you $40 in Free Gas."

If you do not speak English, use your own translator. Do not depend on the "rescue" firm's translator.

ABUSIVE LENDING: A CASE STUDY

This chapter has described several specific types of abusive mortgage loans and scams. There are many other predatory mortgage lending scenarios, however. Many abusive mortgage loans are originated by fraudulent home improvement contractors. Other predatory lenders induce homeowners to refinance into abusive loans with high interest rates, high fees, and abusive terms such as balloon payments and prepayment penalties.

What follows is a case study to help you spot the "red flags" of predatory lending practices. We suggest that you read these materials, consisting of a factual summary, the Truth In Lending Disclosure Statement, and the Settlement Statement. (Lenders are required to give consumers both of these documents at closing. Often the consumer will have them in a packet of loan papers that he or she received at or soon after the closing.)

As you review the case study, list those items which "smell" bad (raise red flags). At the end, you will find a checklist of warning signs that can help to guide you. The author's red flags in this case study can be found in Appendix G below.

A CASE STUDY

Arturo and Maria Homeowner bought their modest row home in 1987 for $45,000 with an FHA loan. Their monthly payment was $460 (P.I. = $328 + T.I. = $132). The interest rate was 8%. Arturo works in the service industry at a hotel. Maria is a nurse's aide at a nursing home. By 1995, the Homeowners had two children to support. In 1998, Maria was out of work for a time and the family balanced its budget by using credit cards. They kept up with the minimum payments and tried to pay more for two years, but the interest rate of 25% (the penalty rate imposed after they were late twice) on their cards meant that they never seemed to be paying down the balance.

In 2000, the Homeowners saw an advertisement on television for home mortgage debt consolidation loans. They thought it would be a good idea since their home was worth $90,000 and the balance on their mortgage loan was less than $37,000. The advertisement said: "No credit check." They thought this was a good idea too, since they had occasionally missed their credit card payments over the years.

The lender was called "WE CAN Mortgage." WE CAN arranged a loan for the Homeowners with TOP QUALITY Mortgage in California. That mortgage amount was $55,000. It paid off the balance of the HUD loan and paid most of their credit cards. The interest rate was over 10%, but the payments were only $400 per month, because a $55,000 balloon was due at the end of 10 years and the monthly payment did not include taxes and insurance. WE CAN did not explain the existence of the balloon payment to Arturo and Maria nor did it tell them that their monthly payment did not include the escrow for taxes and insurance.

About a year or so after this loan was signed, TOP QUALITY contacted Arturo and Maria about refinancing, advising that the balloon payment was not a good idea and claiming that it could get them a better loan and rate. This time, TOP QUALITY made a mortgage loan with an interest rate of 7.55%. The Homeowners were told that the monthly payment would be $456.72. However, TOP Quality did not explain that the loan contained a variable interest rate. When the Homeowners asked about the escrow (because they had gotten the tax bill for the previous two years just about the time TOP QUALITY called), TOP QUALITY told them that it was included in the payment of $456.72.

The Homeowners came to you and brought the attached documents after they received new tax and insurance bills and could not get TOP QUALITY to pay them and then got a notice that their monthly payment was going up. The Homeowners will have difficulty paying the larger payment. Their home is now worth $100,000 because they have taken excellent care of it.

Truth In Lending Disclosure Statement

ANNUAL PERCENTAGE RATE The cost of your credit as a yearly rate.	FINANCE CHARGE The dollar amount the credit will cost you.	Amount Financed The amount of credit provided to you on your behalf.	Total of Payments The amount you will have paid after you have made all payments as scheduled.
12.107%	$163,806.74	$54,811.86	$218,618.60

You have the right to receive at this time an itemization of the Amount Financed.
    ☒ I want an itemization   ☐ I do not want an itemization

Your payment schedule will be:

Number of Payments	Amount of Payments	When Payments Are Due
36	456.72	12/01/2002
6	541.43	06/01/2005
6	586.40	06/01/2006
311	626.34	12/01/2006
1	617.96	01/01/2032

Variable Rate Feature: Your loan contains a variable rate feature. Disclosures about the variable rate feature have been provided to you earlier.

Insurance: You may obtain property insurance from anyone you want that is acceptable to TOP QUALITY.

Security: You are giving a security interest in:
    ☒ the goods or property being purchased
    ☐ (brief description of other property)

Filing fees: $30   **Non-filing insurance $____**

Late Charge: If a payment is late, you will be charged $___ / 5% of the payment.

Prepayment: If you pay off early, you
    ☒ may ☐ will not have to pay a penalty.
    ☐ may ☒ will not be entitled to a refund of part of the finance charge.
See your contract documents for any additional information about nonpayment, default, any required repayment in full before the scheduled date, and prepayment refunds and penalties.

HUD-1 Settlement Statement

D. Name & Address of Borrower: Arturo and Maria Homeowner 123 Main Street Anytown, USA 00000	E. Name & Address of Seller:	F. Name & Address of Lender: TOP QUALITY Mortgage 678 Money Way Anytown, USA 00000

G. Property Location SAME AS ABOVE	H. Settlement Agent: Ed Smith, ESQ	
	Place of Settlement: 678 Money Way Anytown, USA 00000	I. Settlement Date: 10/27/02

J.	Summary of Borrower's Transaction		K.	Summary of Seller's Transaction	
100.	Gross Amount Due From Borrower		400.	Gross Amount Due to Seller	
101.	Contract sales price		401.	Contract sales price	
102.	Personal property		402.	Personal property	
103.	Settlement charges to borrower (line 1400)	13,813	403.		
104.			404.		
105.			405.		
Adjustments for items paid by seller in advance			**Adjustments for items paid by seller in advance**		
106.	City/town taxes to	410	406.	City/town taxes to	
107.	County taxes to		407.	County taxes to	
108.	Assessments to		408.	Assessments to	
109.	TOP QUALITY Acct. # 25240	50,046	409.		
110.			410.		
111.			411.		
112.			412.		
120.	Gross Amount Due From Borrower	64,269	420.	Gross Amount Due To Seller	
200.	Amounts Paid By Or In Behalf of Borrower		500.	Reductions in Amount Due to Seller	
201.	Deposit or earnest money		501.	Excess deposit (see instructions)	
202.	Principal amount of new loan(s)	65,000	502.	Settlement charges to seller (line 1400)	
203.	Existing loan(s) taken subject to		503.	Existing loan(s) taken subject to	
204.			504.	Payoff of first mortgage loan	
205.			505.	Payoff of second mortgage loan	
206.			506.		
207.			507.		
208.			508.		
209.			509.		
Adjustments for items unpaid by seller			**Adjustments for items unpaid by seller**		
210.	City/town taxes to		510.	City/town taxes to	
211.	County taxes to		511.	County taxes to	
212.	Assessments to		512.	Assessments to	
213.			513.		
214.			514.		
215.			515.		
216.			516.		
217.			517.		
218.			518.		
219.			519.		
220.	Total Paid By/For Borrower	65,000	520.	Total Reduction Amount Due Seller	
300.	Cash at Settlement From/To Borrower		600.	Cash At Settlement To/From Seller	
301.	Gross Amount due from borrower (line 120)	64,269	601.	Gross amount due to seller (line 420)	
302.	Less amounts paid by/ for borrower (line 220)	65,000	602.	Less reduction in amt. due seller (line 520)	( )
303.	Cash ☐ From ☒ To Borrower	731	603.	Cash ☐ To ☐ From Seller	

800.	Items Payable In Connection With Loan			
801.	Loan Origination Fee	3.25 %	2,112.50	
802.	Loan Discount	%		
803.	Appraisal Fee	to Top Quality		
804.	Credit Report	to Top Quality		
805.	Lender's Inspection Fee			
806.	Mortgage Insurance Application Fee to			
807.	Loan processing fee to WE CAN		395	
808.	Br. Comp. (WE CAN)		5,000	
809.	(YSP)	(325)		
810.	Underwriting Fee to Top Quality		395	
811.	Tax service fee to Top Quality		81	
812.	Flood certification fee to Top Quality		17	
900.	**Items Required By Lender To Be Paid In Advance**			
901.	Interest from 10/27 to 11/1/04 @$ 13.63 /day	91.78		
902.	Mortgage Insurance Premium for months to			
903.	Hazard Insurance Premium for	years to		
904.		years to		
1000.	**Reserves Deposited With Lender**			
1001.	Hazard insurance	months @$	per month	
1002.	Mortgage insurance	months @$	per month	
1003.	City property taxes	months @$	per month	
1004.	County property taxes	months @$	per month	
1005.	Annual assessments	months @$	per month	
1006.		months @$	per month	
1007.		months @$	per month	
1008.	months @$ per month			
1100.	**Title Charges**			
1101.	Settlement or closing fee	to Ed Smith	450	
1102.	Abstract title search	to		
1103.	Title examination	to Ed Smith		
1104.	Title insurance binder	to		
1105.	Document preparation	to WE CAN	295	
1106.	Notary fees	to		
1107.	Attorney's fees	to Ed Smith		
	(includes above items numbers:)			
1108.	Title insurance	to Title Abstract	295	
	(includes above items numbers:)			
1109.	Lender's coverage	$		
1110.	Owner's coverage	$		
1111.	Endorsement fee		95	
1112.	Express mail		45	
1113.	Courier fees		7.20	
1200.	**Government Recording and Transfer Charges**			
1201.	Recording fees: Deed $; Mortgage $30;	Releases $	30	
1202.	City/county tax/stamps: Deed $	; Mortgage $		
1203.	State tax/stamps: Deed $	; Mortgage $		
1204.				
1205.				
1300.	**Additional Settlement Charges**			
1301.	Survey to			
1302.	Pest inspection	to		
1303.	Appraisal review	to Top Quality	175	
1304.	Funding fee	to Top Quality	175	
1305.	Administrative fee	to WE CAN	795	
1306.	Delinquent county taxes		3,358.52	
1400.				
Total Settlement Charges (enter on lines 103, Section J and 502, Section K)			13, 813	

LOAN NOTE

We the borrowers, Arturo and Maria Homeowner, of 123 Main Street, Anytown, USA, do hereby agree to repay TOP QUALITY Mortgage, Inc., or it transfers and assigns under the following provisions and terms,

Borrowers' Promise to Pay. In return for the loan we have received, we promise to repay $65,000 (the "principal amount"), plus interest to TOP QUALITY Mortgage Co. We understand that this note may be transferred at any time to another holder. If the loan is transferred, we agree to pay the new holder under this contract.

Interest. Interest will be charged on the principal amount until the loan is fully paid. We will pay interest at an initial yearly rate of 7.550%. The interest rate may vary during the loan terms as discussed below.

Interest rate and monthly payment changes.

(A) Change dates. The interest we will pay may change on the first day of June, 2005 and on that day every 6th month thereafter. Each date on which our interest rate could change is called a "Change Date."

(B) Index. Beginning with the first Change Date, our interest rate will be based on an "Index." The Index is the average of interbank offered rates for 6-month U.S. dollar-denominated deposits in the London market based on quotations of major banks, as published in the "Money Rates" section of the Western Edition of the Wall Street Journal. The most recent Index figure available as of the date 45 days before each Change Date is called the "Current Index."

(C) Calculation of Changes. Before each Change Date, the Note Holder will calculate our new interest rate by adding 5.25% to the Current Index. The Note Holder will then round the result of this addition to the nearest one-eighth of one percentage point (0.125%). Subject to the limits stated in Section (D) below, this rounded amount will be our new interest rate until the next Change Date. The Note Holder will then determine the amount of the monthly payment that would be sufficient to repay the unpaid principal that we are expected to owe at the Change Date in full on the Maturity Date at our new interest rate in substantially equal payments. The result of the calculation will be the new amount of our monthly payment.

(D) Limits on Interest Rate Changes. The interest rate we are required to pay at the first Change Date will not be greater than 9.55% or less than 7.55%. Thereafter, our interest rate will never be increased or decreased on any single Change Date by more than 1% from the rate of interest we have been paying for the preceding 6 months. Our interest rate will never be greater than 14.55% or less than 7.55%.

(E) Effective Date of Changes. Our new interest rate will become effective on each Change Date. We will pay the amount of our new monthly payment beginning on the first monthly payment date after the Change Date until the amount of my monthly payment changes again.

(F) Notice of Changes. The Note Holder will deliver or mail to us a notice of any changes in our interest rate and the amount of our monthly payment before the effective date of any change. The notice will include information required by law to be given us and the title and telephone number of a person who will answer any question we may have regarding the notice.

Payments. We will make our principal payment on the first of every month starting on December 1, 2002. The initial monthly payment shall be $456.72. All payments will be paid first to any charges due and owing on the account under the terms of this note, then to interest, then to reduce the principal amount. We will make payments on this account until the principal, interest and other charges due on this account are fully paid. If the note is not fully paid by January 1, 2032, the lender may declare the remaining principal, interest and other charges dues and owing full at that time.

Prepayment. If this loan is prepaid in whole or in part, we agree to pay a penalty of 5% of the principal balance due on the date of prepayment during the first five years of the term.

By signing below, the borrowers agree to all terms and covenants contained in this loan note.

X *Arturo Homeowner*
_____

X *Maria Homeowner*
_____

11/17/2002
_____
Date

CHECKLIST: IDENTIFYING A PREDATORY MORTGAGE LOAN		
#	Indicator	Check if included
Marketing & Sales		
1	Aggressive telephone or mail solicitations to targeted neighborhoods	
2	Door-to-door solicitation by home improvement contractor	
3	Kickbacks to mortgage brokers	
4	Steering to high rate lenders	
5	Promising specific terms, e.g., a fixed rate loan; switching at closing	
6	Property flipping	
The Application		
7	Structuring loans with payments borrowers can't afford	
8	Falsifying loan applications (particularly regarding income level)	
9	Adding "insincere" co-signers	
10	Making loans to mentally incapacitated homeowners	
11	Forging signatures on loan documents (i.e., required disclosures)	
12	Paying off subsidized mortgages or lower interest rate loans	
13	Shifting unsecured debt into mortgages	
14	Loans in excess of 100% LTV	
15	Falsifying appraisals	
The Loan		
16	High annual percentage rate	
17	High points or padded closing costs	
18	ARM sold to borrower with limited/no ability to pay higher payments	
19	Balloon payments	
20	Negative amortization	
21	Bogus broker fees	
22	Requiring credit insurance	
23	Falsely identifying loans as lines of credit or open-end mortgages	
24	Mandatory arbitration clauses	
25	Excessive prepayment penalties	
26	Rushed loan closing	
27	Back-dating documents, esp. the notice of right to cancel	
28	Failing to give copies of documents to homeowner at closing	
After Closing		
29	Loan flipping (repeated refinancing, often after high-pressure sales tactics)	
30	Excessive late fees (including daily interest)	
31	Deliberately posting payments late	
32	Abusive collection practices	
33	Incomplete or shoddy work by home improvement contractor	
34	Shoddy installation of mobile home/damaged mobile home	
35	Failure to pay off debts as promised	
36	Foreclosure "rescue" scams	

Chapter Notes

1. 24 C.F.R. § 203.37a.

2. Cal. Civ. Code §§ 2945.1 to 2945.11 (foreclosure consultants); Cal. Civ. Code §§ 1695.1 to 1695.17 (home equity purchasers); Fla. Stat. §§ 45.031 to 45.035, 501.2078; Ga. Code Ann. § 10-1-393(b)(20)(A); 765 Ill. Comp. Stat. §§ 940/1 to 940/65; Md. Real Prop. Code Ann. § 7-105(A-1); Md. Real Prop. Code Ann. §§ 7-301-321; Mich. Comp. Laws §§ 445.1822 to 445.1825; Minn. Stat. Ann. §§ 325N.01 to .18; Mo. Ann. Stat. §§ 407.935 to 407.943; N.Y. Real Prop. Law § 265-a; R.I. Gen. Laws §§ 5-79-1 to 5-80-9; Wash. Rev. Code §§ 10.134.010 to 10.134.080.

3. A homeowner who is interested in exploring bankruptcy as an option should consult a reputable bankruptcy attorney. The National Association of Consumer Bankruptcy Attorneys lists its members at www.nacba.org.

CHAPTER 4

Homeowner Strategies for Reducing and Prioritizing Debt and Increasing Income

Often dealing with a homeowner's complete financial picture is essential to resolving a threatened foreclosure. Reducing expenses, deferring debts, and increasing income mean there is more money to devote to mortgage payments or a workout plan. Moreover, sometimes other debts also adversely affect the consumer's ability to stay in the home in other ways. Failure to pay utility bills may make the home uninhabitable because of a utility termination. Refinancing credit card debt into a home equity line of credit can lead to foreclosure not based on the first mortgage, but on this junior lien on the home.

This chapter examines a series of issues that can be key to keeping the homeowner in the home, including:

- Reducing utility costs and maintaining or restoring service;
- Dealing with student loan debt;
- Canceling private mortgage insurance;
- Dealing with credit card debt;
- Risks of repaying unsecured debt through repayment companies;
- Avoiding high-cost loans and related products;
- Refinancing of non-mortgage debt;
- Increasing income using the Earned Income and Child Tax Credits; and
- Prioritizing debt.

REDUCING UTILITY COSTS AND MAINTAINING OR RESTORING SERVICE

Utility issues are important in foreclosure prevention for several reasons. First, utility costs can eat up such a substantial portion of a homeowner's income that it becomes impossible to make the mortgage payment. Reducing the cost of utility service can free up income that a homeowner can use to catch up on mortgage payments. In addition, utility service is an essential part of shelter. If the homeowner saves the home, but utility service is disconnected, the family still cannot live in the home in safety and comfort.

Fortunately, there are many avenues to explore to reduce utility costs, and to prevent termination of service or restore service that has already been terminated. This section provides a condensed guide to the rights of customers of electric and gas utilities. For a good overview designed for counselors of this subject area, see the *NCLC Guide to the Rights of Utility Consumers*. For even more in-depth analysis, see NCLC's *Access to Utility Service*.

Every state regulates its electric and gas companies, and those regulations contain important consumer protections. However, we caution that rules governing utility service vary quite widely. When helping a homeowner with utility problems, make sure to check the rules in your state. Go to www.naruc.org, and click on "State Commissions." You will find a map of the United States that will lead you to the home page for the utility regulatory commission in your state.

In every state, "investor owned utilities" (IOUs), which are private and quite often large corporations, are much more closely regulated than municipally-owned or other government-owned entities (munis), or "rural electric cooperatives" (coops). This handbook's discussion of utilities focuses primarily on the rules that apply to IOUs.

Reducing Monthly Energy Bills

Sources of Payment Assistance. The federal Low Income Home Energy Assistance Program (LIHEAP) provides payments to help low-income households with their heating and cooling bills. Some state programs include furnace repair as a part of their assistance. To find out where a homeowner should apply for LIHEAP, send an e-mail to energyassistance @ncat.org, including the homeowner's city, county, and state, or call, toll-free, 866-674-6327.

There are also local fuel funds and, in some areas, water funds which raise charitable donations from various sources. These crisis funds usually help households that do not qualify for LIHEAP or who need additional help paying their energy or water bills. Your local LIHEAP agency is probably the best source for learning about any fuel funds in your area.

Some electric and natural gas utilities have low-income discount programs that can reduce the household's monthly bills. To find out about the availability of utility low-income discounts in your area, contact your electric or natural gas utility or utility commission.

Budget Billing or Levelized Payments. Most utilities offer "budget billing" (also called "levelized payments"). Estimated bills are sent each month for the average monthly bill based on the prior year's total charge. In this way higher winter or summer costs are spread out throughout the year. At some point during the year, the utility will reconcile the actual usage with the estimated usage so that by the end of the year the consumer is billed for what is actually used.

Weatherization Assistance. The federally-funded Low Income Weatherization Assistance Program can help households to significantly reduce their energy consumption, by an average of about 30%. The program is administered by state agencies, which often subcontract with local community action agencies. Some states and utilities also have their own low-income energy efficiency programs. These programs may be administered by the same agencies that administer the federal weatherization program or they may be administered by the local utility. To find out where a homeowner should apply for weatherization assistance, go to www.eere.energy.gov/weatherization/state_contacts.html. It is also worth asking the electric or natural gas utility if they have a low-income energy efficiency program.

Late Charges

Utilities often impose late charges on customers who do not pay their bills by the designated due date. While some states, such as Massachusetts and New Jersey, prohibit utilities from assessing late charges on residential customers, most states allow them. Many states provide a grace period before a utility may deem a bill "delinquent" and subject to the late charge. Utilities are prohibited from assessing late fees on disputed amounts. Thus, the utility should not impose a late charge on the disputed portion of the balance that remains unpaid.

Helping Homeowners Avoid Termination of Service

Most states limit the ability of utility companies to terminate service. A utility cannot terminate for nonpayment until after the bill is formally "due," and most states specify a minimum number of days before a bill can be considered past-due.

Once a utility sends a termination notice, it usually must wait a certain number of days before it can actually terminate the service—as few as 15 days in some states and as many as 40 to 50 days in others. Many states require utilities to provide repeat written notice, phone notice, or in-person notice prior to disconnecting service.

In most states, utilities may not disconnect service during non-business hours (e.g., weekends and holidays). In addition, many states further restrict the hours the utility may disconnect. For example, Maine's rule provides that utilities may disconnect Monday through Thursday 8 A.M.–3 P.M. and may not disconnect on Fridays or on the day of or before a legal holiday. Some states provide that termination notices become void after a given period of time. If the utility fails to disconnect within that time it must start the termination notice procedure over again.

Deferred Payment Plans. Most states require utilities to offer customers the option of entering into a deferred payment plan as a means of avoiding service termination. A typical deferred payment plan requires the customer to pay new bills as they come due while paying a portion of the past-due amount or "arrearage" each month. Some states specify a minimum length for payment plans and the circumstances in which they must be offered.

Serious Illness. Many states prohibit or limit terminations of service if disconnection would threaten the health or safety of one of the household's occupants. In some states, the serious illness provisions may only apply to households experiencing financial hardship. Customers who postpone termination based on the serious illness protections remain responsible for their past and current utility bills and may be required to enter into payment plans as a condition of postponing termination.

Customers will usually need to document the illness with a letter from a doctor or other medical professional. In general, serious illness letters are only valid for limited periods of time, from 30 to 60 days. Customers seeking to continue the postponement must submit renewed letters. Some utilities limit or prohibit renewal even when the illness persists.

Elders and Infants. Quite a few states have enacted age-related protections, limiting or prohibiting terminations of service based on the age of the household members. Most of these protections apply to elders. But one state, Massachusetts, specifically prohibits utilities from disconnecting or refusing to restore a customer's service if there is a child under the age of 12 months.

A number of states also provide elders with enhanced termination notification, e.g., requiring the utility to notify the elder or a third party, either in-person or by phone, of the impending termination. In addition, many utilities offer third party notification programs under which elders may request that a copy of all bills and notices be sent to a third party, often a relative, in addition to the customer.

Cold Weather. Many states have winter utility termination rules in effect that prohibit utilities from terminating or refusing to reinstate services due to nonpayment of heat-related utility bills. Most winter protection provisions apply during a several month period, typically mid-November through mid-April. Some states also extend the winter protection rules to 24-hour periods not falling within the winter months for which the national weather service has predicted temperatures of below 32 degrees Fahrenheit.

Some winter protection provisions apply exclusively to customers who are in financial hardship, while others also apply to households which include children, elders, or infirm individuals. Almost all winter protection provisions require customers taking advantage of the protection to enter into payment plans as a condition of continued service.

Hot Weather. A few states also have rules prohibiting service disconnection for 24-hour periods for which the National Weather Service is predicting unusually high temperatures. Eligibility for protection from termination under the hot weather provisions may depend on financial criteria.

Nonpayment of Disputed Bills. In general, regulations prohibit utilities from terminating service for nonpayment of *disputed* amounts. A minority of state utility regulations provide that customers may be required to put disputed amounts into an escrow account pending dispute resolution.

If the Homeowner's Utility Service Has Been Terminated

Right to Restoration of Service. Some homeowners seeking foreclosure prevention will have suffered such serious financial problems that they have not only fallen behind on their mortgage payments but have also lost utility service. Helping these homeowners restore utility service is an important step in preserving their homeownership.

Customers whose service has been terminated can usually get service restored by:

- Eliminating the reason for disconnection (for example, paying past-due amounts or entering into a payment plan on the past-due amount);
- Showing the utility commission that the disconnection was wrongful; or
- Demonstrating that a statutory protection (for example, winter moratorium or serious illness) applies.

Many states require utilities to reconnect service within a certain amount of time once the reason for the disconnection has been remedied, often within 12 or 24 hours. Most utilities charge a fee to reconnect service. However, utilities may waive or reduce that fee under certain circumstances.

Deposit Requirement. A deposit requirement can be a serious obstacle to restoring utility service. Utilities in every state except Massachusetts may require applicants and existing customers to pay a security deposit in order to receive utility service. Generally, utilities will require a deposit if the applicant cannot provide a satisfactory payment of payment for utility service for the previous 12 months; or has an undisputed past-due unpaid account for previous utility service; or gave the utility bad checks; etc.

Utilities often consider other factors when deciding whether to impose a deposit: an applicant's record of homeownership; proof of regular income; and, sometimes, credit scores. However, some states may prohibit basing the size of a deposit on one or more of these factors.

Utility regulations typically provide that a deposit may not exceed an estimated bill for two to three months of usage. Many utilities allow customers to pay deposits in monthly installments. Keep in mind that deposit requirements may be more flexible for elders, for low-income applicants/customers, and during the winter months. In fact, at least one state prohibits utilities from requiring or retaining deposits from customers aged 60 or older.

Utility companies in most states are required to keep records of deposits, issue receipts to customers, return deposits by a time specified by regulation if the customer has maintained a good payment record, and pay interest on the deposit at a specified rate.

Old, Unpaid Bills. Sometimes, a utility will not restore service because it reaches back into the past and finds old unpaid bills, from prior addresses, or even by prior occupants of the present address. Most states permit utilities to either deny service to or require a deposit from an applicant who has unpaid utility bills from a prior address. Many of those states will still require the utility to provide service at the new address if the customer pays off the unpaid amount, enters into a payment plan to repay the arrearage, or shows that he or she has a dispute regarding the arrearage pending at the state utility commission.

The law in most states is clear that a utility company cannot deny an applicant new service simply because there is an amount due from a prior unrelated occupant of the dwelling or from the owner of the property. If the utility denies service on this basis, contact the utility commission. The rules regarding denial of service based on the debt of a roommate, spouse, or household member are quite varied. Many states follow the rule that a utility cannot deny an applicant service based on anyone else's debt, whether that third party is a completely unrelated prior tenant or a close family member. However, several states have adopted rules which allow utilities to collect bills owed by a roommate, spouse, or household member of the applicant for new service. Since the rules vary, customers with this problem should contact the utility commission and ask what the rules provide.

Reduced Cost Phone Service

Many homeowners can reduce their telephone costs substantially by shopping around and comparing offers from several providers. Canceling optional features can also shave precious dollars off the monthly bill.

Lifeline and Link-Up are federal programs designed to make local phone service affordable for low-income households. The Lifeline program provides a discount on local phone bills and the Link-Up program provides a discount on the connection charge for starting service. To find out who may be eligible, call the local phone company, or contact the Universal Services Administrative Company at www.universalservice.org/li/consumers/lifeline_support .asp or 888-641-8722.

DEALING WITH STUDENT LOAN DEBT

Student loan debt takes an enormous bite out of many homeowners' budgets, impairing their ability to make mortgage payments or make other priority payments. Working out some relief from overwhelming student loan debt can be an important step toward saving their home. Whenever you help a borrower with a student loan problem, it is important to assess the impact on the borrower's credit report and, whenever possible, help to remove negative information about student loans or ensure that lenders do so when required.

Students of all ages and income levels are leaving school with higher levels of student loan debt. This is due to a variety of reasons, including skyrocketing tuition costs and cuts in grant programs. In addition, student loan debt sometimes results from enrollment in a fraudulent trade school. Student loan debt problems are exacerbated by the fact that the government uses harsh methods to collect student loans, such as offsetting the debt against the debtor's federal benefits, garnishing the debtor's wages, and intercepting the debtor's tax refund.

There is almost always something to be done to help a borrower cancel or defer a student loan, or reduce monthly payments. Even when repayment is not feasible, a borrower may be able to reduce the amounts subject to offset, garnishment, or seizure based on a hardship defense. There are special forms available on the Department of Education's website and in NCLC's *Student Loan Law* manual that a borrower must fill out in order to prove hardship. These generally require an accounting of income and expenses and an explanation of the hardship circumstances. Borrowers should aggressively assert their collection appeal rights.

Discharge of Student Loan Debt

In limited circumstances, the federal government will discharge (cancel) a student loan debt. Discharging a student loan debt completely wipes out the current loan. In addition, if a student loan is discharged, the consumer is entitled to get back any money paid on the loan, as well as funds taken by the government when it collected on the loan through tax intercepts, wage garnishment, or other methods.

The following student loans can be discharged through some or all of the federal discharge programs:

- Guaranteed student loans (Stafford).
- Unsubsidized Stafford loans.
- Supplemental loans for students (SLSs).
- PLUS loans.
- Federal direct loans.
- Perkins loans (however, the false certification discharge does not apply).

There are also many private student loans on the market. Private loan borrowers do not participate in the federal discharge program, but the private lender also has fewer collection tools available. Borrowers must contact their lenders to get more information about the terms and conditions of private loans.

For any federal loan discharge application, a critical first step is to figure out what type of federal loan a borrower has, by contacting the National Student Loan Data System (NSLDS) through the Federal Student Aid Information Center, 800-4-FED-AID, TDD 800-730-8913, or on-line at www.nslds.ed.gov. These resources only list federal student loans. Applications for discharges of federal student loans are available on the Department of Education website, www.ed.gov. The most important types of discharges are discussed below:

Closed School Discharge. A student can get a discharge of a student loan in some circumstances if the school closed while the student was enrolled. A closed school discharge is also available if a school closed within 90 days after the student withdrew from the school. This discharge is available for loans received at least in part on or after January 1, 1986. The

Department of Education maintains a list of official closure dates, *available at* http://bcol01.ed.gov/CFAPPS/FSA/closedschool/searchpage.cfm.

False Certification Discharge. Another type of discharge is the false certification discharge. To obtain a false certification discharge, the student must show that his or her eligibility to borrow was falsely certified by the school. For example, the school may have falsely certified the results of an admissions test that it gave to students who did not have high school diplomas. In most cases, a student with a high school diploma or GED at the time of admission cannot qualify for a false certification discharge. A false certification discharge is also available in cases of forgery and, as of July 1, 2006, if there was a false certification due to a crime of identity theft. A false certification discharge is available only for loans received at least in part on or after January 1, 1986. Perkins loans not eligible.

Unpaid Refund Discharge. An unpaid refund discharge cancels the student's liability for loans obtained after January 1, 1986 to the extent of the amount of a refund that a school owed the student and failed to pay. For example, if the student never attended or dropped out soon after enrolling, and the school should have refunded part of the tuition but did not, the student can get a discharge of the amount that should have been refunded.

Disability Discharge. To qualify, a student loan debtor must document a permanent and total disability. Preexisting conditions qualify only if there has been substantial deterioration after the borrower took out the loan.

Other Discharge Options. There are a few federal discharge programs for borrowers who work in certain professions, such as teaching. These programs vary considerably depending on the type of loan the borrower has. Loans should also be discharged if a borrower passes away. Bankruptcy is another way to cancel a student loan debt. However, cancellation of the debt is not automatic, but is only granted if the borrower shows that repayment will "impose an undue hardship on the debtor and debtor's dependents."

Some states have their own student loan discharge programs. Under these programs, a discharge is usually available where a school is insolvent and where the student cannot obtain a federal discharge. A list of these programs can be found in NCLC's *Student Loan Law*.

Deferment and Forbearance

If a homeowner is burdened by student loan debt but is not eligible for a discharge, a deferment or forbearance may be an option.

Deferment. A deferment allows a borrower to delay repayment on a loan for a specified period of time. Interest will not accrue during the deferment period for borrowers with subsidized loans. Interest will accrue for most other borrowers. Only borrowers who are not currently in default may apply for deferments. The primary types of deferments are in-school deferments; unemployment deferments, not to exceed three years; and economic hardship deferments, granted one year at a time for a maximum of three years. There is also a deferment program for members of the military.

Forbearance. A forbearance allows a borrower to temporarily stop payments on a loan. Interest continues to accrue during this period. Forbearances are available regardless of whether a borrower is in default. Under most of the student loan programs, the Department of Education has discretion to grant a forbearance, and in some cases must grant a forbearance, if:

- The borrower is in poor health or has other personal problems that affect the ability to make the scheduled payments;
- The borrower has filed an application for consolidation or discharge that is being considered;
- The borrower has been affected by a military mobilization; or
- The borrower will not be able to repay the loan within the maximum repayment term.

There are also several other grounds for forbearances.

Borrowers may request forbearances orally or in writing. Deferment requests must be in writing. The Department of Education has developed forms for the various deferment programs. These are available on the Department's website, www.ed.gov.

Repayment

For many student loan debtors, discharge of the debt will not be possible, and forbearance or deferment will not be available. These homeowners will have to deal with making payments on the loan. The important goal for the housing counselor is to get the homeowner's student loan payments down to a level that makes it possible for the homeowner to afford the mortgage payment.

Repayment options vary depending on whether the borrower is merely delinquent on the loan or in default. In most cases, a borrower is considered to be in default after having been delinquent for nine consecutive months.

Pre-Default Repayment Options. Borrowers have much more flexibility to choose repayment plans if they are not yet in default on their loans. There are a number of repayment options, depending on the type of loan the borrower has. These options include extended repayment plans as well as income-sensitive plans.

For the lowest income borrowers, the most affordable plan is generally the income-contingent repayment plan, available only through the Department of Education's Direct loan program. The borrower's monthly payments are determined using a formula that takes household income and size into account as well as student loan debt levels. In some cases, borrowers may have to consolidate their loans with the Direct loan program in order to access the income contingent repayment plan. Consolidation is an option to consider both before and after default. Consolidation loans are available through the government's guaranteed loan program (the "FFEL" program) and through the Direct loan program. The FFEL program offers an "income-sensitive" repayment plan, which requires borrowers at a minimum to make payments that cover monthly accrued interest.

Post-Default Repayment Options. As discussed above, the lowest income borrowers will often want to obtain an income contingent repayment plan through the Direct loan program. If the borrower did not originally take out a Direct loan, she will likely have to consolidate with the Direct loan program in order to access this repayment plan.

In order to obtain a FFEL consolidation loan, a borrower who is in default must first either make three monthly payments in an amount determined to be "reasonable and affordable" (see below), or agree to an income sensitive repayment plan (ISRP). Similarly, in order to obtain a Direct consolidation loan, a borrower who is in default must either make three monthly payments in an amount determined to be "reasonable and affordable" or agree to an income contingent repayment plan (ICRP). An on-line calculator can be used to figure out the monthly payment under standard and income-contingent repayment plans. For more information, see www.ed.gov/offices/OSFAP/DirectLoan/calc.html. A more sophisticated calculator program to analyze ICRP payments is available at www.finaid.org/calculators/icr.phtml.

There are advantages and disadvantages to consolidation as well as certain restrictions. Not all loans can be consolidated. Borrowers who are able to consolidate their defaulted loans obtain a fresh start, becoming eligible for new loans, grants, and even deferments. Borrowers will no longer be listed as currently in default and will no longer be subject to tax intercepts, garnishments, or other collection efforts. For more information, see the *NCLC Guide to Surviving Debt* and NCLC's *Student Loan Law*.

Loan rehabilitation is another strategy to get out of default. Borrowers must request this option from their loan holder and must establish a rehabilitation plan in writing. They must make nine timely reasonable and affordable payments within a ten month period as part of the rehabilitation process. The payment amount is negotiated with the loan holder, but must be reasonable and affordable and the loan holder is not permitted to set a minimum amount that all borrowers must pay. Perkins rehabilitation is also available in certain circumstances.

Collection Methods

The government has significant powers to collect federal student loans. There is also no statute of limitations on student loan collections, which means that the government can continue collecting a student loan no matter how old it is. Allowable collection methods include:

Administrative Wage Garnishment. Unlike other creditors, the government does not have to get a judgment from a court to begin garnishing wages. In general, the government can take no more than 15% of disposable pay.

Tax Refund Offset, Including Offsets Against the Earned Income Tax Credit.

Federal Benefits Offsets. The government can seize portions of certain federal benefits, including Social Security Retirement and Disability. No more than 15% of the total benefit may be taken. The first $750 of a borrower's monthly payment may not be taken. SSI benefits are also exempt. Other federal benefits may be offset if the regulatory agency has not requested and received a waiver for those benefits. For more details, see http://fms.treas.gov/debt/dmexmpt.pdf for information on benefits exempted from offset. Some benefits are statutorily exempted, including federal student loan payments and U.S. Department of Veterans Affairs payments.

A borrower may be able to reduce the amounts subject to offset, garnishment, or seizure based on a hardship defense. There are special forms available on the Department's website and in the NCLC's *Student Loan Law* that a borrower must fill out in order to prove hardship. These generally require an accounting of income and expenses and an explanation of the hardship circumstances.

Litigation. The government can sue defaulted borrowers.

CANCELING PRIVATE MORTGAGE INSURANCE

A homeowner whose down payment on a house was less than 20% of the purchase price will probably be required to pay for private mortgage insurance (PMI). This insurance protects the lender if there is a default on the mortgage by allowing it to get paid some of the monies not recovered from the foreclosure process.

The cost of this insurance is added to the mortgage payment and is handled like payments for taxes and property insurance in an escrow account. The premiums are based on the amount and term of the loan, the loan-to-value ratio (LTV), the type of loan, and the amount of coverage required by the lender. The less the borrower puts down, the higher the premium.

The monthly charge for private mortgage insurance can be the factor that makes a homeowner's mortgage unaffordable. For homeowners who are having trouble making their mortgage payments, it is important to find out if their payment includes PMI, and, if it does, whether the equity in the home is sufficient to cancel the PMI.

Cancellation Rights Under Federal Law

The Homeowner's Protection Act of 1998 is a federal law that requires PMI to be canceled automatically or at the homeowner's request when the amount of equity in the home reaches certain levels, as described below. The law does not apply to mortgages made before July 29, 1999, and it does not apply to all mortgages (for example, FHA mortgages are not covered because the FHA has its own rules for cancellation of PMI).

If the homeowner is current on her mortgage payments, PMI may be canceled:

- *Automatically,* if the equity rises to 22% of the value of the home at the time when the homeowner took out the mortgage;
- *When requested in writing,* if the equity increases to 20% of on the value of the home at the time when the homeowner took out the mortgage.

The lender may require evidence that the value of the property has not declined below its original value and that the property does not have a second mortgage, such as a home equity loan.

> Canceling PMI will make the mortgage payment go down and will save money. For example, if the consumer purchased a home for $100,000 by making a 10% down payment ($10,000) and got a $90,000 mortgage loan for the balance of the sale price, the consumer may be paying about $50 per month for PMI. When the mortgage balance reaches $80,000 (creating 20% equity), the consumer can ask that the PMI be canceled. This will save $600 per year and many thousands of dollars over the loan term.

To figure out how much equity a homeowner has for the purposes of this law, you will need to know the balance owed on the mortgage and the original value of the home. To determine the value of the property, the law specifies that the lower of two figures must be used; either the original purchase price of the home or its appraised value at the time the mortgage was originated.

To figure out the balance owed, you can check the mortgage statements or call the servicer. In some cases, you may be able to use a figure for the balance owed based on the original amortization schedule for the mortgage rather than the actual outstanding balance. In the example above, under the original amortization schedule for a fifteen-year $90,000 mortgage at a 6% interest rate, an $80,000 balance owed (20% equity) would be reached after thirty months of payments. If in this example the homeowner did not request cancellation of the PMI at the thirty month point, the lender should automatically cancel the PMI in the thirty-sixth month when the balance owed is down to $78,000 (22% equity). If this mortgage had a higher interest rate, or a longer repayment term, then it would take more time to reach the required equity levels.

Even if the homeowner has an older mortgage or the law does not apply for some other reason, the lender may be willing to cancel the PMI or state law may require it, so you should ask the lender. For example, in California, if PMI is required as a condition of securing a loan, the lender must notify the borrower whether he or she has a right to cancel the insurance and under what conditions the insurance can be canceled. In Connecticut, the lender must notify the borrower whether the borrower has a right to cancel. In Minnesota, borrowers have the right to cancel PMI when the unpaid principal balance of the loan falls below 80% of the current fair market value of the property. These state laws remain relevant to the extent that the 1998 federal law does not override them.

Even where there is no legal requirement, some lenders may agree to cancel PMI if the homeowner has enough equity (usually at least 25%) based on the current market value of the home rather than the original value when the homeowner got the mortgage. The lender will require an appraisal of the home and require that the borrower have a good payment history. This rule can be very helpful if the home has gone up in value since the consumer bought or refinanced it. In this situation, it cannot hurt to ask the servicer or lender about the possibility of canceling the PMI.

Cancellation Rights Offered by Fannie Mae, Freddie Mac, and the FHA

Fannie Mae guidelines provide for cancellation of private mortgage insurance at the borrower's request when the borrower's equity reaches 25% of the *current* value of the home as established by a new appraisal, provided that the borrower has a good payment history and that the loan is at least two years old. For loans made on or after July 29, 1999, Fannie Mae will automatically cancel private mortgage insurance when the loan reaches a loan-to-value ratio (LTV) of 78% based on original value; for loans made before July 29, 1999, PMI is canceled at the half-point of the loan term, provided that payments are current at that time.

Freddie Mac provides that a consumer can request cancellation of PMI coverage when the borrower's equity reaches 25% of the *current* value of the home as established by a new appraisal, provided that the borrower has a good payment history and that the loan is between two and five years old. If five or more years have passed since loan origination, the borrower can request cancellation at 20% equity. Cancellation at 20% equity is also permissible earlier if substantial improvements have increased the market value of the property. For loans originated on or after July 29, 1999, automatic cancellation is available on the date when the loan is scheduled to reach an LTV of 78%, based on the original value, or the midpoint of the amortization schedule, whichever is first, provided that the loan is current. For loans made before July 29, 1999, PMI must be canceled at the half-point of the loan term, provided that loan payments are current.

As with conventional home loans, FHA-insured mortgages require mortgage insurance. The mortgage insurance, referred to as mutual mortgage insurance (MMI), charges 0.5% per year of the loan amount. In addition to the monthly MMI, the FHA charges an up-front mortgage insurance premium (MIP) of 1.50% for 30-year fixed rate mortgages. Any unused portion of the upfront MIP may be refunded within the first 84 months of the loan if the loan is retired.

For FHA loans originated after January 1, 2001, the monthly mortgage insurance payment will be automatically canceled when the outstanding principal balance reaches 78% of the original purchase price (provided that the monthly mortgage insurance payments have been made for a minimum of 5 years for 30-year loans). In addition, a homeowner with a 15-year mortgage will not have to pay the monthly mortgage insurance when the down payment was greater than 10% of the purchase price. Neither section 203k loans nor section 234 (condominium) loans require the upfront MIP but do both require the monthly MIP regardless of the down payment.

Excessive Premiums

Credit Scoring. Abuses in the area of private mortgage insurance have most recently taken the form of extraordinarily high PMI premiums attributable primarily to a borrower's credit score. Whereas premiums used to be priced based upon certain loan characteristics, the addition of credit history as a factor has raised monthly premiums for some borrowers from an average of under $100 to amounts ranging from $200 to over $900. Such a premium increase can raise a consumer's monthly mortgage payment quite dramatically—50% or more. According to Fannie Mae's guidelines, the creditor's determination of the consumer's repayment ability based on the debt-to-income ratio at the time of the loan origination should include the actual PMI payment that the consumer will be required to pay.

The insurance companies that provide private mortgage insurance post prices incorporating credit scores on their websites, but creditors who are dealing directly with consumers (and who themselves choose the PMI provider) generally do not inform borrowers of these prices prior to closing (and at least in some cases do not appear to include the high PMI payment caused by a low credit score in the analysis of a consumer's repayment ability). In addition, many subprime lenders fail to provide consumers with a good faith estimate, which may list the monthly premium. As a result, a borrower could arrive at a loan closing only to find that her monthly payment is several hundred dollars higher than she was expecting. The borrower may not be able to afford this, but may feel pressured to sign the loan papers because she needs the loan. Because no prior notice has been provided, the borrower is not in a position to shop around.

Kickback Arrangements. High costs may also be due to the fact that the insurer has paid illegal kickbacks to the mortgage company for the referral of business. Since lenders, and not borrowers, choose the PMI company, there are strong incentives for lenders to select an insurer that will pay the lender the largest referral fee for selecting that insurer, rather than seeking the insurance policy that is best for the borrower. Additionally, only a few companies provide all of the private mortgage insurance in the country, further decreasing any chance for competition. A consumer whose premium appears to be inflated should explore bringing a claim against the insurer and creditor under the Real Estate Settlement Procedures Act (RESPA). State regulation currently provides no specific protection from such predatory pricing.

Disclosure Requirements

There are several disclosure requirements related to private mortgage insurance. First, RESPA requires that mortgage insurance be disclosed as part of the good faith estimate (GFE). Second, the lender must tell borrowers about "affiliated business relationships" between lenders and a PMI company (if one exists), list the estimated cost of the real estate settlement service, and state that the use of the particular PMI company is not required. If the disclosures about an affiliated business arrangement are not provided, payments between the lender and the insurance company may be illegal. However, the consumer has no right under RESPA to sue the lender if it fails to give the GFE or fails to list the PMI premium on the document. For this latter violation, state deceptive practices laws may provide a remedy.

The Truth in Lending Act (TILA) imposes disclosure requirements that may provide more effective remedies for borrowers. First, TILA requires that mortgage premiums be included in the finance charge and the APR. In addition, TILA requires the creditor to disclose the monthly payment schedule for the loan, including scheduled changes in the payments. Since the federal Homeowners Protection Act requires that mortgage insurance be terminated at a particular time, the schedule of payments must reflect this reduction in the payments. Failure to provide an accurate payment schedule entitles the borrower to money damages and attorney fees. In addition, for most mortgage loans that are for some purpose other than buying the home, it is grounds to rescind the loan. A suit for damages under TILA must be filed within one year of the date of the loan, and there is a three-year deadline for rescission, so whenever there is a violation of these requirements the homeowner should be referred to an attorney promptly.

DEALING WITH CREDIT CARD DEBT

Unsecured Credit Card Debt Should Be Low Priority

Credit cards should be among the lowest priorities for payment for a homeowner who is already having financial problems. The mortgage payment, other shelter costs, food, automobile expenses, health care costs, and other necessities should always come first.

Homeowners may feel pressured by collection calls or other concerns to give credit card debt greater priority than it deserves. As long as the credit card debt is unsecured, however (see the discussion below), the homeowner should give it lower priority than the debts and expenses necessary to save the home, maintain employment, and pay for other necessities.

One reason so many homeowners have unmanageable credit card debt is the aggressive promotion of these cards by the industry. More than five billion credit card offers are mailed to consumers each year. Most of us get several offers for new credit cards every week. In addition, credit cards are advertised everywhere. We see advertisements on television, the Internet, at sporting events, in restaurants, and increasingly on college campuses and even in high schools.

In the past, consumers who had credit problems rarely got new credit card offers. Lenders reviewed credit reports and chose not to offer credit to consumers they considered bad risks. More recently, lenders buy huge mailing lists and offer credit to everyone on the list without an individual evaluation of their credit history. They offer credit cards to anyone with an adequate credit score, whether or not the person can afford the credit or is already over-extended. The result is that credit card debt has grown dramatically, creating pressure on more and more consumers not to pay their other, higher-priority debts.

Distinguishing Unsecured Credit Card Debt from Secured Debt

Before discussing with a homeowner the priority to be given to credit card debt, it is important to determine what kind of credit card debt the homeowner has. If the credit card is secured by the consumer's home or bank account, then it is a higher priority debt than if it is unsecured. (In general, all things being equal, consumers should seek and use credit cards which are unsecured in preference to those that are secured.)

Most credit cards are unsecured. However, there are three ways in which some credit card lenders take collateral:

Credit Cards Secured by Purchases. Some credit card lenders, such as department stores, claim to take collateral in items purchased with their card. If the consumer has problems making payments, those creditors may threaten to repossess the property bought with the card. Creditors rarely follow through with these threats, however, except for unusual big-ticket purchases.

Even if the creditor might follow through with a threat of repossession, a credit card debt that is secured only by the items bought with the card will normally be a lower priority debt than the mortgage payment and other necessities. Losing the items bought with the card is usually a less serious problem than falling behind on the mortgage payment, so debts owed on this type of secured credit card are lower priority than the mortgage payment.

Credit Cards Secured by a Bank Account. Another type of secured credit card provides a credit limit up to the amount the consumer has on deposit in a particular bank account. If the consumer does not make the payments, the creditor takes the money in the account. These cards are usually marketed as a way for a consumer with a bad credit rating or no credit history to establish or reestablish credit.

A credit card secured by a bank account should be given higher priority than an unsecured credit card. Homeowners need to be aware that if they fail to pay, the creditor will take the money from the bank account. Once the money in the account is gone, however, the debt should be the same low priority as an unsecured credit card (as long as the consumer is not depositing more money into that same account).

Credit Cards Secured by the Home. Some lenders offer credit cards in connection with a home equity line of credit. Each time the borrower uses the card, the balance is secured against the home. Some home improvement contractors offer these cards as a way to pay for repairs.

If the homeowner does not pay a credit card debt that is secured by the home, the creditor can foreclose on the home. (For this reason, home-secured credit cards are generally a bad idea for consumers.) If the credit card debt in question is secured by the home, the homeowner should give it the same priority as any other mortgage debt, and should make at least the minimum payments on it.

Can the Homeowner Negotiate a Lower Interest Rate or Other Concessions from the Creditor?

Negotiating a Lower Interest Rate. For many consumers, interest charges make up a substantial portion of their credit card debts. If the interest rate were lower, they could reduce their payments and still pay off the debt just as quickly.

One small survey by U.S. PIRG found that consumers had great success in convincing their credit card companies to lower their interest rates simply by calling their creditors and asking them to do this.[1] The consumers used this sample script:

> Hi. My name is _____. I am a good customer, but I have received several offers in the mail from other credit card companies with lower APRs. I want a lower rate on my card, or I will cancel my card and switch companies.

Fifty-six percent of consumers who called lowered their annual percentage rates (APRs), by an average of more than one-third. It is unclear, however, how well this will work for consumers who are already behind on their credit card payments when they call. The key factors affecting success were:

- Length of time with this particular card (longer is better);
- Credit limit on this card (a higher limit is better);
- How maxed out the consumer is on this card (less is better);
- How maxed out the consumer is on other credit cards (less is better);
- Number of times the consumer missed a payment or paid late on debts other than this credit card (fewer is better).

Any homeowner who is paying interest on a credit card debt should consider calling the credit card company to ask for an interest rate reduction. Even if the factors listed above do not apply to the consumer, making the call cannot do any harm and may result in a reduction.

Asking the Creditor to "Re-age" the Account. Re-aging an account is a way of turning back the clock and wiping away at least some of a credit card debtor's negative credit history. For example, a homeowner who was three months late on credit card payments and then started paying again could ask the creditor to re-age the account. If the creditor agrees, then the homeowner's credit record will not show that the account was late for those three months.

The primary benefit of re-aging a credit card debt is that is reduces the damage to the consumer's credit record. However, the creditor may also forgive any late fees that were imposed when the consumer missed the payments, so re-aging can also free up some money for the consumer's mortgage payments.

Most creditors require the debtor to make at least two or three timely payments before they will consider re-aging an account. Most will consider re-aging only if the consumer has had the account for at least nine months. They usually do not allow a consumer to re-age an account more than once over a twelve-month period or more than twice in a five-year period.

Lump-Sum Settlement. In many cases, a creditor will accept a percentage of a debt as full payment if the money can be paid all at once in a lump sum. A homeowner who is in danger of foreclosure is unlikely to have a lump sum available, so this option is usually not on the table. If a consumer pays a lump sum in return for forgiveness of the remainder of the debt, it is critically important to get the creditor to confirm in writing that the remainder of the debt has been forgiven.

Educating the Homeowner About the Benefits and Disadvantages of Making Minimum Payments

Typically, homeowners who are facing foreclosure are already making only the minimum monthly payments on their credit card debts. For the less-typical homeowner who is paying more than the minimum monthly payment, an easy way to free up more money for the mortgage payment is to reduce the monthly credit card payment to the minimum.

Before recommending this step, the counselor should make sure that the homeowner understands the long-term drawbacks of making only the minimum monthly payment: the credit card debt will hardly be reduced at all, and that it will take years to pay off the debt. For example:[2]

Balance	APR	Min. Mo. Payment	Total Interest	# Mos. to Pay
$4,500	12%	1% plus that month's interest	$ 4,196	291
$4,500	12%	4%	$ 1,455	124
$4,500	18%	1% plus that month's interest	$12,431	307
$4,500	18%	4%	$ 2,615	146

Another problem with making only the minimum monthly payment is that consumers in tight financial circumstances often budget to pay only this amount. Then if the creditor increases the minimum payment, the consumer faces new financial problems.

Despite these long-term concerns, unsecured credit card debts are a low-priority obligation for a homeowner who is in danger of foreclosure. Reducing the credit card payment to the minimum—at least until the foreclosure is resolved—is sound financial advice as long as the homeowner understands the reasons to resume larger payments if possible once the foreclosure crisis is resolved.

Discontinuing Payments on Unsecured Debt if Necessary to Save the Home

In some cases, it will be impossible for the homeowner to make even the minimum payment on a credit card debt and still catch up on the mortgage. In this circumstance, the homeowner should consider discontinuing payments on the credit card debt until the foreclosure crisis is resolved. While collection calls will likely begin, the end of this chapter describes how to stop such calls. Discontinuing payments on credit card debt will harm the consumer's credit rating, but so will a foreclosure. If the homeowner decides to save the home by diverting the credit card payments to the mortgage, the homeowner should be supported in this decision.

The homeowner may want to stay current on payments on one credit card so that it can be used for emergencies. Before selecting one card to continue paying, however, the homeowner should make sure that that card issuer will not cancel the card, lower the credit limit, or raise the interest rate because the consumer has defaulted on payments on a different credit card.

Dealing with Credit Card Debts Where the Amount Claimed Is Wrong

If the homeowner's credit card debt is higher than it should be because of mistakes in the bill—for example, purchases the consumer did not make or charges that were induced by fraud—the homeowner should to dispute the debt with the credit card company. The rights of credit card customers to dispute charges are explained in Chapter 15, below.

Educating the Homeowner About Daily Use of Credit and Debit Cards

Even while implementing a plan to save the home, most homeowners will want at least one debit or a credit card to use when it is inconvenient to pay with cash. *Although they often look the same, there are important differences between credit and debit cards.* When a consumer uses a debit card, the money is immediately taken from the consumer's bank account. This is different from using a credit card, where the consumer is getting money as a loan that has to be paid back only when the credit card bill comes.

Debit Cards with the VISA or MasterCard Brand. If a consumer has a debit card with a VISA or MasterCard logo on it, sometimes when the card is swiped at a point-of-sale device (the card readers at the grocery store or gas station), the consumer is given the option of using the card as "credit" or "debit." The credit option is confusing because really the consumer is still using the card as a debit card. What this choice actually means is: does the consumer want to use the debit card like an ATM card and enter a PIN (Personal Identification Number) for identification, or does the consumer want to use it like a credit card and sign the receipt for identification? Either way, the money is taken out of the consumer's bank account within a short period of time.

Comparing Credit and Debit Cards. There are advantages and disadvantages to using a credit card versus a debit card. The danger with a debit card is that the homeowner may draw down the bank account that has the money for the mortgage payment. Another danger is that many banks automatically place "overdraft protection," an extremely high-cost form of short-term credit, on debit cards. Then the bank allows the consumer to overdraw the account with the debit card, in return for enormous fees.

The danger with a credit card is that the homeowner may run up additional interest-bearing debt that may cause financial hardship in the long run.

The consumer's rights to dispute charges on debit cards (including debit cards with the MasterCard or VISA logo) are more limited than with credit cards. For example, if a consumer buys a vacuum cleaner from a nearby store with a credit card and it breaks during the first week of use and the merchant refuses to fix it, the consumer may withhold payment for the charge for the vacuum on his or her credit card bill. There are *no* similar rights available when a consumer uses a debit card.

The consumer's responsibility for losses from a lost or stolen card is generally much greater for a debit card than for a credit card. The consumer's responsibility for unauthorized credit card charges is limited to $50. Compare that to a debit card where the consumer could be responsible for as much as $500 if the consumer fails to notify the bank within two days after finding out that the card was taken and for an unlimited amount if he or she fails to report an unauthorized transfer within sixty days of when the bank statement is mailed showing these charges.

Both VISA and MasterCard have policies that limit the consumer's debit card losses in most situations to $50. However, these policies do not apply when the debit card is used at an ATM or with some debit card transactions using a PIN.

Finally, the consequences of an unauthorized withdrawal from a bank account through a debit card may be worse than the consequences of an unauthorized charge on a credit card. Since the money to pay the debit comes directly out of the bank account, the consumer may temporarily or permanently lose use of that money—effective immediately. Even if the money is later restored to the account, temporary loss of the money may mean that the consumer cannot pay bills or meet other pressing needs and may also cause checks to bounce.

Educating the Homeowner About Future Credit Card Offers

Credit card offers can be very enticing. Nearly every offer promises some special benefit with a new card. In some cases, the offer is for a low rate. In others, no annual fee is promised. Still others advertise free goods or services, low minimum payments, frequent flyer miles, cash back, special member privileges, and contributions to schools or favorite charities. These offers, however, never discuss the downside of a new card or the potential risks.

Appendix B, below, is a list, suitable for distribution to homeowners, of tips for selecting a new credit card and avoiding problems when using a credit card. These tips are an abridged version of consumer information in the *NCLC Guide to Surviving Debt.* Another useful resource for the consumer is the *NCLC Surviving Credit Card Debt Workbook.*[3]

SPECIAL RIGHTS FOR MEMBERS OF THE MILITARY AND THEIR DEPENDENTS

Members of the military who are on active duty and their dependents have special rights that can significantly reduce their expenses. The interest rate on any obligation taken out *before* the servicemember entered active duty—for example, a mortgage, a car loan, a credit card, a home equity line of credit, a payday loan—is reduced to 6%. If there are co-signers on the obligation, the interest rate has to be reduced for all obligors. Reducing the interest rate can result in a major reduction of the monthly payment, but the servicemember must request the reduction.

Federal law allows servicemembers to get out of vehicle leases without penalty in some circumstances when they enter active duty. Even a servicemember who entered into the vehicle lease while on active duty can get out of it if he or she is transferred overseas or deployed with a military unit for 180 days or more. In addition, when a member of the military is on active duty, federal law prohibits self-help repossession, non-judicial foreclosure, and enforcement of storage liens without a court order. While these prohibitions do not directly reduce the servicemember's monthly expenses, they mean that a servicemember who falls a little behind on these payments is not in danger of immediate loss of property.

Members of the military also have certain extra protections after a foreclosure sale, discussed in Chapter 12, below. In addition, as of October 1, 1007, a new federal law will prohibit certain loans to active duty military personnel from carrying an interest rate greater than 36%.

Tips for Counselors. If the homeowner or a member of the homeowner's family is on active duty, refer them to a JAG Corps attorney to make sure that they have exercised all their rights under the Servicemembers Civil Relief Act.

REPAYING UNSECURED DEBT THROUGH REPAYMENT COMPANIES

Debt Management Plans Obtained Through Credit Counselors

An option for paying unsecured debts is to work with a credit counseling agency that offers debt management plans (DMPs). With a DMP, the consumer sends the credit counseling agency a monthly payment, which the agency then distributes to creditors. In return, creditors usually agree to waive fees and reduce interest rates.

Despite claims of many credit counseling agencies, DMPs are not suitable for everyone. DMPs do not include secured debt, e.g., mortgage or car debt, and generally only include credit card debts. Credit counseling agencies generally do not help directly with secured debt. DMP monthly payments can be considerable. The consumer must have some disposable income each month to make payments. Most credit counseling agencies charge set-up and monthly fees to administer the DMPs. Many credit counseling agencies also get paid by the credit card companies for whom they collect.

A DMP may be useful for a homeowner who is facing foreclosure *if* the credit counseling organization obtains enough concessions from the creditors it is paying so that the homeowner can pay down those debts with a lower monthly payment. On the other hand, the credit counseling organization may charge so many fees that it makes the consumer's financial situation worse. In addition, being in a DMP may put pressure on the homeowner to pay the credit cards at the expense of the mortgage.

Unfortunately, some credit counseling agencies are unscrupulous and it may be difficult to find reputable agencies. Non-profit status is *not* a guarantee of quality. Consumers and their representatives should ask at least the following questions:

- Will you keep my information private?
- What services do you offer? (If the agency says that it only consolidates credit cards or only offers debt management plans, the consumer should look elsewhere.)
- How much do you charge, if anything, for services?
- Do your charges include any "voluntary fees?"
- Do you have a sliding scale for fees?
- Let me tell you about my situation. What do you think are my best options?
- Let me tell you who my creditors are. Do you work with these creditors? If so, what are the typical concessions each of these creditors offer if I sign up for a DMP?
- Can you help me with my secured debt problems?
- Do you provide training for your counselors?
- Are your counselors paid by commission?

Consumers should check for complaints with local consumer affairs or better business offices and with state licensing agencies (about half of the states have laws that require credit counselors to be licensed).

There is a separate provision in the bankruptcy law that requires consumers to get a certificate from a credit counseling agency prior to filing bankruptcy. These agencies must be approved in the consumer's jurisdiction by the U.S. Trustee's office. For more information, see www.usdoj.gov/ust/eo/bapcpa/ccde/index.htm.

NOTE: The Internal Revenue Service is auditing a huge portion of the credit counseling industry. In early 2006, the agency announced that it had revoked tax-exempt/non-profit status of 30 agencies. The identity of these agencies is confidential until the IRS posts the names on its website. Check at www.irs.gov for the release of these names.

Additional Resources: Deanne Loonin and Travis Plunkett, *Credit Counseling in Crisis: The Impact on Consumers of Funding Cuts, Higher Fees and Aggressive New Market Entrants* (2003), *available at* www.nclc.org/action_agenda/credit_counseling/content/creditcounselingreport.pdf.

Other Debt Relief Companies: Beware

Debt Settlement. Negotiation and settlement services are different from debt management services, mainly because the debt settlement agencies do not send regular monthly payments to creditors. Instead, these agencies generally maintain a consumer's funds in a separate account, holding the money until the agency believes it can settle the consumer's debts for less than the full amount owed.

Nearly all debt settlement companies require consumers to set money aside each month. Sometimes the company sets up an account for the consumer. In other cases it will ask for proof that consumer has set up an account. The company will generally take fees directly from the account. The consumer deposits money in the account each month, intended to build up a fund to settle debts. In the meantime, debt collectors and lenders continue to pressure the consumer.

The main problems with debt settlement companies include:

- The consumers targeted by debt settlement companies are generally the least likely to benefit.
- Very few consumers ever complete a debt settlement program. Settling multiple debts, if it ever occurs, is a very long process. In the meantime, consumers in debt settlement programs continue to face collection efforts. Their debts also continue to grow as creditors pile on fees and interest accrues.
- Debt settlement fees are so high that the consumers do not end up saving much in the so-called "reserve accounts."
- It is unclear what if any professional services most debt settlement companies offer to assist debtors during the time they are saving money for settlement.

Additional Resources: Deanne Loonin, National Consumer Law Center, *An Investigation of Debt Settlement Companies: An Unsettling Business for Consumers* (2005), *available at* www.nclc.org/action_agenda/credit_counseling/content/DebtSettleFINALREPORT.pdf.

Debt Elimination/Termination. There are a number of different debt elimination schemes. Some companies offer various instruments, such as a "bond for discharge of debt" or "redemption certificate" that the consumer is to present to the creditor and that supposedly forces the creditor to relinquish the debt. Another scheme sets up an arbitration that is programmed to produce a ruling that the debt is invalid. The Federal Reserve Board and the Office of the Comptroller of the Currency have described these companies as "totally bogus."[4]

Tips for Counselors

1. You should always ask whether a homeowner is already repaying debt through a DMP. Key factors to consider in helping the homeowner decide whether to continue with a DMP include:
   - How is the DMP affecting the homeowner's ability to meet mortgage obligations?
   - If lower priority credit card debt is impeding the work-out process, you and the homeowner should review the other options discussed on pages 55–60 for dealing with credit card debt and the consequences of these choices.
   - How much are the monthly fees for the DMP? Could the borrower continue the plan on his or her own and save the administrative fees?
   - Are there other unsecured debts that are not included in the DMP? What is the status of these debts?

2. If the homeowner has outstanding credit card debt, but has not yet signed up for a DMP, you should consider referring her to a credit counseling agency only if you are familiar with that agency and know that it is a reputable, non-profit agency. In addition, you should go over the homeowner's budget and help to prioritize the debts. The consumer should consider pursuing a DMP only if she has significant income left over each month AFTER paying all high priority expenses, including housing-related debt.

3. If the homeowner is dealing with a debt settlement company, it may be holding a lump sum that could be used to catch up on the mortgage payment. The homeowner should consider demanding that the lump sum be returned. Legal assistance may be necessary.

4. If the homeowner has dealt with a debt termination/elimination scheme, consider making a referral to law enforcement.

AVOIDING HIGH-COST FINANCIAL SERVICES, LOANS, AND RENT-TO-OWN

Always ask homeowners whether they are using fringe financial products such as payday loans, auto title loans, overdraft or "bounce" loans, refund anticipation loans, pawnshop loans, or rent-to-own. Simply discontinuing use of these high-cost financial products can make the difference between saving and losing the home. The high cost of cashing checks, paying bills, renting household goods, and getting small loans in times of need bleed *billions* of dollars from the pockets of those least able to afford it.

If the homeowner already is involved with one or more of these businesses, you also need to understand the priority, if any, that should be accorded the lender and the consequences of nonpayment for the homeowner. You can also help homeowners explore alternatives that may be available. It is critical that the homeowner escape the debt trap that these financial products create, because otherwise the sky-high interest rates will eat up the money that might go to save the home. Finally, in some states these lending schemes are illegal, and you can assist consumers in getting legal assistance to challenge them.

Resources for the Counselor and Homeowner. Homeowners need to know about the cost of credit and how much it affects their budgets. They will also want to know if there are alternatives that will reduce their monthly expenses. Two brochures, suitable for distribution to homeowners in English, Chinese, Korean, Russian, Spanish, and Vietnamese, are available at no cost at NCLC's website: www.nclc.org/action_agenda/seniors_initiative/information.shtml.

- *Cashing Checks and Opening Bank Accounts: How to Save Money and Avoid Theft*
- *Borrower Beware: The High Cost of Small Loans, Pawnbrokers, and Rent-To-Own Stores*

As a counselor, you may wish to read more about these industries and their products. Reports regarding payday, auto title, refund anticipation, and overdraft loans can be found at the following websites:

- National Consumer Law Center: www.nclc.org.
- Consumer Federation of America: www.consumerfed.org.
- Center for Responsible Lending: www.responsiblelending.org.

Alternatives to High-Cost Loans. A homeowner who is already indebted to high-cost lenders will need help finding a way to retire that debt. Similarly, a homeowner who is running short of cash for necessities may need to find some source of short-term credit other than the high-cost lenders discussed in this chapter. Fortunately, alternatives to the high-cost lenders are beginning to emerge.

Using low-cost checking and savings accounts (to the extent they are available in low-income neighborhoods) to avoid the costs of check cashers is a start. A checking account with an overdraft line of credit is *much* less expensive than a checking or savings account with "bounce protection." Credit unions, particularly community development credit unions, may make small loans to their members that could be used to purchase that needed appliance or pay the medical and car repair bills. While some credit cards are fraudulent and even the most legitimate credit card creates a danger of overextension, credit cards usually offer credit at much lower rates than the high-cost credit products described above in this chapter.

In addition, there are non-profits in every state that may make small business loans for individuals who wish to avoid high-cost lenders when starting up their own businesses. You can find the community development credit unions in your area through the National Federation of Community Development Credit Unions at www.natfed.org. You can contact Accion regarding its micro-enterprise programs in the United States at www.accion.org. If the consumer is a member of the military or a dependent of a servicemember, relief societies associated with each branch of the military may have funds to pay off these high-cost loans.

Legal Referrals. Where a high-cost lender has taken advantage of a homeowner, the homeowner may want to explore the possibility of suing the lender. Legal services offices exist in all major cities and serve all rural regions of the country. Referrals should be made to those offices for low-income homeowners. For homeowners who are not eligible for representation by a legal services office, a good resource for a homeowner to locate a private consumer attorney is the website of the National Association of Consumer Advocates, www.naca.net. The "Find a Lawyer" feature allows users to search the organization's list of members by state or zip code and by type of case the attorney is willing to handle. In addition, most state bar associations and many local bar associations operate lawyer referral services.

Payday Loans

Payday loans are also called post-dated check or deferred presentment loans or cash advances. They work this way: the consumer writes a post-dated check to the lender (sometimes a company that also offers check-cashing services) or gives the lender an authorization to electronically debit a bank account on a later date. The borrower then receives an amount less than the face value of the check or debit agreement. For example, if the check or debit agreement is for $256, the cash back may be only $200.

The check or debit agreement is then held for one to four weeks (usually two weeks), at which time the customer has to do one of three things:

1. Pay the entire loan amount, e.g., $256;
2. Allow the lender to cash the check or debit the bank account; or
3. Write another check or debit authorization, pay another service charge, and renew or refinance the original loan.

In this latter situation, the consumer receives no additional cash. For example, if the consumer renewed the loan described above five times, she would owe the $256 at the end of six two-week periods and would have paid $280 in fees alone (more than the face value of the check!).

The loan fees range from 10% to 30% of the cash received. The annual percentage rate on a $256 check with a payout of $200 that is redeemed in two weeks is 730%! Payday lenders do not assess the consumer's ability to repay these loans when due. They typically require proof that the borrower has regular income and a bank account.

The risk to payday lenders of making these loans is relatively low because they hold a live check or debit authorization. The noose around the consumer's neck is effective because the lender can cause havoc by presenting a check at the bank that subsequently bounces, causing other outstanding checks to bounce. Non-sufficient funds fees can multiply quickly. For example, the consumer may suddenly be forced to deal with merchants, creditors, and others who attempted to cash checks written by the consumer that did not clear because the payday lender got paid first. Even worse, the payday lender may submit the check or electronically debit the consumer's account several times, leading to a cascade of problems. Some payday lenders also threaten criminal prosecution, even if that threat is illegal.

Payday loans are widely sold on the Internet and these loans present special problems. For more on this topic, you can obtain a copy of Consumer Federation of America's report entitled *Internet Payday Lending: How Much High-Priced Lenders Use the Internet to Mire Borrowers in Debt and Evade State Consumer Protections*, available at www.consumerfed.org. Click on "Finance," then "Credit and Debt," then "Payday Lending."

Legal Challenges to Payday Loans. Payday loans are illegal in some states. Even where state law allows high-cost payday lending, there are other laws that payday lenders may violate. The following are some of the circumstances in which it may make sense to refer the borrower to an attorney to explore the possibility of a legal challenge:

- Any payday loan made in Arkansas, Connecticut, Georgia, Maine, Maryland, Massachusetts, New Jersey, New York, North Carolina, Pennsylvania, Vermont, West Virginia, Puerto Rico, or the Virgin Islands is probably illegal and subject to challenge. As of early 2007, these states had not legalized payday lending.
- Any payday loan that is made without disclosing the finance charge, the annual percentage rate, and other basic terms probably violates the federal Truth in Lending Act. Violations are especially common in the case of payday loans that are disguised as catalog sales, sale-leasebacks of personal property, or Internet access.
- State law may prohibit check cashers from making loans or, if permitted, require licensing.

A referral to an attorney should also be considered if the payday lender appears to have violated general consumer protection laws, for example by imposing unconscionable terms, using unfair and deceptive acts and practices, or using unfair, deceptive, or abusive debt collection practices.

If any member of the homeowner's household is in the military, special attention should be paid to any payday loans the household has taken out. As of early 2007, at least six states—Georgia, Illinois, Nebraska, Texas, Virginia, and Washington—had special payday loan protections for members of the military. In addition, as of October 1, 2007, a new federal law will prohibit payday lenders from making loans at greater than 36% interest to members of the military on active duty or their dependents.

Tips for Counselors. If a homeowner has any payday loans outstanding, it is important to get them paid off. The snowballing effect of rolling one payday loan over into another at triple-digit interest rates will eat up any funds that might be used to catch up on the mortgage.

Paying off the payday loan all at once is the best strategy. If that is impossible, the homeowner should explore the possibility of installment payments. Payday lenders do not like to accept installment payments, since their business model is to encourage repeat borrowing. A few states, including Florida, Illinois, Michigan, and Oklahoma require the lender to accept installment payments in certain circumstances.

Another possibility is to pay off the payday loan by borrowing from a legitimate lender. A community credit union or a community loan fund, for example, might offer small short-term loans at more reasonable rates.

Stopping payment on the check given to the payday lender, closing the bank account, or setting up a different account at a different bank on which to write checks are other ways to stop the cycle. A homeowner should get legal advice before taking any of these steps, however, because they may be crimes in some states. In addition, merely stopping payment may be insufficient to prevent the check from clearing, because payday lenders use various techniques to evade stop-payment orders.

Bankruptcy is another option. In some circumstances, bankruptcy will likely eliminate the obligation to the payday lender. However, the homeowner should get competent legal advice before assuming that bankruptcy will wipe out a payday loan.

If none of these options is practical, you will need to treat the payday lender as a secured creditor when working out a budget with the homeowner. You should give high priority to this debt and include it in the monthly budget because of the havoc the homeowner will face if the debt is not paid.

Auto Title Loans

Auto title pawn transactions work like this: the car owner pawns the title of her car in exchange for a sum of cash. The amount of the loan is usually no more than 50% of the value of the car, as set by the lender. Because title loans are so well-secured, the lender is protected if the consumer defaults. The lender may then claim title to the car and lease it back to the consumer. Others just hold onto the certificate of title without transferring ownership.

The loans are structured to be repaid in one payment after a short term (usually one month or less). If the customer fails to pay the cash advanced plus interest and fees when due, the pawnbroker may repossess the car. The annual percentage rate on an auto pawn can be astronomical, usually over 200% and sometimes as high as 900%. Like payday loans, the auto title lender does not assess the consumer's ability to repay. Only proof of regular income, title to the car, and a set of car keys are necessary.

This type of pawn presents particular difficulties for consumers because their transportation is at stake if they do not redeem the title to the car by repaying the money borrowed. These lenders often encourage the customer to renew the loan, which pushes the customer further and further into debt.

Legal Challenges to Auto Title Pawn. In contrast to payday lending, auto title loans are illegal in most states, so a referral to an attorney may be helpful. As of early 2007, they were legal only in Alabama, Arizona, Georgia, Idaho, Illinois, Mississippi, Missouri, Montana, New Hampshire, Nevada, New Mexico, Oregon, and Tennessee. Florida, Kentucky, and Minnesota permit auto title lending but significantly restrict the cost.

Even if the state has legalized auto title loans, the consumer should consider legal action if the lender has committed unfair, deceptive, or abusive acts. In addition, as of October 1, 2007, a new federal law will prohibit payday lenders from making loans—including auto title loans—at greater than 36% interest to members of the military on active duty or their dependents. This new law will override state laws that permit title lending.

Tips for Counselors. Auto title lenders hold title and/or a set of keys to the consumer's car. Repossession can occur as soon as one day after the consumer fails to pay the loan or renew it when due. Once the car is repossessed, additional fees will be added to the loan balance making the possibility of redeeming the car more remote. If the car is the consumer's transportation to work, loss of employment could result.

The homeowner should consider a legal challenge, a lump-sum repayment, or refinancing with a legitimate lender. If these options are not practical, the auto title lender should be treated as a secured lender and a consumer who uses the pawned car to get to work should proceed with caution. If funds cannot be found from public or private sources to repay the loan, counselors should encourage the consumer to negotiate a repayment schedule, and, failing that, include the scheduled payment in the monthly budget.

Overdraft Loans

Overdraft or "bounce" loans are a form of overdraft coverage whereby banks or credit unions charge penalty overdraft fees when consumers overdraw their accounts by check, at automated teller machines, or using a debit card. Unlike traditional overdraft protection, these services do not require consumer consent, do not provide cost of credit disclosures under federal lending laws, and do not guarantee that the bank pays the overdrafts.

The bank pays the amount of the overdraft and charges the customer a fee that ranges from $20 to $35. Some banks also charge a daily fee until the loan is paid in full. These fees are triggered regardless of whether the overdraft is $5.00 or $500. When the customer is overdrawing her account through an ATM withdrawal or debit purchase, generally the bank will neither notify the customer of this fact nor give her the option to cancel the transaction. When the customer's next deposit is made to the account, the bank debits the amount of the overdraft, plus the fee.

As a result of the high fees and short repayment time, borrowers pay triple- and even quadruple-digit interest rates. For example, if the overdraft loan fee was calculated as an APR, a $22.50 fee for an $80 overdraft loan translates into a 1,467% APR for a loan paid back in a week and a 733% APR if the loan is repaid in two weeks.

The Center for Responsible Lending estimates that consumers pay about $10 billion each year for overdraft or "bounce" loans, and expects that number to rise if more banks jump on the bandwagon.[5] Some banks ratchet up the fee income intentionally by using a "high-to-low" method of honoring checks and debits to the account, as opposed to paying them (and applying deposits) in chronological order. In other words, the bank will pay the largest obligation first each day and sometimes apply deposits after debits. This practice can trigger a cascade of overdrafts if the account does not have sufficient funds to cover all of the small checks.

Tips for Counselors. Counselors can play a role in educating consumers about the risks of overdraft loan programs. Consumers should ask their banks if they have instituted this program and obtain a list of the fees. Counselors can assist consumers in understanding the effect of using this product on their ability to budget. For example, while covering an overdraft may provide temporary relief, the bank will use the next deposit to cover the full amount of the overdraft. The consumer can get caught in a web of bouncing checks and accumulating fees. For some consumers living on the extreme financial edge, the bank accounts themselves can be a dangerous drain on the family income.

The best recommendation for consumers is to ask the bank not to include bounce protection as a feature of their bank accounts. By contrast, an overdraft line of credit, often offered by banks in connection with credit cards, provides similar protection and is far less costly.

Refund Anticipation Loans

Refund Anticipation Loans (RALs) are extremely high-cost bank loans secured by the taxpayer's expected tax refund—loans that last about 7 to 14 days until the IRS refund repays the loan. These loans go by various names, such as "Fast Cash Refunds," "Express Money," or "Instant Refunds." These loans are made on behalf of a bank through a tax preparer who files the return for the taxpayer. The effective annual interest rate (APR) for a RAL can range from about 40% (for a loan of $9,999) to over 700% (for a loan of $200). If administrative fees are charged and included in the calculation, RALs cost from about 70% to over 1,800% APR.

In 2006, a RAL for the average refund of around $2,150 cost about $100. A loan under those terms bears an effective APR of about 178%. If the taxpayer goes to a preparer who charges an additional $30 administrative fee, the effective APR including the administrative fee would be 235%. These loan charges are in addition to tax preparation fees averaging $146, so the grand total could be as high as $276. Approximately 12.38 million taxpayers—about 1 in 10 tax returns—received RALs in the 2004 tax filing season. These consumers paid a total of $1.24 billion in loan fees, plus $360 million in administrative fees for these loans.[6]

Recently, RAL lenders have started promoting pay stub RALs and holiday RALs in addition to RALs based on the tax payer's actual W-2 form. Pay stub RALs are offered in January, using the borrower's year-end pay stub information rather than a W-2 form. Holiday RALs are offered even earlier—in November and December—before the borrower has even received a year-end pay stub. These RAL loans present additional risks and costs to borrowers.

In addition to the high cost, RALs can be risky. Since a RAL is a loan from a bank in partnership with a tax preparer, it must be repaid even if the IRS denies or delays the refund, or the refund is smaller than expected. If the consumer does not pay back the RAL, the lender may report the delinquency to a credit reporting bureau, send the account to a debt collector, or use the tax refund to pay for old tax debts that the lender claims the consumer owes it or other banks.

Tips for Counselors. A taxpayer who files a return electronically can expect to receive the refund in 14 days or less, as long as the refund will be directly deposited into a bank account. If the taxpayer files a paper return with direct deposit, the refund should arrive in 30 days or less from the date of filing. The worst case scenario occurs when the taxpayer files a paper return and waits for a check to arrive in the mail from the IRS. That could take up to 45 days.

Counselors can educate consumers about the costs of this loan product. More importantly, consumers should understand that they can get their refunds in 14 days or less without paying for a RAL.

When discussing a monthly budget that relies upon an expected tax refund, counselors should inquire about whether the consumer obtained a RAL in a prior tax year that is unpaid or if there are other debts outstanding that could be offset by the refund, for example, unpaid student loans and child support. If so, the homeowner cannot rely on the refund to help fund a proposed mortgage repayment plan. For more information, see the *NCLC Guide to Surviving Debt.*

Pawns

Pawnbrokers have been around for centuries. They provide short-term loans based on the value of personal property that the pawnbroker holds for the consumer during the term of the loan. Many pawnbrokers charge up to 200% annually on their loans. Typically, pawnbrokers never loan more than 50% of the value of the goods pawned. If the goods are never redeemed, the pawnbroker can make a substantial profit from the sale of the goods. If the property is redeemed, the customer must repay the amount of cash advanced plus interest and fees. Since the vast majority of customers redeem their pledges, however, pawnbrokers are really engaged in the business of making small, secured, short-term consumer loans.

State Regulation. Almost every state has enacted laws that regulate pawnbrokers in some way. Generally, the state law permits regulation at the municipal level, so there are often applicable local ordinances. Typically, when someone pawns a good, the terms of the agreement must be specified on the pawn ticket. The ticket may also state the customer's name and address, a description of the pledged good, the amount loaned, the maturity date, and the amount that must be paid to redeem the item. Most states set ceilings on interest rates and other fees that pawnshops can charge on loans. Finally, licensing of the pawnbroker is almost universally required.

Tips for Counselors. The worst consequence to the consumer if she does not redeem the property is that the item will be sold. Unless the pawned item has significant value which, if sold directly by the consumer could yield a sizeable amount of cash to put toward a repayment plan, counselors typically need not include this debt in a budget plan. However, the counselor should warn the consumer of the consequences if the consumer cannot resist diverting money from a tight budget to redeem the property.

Rent-to-Own

Rent-to-Own (RTO) businesses are essentially appliance, electronics, and furniture retailers that arrange lease agreements for those customers who cannot purchase goods with cash. These lease agreements contain several special features. They contain purchase options which typically enable the lessees to obtain title to the goods by making a series of payments over a term, such as 18 months. "Rental payments" are due weekly or monthly, terminable "at will," meaning the leases theoretically need not be renewed at the end of each weekly or monthly term.

The RTO industry aims its marketing efforts primarily at low-income consumers by advertising in ethnic media, public transportation, and in public housing projects. The sales pitch suggests that RTO has many attractive features: no credit checks, quick delivery, weekly payments, no or small down payments, quick repair service, and no harm to one's credit rating if the transaction is canceled.

Most customers, however, hope to ultimately own the goods that they are renting. This attitude is encouraged by the RTO dealers who emphasize the purchase option in their marketing even while they are minimizing its importance in the written contract.

The chief problem with RTO contracts is that these "leases" are disguised sales made at astronomic and undisclosed effective interest rates. For example, a brand new 19-inch color TV with standard features may sell for less than $300. An RTO dealer may lease this TV for $16 per week for 52 weeks, making the annual percentage rate (interest rate) about 254%. The total of payments would be $832, almost three times the retail sales price. If the customer misses a payment, the TV will be repossessed and the customer loses all of the payments made.

State Regulation. Over the last 20 years, the RTO industry has aggressively (and successfully in most cases) lobbied state legislatures for statutory exemptions from consumer protection statutes, annual percentage rate disclosure requirements, and usury rate limitations. In nearly every state there are now RTO statutes which were carefully drafted by the industry to insulate dealers from claims of consumer abuse.

Tips for Counselors. If homeowners need appliances or furniture, it is wiser to try second-hand stores for these purchases. Some non-profit organizations refurbish washers, dryers, and other appliances and then sell them at very reasonable prices. Some retail stores may have a "lay-away" plan which allows consumers to pay for the item over time without interest in advance of obtaining physical possession of the purchase.

If the homeowner is purchasing goods under an RTO contract, the counselor can educate the consumer regarding the possible options. The best option for a consumer who is close to the end of the contract term may be to continue to pay off the lease. However, if the consumer has not invested much for the items (that is, has not made many payments under the contract), the best option may be to cancel the contract, give some or all of the items back, and reduce or eliminate the RTO payments from the budget.

Check Cashers

Check-cashing fees can add up, particularly for families who do not have a bank account and are living on a budget where every penny counts. For example, a worker who cashes fifty $320 payroll checks can pay from $160 to $960 (average of $374.50) to the check casher per year. A public benefits recipient who cashes 12 government checks of $500 can spend from $48 to $360 (average of $132) per year.

State Regulation. Check-cashing companies are "regulated" in varying degrees in more than half of the states. Many states cap fees at 1% to 10% of the check amount (or a certain minimum fee, whichever is greater). The rate caps sometimes vary depending on the type of check to be cashed, i.e., payroll, government, or personal. Most of these states require that the check cashers be licensed. Some of the statutes mandate that the check casher post its fees in a prominent location in the store and give the customer a receipt.

Tips for Counselors. Consumers without bank accounts may get free check-cashing in several ways, such as:

- The employer may cash its own payroll check for the employee;
- The bank the employer uses may cash the check at no cost;
- Banks may cash government checks for free; and
- The bank whose name is on the check may cash it for free.

Counselors may suggest the consumer open a "no-frills" bank account that provides free or low cost checking and savings services. However, this may not be possible if the consumer has a poor credit history or has previously bounced a check. If the consumer is eligible to open an account, the counselor should educate the consumer about the pitfalls of overdraft loans, discussed above.

REFINANCING OF NON-MORTGAGE DEBT INTO A MORTGAGE LOAN

Refinancing is a process in which the consumer pays off one or more debts by borrowing new money from an existing creditor or a new creditor. It is sometimes suggested as a good way for people with financial problems to address their difficulties.

Refinancing of mortgage loans is discussed in Chapter 3, above. Be very careful also when counseling about refinancing other forms of debt. Refinancing an unaffordable amount of debt is one of the most tempting but risky steps one can take when in financial trouble. Many refinancing loans will hurt more than they help.

Homeowners in financial trouble are preyed upon by predatory lenders that often come to the consumer's home. You should urge the homeowner to get independent advice about the terms of any new loan. If the homeowner is considering refinancing as a way of paying off unsecured debts such as credit cards, remember that this will put the home at risk for not just the mortgage debt but also the unsecured debt. In addition, many refinancings have teaser rates that increase after a year or two. What may look affordable then becomes unaffordable. Some refinancing loans start the homeowner off with an artificially low monthly payment that may not even pay the interest on the loan. When the monthly payment increases after the initial period, the payment shock can be severe. These types of mortgage loans are discussed in more detail in Chapter 3, above.

Thirteen Refinancing Rules for Homeowners

1. **When in doubt, do not refinance or consolidate debts.** Refinancing deals almost always come with significant costs. These costs will usually just make matters worse in the long term.

2. **Do not let debt collectors pressure you into refinancing.** Debt collectors may try to scare you into refinancing because they have no other way to get their money. Better ways to address debt collection problems are discussed at the end of this chapter and in the NCLC Guide to Surviving Debt.

3. **Never (or almost never) refinance unsecured debt into secured debt.** Unsecured debt, such as medical bills and most credit card debt, should be lower priority for a homeowner than paying the mortgage. But if unsecured debt is refinanced into a mortgage loan, you face loss of your home if you continue to have financial problems. Do not refinance unsecured debt, that is, most credit card debt, into secured debt even if this allows you to lower the interest rate you are paying. The interest rate on a mortgage loan may be lower, but these are usually at least 20- and more commonly 30-year loans. Paying at a lower rate for such a long time will almost always cost you more than a higher rate on a shorter-term loan. Think of it this way: Would you ever want to pay off the pizza you bought for dinner with a credit card by stretching the payments out for thirty years? This is the result of adding your credit card debt to a mortgage loan.

4. **If you have an existing debt with a finance company or high-rate second mortgage lender, do not refinance that debt with the same lender.** Ask the company to agree to lower payments on the existing loan, but do not allow the lender to refinance that loan, which may involve new closing costs and perhaps even a higher interest rate.

5. **Do not turn your car loan into a second mortgage unless you would rather lose your home than your car.** If you are in danger of losing your car, you may be tempted to pay off your car loan by taking out a second mortgage on your home. You may save your car temporarily this way, but you are putting your home in danger. Although repossession is bad, foreclosure is worse. This type of refinancing adds the car loan into the mortgage loan, turning a 5-year car loan into a 30-year mortgage. This greatly increases the amount of interest you pay.

6. **Do not refinance low-interest debts with higher interest loans.** You should always evaluate the interest rate on the new debt and look for a lower rate than on the old debts. You have already paid certain fees in the old loan, and you must make sure that a new lower rate is actually lower after both the old and new fees are accounted for. Furthermore, the "APR" (Annual Percentage Rate) of the new loan must be lower than the interest rate stated in the note of the old loan, or you will be losing money. The APR is the cost of credit as a yearly rate. It is often higher than the interest rate on your promissory note because the APR takes into account both the interest plus certain fees that the lenders add to the cost of the loan.

    The interest rate is not the only consideration when evaluating a loan. Other fees, charges, and expenses which are not considered interest may turn a loan which looks cheaper into one which is actually more expensive.

7. **Do not include your long-term first mortgage in a refinancing package.** Do not let potential lenders pay off your first mortgage and give you a new mortgage equal to the first mortgage plus the new loan amount. The only exception is if the new mortgage is for the equivalent length of time and the APR is significantly *lower* than the interest rate on the old first mortgage—to offset prepayment penalties and fees and charges.

8. **Be careful about variable rates.** Variable-rate refinancing loans can be tricky. In any variable-rate transaction, the monthly payment can increase drastically when you can least afford it. Some loans have artificially low rates (and payments) during the first months or years, called "teaser rates." Other variable-rate loans provide that the rate will only go up, never down.

9. **Do not refinance a debt if you have valid legal reasons not to pay it.** If you have a legal defense to repayment of a debt, such as lender fraud, you can raise that defense in court. If you refinance with a new lender, the defense may not be available against the new creditor. If you need legal help to determine if you have a defense, you should get that help *before* entering the refinancing deal.

10. **Be wary of claims that you will get a tax advantage from a debt consolidation loan.** Many lenders offering bad refinancing deals talk about the benefit of the tax deductibility of mortgage interest. Make sure you understand how your personal tax situation will be affected. For example, if you do not itemize deductions, the tax deductibility of mortgages interest is worthless.

11. **Avoid refinancing deals that are scams.** Refinancing involves great potential for hidden costs, fees, and other unfair loan terms. Even some reputable lenders make unfair refinancing deals. When in doubt, get help in reviewing the loan papers *before* you sign anything. You can walk away from a bad deal even at the last minute. A lender that is unwilling to let you get outside help should not be trusted. Another way to avoid scams is never to let a contractor or salesperson arrange financing for you and be wary of mortgage brokers. Unfortunately, some brokers find you refinancing deals which involve big commissions for them rather than good loans for you.

12. **If your home is collateral in a refinancing deal, remember that you have three days to cancel.** In most refinancings in which you give the lender a mortgage, federal law gives you the right to cancel for any reason for three business days from the date you sign the papers. If you wish to cancel, make sure you do so in writing before the deadline. The lender is required to give you a form for this purpose. You can, but need not, use the cancellation form provided by the lender. You may cancel the loan by sending a signed, dated letter indicating your desire to cancel the refinancing. You should keep a copy of this letter and be sure to send it by registered or certified mail.

13. **If it seems too good to be true, it is not true.**

STRATEGIES FOR INCREASING INCOME— THE EARNED INCOME AND CHILD TAX CREDITS

The Earned Income Tax Credit and Child Tax Credit may be sources of income that a homeowner can use to catch up on mortgage payments. Earned Income Tax Credit (EITC) refunds can be quite substantial, especially for working families with children—up to $4,400 in the 2006 filing season. The Child Tax Credit is worth up to $1,000. An eligible taxpayer who overlooked these credits might even be able to claim up to 3 years worth by filing back returns.

In order to qualify for the EITC, the taxpayer must have worked and her income must be below a certain amount. The taxpayer must file a tax return to receive the EITC. Even a taxpayer whose earnings are so small that she does not owe any taxes can get cash back through an EITC if she meets these requirements.

The tax credit is larger and the income cut-off is higher if the taxpayer had a "qualifying child" living with her for over six months of the year. (The six months need not be consecutive.) A "qualifying child" is:

- A son, daughter, stepchild, grandchild, or adopted child;
- A brother, sister, stepbrother, stepsister, or a descendent of one of these relatives; or
- A foster child who was placed with the taxpayer by an authorized government or a private placement agency.

The child must be under age 19, or under 24 if a full-time student, but children of any age who have total and permanent disabilities may qualify.

Even if the taxpayer has not qualified for this credit in the past, she may now qualify due to changed circumstances such as divorce or separation. The taxpayer can even get advance payments on part of the EITC, which could help her balance her budget, by giving an IRS Form W-5 to her employer.

An excerpt from the Center on Budget and Policy Priority's publication *Facts About Tax Credits for Working Families 2006* is reprinted with permission at Appendix C, below. More information on the EITC and Child Tax Credit is available from the Center on Budget and Policy Priority at www.cbpp.org/eic2006.

PRIORITIZING DEBT

The preceding discussions in this chapter have suggested ways that homeowners can reduce expenses and increase income. Even after following these recommendations, however, many homeowners who are in danger of foreclosure will have more obligations than their monthly income covers.

These homeowners should not give up. By prioritizing their debts they may still be able to save the home. By prioritizing their debts, the homeowners may find that they can defer paying certain low-priority debts in order to free up enough money to catch up on mortgage payments and pay other essential bills. This strategy will result in debt collection calls, but these can be stopped, as described at the end of the chapter. It will also result in damage to their credit rating, but the same is true if they fall behind on the mortgage. After they have saved their home they can begin the process of rebuilding their credit rating.

Distinguishing Between Secured and Unsecured Credit

In prioritizing debt, it is important to distinguish between secured and unsecured debt. With secured debt, the consumer puts up collateral—property that the creditor has the right to take if the consumer does not pay that debt. The most common types of secured debts are home mortgages and car loans. If the debtor fails to pay a home mortgage, the creditor can take the home by foreclosure. If a consumer fails to pay a car loan, the creditor can repossess the car.

A creditor may also have collateral in a consumer's household goods, business property, bank account, or even wages. Collateral can take many forms. When a creditor has taken collateral for a loan, it has a "lien" on that property. Creditors who have collateral are usually referred to as "secured" creditors. They know that if the debtor does not pay, they can take the collateral and sell it to get their money.

Creditors without collateral are often referred to as "unsecured." It is usually hard for unsecured creditors to collect what they are owed unless the debtor pays pay voluntarily. To force the debtor to pay, they have to bring and win a lawsuit, and even then they must go through further steps before they can take money or property from the debtor.

Examples of unsecured debts are:

- Most credit and charge cards;
- Lawyer or medical bills;
- Most loans from friends or relatives;
- Most department store and gasoline card charges.

Which Debts Are High and Which Are Low Priority?

Debts with collateral should almost always be highest priority. How important it is to repay other debts, particularly in the short-term, depends a lot on the homeowner's individual circumstances. The creditor making the most noise is not necessarily the most important creditor. Creditors who yell the loudest often do so only because they have no better way to get their money. You can use the following sixteen rules as guidance when helping homeowners prioritize their debts.

1. The homeowner should always pay family necessities first. Usually this means food and unavoidable medical expenses if the medical provider requires pre-payment. (The homeowner should *not* pay old medical bills first.)
2. The homeowner should pay housing-related bills next. The payments you work out for the homeowner to save the home should be the next priority. Real estate taxes and insurance must also be paid unless they are included in the monthly mortgage payment. Failure to pay these debts can lead to loss of the home.

3. The homeowner should pay the minimum required to keep essential utility service. At the very least, the homeowner should pay the minimum payment necessary to avoid disconnection. Working hard to keep the house makes little sense if the homeowner cannot live there because the utility service has been terminated. Options for dealing with utility payments and disconnections are discussed at the beginning of this chapter.

4. The homeowner should pay car loans or leases next for any car that is essential. If the homeowner needs a car to get to work or for other essential transportation, the car loan or lease payments should usually be the priority after food, housing costs, unavoidable medical expenses, and utilities. The homeowner may even want to pay for the car first if the car is necessary to keep a job.

    It is important to stay up to date on car insurance payments as well. Otherwise the creditor may buy costly replacement insurance at *the homeowner's* expense that provides *less* protection. And in most states it is illegal not to have automobile liability coverage.

    If you the homeowner can give up a car (or one of the household's cars), this will not only save on car payments, but also on gasoline, repairs, insurance, and automobile taxes.

5. The homeowner must pay child support debts. These debts will not go away and can result in very serious problems, including prison, for nonpayment.

6. Income tax debts are also high priority. The homeowner must pay any income taxes that are not automatically deducted from his or her wages, and must file a federal income tax return every year (even if the homeowner cannot afford to pay any balance due). The government has many collection rights that other creditors do not have, particularly if a person does not file a tax return.

7. Loans without collateral are low priority. Most credit card debts, attorney, doctor and hospital bills, other debts to professionals, open accounts with merchants, and similar debts are low priority. The homeowner has not pledged any collateral for these loans, and there is rarely anything that these creditors can do to hurt the homeowner in the short term.

8. Loans with only household goods as collateral are also low priority. Sometimes a creditor requires a consumer to place some household goods as collateral on a loan. A homeowner should generally treat this loan the same as an unsecured debt—as a low priority. Creditors rarely seize household goods because they have little market value, it is hard to take them without involving the courts, and it is time-consuming and expensive to use the courts to seize them.

9. The homeowner should not move a debt up in priority because the creditor or collector threatens suit. Many threats to sue are not carried out. Even if the creditor does sue, it will take a while for the collector to be able to seize property, and much of the homeowner's property may be exempt from seizure. On the other hand, nonpayment the mortgage or a car loan may result in immediate loss of the home or car.

10. The homeowner should evaluate legal defenses to repayment. Some examples of legal defenses are that the goods purchased were defective or that the creditor is asking for more money than it is entitled to. A homeowner who has a potential defense to a debt should obtain legal advice. Withholding payments may be an option, but the homeowner should obtain a legal evaluation of the risks of doing so. It is especially dangerous to withhold mortgage payments without legal advice.

11. **Court judgments move debts up in priority, but often less than the homeowner may think.** After a collector obtains a court judgment, that debt often should move up in priority, because the creditor can enforce that judgment by asking the court to seize certain pieces of the debtor's property, wages, and bank accounts. How serious a threat this really is will depend on the state's law, the value of the homeowner's property, and the homeowner's income. It may be that all the homeowner's property and wages are protected under state law. For example, the state's homestead exemption may fully protect the home from seizure by a lender other than the mortgage lender.

    In some circumstances, all of the homeowner's income and assets may be fully protected from seizure. In that case, the homeowner does not really have to worry about the judgment unless his or her financial situation gets much better. A homeowner who has income and assets that can be seized will need to evaluate whether the consequences of not paying these debts are likely to be worse than the costs of paying them. The homeowner might also want to consider whether bankruptcy is a useful option. This is a good time for the homeowner to obtain legal advice.

12. **Student loans are medium-priority debts.** Student loans should generally be paid ahead of low-priority debts, but after top-priority debts. Most delinquent student loans are federal government loans. The law provides special collection remedies to the government that are not available to other creditors. These include seizure of the debtor's tax refunds, special wage garnishment rules, denial of new student loans and grants, and, in some cases, seizure of federal benefits such as Social Security. The law also provides special remedies for borrowers hoping to get out of default. These include reasonable and affordable payment plans, loan consolidation, and even cancellation in some circumstances. These issues are discussed earlier in this chapter.

13. **Debt collection efforts should never move up a debt's priority.** The homeowner should be polite to debt collectors, but should make her own choices about which debts to pay based on what is best for her family. Debt collectors are unlikely to give good advice to the debtor. Debt collectors may be most aggressive when trying to get a homeowner to pay debts that should actually be paid last. Debtors can stop most debt collection contacts and have legal remedies to deal with collection harassment, as described below.

14. **Threats to ruin the homeowner's credit record should never move up a debt's priority.** Many collectors who threaten to report a delinquency to a credit bureau have already done so. If the creditor has not yet reported the status of the homeowner's account to a credit bureau, it is unlikely that a collector hired by that creditor will do so. In fact, a mortgage lender, car creditor, and other big creditors are *much* more likely to report a delinquency (without any threat) than is a debt collector who threatens you about your credit record. If the homeowner has the financial ability to pay all low-priority debts *and* high-priority debts, this will prevent damage to his or her credit record. But paying a low-priority bill *instead of* a high-priority bill will just make a difference in the source from which the damage to the homeowner's credit record comes.

15. **Cosigned debts should be treated like other debts.** The homeowner may have cosigned for someone else and put up the home or a car as collateral. If the other cosigner on the loan is not keeping the debt current, the homeowner should treat that loan as a high-priority debt. If the homeowner has *not* put up such collateral, cosigned debts should be treated as a lower priority.

Or others may have cosigned for the homeowner. A homeowner who is unable to pay the debt should tell the cosigners so that they can decide what to do.

16. Refinancing is rarely the answer.   The homeowner should always be careful about refinancing. It can be very expensive and it can give creditors more opportunities to seize important assets. A short-term fix can lead to long-term problems. Some refinancing rules and techniques to avoid scams are discussed earlier in this chapter.

HOW THE HOMEOWNER CAN STOP DEBT COLLECTION HARASSMENT

A homeowner who decides not to pay certain debts is likely to face debt collection harassment. Debt collection harassment should not force the homeowner into making bad decisions. The recommendations for homeowners immediately below may help them effectively face debt collectors.

In addition, consumers have the right to instruct debt collectors to stop contacting them. It is a violation of federal law for a debt collector to continue to make collection calls to consumers after receiving a *written request* to stop calling. (The federal law only applies to independent debt collection agencies, not to creditors who collecting their own debts, but even these creditors will often honor such requests.)

The consumer does not have to give any special explanation why the collector should cease contacts. Nevertheless, it is generally a good idea for the consumer to explain the current financial problem and any financial plans for the future. The letter might also describe prior abusive tactics of the collector's employees and any resulting distress this has caused.

ADVICE FOR HOMEOWNERS
DO NOT LET DEBT COLLECTORS PRESSURE YOU

It is important not to let debt collection harassment force you into making decisions that will hurt you later. Although this can be difficult when you are feeling pressured, it is important to make your own choices about which debts to pay based on what is best for you and your family.

Try to keep in mind that as bad as you may feel, you are not a deadbeat when circumstances outside your control prevent you from paying your debts. Believe it or not, the collector knows this even better than you do. Creditors and collectors know from long experience that most people pay their bills and, when they do not, it is usually because of job loss, illness, divorce, or other unexpected events. Creditors take this risk of default into account when they set the interest rate—creditors make enough money from you and others in good times so that when you default, the creditor is covered.

Do not be fooled by collector statements to the contrary. Debt collectors are *instructed* to ignore your reasons for falling behind on your debts, to show no sympathy, and not to listen to reason.

You have no moral obligation to pay one debt before you pay another debt, particularly when the debt you do pay is more central to your family's survival. Creditors know this. They should not be rewarded for trying to pressure you to pay them off at the expense of another creditor or, more importantly, at the expense of your family.

Sample "Cease Debt Collection Communication" Letter

(You should delete references to billing errors, debt harassment, or any other statements that do not apply to you—a simple request to stop collection contacts is sufficient.)

Sam Consumer
10 Cherry Lane
Flint, MI 10886

January 1, 2006

NBC Collection Agency
1 Main Street
Flint, MI 10887

Dear Sir or Madam:

I am writing to request that you stop communications to me about my account number 000723 with Amy's Department Store, as required by the Fair Debt Collection Practices Act, 15 U.S.C. § 1692c(c). [NOTE: Delete reference to the Fair Debt Collection Practices Act where the letter is to a creditor instead of to a collection agency.]

I was laid off from work two months ago and cannot pay this bill at this time. I am enrolled in a training program which I will complete in March and hope to find work that will allow me to resume payments soon after that. Please also note that your letters mistakenly list the balance on the account as $245. My records indicate that the balance is less than that.

You should be aware that your employees have engaged in illegal collection practices. For example, I received a phone call at 6:30 a.m. from one of them last week. Later that day I was called by the same person at my training program which does not permit personal phone calls except for emergencies. My family and I were very upset by these tactics.

This letter is not meant in any way to be an acknowledgment that I owe this money. I will take care of this matter when I can. Your cooperation will be appreciated.

Very truly yours,

Sam Consumer

It is very important to keep a copy of the written request and to send it by certified mail, return receipt requested. This will serve as proof that the collector received the letter. A sample letter follows:

If a debt collector continues to contact the homeowner after receiving a "cease communication" letter, the homeowner should:

1. Consider sending another letter by certified mail, once again keeping a copy. This second letter should tell the collector that the homeowner is aware that they are violating the federal law by continuing the collection calls.

2. Keep a careful record of any letters and phone calls received after sending the letter.

3. Consider contacting a lawyer. If a lawyer sends a letter saying that he or she is representing the homeowner, the collector will be subject to additional federal

restrictions on collection calls. The lawyer can also evaluate the merits of suing the collector for violating the federal law.

Chapter Notes

1. Bradley Bakake and the State PIRG Consumer Team, Deflate Your Rate: How to Lower Your Credit Card APR (Mar. 2003).
2. The calculator used to create this chart can be found at www.bankrate.com/brm/calc/MinPayment.asp. The federal banking agencies instructed banks to start requiring higher monthly payments that at least cover the interest earned that month, plus fees, plus at least 1% of the monthly balance. This change should have occurred in 2006. This chart compares the repayment term when using that formula (assuming no late or other fees) compared to a formula in based on 4% of the monthly balance. The 4% formula saves the consumer interest and substantially reduces the term.
3. Both books can be ordered securely on-line at www.consumerlaw.org, or by calling NCLC publications at 617-542-9595. Workbook purchases require a minimum order of 20 copies.
4. *See* Federal Reserve Board, Letter on Debt Elimination Scams (Jan. 2004), *available at* www.federalreserve .gov/boarddocs/SRLETTERS/2004/sr0403.htm; Office of the Comptroller of the Currency, Alert 2003-12 (Oct. 1, 2003), *available at* www.occ.treas.gov/ftp/alert/2003-12.doc.
5. Center for Responsible Lending, *High Cost & Hidden from View: The $10 Billion Overdraft Loan Market* (May 26, 2005), *available at* www.responsiblelending.org/pdfs/ip009-High_Cost_Overdraft-0505.pdf.
6. National Consumer Law Center and Consumer Federation of America, *Press Release: Refund Anticipation Loans—Updated Facts and Figures* (Jan. 17, 2006), *available at* www.nclc.org/action_agenda/refund_ anticipation/content/2006RAL_Early%20info.pdf.

PART
II

The Workout Process

CHAPTER 5

Getting a Deal: The Mechanics of Arranging a Workout

This chapter describes the mechanics of arranging a workout:

- An introduction to the parties who will play important roles in a mortgage workout.
- Which players to contact to arrange a workout.
- Gathering basic information about the mortgage loan: the terms of the loan; the amount in arrears; and the total amount due.
- Calculating the reinstatement and payoff amounts.
- Circumstances in which the homeowner will be entitled to cancel private mortgage insurance PMI—an important way to make the monthly mortgage payment affordable.
- Putting together a workout proposal, with a sample proposal.
- Information about contacting and advocating with the servicer on behalf of the homeowner.
- A decision tree that summarizes the essential issues that counselors and homeowners will have to address.
- Tips for counselors.

The specific workout options open to the homeowner and the process for seeking them vary by the type of loan. Workouts for loans purchased by Fannie Mae and Freddie Mac, and loans serviced by subprime companies are discussed in Chapter 6 of this handbook. The options for FHA-insured loans are examined in Chapter 7. Workouts for VA-guaranteed mortgages, RHS direct loans, and RHS-guaranteed loans are covered in Chapter 8.

KNOWING THE PLAYERS

Most workout negotiations involve multiple parties. These may include the mortgage holder, the servicer, the foreclosure attorney, and a mortgage insurer. In some cases, the mortgage holder has a separate servicer for foreclosure. Determining the identity and relationship of the parties to a loan is an essential first step in the workout process because this information tells the counselor who the decision maker is and which workout options are available.

Under the 1995 amendments to the Truth in Lending Act, the servicer is required, upon written request, to provide the homeowner with the name, address, and telephone number of the owner of the mortgage or the master servicer of the mortgage.[1] Thus, homeowners should be able to find out the identity of key parties by writing to the loan servicer, which is generally the entity to which the borrower makes payments.

The Secondary Market.   The secondary market is not a real place. Instead the term refers to the fact that mortgages are frequently sold immediately or shortly after they are made, to other lenders who hold them or to investors. See the discussion of *securitization* below and in Chapter 14 for more information.

Mortgage Originator.   The mortgage originator is the bank or mortgage company that makes the loan to the borrower. When originators keep the loans they have made, the loans are called "portfolio loans." However, nearly 90% of all new loans are sold to other banks or investors shortly after funding. Loans can be sold with servicing released, which means that the original lender will not act as servicer for the loan after it is sold. In that case, the borrower must be formally notified of the transfer to the new servicer, as required by the Real Estate Settlement and Procedures Act. Alternately, the originator may sell the loan but continue to service the loan for a fee, in which case the borrower need not be notified. The purchaser of the loan becomes the mortgage holder.

Mortgage Holder.   The mortgage holder "owns" the borrower's mortgage. This is the party that has the right to foreclose and generally will determine policies and make decisions regarding loan workouts. The mortgage holder may be the originating lender, or may have purchased the loan from the originating lender.

A high percentage of mortgages are assigned (sold) by mortgage originators to secondary market investors, such as Fannie Mae and Freddie Mac. Fannie Mae is the common name for a quasi-governmental agency known more formally as the Federal National Mortgage Association. Freddie Mac is the colloquial name for the Federal Home Loan Mortgage Corporation. The objective of both entities is to provide liquidity in the housing market by purchasing mortgages. Their purchases help put capital back into the hands of the originating lender so that new loans can be made. Some mortgages are "pooled" and sold pursuant to a trust agreement so that the mortgage holder is a trustee for a larger group of investors. Although the mortgage holder has ultimate authority to decide whether or not to accept a workout, some or all of this authority will be delegated to a servicer.

Mortgage Servicer.   The company that collects the borrower's payments, manages escrow accounts, processes payoffs, and performs other loan activities is the mortgage servicer. A mortgage holder may service its own loans or pay another company to perform loan servicing functions. Loan servicing is a large and profitable business within the mortgage industry. Some firms service thousands or hundreds of thousands of mortgages owned by others, though they neither originate nor own any loans.

When mortgages are sold to the secondary market, the selling lender often remains responsible for servicing. Fannie Mae, Freddie Mac, and a variety of investors give servicers differing amounts of authority to act on their behalf. The scope of that authority is generally spelled out in servicing contracts and/or in servicing guidebooks.

Frequently, the servicer will be the only party with whom the borrower has had any contact. Only on investigation will it become apparent that the servicer is acting on another company's behalf.

Lender's Attorney. The lender's attorney is also an agent with delegated authority from the mortgage holder, although usually the attorney is hired by the servicer. Attorneys are generally retained to pursue foreclosure. Sometimes after foreclosure has started, the attorney will refuse to consider workout options. Although some attorneys will readily participate in workout discussions or give you permission to speak with their client directly, others will need to be pushed to communicate offers to their client. Since a workout is a form of legal settlement, attorneys should be reminded when necessary of their ethical responsibility to communicate offers of settlement to their client.

Private Mortgage Insurer. Private mortgage insurance (PMI) is generally required when the borrower's down payment is less than twenty percent of the purchase price. PMI premiums are paid by the borrower, even though the insurance benefits the mortgage holder. If the borrower defaults, the mortgage insurer generally will pay some or all of the monies not recouped in the foreclosure process, up to the policy limits.

Sometimes, the existence of mortgage insurance creates a dynamic in favor of foreclosure and against workouts, because the lender is guaranteed to be made whole or nearly whole in the event of foreclosure. However, the good news is that mortgage insurers realize they have an interest in preventing foreclosure in many cases. They will often step in to insist on acceptance of proposed workout terms. Alternatively, they may agree to pay a small arrearage or provide other limited relief in order to keep the borrower in the home. They do so in order to prevent a potential larger loss in the event of foreclosure.

If the homeowner is paying for private mortgage insurance, it is important to find out the name of the insurer and the certificate number of the policy. This may be difficult to figure out. A charge for mortgage insurance should appear in the settlement statement a.k.a. the HUD-1 statement (the itemization provided at the time a real estate loan is closed) or other document itemizing disbursements. It may be necessary to obtain more information about the mortgage insurer directly from the lender or servicer. (Since the homeowners are paying for the PMI, they are entitled to know who is providing it.) See pages 93–94 for a discussion of ways to get information from the servicer.

Many PMI companies are willing to actively participate in the workout discussions. However, even if they are not, keeping them informed of the progress of the workout negotiations will keep the mortgage holder on its best behavior.

Government Mortgage Guarantors. In other cases, mortgages are guaranteed by the federal government, by the Federal Housing Administration (FHA), the Rural Housing Service (RHS), or the Department of Veterans Affairs (VA), or by a state housing finance agency. Like PMI, mortgage holders are protected against the risk of default by guarantee fees or insurance premiums paid to these government agencies by borrowers. Though coverage amounts differ by program, FHA loans, which account for the vast majority of all government-insured loans, provide 100% loss protection. Just as with PMI loans, this protection is sometimes a disincentive to pursue a workout because the lender has virtually no financial risk.

The FHA and RHS, in particular, have instituted both incentives for lenders who offer workouts and financial penalties for those who do not offer assistance. The VA also has some special prerequisites to foreclosure. The various foreclosure alternatives for these government-insured mortgages are discussed in Chapters 7 and 8, below.

Ginnie Mae. Ginnie Mae stands for the Government National Mortgage Association, a government corporation. Ginnie Mae guarantees mortgage-backed securities composed of

FHA-insured or VA-guaranteed mortgage loans that are issued by private lenders. This guarantee is important to investors. Through its mortgage-backed securities programs, Ginnie Mae increases the overall supply of credit available for housing by providing a vehicle for channeling funds from the securities markets into the mortgage market.

Securitization. The majority of mortgages in this country are packaged into pools that are sold to institutional and individual investors. For example, you may have heard of a "Ginnie Mae" mutual fund. This is simply a pool of mortgages from all over the country that produces a stream of income from the principal and interest paid by homeowners. Rather than buying a mortgage or a group of mortgages outright, investors in a mutual fund buy a share or shares of stock in all of the mortgages held in a particular Ginnie Mae pool and are entitled to returns based on the income generated by that pool.

Since most of the loans in a Ginnie Mae pool are HUD insured, HUD supervises the lenders that make these loans. Fannie Mae and Freddie Mac also pool mortgages and make them available to investors. Fannie and Freddie pools may include both conventional and government-insured loans.

When a loan is securitized, each party in the chain is compensated in one form or another. Not all of the income from the loan is passed on to the investors. The servicer gets a piece, the mortgage holder gets a piece, and the company managing the pool, if different, gets a piece as well. The arrangement for this compensation is set out in complicated contracts between the various parties.

Once a loan is securitized and placed in a pool, the investors in the pool have some risk because of fluctuating interest rates on mortgages. However, the investors generally do not share the risks associated with default, because the lender, the servicer, the mortgage holder, or an insurance company normally covers losses that occur because of a default. Whichever party covers the risk of loss due to default is typically compensated for its risk by its share of the stream of income from the mortgage.

The existence of securitization pools makes more capital available for lenders. However, it can sometimes complicate the process of a workout for individual homeowners, because the servicer's hands are tied by the agreements under which the mortgages are sold into the pool. Some of the companies and agencies that manage pools require a lender who wishes to modify a mortgage to buy the loan back out of the pool as a precondition to the modification. Depending on the terms of the modification the lender may be unable to re-pool the loan after modification and may have to keep it in portfolio.

Since pools usually consist of vast numbers of mortgages, the overseers or trustees of the pool generally have little interest in what happens to a particular homeowner. Big mortgage holders such as Fannie Mae and Freddie Mac have created detailed policies to deal with defaulted mortgages in pools, but sometimes other smaller entities that supervise pools (usually as trustees) may have less flexibility.

Understanding Who Owns the Risk of Loss

When a loan is sold or securitized, it is sometimes difficult to know who bears the risk of loss without reviewing the contracts between the servicer, the mortgage holder, the insurer, and the pool administrator. The entity that bears the risk of loss is almost always the loss mitigation decision maker. Determining who owns the risk is critical to the workout process.

Case Study As to How the Secondary Market Works

Joe and Suzie Homebuyer have approached SouthSide Neighborhood Housing to help them buy a home. SouthSide provided pre-purchase counseling and eventually pre-qualified Joe and Suzie for a 95% LTV (loan to value) ratio loan through We Care Community Bank.

SouthSide also sent a preliminary underwriting package to Neighborhood Housing Services of America (NHSA), who issued a purchase commitment letter to We Care Bank. Based on that commitment, We Care completed the final underwriting and closed the loan. Joe and Suzie are homeowners for the first time!

After a few days (or weeks or months), We Care packaged the loan with a few other loans to be sold to NHSA and sent all of the original loan documentation to them. NHSA's loan purchase staff reviewed the documentation and issued We Care a check to purchase the loans. At purchase, servicing was transferred to NHSA. Both We Care and NHSA notified the Homebuyers that their payments should be sent to a new address.

NHSA combined documentation describing the Homebuyer's loan with that of several hundred similar loans, and forwarded the package to Freddie Mac for purchase consideration. NHSA was required to send certain original documents as well as provide a certification that other documents, which met all of Freddie Mac's requirements, were in its loan files. Freddie Mac agreed to purchase the NHSA loans and issued a wire transfer for the full face value of the loans. NHSA will continue to service the loans and each month will send the payments received from the Homebuyers and all the other borrowers to Freddie Mac after deducting a small servicing fee.

Freddie Mac combined the NHSA loans with several thousand loans with similar interest rates, terms, credit scores, LTVs, and maturity dates. It then sent the package to a securities broker on Wall Street. These loans became collateral for a pool of Mortgage Backed Securities (MBS). Shares of stock in this pool were offered through the stock exchange to individual and institutional investors. Freddie Mac was paid for the loans with the income from the stock sale. The investors are entitled to an agreed-upon rate of return that is less than the principal and interest being paid to Freddie Mac by NHSA.

Each month, the servicer will send the agreed upon percentage of the principal and interest due on the loans in the MBS pool to the Pool Trustee. If any loan goes into serious default (more than 120 days delinquent), Freddie Mac is required to buy the defaulted loan out of the pool by sending the Trustee the full amount of the outstanding principal balance.

Through Suzie Homebuyer's new job she has a 401k personal retirement plan. Suzie elected to invest her 401k contributions in a mutual fund that has purchased shares of a Freddie Mac MBS Loan Pool. Joe and Suzie have invested in their own home!

FHA. The FHA owns 100% of the risk of loss for the mortgages it insures. Though the FHA has delegated the initial decision-making authority for loss mitigation to its loan servicers, it encourages housing counselors to call the Oklahoma City office for assistance. Contact information is found at pages 101–102.

Department of Veterans Affairs. The Department of Veterans Affairs (VA) owns the risk of loss for VA-guaranteed loans. Though the VA has delegated some loss mitigation authority to its servicers, VA staff is available to intervene on behalf of borrowers. Contact the VA at one of its nine regional loan centers; contact information is available at 800-827-1000 or www.homeloans.va.gov/rlcweb.htm.

PMI. In loans with private mortgage insurance (PMI), the insurance company absorbs the first loss in the event of default. Accordingly, the insurance company is often very interested in a workout that will reduce its losses. Although PMI companies encourage borrowers to communicate primarily with servicers, all workout decisions must be approved by PMI staff, who will become directly involved in a workout negotiation as necessary.

Fannie Mae/Freddie Mac. If a conventional loan is owned by Fannie Mae or Freddie Mac, that agency generally bears the risk of loss in the event of foreclosure and therefore controls the ultimate workout decision. Both agencies have loss mitigation departments that will intervene to address a proposed workout. If the conventional loan also has PMI, Freddie Mac and Fannie Mae will defer to the private mortgage insurance company to make the workout decision. If a Freddie Mac or Fannie Mae loan is government insured, Freddie or Fannie will not get involved in the loan workout process.

Portfolio Loans. Conventional loans held by lenders in their own portfolios are often the easiest workout candidates because the lender is acting its own servicer and has complete authority to make decisions. It will experience the full impact of the loss if the loan is foreclosed.

Loans Serviced for Others. When servicers are managing loans for other banks or for private investors, the risk of loss will be covered by the servicing contracts between the various parties. Generally, the mortgage holder bears the risk, but the mortgage holder may be unwilling or unable (in the case of a securitized loan managed by a trustee) to intervene in the workout decision process.

How the Financial Dynamics of Foreclosure Affect the Risk of Loss

The preceding pages described which of the players bears the risk of loss in the event of a foreclosure. In some cases, the potential amount of the loss will be significant, giving that player a powerful incentive to avoid foreclosure. In other cases, however, the potential amount of the loss will be so small that the player who bears the risk of loss will not be concerned about it.

The potential amount of the loss depends primarily on how much equity there is in the home and who will get that equity if the home is sold. Although differences in state law make is impossible to generalize about exact rules, the examples on pages 89–90 illustrate several common scenarios.

Who Loses

Example where the home is worth more than the amount outstanding:

    $100,000 home (fair market value)
    $ 65,000 foreclosure sale price
    $ 20,000 mortgage

In this example, the mortgage lender receives $20,000, which pays off the mortgage. The mortgage lender suffers no loss.

The purchaser gets a home worth $100,000 for $65,000.

The homeowner receives $45,000, which is the excess of the foreclosure sale price over the mortgage. The homeowner has thus lost $35,000 of the original $80,000 equity in the home. Because of the substantial original equity in the home, the homeowner could probably have saved the home by refinancing it, or could have sold it for its fair market value.

Example where there is both a mortgage and another lien on the home:

    $100,000 home (fair market value)
    $ 70,000 foreclosure sale price
    $ 60,000 first mortgage and foreclosure costs
    $ 10,000 real estate tax lien

In this example, the mortgage lender receives $60,000, which pays off the mortgage. The mortgage lender is secure as long as the home sells for $70,000 or more, but, since there is less of an equity cushion, the mortgage lender may be concerned that there is a risk of loss.

The purchaser gets a home worth $100,000 for $70,000.

The taxing authority receives $10,000.

The homeowner receives nothing. The proceeds of the foreclosure sale are entirely consumed by the mortgage debt and the real estate taxes.

Example where there is a mortgage, judgment lien, and homestead exemption:

A judgment lien is a lien placed on the home by a creditor who has won a judgment in court against the homeowner. For example, imagine that the homeowner was sued on an unpaid medical bill for $10,000. If the medical provider won the case and the homeowner did not pay the debt, in most states the provider would be able to place a $10,000 lien on the home. However, most states provide a "homestead exemption," meaning that the home is exempt from judgment liens up to a certain amount.

    $100,000 home (fair market value)
    $100,000 foreclosure sale price
    $ 90,000 first mortgage and foreclosure costs
    $ 25,000 homestead exemption
    $ 20,000 judgment creditor

The mortgage lender receives $90,000, assuming that the mortgage debt has priority over the judgment creditor. The mortgage lender is secure as long as the home sells for $90,000 or more. But since there is only a small equity cushion, the mortgage lender may be concerned that there is a risk of loss.

The judgment creditor receives nothing. The homestead exemption of $25,000 protects the home from the judgment creditor's claim.

What does the homeowner receive? The homeowner receives $10,000, which is the amount by which the foreclosure sale proceeds exceed the first mortgage and foreclosure costs.

Example where there is a first and second mortgage:

$100,000 home (fair market value)
$ 90,000 foreclosure sale price
$ 95,000 first mortgage and foreclosure costs
$ 25,000 second mortgage lender

The first mortgage lender receives $90,000, and loses $5,000. In some states it may be able to obtain a deficiency judgment against the homeowner for the $5,000 shortfall.

The second mortgage lender receives nothing. The foreclosure sale price is not even sufficient to pay off the first mortgage.

The homeowner receives nothing.

WHO TO CONTACT FOR A WORKOUT

Start with the Servicer. It is always appropriate to begin the workout process with the servicer. The servicer should have workout specialists who will take applications and provide information on the requirements and standards for a workout. Usually, these employees will work in the "loss mitigation" department, rather than in "collections" or "foreclosure." As with any negotiation, a record should be made of contacts with the servicer and significant communications should be confirmed in writing.

The scope of a servicer's authority to arrange workout terms may be less than clear. Although some servicers have substantial delegated authority, complicated or unusual workout terms generally have to be cleared with the mortgage holder whoever bears the risk of loss. It may be necessary to push the servicer to take a proposal to the mortgage holder rather than simply allow the servicer to refuse the proposal as the path of least resistance.

Unfortunately, one of the problems that have plagued the modern mortgage lending industry is unresponsive loan servicers. Although not all servicers are bad, some servicers have inadequate resources to meet the needs of a national portfolio. Other problems arise because servicers are not traditionally held accountable by mortgage holders for their foreclosure avoidance activities. More promisingly, in recent years Fannie Mae and Freddie Mac have begun the process of upgrading their servicers by tightening policies and by providing incentives to their servicers for arranging workouts.

When a Servicer Is Unresponsive. When a servicer is unresponsive to a workout proposal, it is usually appropriate to appeal directly to the owner at risk—the player that bears the risk of loss. It is a good idea to develop a database of names and contact numbers from different agencies and servicers. It is best to ask to speak with someone in "loss mitigation" or "workouts." Contacts with helpful employees should be fostered and carefully maintained.

CALCULATING REINSTATEMENT AND PAYOFF AMOUNTS

The first step in arranging a workout is gathering some basic information about the loan. The following is a worksheet for recording and calculating this information. Only some of this information will be available from the homeowner, so it will be necessary to obtain information from the servicer as well. How to get information from the servicer is described later in this chapter.

Loan Information Worksheet

Original Loan Terms
Principal Amount   _____
Interest Rate   _____
Loan Term (in months)   _____
Principal and Interest Payment   _____
Escrow Payment   _____
Total Monthly Payment   _____

Arrears Calculation
Total Number of Missed Payments _____ × Amount of Each Payment _____
Late Charges (usually can be waived)   _____
Foreclosure Fees   _____
Foreclosure Costs   _____

Total Amount Due on the Loan
Unpaid Principal Balance   _____
Back Due Interest   _____
Delinquent Escrow Amount (property taxes, insurance)   _____
Late Charges   _____
Foreclosure Fees   _____
Foreclosure Costs   _____

Modification Fee (if any)   _____
(Some workouts will require a modification fee. A request for waiver of any modification fee should be included in the workout proposal.)

Current Value of the Home   _____

Once the basic information about the mortgage loan has been obtained, the next step is to calculate the amount to reinstate the mortgage. By reinstating the mortgage, the homeowner brings the loan current, and can resume monthly payments. The amount to pay off the whole mortgage debt should also be calculated, as this figure is important when considering workout options such as a short sale or HUD's Streamline refinance option.

How to Calculate the Reinstatement Amount

1. Multiply the number of months behind by the monthly payment amount.

2. Add late fees and any additional accrued costs, if reasonable and justifiable.

For example:

Months behind:	4
Monthly payment of principal, interest, taxes, and insurance (PITI):	$1,500
Past-due payments ($1,500 × 4) =	$6,000
Late Fees ($50/month × 4):	$ 200
Foreclosure Fees:	$ 600
Foreclosure Costs:	$ 150
Inspection Fees:	$ 50
Total Reinstatement Amount:	$7,000

How to Calculate the Payoff Amount

1. Obtain the daily interest rate from the lender or approximate it yourself by dividing the annual interest rate by 365 or 360. (Dividing by 365 days is more accurate, but some lenders use 360 days, as it increases the amount of interest they can charge. The loan documents or mortgage may state whether the lender is using 365 of 360. If unclear, ask the lender.)

For example:

Principal amount due on loan:	$120,000
Annual interest rate:	8%
Accrued fees (see above):	$1,000
# of days in arrears:	120 (30 × 4)
Escrow due:	$800 ($200 × 4)

To calculate the daily interest, divide the annual interest rate of 8% (or .08) by 365.
.08 divided by 365 = .0002191

2.   Multiply the daily interest rate by the number of days that have elapsed since last paid installment.

     For example:

     Daily interest rate of .0002191 x 120 (number of days since last paid installment) = .026292

3.   Multiply that result by the principal balance owed on the loan.

     $120,000 × .026292 = $3,155.04

4.   Add late fees and any additional accrued costs, if reasonable and justified.

     For example:

     $3,155.04 + $1,000 (accrued fees) = $4,155.04

5.   Add the total monthly escrow amount due.

     For example:

     $4,155.04 + $800 = $4,855.04

6.   Add this sum to the principal amount due on the loan.

     For example:

     $120,000 + $4,855.04 = $124,855.04

     Total Payoff Amount: $124,855.04

HOW TO OBTAIN LOAN INFORMATION FROM RELUCTANT SERVICERS: THE QUALIFIED WRITTEN REQUEST

Often the homeowner does not have all the information necessary to make the calculations described above, and a simple telephone call to the servicer may be all that is needed to get the missing information. But other times the servicer is non-responsive.

In 1990, Congress added a new section to the Real Estate Settlement Procedures Act (RESPA).[2] This amendment, known as the Servicer Act, creates a mechanism for borrowers to obtain answers from lenders or loan servicers to questions or disputes they have about their accounts and to obtain corrections to their accounts where appropriate.

When a borrower has a question or a dispute concerning the account, including the escrow, a written inquiry triggers certain obligations on the part of the servicer as long as the consumer includes identifying information and a statement of the reasons why the account is in error or clear information about the consumer's question. This is called a *qualified written request*. The servicer must acknowledge the request within 20 days of receipt.

Within 60 days of receipt (not including Saturdays, Sundays, and legal holidays) of a qualified written request from the consumer, the servicer must conduct an investigation if the borrower claims an error; provide the information requested, if available; make any necessary correction to the account; and, inform the consumer of its actions. During this 60-day period, the servicer cannot give any information to a credit reporting agency if a payment related to the inquiry is overdue.[3]

How and Where to Send the Qualified Written Request

To be a qualified written request, the inquiry must be in writing, but it does not need to be in any particular form or even be called "qualified written request." The qualified written request should not be written on a payment coupon or included with the borrower's payment. Instead, it should be a separate letter sent to the servicer's customer service address.

If the homeowner has received a notice from the servicer listing an address where qualified written requests are to be sent, then the homeowner must send it there. This designated address for borrower requests may be listed on the original loan documents, a transfer of servicing statement, an annual escrow statement, or a monthly billing statement. If the homeowner did not get such a notice or does not remember, you or the homeowner should call the servicer's customer service center (a toll-free number may be listed on account statements and is usually available on the servicer's website) and ask for the address to send requests.

If the proper address cannot be confirmed and the homeowner has several addresses for the servicer, then it should be sent to all of these addresses. However, the request should not be sent to the "lock box" address on the payment coupon. This may be the post office box for a third-party company hired by the lender to process payments.

The letter must include enough information to allow the servicer to identify the borrower or the borrower's account. Usually an account number, along with the borrower's name and the address of the property is sufficient. The only other requirement is that the request must include a statement of the reasons why the borrower believes the account is in error and/or provide sufficient detail to the servicer concerning the borrower's question or the information sought. The request should be as specific as possible. An example is found on the next page.

Example of a "Qualified Written Request"

Ken and Susan Starr
12 Budding Bloom Lane
Elizabeth, New Jersey

January 1, 2006

Last Dollar Mortgage Co.
398 Rockefeller Drive
St. Albans, WV 25177

Attention: Customer Service Department
RE: Account #333234

Dear Last Dollar Mortgage Co.:

We are requesting information about the foreclosure fees and costs, and escrow accounting, on our loan. Please treat this letter as a "qualified written request" under the Real Estate Settlement and Procedures Act (section 2605(e)).

Specifically, we are requesting the following information:

- The payment dates, purpose of payment, and recipient of all foreclosure fees and costs that have been charged to our account or have been advanced on our behalf in the last 24 months;
- The payment dates, purpose of payment, and recipient of all escrow items that have been charged to our account or have been advanced on our behalf in the last 24 months; and
- A breakdown of our current escrow payment showing how it was calculated and the reasons for any increase in the last 24 months (include a copy of any annual escrow statement prepared within the last 24 months).
- A payment history that can be easily read and understood listing the dates and amounts of all payments for the last 24 months, showing how they have been applied or credited, or if not applied, showing how they have been treated.

Also, on March 1, 2005, we sent our March payment to First Dollar Mortgage Co., which had been servicing our mortgage before it was transferred to you. Our March payment was never credited to our account. Please correct this error.

Thank you for taking the time to acknowledge and answer this request as required by the Real Estate Settlement Procedures Act (section 2605(e)).

Very truly yours,

Ken and Susan Starr

[certified mail]

If the Servicer Fails to Respond to the Qualified Written Request

A homeowner has a legal right of action against a servicer who fails to comply with the RESPA requirements for responding to a qualified written request.[4] An individual consumer may recover damages, costs, and reasonable attorney fees for "each such failure." If the evidence reveals a pattern or practice of noncompliance, the court may award "additional" damages for each violation up to $1,000. The homeowner must file suit within three years of the violation.[5]

PUTTING TOGETHER THE WORKOUT PACKAGE

The complete package submitted to the lender for its consideration should include the following documents:

- **Hardship Letter:** The hardship letter is optional for FHA-insured loans, but required for other lenders. (The hardship letter is described below.)
- **Workout Proposal** (if the terms are not included in the hardship letter).
- **Financial Statement** (listing income, expenses, assets, liabilities).
- **Other Documentation:** In addition to the items listed above, a lender may require:
  - Tax returns for prior years.
  - Current pay stubs.
  - BPO/Appraisal.
  - Documentation supporting the specific proposal. For example, if the homeowner proposes to make a cash contribution, the lender may require proof in the form of an account statement showing that the cash is available; if an asset will be liquidated, proof of the value of the asset; or if the homeowner's income will change in the near future, proof of the new income and when it will start.
  - A signed listing agreement or purchase and sale agreement if the homeowner proposes a pre-foreclosure sale.
- The lender may order a title report, credit report, or BPO/Appraisal.

Determining Financial Hardship

Some, but not all lenders and investors require that certain workout options be offered only to borrowers experiencing financial hardship. In general, these lenders require a "hardship" that results from a involuntary reduction of income or an unavoidable increase in expenses.

Involuntary Reduction of Income. Examples of circumstances that may demonstrate to a lender that the homeowner has suffered an involuntary reduction in income are:

- Unemployment;
- Mandatory reduction in hours or wage rate;
- Under-employment after loss of a previous job;
- Death of a borrower;
- Decline in business earnings if self-employed;
- Permanent or short-term disability;
- Serious illness of a household member;
- Divorce.

Unavoidable Increase in Expenses. Examples of circumstances that may demonstrate to a lender that the homeowner has suffered an unavoidable increase in expenses are:

- Disability or illness and increase in uninsured major medical expenses;
- Natural or man-made disaster damaging the property;
- Unanticipated capital expenses for urgent property repairs;
- Unavoidable child care expenses.

Voluntary Income Reductions That May Not Be Considered Financial Hardship. Examples of circumstances that a lender may consider insufficient to show financial hardship are:

- Quitting a job without a valid reason;
- Leaving job to stay home and care for children (without documentation that no alternative affordable child care is available);
- Voluntary decrease in hours;
- Normal seasonal layoffs.

Suggested Contents of a Hardship Letter

To qualify for some workout options, the holder of the mortgage will require the homeowner to submit a letter. (A hardship letter is not required for FHA-insured loans, but may still be helpful.) The hardship letter explains the cause of the default, whether the homeowner intends to remain in the property, and how the homeowner intends to resolve the default. The letter should be signed by the homeowner, though the counselor could assist in drafting the letter.

An effective hardship letter will include:

- Identifying information, including the homeowner's names, address, and account number.
- The introductory paragraph should state the foreclosure prevention tool (for example, reinstatement, special forbearance, or streamline refinance) that the homeowner is seeking.
- The second paragraph should describe the hardship and the reasons for the hardship in detail.
- The next paragraph should give an overview of the homeowner's income and expenses and explain any anticipated changes in income (or expenses) and when the changes may occur. It should also state whether the homeowner has a lump sum saved to offset any delinquency.
- Then, describe the proposed plan. The description should state when the plan will be effective, list the reasons why the homeowner believes it will work, and include a statement about why the homeowner is committed to see the plan through to its conclusion.
- The closing paragraph should state the methods and times to contact the homeowner and counselor.
- Attachments—the attachments that lenders typically require are discussed later in this chapter.

There is no one "right" approach to a hardship letter. The letter should, of course, avoid disparaging the servicer, the homeowner's employer, or other third parties. Some good points that the sample letter on pages 98–99 illustrates are:

1. Outlining the workout option or plan to cure the default;
2. Reason for the default;
3. Intention to remain in the home;
4. Prospects for increase in income;
5. Fact that the income will be more stable than before;
6. Reason why the money that was returned by the servicer (and should have been saved) was spent—otherwise the servicer may assume that the homeowner has a lump-sum amount available to cure the mortgage;
7. Other lump-sum amounts saved to help cure the default;
8. Whom to contact (counselor or homeowner) and contact information.

Sample Hardship Letter

June 1, 2006

Darleen Smith
Loss Mitigation Specialist
ABC Mortgage Co.
1234 River Road
Milwaukee, WI, 33333

RE: John and Joan Borrower
271 Lake Street
Dover, Delaware 12345
Account number: 987654321

Dear Ms. Smith:

This letter is to support our application for a forbearance plan that will help us get our mortgage payments back on track. We have lived in our home for 20 years and we want to work hard and keep it.

Our youngest child is learning disabled and attends a special program at school. If we lose the home we will probably have to move out of this school district. (There are very few rental properties.) Our doctor has said that moving is likely to disrupt our boy's development.

We fell behind on our mortgage payments due to loss of income because of a lay-off. We had a very hard time dealing with our debts, because we never had financial problems before. There are so many expenses and managing a home and family of 5 is very hard.

John has been employed in the construction business for more than 20 years as a plasterer and mason. He was laid off by his prior employer last September and his unemployment compensation was only 60% of his prior income. Joan was able to increase her hours as a school aid as of December 1 to make up part of the difference, but we were unable to make full mortgage payments for December through April. Our partial payments were returned by you.

We will be able to start making full payments again soon. John obtained part time work as of April 15, and this job can expand to full time as of July 1. He will be paid less than his prior job, but with Joan's increase in hours our income will be approximately 90% of what it was before the lay-off.

One other good thing is that John's new job is indoor work, which will be steady, and his new employer is a construction company that has been in business for 35 years. Unlike some of John's past jobs, he is not going to be laid off for the winter. John is a good worker and we know he will stick.

We had saved about $2,700 toward the mortgage as of March 1. This is the money you had returned to us. We had hoped to use this money as part of a plan to get caught up on our payments. However, we discovered last month that our 1996 Nissan Maxima could no longer be fixed. Since John's new job is in Wilmington, he needs a car and we have spent about $2,000 of the money we had saved as a down payment for a used (2000) Ford truck. We still have the other $700 and we expect to put aside $800 (the amount of our regular payment) each month starting August 1.

Our financial information is enclosed with this letter. If we can have a forbearance plan that involves payments of no more than $800 per month, we know we can make it. You will see that we have minimized all our expenses and it is most important to us to keep this home. Please put yourself in our position and try to help. We thank you very much for any effort you can make.

Please contact our foreclosure prevention counselor, Jane Dean, at 312-555-1213, to discuss this further.

Sincerely,

John Borrower

Joan Borrower

TIPS FOR COUNSELORS ESTABLISHING A WORKOUT PLAN

1. Time is of the essence in working out a foreclosure. Make sure you know what the timeline is in your state and where in the timeline the borrower you are assisting is.

2. Keep track of deadlines. Negotiating a workout may take months. Servicers may neglect to tell the foreclosure attorney that they are talking to you. Do not let deadlines pass without an agreement in writing as to an extension.

3. Confirm with the servicer any extension of deadlines in writing. Do not rely on oral assurances that everything is taken care of.

4. Be careful that workout agreements do not waive borrowers' rights. Borrowers should never waive their rights unless they have had a legal review of their loan.

NAVIGATING THE SERVICER SHOP

Anatomy of a Servicer Shop

The servicing company performs a variety of functions on behalf of the mortgage holder. General servicing functions include payment processing, escrow, and loan administration. Once the loan is delinquent, servicing functions include collections, loss mitigation, monitoring bankruptcy, overseeing the foreclosure process, and administering real estate owned properties. Frequently, the servicer will be the only party with whom the borrower has had any contact.

Each servicing company is organized differently. However, servicers often will be divided into the following departments. Please note that not every servicer will have a department listed below or call the department by the name listed below.

The Escrow Department. The escrow department collects money to pay for hazard insurance, property taxes, mortgage insurance premiums, and other assessments, and prepares annual escrow statements. Call this department if there is a question about the escrow account. For example, if there is a deficiency (negative balance) in the escrow account, a repayment plan can be worked out with this department.

Collections Department. Once the homeowner has missed a payment, this is the department that will call and send letters to the homeowner demanding payment and assessing late penalties. Your call may be routed to collections. In addition to monitoring the delinquency, the collections department may initiate a conversation about loss mitigation and workouts, but may only be authorized to put simple workouts (typically a full reinstatement or short-term repayment plan) in place.

The Loss Mitigation Department. The loss mitigation department will negotiate a workout plan or other foreclosure alternative. This department has the full authority to offer a wide range of workout options. If the servicer has a loss mitigation department, it is appropriate to contact this department to begin workout discussions.

Bankruptcy Department. If the homeowner has filed for bankruptcy, this department will track and monitor the bankruptcy case and repayment plans. If the homeowner is in bankruptcy, you may be referred to this department when you call the servicer.

The Foreclosure Department. The foreclosure department monitors the foreclosure process. You can call this department to get copies of default or foreclosure notices, to check on the status of a foreclosure, and to obtain a breakdown of the foreclosure costs.

The Real Estate Owned Department. The real estate owned department assumes all the responsibilities of ownership for the foreclosed real estate. This includes the responsibility for vacating the property by providing tenants with time to move, giving them a cash incentive, or initiating eviction procedures. You would call this department if the homeowner has decided to move out of the home. If you are helping the homeowner's tenants this department may also be of assistance.

Helpful Hints When Working with Servicers

Get Thee to Loss Mitigation. Unless the counselor has a direct phone number, the call to the servicer will be routed to the collection department or to a customer service agent. While the collection department may be helpful with simple requests, they usually have limited information about the account, and may lack the authority to negotiate complex workouts. After stating the purpose of the call and establishing your authority to speak on behalf of the homeowner, you should ask to be transferred to the loss mitigation department. This department is most knowledgeable about workout terms and investor guidelines, and has the authority to approve workouts and make key decisions.

Establish Your Authority to Speak on Behalf of the Homeowner. Servicers will refuse to give counselors any information about the homeowner's account without the homeowner's written authorization. The counselor should introduce herself and her organization, state the purpose of the call, and provide the servicer with an authorization form immediately. A sample form is included in Appendix A, below.

Be Prepared. It is helpful to know exactly what information you will need from the servicer at the time of your call, and when you need this information. The servicer's agent will then know best how to direct your call.

Tell a Story. When submitting a workout package, emphasize the sympathetic aspects of the homeowner's story. The servicer's agent may be more motivated to help the homeowner if the sympathetic facts are brought forth.

Be Accurate. The information submitted in the loan workout package needs to be as accurate as possible. The servicer will compare this information with information it already has on file. Explain any discrepancy between the information submitted in the workout proposal and information submitted in the past. The counselor and the homeowner will maintain credibility by submitting realistic workouts with information that is as accurate as possible.

Make Sure the Escrow Department Is Aware of the Workout Proposal. Do not assume that information told to servicer employees in the loss mitigation department will be transmitted to the escrow department. The escrow department may be unaware that delinquent escrow amounts are being repaid through a workout plan. After a workout plan is put in place, homeowners should be on the lookout for a notice or escrow statement raising the total monthly payment because of an alleged escrow shortage or deficiency.

This breakdown in communication can occur between other departments as well. If you are concerned, make sure you remind the servicer's agent to record key information in the servicer's database.

Build Relationships. Cultivate helpful people and build strong relationships with the personnel in the loss mitigation department. However, if the servicer's agents are not being responsive or timely, ask to speak to a supervisor. Always be polite but persistent in getting the help the homeowner needs.

Thank the Servicer. When the servicer says yes to a workout proposal, have the homeowner write a thank you letter. If a servicer employee has been extra helpful, send a letter to a supervisor praising the employee.

Appeal to the Insurer or Investor. If the servicer rejects the workout proposal, it is possible to appeal to the insurer or investor. For FHA-insured loans, ask for help from HUD's Oklahoma City Office: 888-297-8685 or write to the Oklahoma City Office with a copy to the servicer:

Department of Housing and Urban Development
National Servicing Center
310 N.W. 6th Street, Suite 200
Oklahoma City, OK 73102
ATTENTION: [name], Housing Specialist

Information on appealing to Freddie Mac and Fannie Mae is contained in Chapter 6, below.

Getting to YES!

If a servicer says no to the workout proposal, do not give up. First, find out the reason the proposal was rejected and make sure that the "no" is not based on a misunderstanding about the facts or the workout proposal:

- Correct mistakes in the proposal, if any were made, and resubmit it quickly.
- Find out if the servicer has an alternative proposal that can be presented to the homeowner.
- Remember to use qualified written requests to get information on the loan that may not be readily available.
- Remember to dispute overcharges or ask for waivers.
- Review waivers of legal rights the servicer may insert into a workout agreement; highlight these for the homeowner and suggest getting legal advice before signing.

LOSS MITIGATION DECISION TREE

(This is a simple distillation of the fuller information contained in the elsewhere in this handbook and should not be attempted by a counselor without understanding the shorthand implied within.)

Step One: Are there any predatory markers in the loan documents, settlement sheets, HUD-1, correspondence, etc., that should be investigated? See Chapter 3, above, for a list of red flags.

If YES, send to a qualified attorney who specializes in these types of cases.

If NO, go to Step Two.

Step Two: Does the homeowner want to keep the house?

If NO, skip to Step Eight.

If YES, go to Step Three.

Step Three: Does the budget balance?

If YES, skip to Step Five.

If NO, go to Step Four.

Step Four: To help balance the budget, help the homeowner apply for all eligible programs; reorder priorities; increase income; decrease expenses; raise a lump sum. See Chapter 4, above. After all of these, does the budget balance?

If NO, skip to Step Seven.

If YES, go to Step Five.

Step Five: Is there a monthly surplus in the budget?

If YES, go to Step Six.

If NO, consider Special Forbearance (for FHA loans) if the homeowner has good future prospects (such as a raise in salary, prospect of more hours, a court settlement, etc.). If FHA, consider a Partial Claim to reinstate the mortgage. See Chapter 7, below, for further discussion. For all loans, consider a Loan Modification to capitalize the defaulted amount combined with interest rate decrease and/or term lengthening to ensure monthly payment meets budget.

Step Six: When there is a monthly budget surplus, consider a traditional forbearance plan to spread the default over a series of monthly repayments. If there are other problems, a bankruptcy plan might be considered.

STOP.

Step Seven: When the budget does not balance and the borrower wants to keep the house, a loan modification may work to lower the payments sufficiently to satisfy the budget. Also, with an FHA loan, the borrower might seek a Special Forbearance to temporarily reduce the payments if there are good prospects for an increase in income or decrease in expenses to make the budget balance in the future. See Chapter 7, below. Although many mortgage contracts may preclude this option, the homeowner might rent the house temporarily while living in a less expensive place until the situation improves.

STOP.

Step Eight: For homeowners who are ready to let go of the home or for homeowners who do not have the income to support the mortgage, these are the disposition options: lender forbearance while homeowner seeks full sale; deed in lieu of foreclosure; pre-foreclosure sale; assumption by another borrower; allowing the foreclosure and saving money before eviction; and bankruptcy liquidation.

STOP.

Chapter Notes

1. 15 U.S.C. § 1641(f).
2. 12 U.S.C. § 2605(f).
3. 12 U.S.C. § 2605(e); Reg. X § 3500.21(e).
4. 12 U.S.C. § 2605(f). The law provides that a servicer can avoid liability for a violation of the servicing provisions of RESPA by making the appropriate adjustment to the account, as long as this is done within 60 days of discovering the error and before the homeowner files suit, but it is unlikely that this defense would apply to a failure to respond to a qualified written request altogether.
5. 12 U.S.C. § 2614.

CHAPTER 6

Fannie, Freddie, and Subprime Workouts

FANNIE MAE LOAN OPTIONS

Who Is Fannie Mae?

Fannie Mae is the common name for a quasi-governmental agency known more formally as the Federal National Mortgage Association. The aim of the corporation is to provide liquidity in the housing market by purchasing and investing in mortgage loans. As a result of these activities, Fannie Mae puts capital (cash) into the hands of originating lenders who fund new loans.

Fannie Mae, as the largest purchaser of mortgages on the secondary market, sets the standard for the industry on workout options. Its workout policies tend to be used generically by many servicers, as well as by some lenders acting for themselves. The Fannie Mae *Single-Family Servicing Guide,* together with its periodic updates, outlines the company's workout policy. The *Servicing Guide,* which includes a copy of the servicing contract between Fannie Mae and its vendors, is available on-line for free at www.allregs.com/efnma. The *Servicing Guide* is updated periodically through Lender Announcements and Lender Letters, available at www.efanniemae.com/sf/guides/ssg.

The Hardship Requirement and Fannie Mae Workout Options

Fannie Mae workout options are offered to homeowners experiencing financial hardship. In general, the homeowner's financial hardship must be the result of an involuntary reduction in income or an unavoidable increase in expenses. The servicer can consider any substantial reduction in income that the homeowner could not prevent, including, for example, reductions in income due to separation or divorce, or other unusual circumstances that are well-documented. Fannie Mae's *Servicing Guide* gives these examples:

- Unemployment or a long-term job layoff.
- Mandatory pay reduction.
- Disability or illness that results in a decrease in income or in major medical expenses.
- Death of a family member who made a significant contribution toward the mortgage payment.
- A natural disaster.
- A decline in a self-employed homeowner's earnings.

Fannie Mae offers at least four types of accommodations for homeowners experiencing hardship: (1) waiver or deferral of late fees; (2) special measures for those experiencing temporary hardship; (3) loss mitigation for those experiencing long-term reductions in the ability to pay the mortgage; and (4) the charging off of second mortgages in certain situations. Fannie Mae delegates considerable discretion to its servicers to implement most of these options and servicers are charged with evaluating each homeowner's circumstance on a case-by-case basis.

Waiver of Late Charges

Late charges can only aggravate the situation for a homeowner having difficulty making mortgage payments. The servicer has the discretion, in certain hardship cases, to waive late charges or defer late charges to a future date. This waiver may allow the homeowner to keep current on mortgage payments or at least reduce the amount due that must be addressed in a workout.

Special Relief Measures for Those Experiencing Temporary Hardship

Fannie Mae offers certain short-term workout options to those who can quickly bring the mortgage current, or to homeowners who will have a reasonable opportunity avoid foreclosure by selling their property. Special Relief Measures include:

Temporary Indulgence. A temporary indulgence may be appropriate when the sale of the home is pending or the homeowner is expecting a lump-sum settlement from insurance or assistance from a social service agency. The servicer may grant the homeowner a 30-day "grace period" to enable the homeowner to repay all past-due installments at once.

Repayment Plan. A servicer may grant a repayment plan if the homeowner is able to resume regularly scheduled payments and pay additional amounts at scheduled intervals to cure the delinquency. The agreement must be in writing if the homeowner is delinquent on three or more monthly payments.

Special Forbearance. The servicer can agree in writing to reduce or suspend a homeowner's monthly payments for a specific period. Generally, the special forbearance should end no later than 18 months from the date of the first reduced or suspended payment. The servicer may consider longer terms for special situations, and the homeowner must document financial hardship. After the forbearance period is over, the homeowner must resume regular monthly payments as well as pay additional funds toward the delinquency at scheduled intervals. The servicer needs Fannie Mae's and the mortgage insurer's approval for a repayment period that exceeds 18 months.

Loss Mitigation Alternatives for Long-Term or Serious Hardship Cases

These alternatives should be considered where the reason for default appears to be long term or too serious for short-term relief measures. Fannie Mae and the mortgage insurer must approve all loss mitigation alternatives.

Loan Modification. A loan modification is a written agreement between the servicer and the homeowner that permanently changes one or more of the original terms of the note in order to help the homeowner bring a defaulted loan current and prevent foreclosure. Fannie Mae will consider modifications that reduce the interest rate on the mortgage, that change the mortgage product (for example, from an adjustable rate to a fixed rate), that extend the term of the mortgage, and that capitalize the delinquent payments.

Fannie Mae requires the homeowner to make a cash contribution to reduce the delinquency, *if financially feasible,* before it will agree to modify a conventional mortgage. The servicer can charge a $500 fee to cover its administrative expenses, plus actual out-of-pocket costs to cover a credit report, a title examination, or other services, if permitted under the terms of the note, security instrument, and applicable law. If the homeowner is unable to pay all or a portion of the processing fee, Fannie Mae may reimburse the servicer the difference between what the homeowner can pay and the amount of the fee for a portfolio mortgage, or capitalizing all or a part of the fee.

According to Fannie Mae guidelines, a servicer should consider a modification for a delinquent homeowner who has experienced a permanent or long-term reduction in income and is unable to continue making the mortgage payments; if the terms of the mortgage (such as those imposed by a nonstandard adjustable-rate mortgage) contribute toward a greater risk of homeowner default; or *any other* situation in which changing the terms of the mortgage would cure the delinquency, avoid foreclosure, or prevent future delinquencies.

Mortgage Assumption. A mortgage assumption permits a qualified applicant to assume both the title to the property and the mortgage obligation from a homeowner who is currently delinquent in the mortgage payments. An assumption may be considered if the current market value of the property equals or exceeds the unpaid principal balance of the loan plus interest due and expected sales costs. Fannie Mae will also consider granting permission for an assumption when the current market value of the property is slightly less than the outstanding indebtedness since the property purchaser may be willing to make up the difference in cash because of the lower closing costs associated with a mortgage assumption. In all cases, the property purchaser must qualify for the mortgage under Fannie Mae's current underwriting guidelines.

The servicer can charge the purchaser a fee of 1% of the unpaid principal balance with a minimum of $400 and up to a maximum of $900. Servicers, however, cannot charge the purchaser an assumption fee unless it is permitted under the terms of the note, security instrument, and applicable law. Fannie Mae will not approve an assumption on a property with subordinate liens unless they can be paid off.

Pre-Foreclosure Sale. A pre-foreclosure sale is a sale of the property in which Fannie Mae and the homeowner agree to accept the proceeds of the sale to satisfy the defaulted mortgage, even though this may be less than the amount owed on the mortgage, in order to avoid foreclosing on the property. The homeowner's financial hardship must be a result of an involuntary loss of income or unavoidable increase in expenses. All other workout options must be considered prior to the use of a pre-foreclosure sale procedure. The lender may require the homeowner to contribute funds to reduce the deficiency. For example, if there are unused funds in the borrower's escrow account, the lender may require the borrower to waive his or her rights to the funds so that they can be applied toward the deficiency. In the alternative, the borrower may be required to execute a promissory note.

When appropriate, the homeowner should request a delay of the foreclosure sale to complete the pre-foreclosure sale of the property. Unless a delay is approved, the servicer will continue the foreclosure process even if the property is listed for sale. However, the terms of any pre-foreclosure sale agreement will be honored as long as the property is sold before the foreclosure sale date. Fannie Mae and the insurer must approve the delay of the foreclosure proceedings. To offset a servicer's expenses for handling a pre-foreclosure sale for a conventional mortgage, Fannie Mae will pay the servicer a processing fee of $1,000. The forgiveness of debt as a result of a pre-foreclosure sale may have tax consequences, as described in Chapter 9, below.

Deed in Lieu of Foreclosure. A deed in lieu of foreclosure is a workout option in which a homeowner voluntarily conveys clear property title to the lender in exchange for a discharge of the debt. Fannie Mae views this as a last resort. Fannie Mae may agree to a deed in lieu when the property has been on the market as a pre-foreclosure sale for at least three months without a reasonable sales offer; when there are legal impediments to pursuing foreclosure; or when acceptance of a deed in lieu will allow Fannie Mae to obtain title earlier than if a foreclosure action is pursued. Except in special circumstances, the homeowner will receive no compensation from Fannie Mae for a deed in lieu, and may be asked to make a cash contribution or sign a promissory note to reduce the delinquency. The property must not be subject to any other liens (subordinate or otherwise), judgments, or attachments, and, unless waived by the mortgage insurer or guarantor, the property must be vacant.

For each completed deed in lieu for a conventional mortgage, the servicer receives a $500 processing fee. The servicer is reimbursed for attorney fees (of up to $350) and for the costs for obtaining a title update if the homeowner is unable to pay. The approval of Fannie Mae and the mortgage insurer is required. The forgiveness of any debt as a result of the deed in lieu will be reported to the IRS and may have tax consequences, as described in Chapter 9, below.

Charging Off a Second Mortgage

In certain circumstances Fannie Mae will consider a charge-off on a second mortgage instead of foreclosure, such as where there is a small monetary delinquency that is deemed uncollectible and accompanied by serious, uninsured damage to the property (i.e., natural disaster or presence of a hazardous substance). A charge-off ceases collection efforts on a mortgage when the debt is deemed to be uncollectible. All other workout options must be explored before a recommendation for a charge-off is considered.

Fannie Mae's decision on the second mortgage will be affected by who owns the first mortgage. If another investor holds the first mortgage, Fannie Mae may charge off the second mortgage, or instead decide to pursue a workout for the second mortgage or pay off the first mortgage and foreclose the second mortgage. When Fannie Mae has an interest in both the first and second mortgages, it may consolidate the two mortgages and modify the homeowner's payments instead of charging off the debt.

Helpful Contacts at Fannie Mae

When a servicer is unresponsive to a workout proposal, it is appropriate to contact Fannie Mae:

> The **Midwestern Regional Office**, 312-368-6200, serves Illinois, Indiana, Iowa, Michigan, Minnesota, Nebraska, North Dakota, Ohio, South Dakota, and Wisconsin.
> The **Northeastern Regional Office**, 215-575-1400, serves Connecticut, Delaware, Maine, Massachusetts, New Hampshire, New Jersey, New York, Pennsylvania, Puerto Rico, Rhode Island, Vermont, and the Virgin Islands.

The **Southeastern Regional Office**, 404-398-6000, serves Alabama, the District of Columbia, Florida, Georgia, Kentucky, Maryland, Mississippi, North Carolina, South Carolina, Tennessee, Virginia, and West Virginia.

The **Southwestern Regional Office**, 972-773-HOME (4663), serves Arizona, Arkansas, Colorado, Kansas, Louisiana, Missouri, New Mexico, Oklahoma, Texas, and Utah.

The **Western Regional Office**, 626-396-5100, serves Alaska, California, Guam, Hawaii, Idaho, Montana, Nevada, Oregon, Washington, and Wyoming.

FREDDIE MAC LOAN OPTIONS

Who Is Freddie Mac?

Freddie Mac is the colloquial name for the Federal Home Loan Mortgage Corporation. Like its sister corporation, Freddie Mac is one of the largest investors in the mortgage marketplace. The company purchases mortgages, packages these loans into securities, and sells them to investors on Wall Street, allowing capital to flow back into the hands of the originating lender so that new loans can be made.

The Hardship Requirement and Workout Options

In general, to be considered for a workout, homeowners must be delinquent in their mortgage payments or be in imminent danger of default. In most instances, workout options are offered only to homeowners experiencing an involuntary reduction of income or increase in expenses. However, homeowners do not have to demonstrate hardship for relief options with repayment plans of twelve months or less in duration. Manufactured home owners also are not required to demonstrate hardship for many workout options.

Examples of an involuntary reduction in income include:

- Unemployment or a mandatory pay reduction.
- Underemployment following a previous job loss.
- Death of a homeowner or primary wage earner in the household.
- A decline in business earnings for a self-employed homeowner.
- Incarceration of a spouse or co-homeowner.
- Illness, disability, separation, divorce.
- A natural or man-made disaster.

An unavoidable increase in expenses may result from:

- An unanticipated repair that affects the value or habitability of the property.
- Overextension on credit resulting from a homeowner using credit to make mortgage payments.
- Medical debt.
- Food expenses or utility bills.

Freddie Mac divides its workout options into three broad categories: reinstatements; relief options; and workout options. With reinstatement, the homeowner brings the mortgage current by paying all past-due amounts. Relief options provide a homeowner with temporary relief and will cure a delinquency over a defined period of time. The workout options lead to a long-term cure of the delinquency or transfer of property other than through a foreclosure sale. Many of the relief and workout options can be offered to homeowners who are not delinquent, but may become delinquent in the near future. Freddie Mac compensates servicers for implementing certain options.

Reinstatement

Servicers are required to pursue a reinstatement as the first option for resolving a delinquency. A reinstatement occurs when a homeowner pays all delinquent mortgage payments and past-due amounts, making the mortgage current. A homeowner may reinstate a delinquent mortgage at any time, even after foreclosure proceedings begin or while a relief or workout plan is in progress.

Full Reinstatement. A full reinstatement restores a delinquent mortgage to current status by paying the total amount delinquent, including advances, accrued interest, legal costs, and other expenses allowed by the security agreement and state law. The servicer does not have the discretion to reject a full reinstatement if the payment includes the total amount delinquent, as enumerated above, even if it does not include other expenses incurred such as the cost of a broker's price opinion (BPO), inspection fees, and accrued late charges.

Partial Reinstatement. In a partial reinstatement, the homeowner pays an amount less than the total due (including advances, legal fees, and expenses) and executes a repayment plan for the remainder, except accrued late charges and the cost of a BPO. The repayment period may last up to 12 months if there is an escrow account on the mortgage. If there is no escrow account, the servicer must establish one, and then may extend the repayment period up to 18 months without Freddie Mac's approval. The homeowner completely reinstates the mortgage when all of the payments specified in the repayment plan are made. The servicer must accept partial reinstatement of the mortgage if the homeowner pays at a minimum all outstanding legal fees and related expenses, plus the first payment due under the repayment plan. In addition, the homeowner must execute a written repayment plan for the remaining delinquent interest, principal, and escrow (if applicable), plus the scheduled monthly payments.

Relief Options

Relief options allow homeowners to gradually pay back delinquent amounts or temporarily reduce the amount of the mortgage payment or temporarily stop making mortgage payments. All relief options must result in the homeowner bringing the mortgage current or paying the mortgage in full. Freddie Mac will consider proposals from homeowners who do not meet all the eligibility requirements for a proposed relief option if the relief option is the best possible solution to cure the delinquency. Relief options include the following:

Repayment Plan. A repayment plan is an agreement that gives the homeowner a fixed amount of time to bring delinquent mortgage payments current by paying the normal monthly payment plus an additional amount. A repayment plan can stand alone as a relief option or can be combined with short-term forbearance, long-term forbearance, or a partial reinstatement. If a repayment plan stands alone, the repayment period must not last longer than 12 months from the date of the agreement, unless approved by Freddie Mac. If the repayment period lasts more than three months and the homeowner is 90 or more days delinquent, the homeowner must be experiencing (or have experienced) financial hardship or have a signed sales contract to sell the home. If a repayment plan is combined with another relief option, the maximum repayment period can vary.

Short-Term Forbearance. A short-term forbearance is a written agreement to temporarily let a homeowner reduce or suspend monthly payments during the forbearance period. Payments may be suspended for up to 3 months or reduced for up to 6 months from the date of the agreement. At the end of the forbearance period, the homeowner must bring the mortgage current through payment in full or begin a repayment plan (lasting no longer than 12 months from the date of the plan), or pay off the mortgage in full. To qualify, a homeowner must meet the financial hardship criteria or have a signed sales contract for the sale of the home. The homeowner also qualifies if he or she is current on the mortgage payment. Freddie Mac's approval is not necessary.

Long-Term Forbearance. A long-term forbearance is an agreement to temporarily let a homeowner reduce or suspend mortgage payments during the forbearance period, which may last up to 12 months from the date of the agreement. At the end of the forbearance period, the homeowner must either bring the mortgage current, begin a repayment plan (lasting no longer than 12 months from when the forbearance ends), or pay off the mortgage in full. Long-term forbearances are typically granted when the property was damaged by a disaster, causing financial hardship; or a homeowner is waiting for an outstanding major medical claim, causing financial hardship; or a homeowner is deceased and the estate is in probate; or a lawsuit is pending that may jeopardize Freddie Mac's lien position; or a homeowner's place of employment was damaged by a natural or man-made disaster. Freddie Mac must approve this option.

Workout Options

Freddie Mac will consider workout proposals that do not meet published guidelines if the option is the best solution to resolve the delinquency. Approval from Freddie Mac and the mortgage insurer is required for most workout options. Workout options include the following:

Loan Modification. A loan modification is a written agreement between the servicer and the homeowner that permanently changes one or more of the original terms of the note. Freddie Mac will consider reducing the interest rate, changing the term or type of mortgage (for example, from an adjustable to a fixed rate mortgage), and capitalizing the arrears. However, no write-off or permanent reduction of the unpaid principal balance is allowed.

Freddie Mac will consider a modification for first-lien loans at least twelve months old at the time of application. The company will also consider a loan modification on a second mortgage if its existing lien status will be maintained. The homeowner must show financial hardship or an allowable reason to warrant the modification and contribute money, if possible, to reduce the delinquency or the amount capitalized. The homeowner also must have a stable income to support some level of monthly payment and pay a $300 processing fee and expenses. All of the modification fees and expenses (i.e., title, notary, recording, broker's price opinion), except for the $300 processing fee, can be capitalized. Approval from Freddie Mac *and* the mortgage insurer is required.

Mortgage Assumption. A mortgage assumption permits a qualified applicant to assume both the title to the property and the mortgage obligation from a homeowner who is currently delinquent in the mortgage payments (or in imminent danger of default). The current homeowner must show financial hardship. The servicer may charge the applicant a fee not to exceed the greater of $400 or 1% of the mortgage's unpaid principal balance, up to a maximum of $900. The applicant must meet underwriting guidelines and pay a down payment of at least 5% of the total indebtedness. The mortgage must have an indebtedness-to-value (ITV) ratio of 85% or greater. (The ITV is the unpaid principal balance, accrued interest, escrow advances, and expenses, divided by the probable sales price. The probable sales price is established by the broker's price opinion.) In most cases, the expenses for the assumption, including the expense for the broker's price opinion, will be paid by the homeowner or the applicant. Approval from Freddie Mac *and* the mortgage insurer is required.

Short Payoff. A short payoff is the sale of the property for less than the total amount necessary to satisfy the mortgage obligation. The homeowner must have the property listed for sale at the current market price and show financial hardship. Freddie Mac will also consider this option if the homeowner defaults on a modification plan. To make up any deficiency from the sale of the property, the homeowner may be required to make a cash contribution and/or sign a promissory note, as well as assign Freddie Mac the proceeds of any hazard insurance. The servicer is required to waive its right to any accrued late fees or property inspection costs. Freddie Mac and the mortgage insurer must approve this option. The forgiveness of debt as a result of a short payoff may have tax consequences, as set out in Chapter 9, below.

Deed in Lieu of Foreclosure. A deed in lieu of foreclosure is a workout option in which a homeowner voluntarily conveys clear property title to Freddie Mac in exchange for a discharge of the debt. The homeowner must generally demonstrate financial hardship. The servicer must determine that no other relief or workout options are appropriate and the property has not significantly deteriorated (i.e., no structural damage, environmental hazard, or condition that would pose a health or safety risk) or have any liens filed against it. The homeowner must have listed the property for sale for at least 90 days, at no more than 110% of market value and all attempts to sell the property must have been unsuccessful. The homeowner may be required to pay costs associated with the deed in lieu, or contribute to any loss. Approval from Freddie Mac and the mortgage insurer is required. The forgiveness of any debt as a result of the deed in lieu will be reported to the IRS and may have tax consequences, as set out in Chapter 9, below.

Charging Off of a Loan

In certain circumstances Freddie Mac will consider a charge-off of the loan instead of foreclosure. A charge-off ceases collection efforts on a mortgage when the debt is deemed to be uncollectible. Freddie Mac will consider a charge-off if no other relief or workout option is appropriate, the property was condemned because of a hazardous substance, deterioration or a natural disaster; and one or more of the following is true:

- The damage to the property is uninsured;
- It is not economically feasible to repair the property and the land has little or no value;
- There is no legal recourse against the homeowner or third party for property damage; or
- There is a small debt that is deemed uncollectible.

Late Charges and Other Fees

The servicer is prohibited from charging additional fees to the homeowner other than those approved by Freddie Mac for each relief or workout option. In addition, the servicer may not refuse to consider a workout option or require payment of accrued late charges as a condition of doing a workout.

Helpful Contacts at Freddie Mac

To get help with difficulties with a Freddie Mac servicer, call 800-FREDDIE and access the customer service representative from the initial menu. Ask the customer service representative for the name and number of someone in the loss mitigation department who can review a workout proposal.

Comparison of Fannie Mae and Freddie Mac Options	
Fannie Mae	**Freddie Mac**
Temporary Indulgence: A thirty day grace period to repay all the arrears.	*Reinstatement:* In a full reinstatement the homeowner repays all the arrears. In a partial reinstatement, the homeowner pays less than the amount due and enters into a repayment plan for the remainder.
Repayment Plan: A plan to resume making monthly payments plus additional amounts to repay the arrears.	*Same.*
Special Forbearance: A written agreement to reduce or suspend monthly payments for a specific period. Repayment must occur within 18 months.	*Short-Term Forbearance:* A written agreement to reduce monthly payments for up to 6 months or suspend payments for up to 3 months. Repayment must occur within 12 mos.
N/A	*Long-Term Forbearance:* A written agreement to reduce or suspend monthly payments for up to 12 months. Repayment must occur within 12 months.
Modification: A permanent change in one or more of the original terms of the note.	*Same.*
Assumption: Third party assumes title to the property and the mortgage from delinquent homeowner.	*Same.*
Pre-Foreclosure Sale: Sale of the property for less than the amount owed on the mortgage.	*Short Payoff:* Same.
Deed in Lieu: Homeowner voluntarily conveys marketable title to the lender in exchange for discharge of debt.	*Same.*
Charge-Off: Cease collection on small second mortgage debt on property with serious, uninsured damage.	*Charge-Off:* Cease collection on a small loan where property is condemned or deteriorated.

WORKOUTS WITH SUBPRIME LENDERS AND SERVICERS

Subprime mortgage holders and servicers are less likely to have established workout criteria, such as those Fannie Mae and Freddie Mac publish. Nevertheless, the counselor should check the servicer's website to see if there is any information posted regarding default servicing or forbearance programs.

On the other hand, subprime lenders and servicers may be more subject to public relations considerations than similar entities in the standard mortgage market, particularly if a class action or government investigation is pending or has been recently concluded. Do a Google search to see if there are any large class action lawsuits pending or government agency investigations. You may also want to contact the lead lawyers or the regulatory agency if you need help resolving the problem.

A servicer who was the recent target of a regulatory action may be more responsive than a servicer who has not been publicly censured. Similarly, some individuals at the servicer will be more responsive and more able to resolve disputes than others. If your borrower is in trouble for the same reasons the servicer was recently in the news, this may dramatically improve your chances of resolving the situation quickly and fairly. In that situation, it is often helpful to work down, instead of up at the servicer or lender. Try to find a contact in the government relations department or the general counsel's office. If, for example, a particular servicer was in trouble recently for its failure to promptly post payments, and that appears to be why the borrower is delinquent, talk to someone in the government relations department or the general counsel's office.

What a subprime servicer is able and willing to do to address a deficiency varies greatly. Some subprime servicers, either as part of a settlement of litigation or in an effort to improve their reputation, have adopted formal loan resolution programs. Others are more ad hoc. In any event, the more you know, the better able you will be to assist the borrower. Most subprime loans are securitized. For a description of securitization, see Chapter 14, below. The obligations of the servicer over a pool of securitized loans is governed by the "Pooling and Servicing Agreement." If the servicer tells you that loss mitigation is not possible because the loan is securitized, you can dig deeper to find out if this is accurate. To do that digging, go to the CD-Rom accompanying this handbook and follow the instruction in "Finding Pooling and Servicing Agreements for Securitized Mortgage Loans." An actual agreement is included on the CD-Rom for your education.

In general, a servicer is paid a percentage of the total principal balances of all the loans it services. In addition, the servicer may usually keep late fees and other charges it imposes when collecting on the loan, foreclosing, and preserving the quality of the property. Retention of these fees provides the servicer an incentive to collect junk or duplicative charges. However, the servicer is normally obligated to pass on to the mortgage holder monthly payments for all loans in its servicing portfolio, subject to explicit provisions that permit workouts in written agreements with the holder. Other factors that may be helpful in working with a subprime servicer include:

- How long has the servicer had the borrower's loan?
- Did the servicer obtain servicing rights before or after default?
- Does the servicer have a reputation for working with borrowers?
- Does the servicer have a reputation for making certain kinds of mistakes?
- Do you have a contact with someone at the servicer who will work with you to resolve the problem?

When dealing with a subprime servicer, use your imagination to identify a workout plan that will work for the borrower you are assisting. Then, find someone at the servicer with the authority and desire to assist you. Among the possible loan resolution options from a subprime servicer are the following:

- *Partial Reinstatement.* The servicer suspends foreclosure proceedings for a time, after the borrower makes a payment equal to some percentage of the delinquency (the borrower must then catch up in full).
- *Forbearance Agreement.* An agreement that can last up to two years in duration and that permits the borrower to catch up on payments while making full current payments.
- *Special Forbearance Agreement.* An agreement that can last up to a year and that allows the borrower to make partial payments (typically, the arrearage must then be paid in full at the end of the agreement period).
- *Loan Modification.* A modification of the existing loan terms that includes significant reductions in interest rate (down to 0%) or converts an adjustable rate mortgage to a fixed rate.
- *Waiving Certain Fees.* Since the servicer keeps all fees collected from the borrower, the servicer has complete discretion to waive these fees in order to help make a workout successful.

No matter the nature of the workout, always, always get all agreements in writing. Also be cautious of agreements that require the borrower to waive rights.

CHAPTER 7

Loan Workout Options for FHA-Insured Loans

THE FHA-INSURED LOAN PROGRAM

The Federal Housing Administration's (FHA) purpose is to expand homeownership and rental housing opportunities for people not adequately served by the private mortgage markets. FHA is a part of the Department of Housing and Urban Development (HUD) and administers a variety of single-family mortgage insurance programs designed to make homeownership more readily available. These programs operate through HUD-approved lending institutions such as banks, savings and loan associations, and mortgage companies.

The lenders fund the mortgage which the FHA insures. HUD does not provide direct loans to purchase a house. Homeowners pay premiums for the insurance through which FHA guarantees the lender that it will earn a return for taking the risk of lending money to the homeowner. If the lender forecloses, the lender receives most of the principal, interest, and costs from the FHA insurance fund.

History

Congress created the FHA in 1934 to help the country get back on the road to economic recovery. At the time, the housing industry was in a deep recession. Two million construction workers had lost their jobs. Terms were difficult to meet for homebuyers seeking mortgages. Mortgage loans were limited to 50% of the property's market value, with a repayment period spread over three to five years and ending with a balloon payment. America was primarily a nation of renters. Only 4-in-10 households owned homes. Today, the U.S. homeownership rate exceeds 68%.

During the 1940s, FHA programs helped to finance military housing and then homes for returning veterans and their families. In the 1950s, 1960s and 1970s, the FHA stimulated production of millions of units of privately-owned apartments for elders, the disabled, and lower income Americans. When soaring inflation and energy costs in the 1970s threatened the economic viability of thousands of private apartment buildings, the FHA's emergency financing kept cash-strapped properties afloat. When a deep recession prompted private mortgage insurers to pull out of oil producing states in the 1980s, the FHA moved in to stabilize falling home prices and ensure purchasers could find financing for homes they wanted to buy. Today, the FHA concentrates its efforts on first-time and lower income homebuyers and is active in urban neighborhoods.

Who Owns and Services FHA Loans?

The lender who originates an FHA-insured loan usually packages the mortgage into a "pool" of other mortgages that is purchased by investors on the secondary market. Investors feel confident in their purchase because the loans are guaranteed by the Government National Mortgage Association (a.k.a. Ginnie Mae), a government corporation.

Ginnie Mae's purpose is to support the government's housing objectives by establishing secondary market facilities for residential mortgages. Ginnie Mae guarantees mortgage-backed securities composed of FHA-insured or VA-guaranteed mortgage loans that are issued by private lenders (issuers) and guaranteed by Ginnie Mae. Through its mortgage-backed securities programs, Ginnie Mae increases the overall supply of credit available for housing by providing a vehicle for channeling funds from the securities markets into the mortgage market.

With the loans no longer owned by the original lender, but by a number of secondary market investors, it is essential that a servicer handle the business on behalf of the investors, collecting the monthly payments and disbursing payments for escrow items (property taxes, insurance, ground rents, mortgage insurance premiums, etc). The servicer of an FHA-insured mortgage must follow guidelines published by HUD in the *Federal Register* and incorporated in its handbooks and Mortgagee Letters.

Types of FHA-Insured Loans

There are many FHA insurance programs, but this chapter focuses on the most popular—the insurance program for single-family homes. FHA programs include:

- Mortgage Insurance for One-to-Four Family Homes (Section 203(b));
- Mortgage Insurance for Disaster Victims (Section 203(h));
- Mortgage Insurance for Outlying Areas (Section 203(i));
- Mortgage Insurance for Older, Declining Areas (Section 223(e));
- Mortgage Insurance for Members of the Armed Forces (Section 222);
- Rehabilitation Mortgage Insurance (Section 203(k));
- Cooperative Program (Section 203(n));
- Graduated Payment Mortgage Insurance (Section 245(a));
- Growing Equity Mortgage Insurance (Section 245(a));
- Mortgage Insurance for Low- or Moderate-Income Buyers (Section 221(d)(2));
- Mortgage Insurance for Condominium Units (Section 234(c));
- Mortgage Insurance for Adjustable Rate Mortgages (Section 251);
- Energy Efficient Mortgages Program;
- Home Equity Conversion Mortgage Program (Reverse Mortgages) (Section 255);
- Manufactured Home Loan Insurance;
- Manufactured Home Lot and Combination Loan Insurance;
- Property Improvement Loan Insurance.

Eligibility for the Single-Family Program

The most popular FHA-insured loans are Section 203(b) mortgages, allowing a person to purchase or refinance a principal residence. To be eligible, the borrower must meet standard FHA credit qualifications and occupy the property as a primary residence. One- to four-unit structures are eligible. The maximum size mortgage for a single-family unit is 95% of the median house price in the borrower's area. The borrower is eligible for approximately 97% financing, and can finance closing costs and the up-front mortgage insurance premium into the mortgage. The borrower will also be responsible for paying an annual premium.

THE FHA LOSS MITIGATION PROGRAM

The FHA's Loss Mitigation Program is designed to address serious defaults, those that continue for 90 days or more. The program was started in 1996 after the FHA stopped accepting applications for the assignment of insured loans. The program delegates responsibility to the lender for managing loans in default, including assisting homeowners to utilize the various workout options. Lenders receive financial incentives for complying with the guidelines.

The guidelines set forth six different options that lenders can offer homeowners:

- Special forbearance;
- Streamlined refinancing;
- Loan modification;
- Partial claim;
- Pre-foreclosure sale; and
- Deed in lieu of foreclosure.

Each of these options are discussed on pages 122–132 later in this chapter.

Eligibility for Loss Mitigation

The homeowner must occupy the property as a principal residence to be eligible for most of the options, unless the homeowner's need to vacate the property is related to the cause of the default (i.e., job loss, transfer, divorce, or death), or if the property was not originally purchased for investment. Homeowners must demonstrate that they have experienced a verifiable loss of income or increase in living expenses to the point where the mortgage payments are no longer sustainable. Homeowners need not justify the loss of income or increase in living expenses as beyond their control or otherwise for good cause.

The homeowner may not own other real estate subject to FHA insurance, or have been the borrower on any loan on which the FHA has paid an insurance claim within the past three years. Exceptions may be made for those who inherited the property or co-signed for an FHA-insured loan.

Homeowners who have filed for bankruptcy are not eligible for any loss mitigation option except the partial claim option discussed on pages 128–130 later in this chapter. Homeowners who have had a bankruptcy discharged or dismissed may be considered for all loss mitigation options including pre-foreclosure sale.

Required Lender Loss Mitigation Efforts and Foreclosure Timelines

HUD regulates lender responses to a homeowner's delinquency on mortgage payments. Lenders may not initiate foreclosure until all loss mitigation options have been considered. However, it is very important to understand that a lender, after considering such options, can proceed to foreclosure, *even if a workout is pending.* Lenders have to review loss mitigation efforts before they initiate foreclosure proceedings, but can simultaneously negotiate workout plans and proceed with the foreclosure process.

Here is the timeline that HUD requires of lenders. Before the 90th day of delinquency, the lender must inform homeowners in writing of all loss mitigation options, provide information about housing counseling, and send a copy of HUD Publication PA 426-H, *How to Avoid Foreclosure*. Also within 90 days of default, the lender must evaluate the loan to determine whether loss mitigation is appropriate. Lenders must also document monthly evaluations of homeowners in default to determine appropriate loss mitigation options and maintain this documentation.

Lenders must initiate foreclosure OR utilize one or more of the loss mitigation options within 6 months from the date of default, although time extensions are allowed in certain circumstances. For special forbearance, loan modifications, or partial claim, the lender may automatically take an additional 90 days provided the workout option is begun prior to the expiration of the initial 6 months. In addition, lenders may request an additional extension of time in writing from the local HUD office.

Lenders have the discretion, without HUD approval, to utilize any loss mitigation option, but they must follow program guidelines. When a lender employs a loss mitigation tool, HUD allows the foreclosure time frame to be stayed as long as the rules for that tool are followed (this is geared primarily towards states with lengthy judicial proceedings). In nonjudicial foreclosure states, where foreclosure proceedings move rapidly, the lender should remove the loan from foreclosure in order to successfully utilize loss mitigation tools—and is encouraged to do so by HUD—but may choose not to do so. *The lender is not required to stop foreclosure proceedings.*

The use of any option, except the deed in lieu, extends the time the lender has to initiate foreclosure. If a lender has tried special forbearance, HUD will allow a larger claim for unpaid interest if the loan later goes to foreclosure. If the homeowner fails to meet the requirements of a special forbearance and the failure continues for at least 60 days, the lender must start the foreclosure no later than 90 days after the homeowner's failure to meet the special forbearance requirements.

HUD's Monitoring of Lender Performance

The lender must report loss mitigation progress to HUD, and HUD does post-claim reviews of individual cases to make sure loss mitigation was handled appropriately, as well as Quality Assurance Reviews on a lender's entire portfolio. The Loss Mitigation Tier Ranking System tracks the performance of lenders. A lender's tier ranking will affect incentive payments, claim reimbursements, and delegated program authority. For example, Tier 1 lenders are eligible for an additional $100 for each special forbearance agreement; a two month extension of the preforeclosure time frame without HUD approval; and additional compensation for foreclosure costs. Eligibility for performance incentives under the Tier Ranking System is determined annually.

Failure to comply with the Loss Mitigation Program may result in: loss of incentive compensation and other benefits; reduced reimbursement of foreclosure costs; and interest curtailment related to foreclosure delays. Depending on the severity of the noncompliance, HUD may refer the lender to the Mortgagee Review Board, whose sanctions include civil monetary penalties and termination of the lender's approval to participate in HUD programs.

Incentive Payments to Lenders

Because FHA loans are insured, the lender has limited incentive on its own to engage in loss mitigation. If the homeowner defaults, the lender recovers the loan amount from HUD. As a result, HUD offers the following cash incentive payments to lenders engaging in loss mitigation:

Special Forbearance . . . . $ 100
Special Forbearance fee for Lenders in the Top Tier . . . . $ 200
Modification . . . . $ 750
Partial Claim . . . . $ 500
Pre-foreclosure Sale $1,000
Deed in Lieu . . . . $ 250

These incentive fees are in addition to reimbursement of actual (allowable) expenses, such as the cost of a title search or recording fees, up to the limits that HUD has established. Note that the homeowner may be responsible for late fees and foreclosure costs.

HUD's Foreclosure Timeline

Listed below are HUD's time guidelines for their lenders. These are estimates, and a foreclosure may take *less* time than allotted by HUD under these guidelines. In fact, the average foreclosure time may well be shorter. Homeowners should not rely on these numbers, since the actual foreclosure time is often much faster.

STATE	MONTHS	FORECLOSURE METHOD	INITIAL ACTION
Alabama	4	Non-Judicial	Publication
Alaska	5	Non-Judicial	Recording Notice of Default
Arkansas	5	Non-Judicial	Recording Notice of Default
Arizona	4	Non-Judicial	Recording Notice of Sale
California	7	Non-Judicial	Recording Notice of Default
Colorado	7	Non-Judicial	Filing with Public Trustee
Connecticut	9	Judicial	Complaint to Sheriff
Delaware	8	Judicial	Complaint
District of Columbia	7	Non-Judicial	Recording Notice of Default
Florida	7	Judicial	Complaint
Georgia	4	Non-Judicial	Publication
Guam	10	Non-Judicial	
Hawaii	9	Judicial	Complaint
Idaho	6	Non-Judicial	Recording Notice of Default
Illinois	12	Judicial	Complaint
Indiana	10	Judicial	Complaint
Iowa	17	Judicial	Petition
Kansas	9	Judicial	Complaint
Kentucky	7	Judicial	Complaint
Louisiana	7	Judicial	Petition Executory Process
Maine	12	Judicial	Complaint
Maryland	6	Non-Judicial	File Order to Docket
Massachusetts	8	Non-Judicial	Filing of Complaint
Michigan	9	Non-Judicial	Publication
Minnesota	10	Non-Judicial	Publication
Mississippi	4	Non-Judicial	Publication

Missouri	3	Non-Judicial	Publication
Montana	7	Non-Judicial	Recording Notice of Sale
Nebraska	5	Judicial	Petition
Nevada	6	Non-Judicial	Recording Notice of Default
New Hampshire	4	Non-Judicial	Publication
New Jersey	14	Judicial	Complaint
New Mexico	7	Judicial	Complaint
New York	13	Judicial	Complaint
North Carolina	5	Non-Judicial	Notice of Hearing
North Dakota	8	Judicial	Complaint
Ohio	12	Judicial	Complaint
Oklahoma	7	Judicial	Petition
Oregon	7	Non-Judicial	Recording the Notice of Default
Pennsylvania	10	Judicial	Complaint
Rhode Island	3	Non-Judicial	Publication
South Carolina	7	Judicial	Complaint
South Dakota	10	Judicial	Complaint
Tennessee	4	Non-Judicial	Publication
Texas	3	Non-Judicial	Posting and Filing of Notice of Default
Utah	5	Non-Judicial	Recording the Notice of Default
Vermont	14	Judicial	
Virginia	4	Non-Judicial	Publication
Washington	6	Non-Judicial	Recording Notice of Sale
West Virginia	5	Non-Judicial	Publication
Wisconsin	12	Judicial	Complaint
Wyoming	6	Non-Judicial	Publication

SPECIAL FORBEARANCE

One of the six HUD forms of loss-mitigation is special forbearance.[1] A special forbearance is written agreement between the lender and borrower that contains a plan to repay a loan. The homeowner is eligible if the lender determines the borrower has a reasonable ability to cure default through a plan. No hardship showing is necessary.

The lender will receive an incentive payment for entering into a special forbearance only if the homeowner is at least three payments behind, so lenders are unlikely to agree to special forbearance for a homeowner with a shorter default. Plans can allow homeowner to become up to 12 months behind in payments of principal, interest, taxes, and insurance. There are two types of Special Forbearance:

Type I Special Forbearance. Type I Special Forbearance provides relief that is not typically offered under an informal forbearance plan (a verbal agreement to repay up to 3 months of arrears). For example, the plan may allow for the temporary suspension or reduction of monthly payments to allow the borrower to recover from the cause of the default; or the borrower may be required to make regular monthly mortgage payment for a set period before beginning to repay the arrearage. The plan must be for a minimum of four months. There is no maximum length of time to repay the arrearage.

HUD specifically permits a lender to enter into a Type I Special Forbearance agreement with a borrower who is unemployed and has a reasonable prospect of finding employment in the future. Once the borrower is employed, the terms of the plan will be adjusted to reflect the change in income.

Type II Special Forbearance. Type II Special Forbearance combines a short-term special forbearance plan and a modification or partial claim, as described on pages 128–130 later in this chapter. The borrower must make at least three monthly payments prior to the execution of a modification or partial claim.

How Special Forbearance Works

The Lender's Incentive. For granting a Type I Special Forbearance, the lender receives a $100 incentive fee ($200 if the lender is in the top tier). The lender also gets two months more interest if the loan later goes to foreclosure. Moreover, there is a chance to make a loan perform again if the plan succeeds, which might cost the lender less than if loan goes to foreclosure. The forbearance may also improve the lender's score with HUD, allowing increased incentive payments in the future. If a Type II Special Forbearance is used, the lender will receive the incentive payment for a modification or partial claim.

Information the Lender Needs. To process a special forbearance, the lender needs independent verification of income, a written agreement defining the term, frequency of payments and amount of payments; and a budget and financial statement of assets and liabilities.

Foreclosure Costs and Late Fees. Reasonable foreclosure costs and late fees may be included in the repayment plan, and will be collected after the loan has been reinstated through payment of all principal, interest, and escrow advances. The loan will not be considered delinquent solely because the borrower has not paid late fees or foreclosure costs. The borrower will not be assessed a late fee while she is performing under the terms of the plan. Since a Type II Special Forbearance plan culminates in either a modification or partial claim, foreclosure costs and late fees are collected in accordance with the requirements for those options.

Renegotiation; Relationship to Foreclosure. A special forbearance can be renegotiated. Loans must be at least 3 months in arrears, but not more than 12 months in arrears, and may not be in foreclosure when the special forbearance is executed. Loans referred to foreclosure may be removed from the foreclosure process.

A Special Forbearance Example

Elaine and Derwood Chaney have arrived at your office seeking help with their four month mortgage default. Both were working, together bringing home $5,000 each month, when she was laid off 12 months ago. Mr. Chaney is still working.

Ms. Chaney received unemployment of $1,000 for three months and then they exhausted most of their savings to keep up with the mortgage before finally falling behind. Mr. Chaney's monthly take-home of $3,000 must cover all of their *minimum* monthly expenses of $2,500 in addition to their monthly mortgage payment of $2,000 ($1,645 P&I and $355 escrow). Mrs. Chaney's past employer cannot promise her anything, and work (except for low wage tourism jobs) is hard to find in this high-cost area near Jackson Hole (and they cannot quit this area). Since the default, they have saved $1,000.

Because they have only been in the house two years, have little equity, and have a low fixed interest rate (6.25%) 30-year mortgage, you suggest a *Special Forbearance*. You call the mortgage servicer and work out the following *special forbearance plan:*

(1) The Chaneys will make a payment of $1,000 due immediately, bringing the amount in default down from $8,000 to $7,000.

(2) Then they will make four monthly $500 payments (instead of the scheduled $2,000 payments). Because these payments are short by $1,500 a month, this will increase the amount in default by another $6,000, for a total of $13,000 remaining in default.

The agreement is that after this four month period of time, you, the Chaneys, and the mortgage servicer will speak and decide if a repayment plan is possible (maybe Elaine will be successful in finding work). If not, a more drastic remedy must be pursued.

In the package, you send to the mortgage servicer you will include:

- A cover letter, describing the plan to which everyone agreed;
- A budget, including current financial information of assets and liabilities;
- Verification of Mr. Chaney's income;
- The Chaneys' check for $1,000.

Four months later . . .

Good news & bad news!

Good news: Elaine Chaney was called back to work and is earning her regular salary plus an increase. Also, Derwood Chaney's supervisor has promised him overtime of at least $600 each month for the next year.

Bad news: The furnace went kaput; the lowest bid is $3,000; and the Chaneys have no credit cards (they listened to you and cut them up).

Create a new plan, assuming:

1. They must replace the furnace with cash; and
2. That they have $1,000 extra each month towards repayment.

One option would be to ask the lender to let them skip a month, so as to pay $3,000 for the furnace, and then to resume payments at the higher amount of $3,000 to catch up. This is how such an *amended special forbearance plan* would work:

(1) Skip any payment for the next month. Because the scheduled payment would have been $2,000, this will increase the amount in default from $13,000 (see the special forbearance plan above) to $15,000.

(2) Make 15 monthly payments of $3,000 (instead of the scheduled $2,000), catching up $1,000 a month. After 15 months, the amount in default would be zero.

STREAMLINE REFINANCE

Another of the six HUD forms of loss mitigation is called streamline refinance. This approach replaces the existing FHA-insured loan with a new FHA-insured loan that has different terms—by a refinancing process. Since HUD's guarantee amount does not change, HUD does not require the lender to underwrite the refinanced loan, so the lender's risk does not change. Here are the basics of how streamline refinance works:[2]

Eligibility. Streamline refinance is only available if the loan is two months delinquent or less. The borrower can pay cash to bring loan no more than two months behind, and then obtain a streamline refinance. Review the other eligibility requirements that apply to all HUD loss mitigation options on page 119 at the beginning of this chapter.

Loan Terms That Can Change in the Refinance. The interest rate can always decrease to the current market rate, but HUD does not allow the interest rate to increase except when the refinance is done with no closing costs. In that case only, the lender can charge a higher interest rate in lieu of closing costs. Also the loan can be converted from adjustable to fixed rate and *vice versa,* and the loan can be converted from one FHA-insured loan product to another. The loan term can be changed to the lesser of:

> A new thirty year term; or
> The current unexpired term plus twelve years.

Payment Changes. An extension of the loan term or a decrease of the interest rate may result in lower monthly payments.

Ginnie Mae Repooling Requirements. Ginnie Mae is paid off by the proceeds of the refinancing. After refinance, the loan is treated as a new loan.

Other Considerations. No cash can be provided to the borrower other than minor adjustments at closing not to exceed $250. Borrowers may be required to pay all closing costs. (In a "no cost" refinance, these fees are actually being paid by an interest rate premium.) For the new loan, the borrower need not use the holder of the existing FHA-insured loan, but can use any new lender eligible for FHA insurance. This new lender may be eager to take care of the paperwork necessary to close the refinancing because it will be paid only if the loan closes.

What Information a Lender Needs to Process a Streamline Refinance. HUD does not require underwriting, but the lender may request income verification, credit report, title search, and broker's price opinion. The lender may calculate the loan-to-value and debt-to-income ratios.

Advantages of Streamline Refinance for the Lender. The lender obtains new settlement costs, and the loan becomes a performing loan, while FHA insurance continues to cover the lender's risk.

Why HUD Would Consider a Streamline Refinance. HUD is not advancing anything on an insurance claim or taking on more risk. The loan may become more affordable and make the possibility more remote that HUD would have to pay the lender on an insurance claim.

Cost to the Homeowner of the Refinance. The homeowner must pay closing costs or an interest rate premium in lieu of closing costs.

STREAMLINE REFINANCE EXAMPLE

Kirby and Kitty Kettel bought their home 10 years ago at a time of higher interest rates—8.25%. They did not realize they could refinance their FHA mortgage until they came to you. Being very conservative and "old school," they had resisted all offers to refinance, even though they received numerous mailings and cold calls (*they had listened to their pre-purchase counselor who had warned them of consumer traps and mortgage scams*).

They are not behind yet, but are sick to death about what will happen when Kirby's rust-belt employer, Schmelta Auto, emerges from bankruptcy and cuts wages by 50%. With their joint income and careful analysis of the budget, they would feel comfortable with a $750 monthly payment. They have savings to cover settlement expenses.

Here is what a Streamline Refinance might look like for the Kettels. This example assumes that ten years ago they took out a 30 year $93,175 mortgage on their home valued at $95,000. The principal amount outstanding by now has been reduced to $82,152. Although there is only 20 years left on the mortgage, they refinance into a new 30 year mortgage.

	Original	As Refinanced
Interest rate	8.25%	6.25%
P & I (per month)	$699.99	$505.82
Escrow (per month)	$202.01	$202.18
Total monthly payment	$902.00	$708.00

Does the value of the home now (ten years later) matter? It does not matter if the Kettels home is now worth less than when they first bought it. A loan-to-value analysis is not required to do a Streamline Refinance. A lender may throw out the appraisal if it is not in the homeowner's interest for the value of the home to be considered. But if the home has increased in value, this might make the loan less than 80% of the home's value, so no mortgage insurance premium would be due. If a mortgage insurance premium is paid, assume for purposes of this example that it is paid at settlement and was not included in their new balance.

Can other loans be refinanced as well? What if the Kettels had a $3,000 car loan that they wanted to include in the refinance? According to HUD's rules, this is *not* allowed. This is just as well. Given their equity, many lenders would love to refinance the Kettels' loans in a regular refinance. However, it is not advisable to refinance unsecured debt into secured debt because it could cause them problems in the future—maybe even the loss of their home. Better to pay off the car loan in other ways. Strategies for dealing with debt are discussed in Chapter 4, above.

LOAN MODIFICATION

Another form of HUD-approved loss mitigation is called *loan modification.*[3] Loan modification involves an agreement to permanently change the original terms of the loan in order to make the payments more affordable for the homeowner. The interest rate or the remaining term of the loan can be changed. Arrears can be added to the principal balance of the new loan.

Changes to the Interest Rate. The interest rate can decrease or increase. The lender has discretion to reduce interest rate to below current market rate. However, the lender will not be reimbursed for fees associated with rate reduction. Any increase in interest rate or monthly payment must be supported by the borrowers' ability to pay.

Length of the Loan Term. The term of the loan cannot be extended more than 10 years beyond the original maturity date of the loan or 360 months from the due date of the first installment required under the modified mortgage, whichever is less. If arrears are capitalized (added to the principal balance of the new loan), the term will usually be extended. This means that the amount of the monthly payment will often go down.

No Adjustable Rate Loans. Modification must result in a fixed rate loan. A required part of loan modification is that any adjustable rate loans must be converted to fixed rate.

Limits on What Can Be Capitalized (Added to the Principal Balance of the Modified Loan) and Relation to Junior Lienholders. At least where there is no junior lienholder, the modified principal balance may exceed the principal balance at origination, and even result in a loan-to-value ratio greater than 100%. Nevertheless, late fees, foreclosure fees, and costs *cannot* be capitalized. They must be paid in a lump sum at the time the loan is modified or through a repayment plan. Only delinquent interest, taxes, and insurance may be capitalized.

State law may limit the ability of the modified mortgage to exceed the original balance. HUD requires that the modified mortgage retain its first lien position. But some states have limits on loan modifications if there are junior lienholders, so that the first mortgage may be limited to a modified principal amount no larger than the original principal balance.

Ginnie Mae Repooling Requirements. To modify a mortgage, the lender generally must buy the loan out of a Ginnie Mae pool. Once the loan is modified, it then may be repooled with other similar loans. Many lenders are unwilling to buy loans out of Ginnie Mae pools in order to modify them.

Relation to Other Forms of Loss Mitigation. Loan modification may be used after a special forbearance agreement. When combined with a short-term special forbearance plan, it becomes a Type II Special Forbearance Plan, as described above. Loan modification may not be used in conjunction with a partial claim, as described below.

What the Lender Needs in Order to Process a Loan Modification. The lender needs verification of income, a credit report, title search, and a written modification agreement signed by all parties. A broker's price opinion is optional, but it will usually be obtained by the lender.

Why Lender Would Consider a Loan Modification. The lender turns a non-performing loan into a performing loan and gets a $750 processing fee plus up to $250 for a title search.

Homeowner's Costs. The lender can require that the homeowner pay legal fees to close the loan as modified.

LOAN MODIFICATION EXAMPLE

Wanda Van Gogh and her husband Pablo Picasso are four months behind in their mortgage payments. They purchased their home eight years ago, for $135,000, with a $125,140 mortgage.

Ms. Van Gogh directs a thriving non-profit agency while Mr. Picasso has struggled lately as an entrepreneur in search of a good idea. (His real passion is painting.) He created Pablo's Tchotkes and earned a respectable income through Ebay, except for the fact he did not pay sales tax or income taxes and owes the government $10,000. The feds have threatened to seize all of the family's savings.

After carefully examining the budget, the three of you agree that they can afford a payment of $1,000 each month.

Here is a loan modification plan that you could propose to the lender:

1.   Add all unpaid interest and delinquent escrow payments to a new principal balance thus:

Existing outstanding principal balance:	$112,974
Four months of unpaid interest:	$ 2,824
Four months of delinquent escrow	$ 680
Foreclosure costs and fees	$ 0
New Principal Balance	**$116,478**

2.   Then you will try to negotiate with the lender to reduce the interest rate down half a percentage point, and allow the new principle balance to be paid out over 30 years.
     Here is a comparison of the original loan and the loan modification.

	Original	**Modified Terms**
Loan Balance	$125,140	$116,478
Interest rate	7.5%	7%
P & I (per month)	$875	$770
Escrow (per month)	$170	$170
Total monthly payment	$1,045	$940
Term	30 years (22 years remaining)	New 30 year

What if they had late charges, foreclosure costs, or fees? How would this have affected the *Loan Modification*? Late fees and foreclosure costs cannot be included in the new principal of a modified mortgage. These would have to be waived or paid separately for the loan modification to happen.

PARTIAL CLAIM

A partial claim is another form of HUD-approved loss mitigation. A partial claim results in HUD granting a junior mortgage loan to the homeowner in the amount of up to 12 months of defaulted mortgage payments (PITI) to bring the mortgage current.[4] The partial claim cannot cover late fees or foreclosure costs—these must be handled in some other way. The homeowner can repay this junior mortgage loan at any time.

How the Partial Claim Loan Works. The homeowner pays no interest, no prepayment penalty, and has no required monthly or periodic payment. The partial claim becomes a junior lien behind all other existing liens. It need not be the second lien. The loan must be repaid when the first mortgage is paid off or when the homeowner no longer owns the property.

Eligibility. To be eligible for a partial claim, the homeowner must:

- Be at least four months, but no more than twelve months in arrears.
- Have the long-term financial stability to support the mortgage debt.
- Not have the ability to repay the arrearage through a special forbearance plan or modification.
- Be committed to continuing to occupy the property as a primary residence. (A partial claim cannot be used to reinstate a loan prior to a sale or assumption.)
- Have overcome the cause of the default.
- Have sufficient income to resume monthly mortgage payments.
- Not be eligible for a loan modification.

Review the other eligibility requirements that apply to all HUD loss mitigation, discussed on pages 118–119 at the beginning of this chapter.

Preconditions. Prior to the execution of a partial claim:

- The lender must remove the loan from foreclosure.
- The homeowner may be required to contribute funds to pay down the default.
- If a homeowner is in chapter 7 or 13 bankruptcy, the homeowner can obtain a partial claim with the approval of the Bankruptcy Court, but the debtor must reaffirm the debt.

Relationship to Other Forms of Loss Mitigation. A partial claim can be used in conjunction with special forbearance. When a partial claim is combined with a short-term special forbearance plan it is a Type II Special Forbearance, described on pages 123–124 earlier in this chapter. Mortgage modification must be considered before partial claim. In addition, a modification cannot be combined with a partial claim.

Availability of a Second Partial Claim. A homeowner can qualify for a second partial claim if circumstances warrant in the future. However, the total of all partial claims cannot exceed 12 times the monthly PITI.

What the Lender Needs to Process a Partial Claim. The lender needs a credit report, a budget and financial statement of assets and liabilities, and independent verification of homeowner's income. The lender must also use HUD's model forms to use for the mortgage and note.

Why the Lender Would Consider a Partial Claim. The lender gets a mortgage brought current and receives a $500 incentive fee and a $250 processing fee, which covers recordation costs of the partial claim mortgage and note. The lender can also collect double interest on defaulted payments if the loan goes to foreclosure.

Homeowner's Costs. The homeowner may not be charged any additional costs for receiving this loss mitigation workout option. However, the lender may collect legal costs and fees related to a canceled foreclosure action directly from the homeowner.

PARTIAL CLAIM EXAMPLE

Mr. and Mrs. Chaney come back to you two months after your last, renegotiated plan. Mrs. Chaney's employer did, in fact, call her back. However, shortly thereafter the company went out of business after it out-sourced its counseling services via the Internet to India. Mrs. Chaney has found another job as an assistant teacher for a daycare center. They can no longer maintain the $3,000 monthly Special Forbearance payment plan. Their financial picture now:

Mr. Chaney's take home:	$3,500
Mrs. Chaney's take home:	$1,200
Sensible monthly budget, including home maintenance:	$2,700
Amount available for the mortgage (originally $2000 a month)	$2,000

Because their original interest rate was low, Streamline Refinancing would not help them. A Loan Modification might work for them, but, because the loan is so young and the interest rate already low, the lender agrees it is not a good option. Before they came to you, they were four payments behind and made these payments under their Special Forbearance plan:

To sum up their recent payment history under the Special Forbearance Plan # 1:

Monthly Payment History	Remaining Default Amount
Amount in default prior to the plan	$8000
Immediate First payment of $1,000	$7,000
First of four $500 payments (each creating an additional $1,500 in default)	$8,500
Second of four $500 payments	$10,000
Third of four $500 payments	$11,500
Fourth of four $500 payments	$13,000
No payment one month (to fix the furnace) pursuant to amended Special Forbearance plan	$15,000
$3,000 payment under amended plan to catch up $1,000 a month	$14,000
A second $3,000 payment	$13,000

Amount of the Partial Claim: $13,000

Remember foreclosure costs and late charges cannot be included in the Partial Claim.

PRE-FORECLOSURE SALE

The fifth form of HUD loss mitigation is a pre-foreclosure sale (PFS). This is the market sale of the borrower's home to satisfy the mortgage debt even if the proceeds of the sale are less than the amount owed on the mortgage.[5] HUD waives the right to any deficiency. If the sale price is *more* than the amount due on the mortgage, this is considered a "full sale."

If the sale of the home will not be completed prior to the date of the foreclosure sale, HUD approval is required to delay the foreclosure sale. If the home is actively marketed for 4 to 6 months, the lender will delay the foreclosure process during this period. (If the lender is in the top tier of Loss Mitigation Tier Ranking System, the lender gets two additional months to complete a sale.)

To qualify for a PFS, the home must have marketable title. There can be no junior liens that cannot be discharged and no irresolvable title problems. In addition, the home must be appraised for at least 63% of total due on the mortgage (the total due includes any partial claim, described above) and the "net sales proceeds" must be at least 82% of that appraised value.

Theoretical minimums for a PFS using a $100,000 mortgage balance:	
$63,000	63% minimum appraisal of home value compared to mortgage balance
$51,660	minimum "net sales proceeds" to HUD (82% of appraisal)

"Net sales proceeds" is a measure of how much HUD will recover, and is defined as the contract price minus any sales commission (6% or less), consideration paid to the seller ($750 or $1,000), money paid to discharge junior liens (not to exceed $1,000); property repairs required by the appraisal; and local/state transfer tax stamps and other customary closing costs. Some settlement costs may not be included in the net sales proceeds, including tax service fees and other property transfer costs normally paid by the buyer, home warranty fees, survey costs, repairs not stipulated in the appraisal, and the seller's lawyer fees.

Eligibility. In addition to HUD's general eligibility requirements for loss mitigation, described at pages 118–119, for a homeowner to be eligible for the PFS program:

- HUD must approve the homeowner's participation.
- The loan must be at least 30-days delinquent prior to the closing date of the PFS sale.
- The homeowner occupies the home as a primary residence. An exception will be made if homeowner's need to vacate the property was related to the cause of the default (i.e., job loss, transfer, divorce, or death).

Advantages for the Homeowner. Homeowners who participate in the PFS program will not be pursued for a deficiency if they are unsuccessful in selling their property and foreclosure occurs. If the homeowner does succeed in selling the property, any deficiency is waived, and the homeowner may receive $750. If the sale closes within 3 months of the lender's approval, the homeowner may receive $1,000. However, if there is a lien on the property, this payment will first be applied toward discharge of the lien. If that is not sufficient, the lender can allocate an additional $1,000 from the sales proceeds to discharge the lien.

Disadvantages for the Homeowner. In addition to the loss of the home, there may be tax consequences to the homeowner for using this option. The homeowner will also receive a "Short Sale" notation on their credit report, which could affect eligibility for another FHA-insured loan for 3 years. There may be other credit reporting consequences as well. Both the tax and credit reporting implications are examined in Chapter 9, below.

Peculiarities of a PFS. Generally, HUD will reduce the realtor's commission in a PFS. This results in some realtors specializing in this type of transaction while others refuse to do them at all. Additionally, the lender has discretion over judging the qualifications of the buyer and making the decision to approve or decline each purchase offer.

What the Lender Needs to Process a Pre-Foreclosure Sale. The lender needs an Application to Participate and Approval to Participate, a credit report, a broker's price opinion, a budget, and independent verification of the homeowner's income.

Why a Lender Would Consider a Pre-Foreclosure Sale. The lender gets a potential or actual non-performing loan off of the books and receives a $1,000 fee.

Pre-Foreclosure Sale Example

Wanda Van Gogh returns to you shocked, not to mention ticked off. Her husband, Pablo Picasso, left the family home to take up a painting career. He also had sucked the household funds dry due to his failed Ebay business.

Wanda cannot manage the mortgage on her non-profit salary and wants to sell. She has no resources (see above) and cannot make any of the $1,045 mortgage payments.

Here is how a PFS would work:

Mortgage balance:	$116,478
Appraised value of the home:	$135,000 (far in excess of the 63% minimum)
Minimum net price to HUD after settlement costs:	$110,700 (82% of $135,000)

DEED IN LIEU OF FORECLOSURE

A deed in lieu of foreclosure is a written agreement transferring title to the home to HUD in exchange for cancellation of the loan and mortgage/deed.[6] The loan must be at least 30 days delinquent prior to transfer of the deed. Moreover, the home must have first been offered for sale through the pre-foreclosure sale process, as described immediately above. There can be no tenants residing in the home, unless HUD approves, and there can be no junior liens, including IRS liens, except Section 235 assistance payments, partial claim advances, and Title I liens. Other liens must be discharged.

Homeowner Eligibility. To be eligible: the homeowner must meet the general loss mitigation prerequisites described on pages 118–119 at the beginning of this chapter; the home must be the homeowner's principal residence; and the homeowner must not be in default on any other FHA-insured mortgage.

Other Advantages to the Homeowner. The homeowner may be compensated by the lender up to $2,000. No fee will be paid if the property is occupied at the time of conveyance. If there are junior liens on the property, this fee may be used to discharge the liens and clear title.

Disadvantages to the Homeowner. Besides loss of the home, there may be tax consequences as a result of the deed in lieu, because HUD is not pursuing any deficiency. HUD will not report any discharge of indebtedness income to the IRS. But, if a Form 1099 is sent to the IRS, indicating income to the homeowner from the discharge of indebtedness, consult Chapter 9, below. A deed in lieu will also be reported to the credit reporting bureaus.

What the Lender Needs to Process a Deed In Lieu. The lender needs certification that the homeowner does not own any other FHA-insured mortgages in default. Lenders are expected to contact junior lienholders in an effort to clear title to the property.

Why a Lender Would Consider a Deed In Lieu. The lender receives an incentive fee of $250. The lender also avoids some of the costs of foreclosure and removes a non-performing loan from its portfolio.

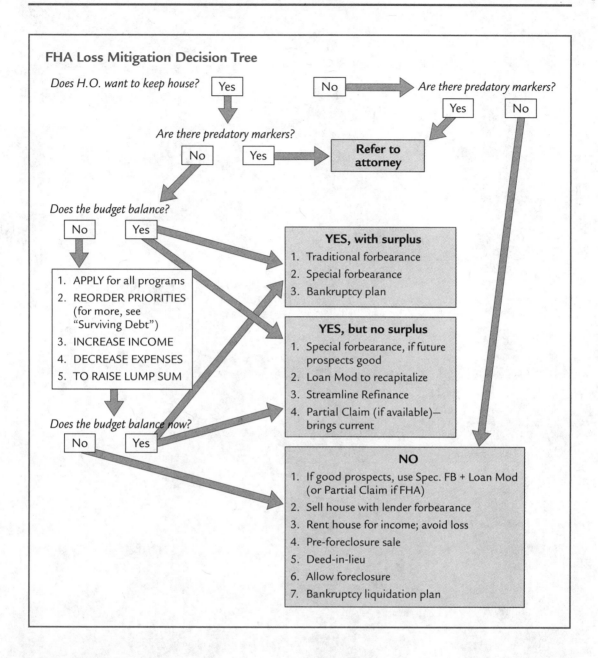

FHA Loss Mitigation Decision Tree

Chapter Notes

1. Detailed information on the HUD special forbearance option is found in Mortgagee Letters 00-05, 01-14, 02-17, 05-18, *available at,* 62 Fed. Reg. 60124 (Nov. 6, 1997).
2. Source: Mortgagee Letters 01-12, 05-03; HUD Handbook 4155.1.
3. Source: Mortgagee Letters 00-05, 01-14, 05-18.
4. Source: Mortgagee Letters 00-05, 03-19, 05-18.
5. Source: Mortgagee Letters 00-05, 05-47.
6. Source: Mortgagee Letter 00-05, 02-13.

CHAPTER 8

VA and RHS Loan Workouts

OPTIONS FOR VA-GUARANTEED LOANS

The Department of Veterans Affairs (VA) guarantees loans made by private lenders to veterans for the purchase, construction, or refinancing of homes owned and occupied by veterans. The VA has established guidelines and procedures for workouts of delinquent loans insured by the agency. The VA expects the mortgage holder to exhaust all possible alternatives before pursuing foreclosure. Here are the current options for VA-guaranteed loans (Note: see the box below that discusses possible changes to these options in the near future):

Forbearance. The lender may grant forbearance by allowing payments to remain delinquent for up to twelve months. Forbearance is followed by a lump-sum repayment or a payment plan. A written forbearance is required if the forbearance will extend beyond the first 60 days of a missed installment. Under written repayment or forbearance plans, lenders must accept partial payments of installments. However, they may return the partial payments if the foreclosure process has started. The guidelines do not limit the repayment period, which can make repayment very flexible.

Modification. A delinquent loan or one where default is imminent may be modified. The lender may extend the term or reamortize the loan provided that at least 80% of the loan balance extended will amortize over the remaining term of the loan, or, for loans with terms of less than thirty years, the lesser of the economic life of the security or thirty years from the date of origination. Unpaid interest, taxes, and insurance may be added to the newly modified balance. Lenders are not allowed to increase the interest rate on a modified mortgage. Modifications will be offered to homeowners whose incomes have been reduced making them financially unable to pay their loan or make up the arrears.

Assumption. If a workout is unsuccessful, a lender may grant a homeowner forbearance for a reasonable period of time to permit the sale or transfer of the property. For loans made prior to March 1, 1988, a homeowner may transfer property to a third party without the approval of the VA. The original homeowner remains liable, however, unless he or she obtains a release from the VA permitting such an assumption. For loans made on or after March 1, 1988, the approval of the VA is needed for an assumption. In addition, most buyers must pay a funding fee equal to one-half of 1% of the loan balance as of the date of transfer. There is also a processing charge, whose maximum is the lesser of: (1) $300 and the cost of a credit report; or (2) the maximum fee prescribed by state law.

Compromise Claim. If the proceeds of a private sale are insufficient to pay the loan, or to pay the delinquency in the case of the assumption, the VA may pay the buyer a "compromise claim" to facilitate the sale. This option is akin to a "short sale" and the lender claims payment from the VA for any deficiency between the sale price and the amount due on the mortgage. If the loan is assumed, and the fair market value of the property is less than the unpaid principal balance, the payment may be applied to the principal to reduce the loan balance and the amount the third party has to assume. The VA, not the lender, processes a compromise claim payment. Any purchaser assuming a VA loan involving a compromise claim must be qualified by the VA, assume responsibility for repayment of the loan, and indemnify the VA against loss in the event of future default. Debt forgiveness as a result of the compromise claim may have tax consequences, as detailed in Chapter 9, below.

Refinance. A homeowner may refinance a high interest rate loan at a current, lower rate under the VA's interest rate reduction refinancing program. If the loan is current, no underwriting is necessary. If the loan is delinquent, the VA must approve this option.

Refunding. The VA has the authority to buy a loan in default from the lender and take over its servicing. However, this option, called "refunding," is to be exercised at the VA's discretion. Though the VA makes very limited use of this option, the VA says it reviews every loan in default to determine whether to refund the loan. There is no formal application process. The objective of refunding is to avoid foreclosure when the VA determines that the default can be cured through various relief measures and the lender is unable or unwilling to grant further relief. Other loss mitigation options may then be available to the homeowner.

Deed in Lieu. The VA must approve any deed in lieu, although it strongly encourages lenders to accept the voluntary transfer of the property if there is no alternative to terminating the loan, But the deed in lieu will usually not be accepted if there are any junior liens on the property. In any deed in lieu, the lender provides the homeowner with a complete release of liability for the deficiency, but will report the forgiveness to the IRS, which may have tax consequences as detailed in Chapter 9, below.

Important Note: In 2005, the VA issued proposed rules which would significantly amend the loan guaranty regulations related to servicing, loss mitigation, and foreclosure of VA-guaranteed loans, to encourage more action by lenders, thereby reducing the amount of refunding that the VA will be required to perform. The proposed rules:

- Delegate more authority to servicers to implement loss mitigation options;
- Increase incentive payments to servicers for using various options;
- Establish a system for measuring servicer performance;
- Set limits on the amount of fees and costs that can be included in a guaranty claim;
- Increase the interest rate cap on modified loans;
- Delegate authority to the servicer to approve a compromise sale or deed in lieu based on new guidelines; and
- Add a new section regarding repayment agreements which would reduce the amount obligors have to repay the VA if the property is transferred through a compromise sale or deed in lieu.

As of early 2007, these proposed rules had not yet been adopted as final.

OPTIONS FOR RHS DIRECT LOANS

The Section 502 Single-Family Housing Program provides direct loans to low-income individuals for the purchase, construction, or rehabilitation of single-family homes located in rural areas. The program is administered by an agency of the U.S. Department of Agriculture, the Rural Housing Service (RHS), formerly known as the Farmers Home Administration (FmHA). The RHS is one of three agencies comprising the Department of Agriculture's Rural Development Mission.

Certain workout options are available for homeowners facing foreclosure of an RHS Section 502 Single-Family Housing Direct Loan, whenever the homeowner is at least two months delinquent. There is no third party servicer, and instead these options should be arranged directly with RHS, through its Centralized Servicing Center in St. Louis, Missouri, at 800-793-8861, but with some assistance from local Rural Development field offices. There are four available options:

Interest Credit and Payment Assistance. Interest credit and payment assistance are two types of payment subsidies for section 502 direct loan homeowners. With interest credit, the agency subsidizes the interest portion of a homeowner's monthly payment in an effort to reduce the monthly payment to an affordable amount. With payment assistance, the homeowner is required to repay the subsidy when he or she sells the property, moves out of the property, or pays off the loan in full. Both interest credit and payment assistance are recalculated annually, and the homeowner must notify RHS of household, employment, and income changes. For both programs, RHS will send a notice of review ninety days before the expiration of the agreement. To be eligible for assistance the homeowner must demonstrate a decrease in income.

Payment Moratorium. A payment moratorium is available when a homeowner can show that due to circumstances beyond his or her control, the homeowner is unable to continue making payments of principal and interest when due without "unduly impairing his standard of living." With a moratorium, the homeowner's scheduled monthly payments may be deferred for up to two years. At the end of two years, or at an earlier date if it is determined that the homeowner no longer needs moratorium assistance, the loan will be reamortized. If the homeowner is unable to afford the new payments on the reamortized loan, all or part of the interest that accrued during the moratorium may be forgiven. The loan will be accelerated at the end of two years if the homeowner is unable to resume monthly payments and maintain the loan. Eligibility for the moratorium is reviewed every six months, and the homeowner should be provided with sixty days notice before the moratorium is terminated.

Delinquency Workout Agreement. A delinquency workout agreement (DWA) allows a homeowner to cure a delinquency, either by making a single lump payment or by paying the delinquent amount, in addition to the scheduled mortgage payment, through monthly installments not to exceed two years.

Protective Advances. RHS also has the ability to advance funds to cover the cost of taxes, insurance, and emergency repairs necessary to protect the government's interest in the property. The payments are then charged to the homeowner's account. Repayment terms are to be consistent with the homeowner's ability to repay or the loan can be reamortized to include the amount of the advance.

OPTIONS FOR RHS-GUARANTEED LOANS

Under Section 502, the RHS also guarantees loans made by private lenders to low- and moderate-income individuals living in rural areas. These loans may be made for up to 102% of the value of the property that secures the loan. RHS also has a loss-mitigation program designed to address serious defaults for these guaranteed loans—generally those loans 90 or more days past due. The agency's *Loss Mitigation Guide* outlines the workout options and policies that apply to guaranteed loans—these options are very similar to those offered by HUD under its Loss Mitigation Program. The *Guide* is contained as an attachment to an Administrative Notice, RD AN No. 4025 (1980-D) (November 30, 2004); a copy of this *Guide* is contained on the CD-Rom accompanying this handbook.

These guidelines require the lender to evaluate each delinquent loan that is 90 or more days past due to determine if a loss mitigation option is appropriate. The options fall into two broad categories: *options to cure* a default, and *disposition options* that result in the homeowner transferring the property.

Options to Cure

Special Forbearance. A special forbearance is a written agreement to cure the mortgage arrears. The agreement may include a plan to reduce or suspend payments for one or more months to allow the homeowner to recover from the cause of the default; or an agreement to allow the homeowner to resume making full monthly payments while delaying repayment of the arrears. The period of reduced or suspended payments is followed by a repayment plan. There is no time limit on the repayment plan, so long as during the term of the plan the accumulated arrears do not exceed the equivalent of twelve monthly mortgage payments.

Special forbearance may be offered to homeowners who have experienced a verifiable loss of income or increase in living expenses, but who will have sufficient income to repay the arrears during the term of the plan. The homeowner must occupy the property and be committed to occupying the property as a primary residence during the term of the special forbearance agreement. RHS allows for the repayment of foreclosure costs and late fees through the special forbearance repayment plan. A special forbearance may be used alone or combined with a loan modification.

Modification. A modification is a permanent change in one or more terms of the loan. A modification is appropriate for homeowners who have experienced a permanent or long-term reduction in income or an increase in expenses, or who have recovered from the cause of the default but do not have sufficient surplus income to repay the arrears through a repayment plan. Lenders may reamortize the arrearage over the remaining term of the loan, capitalize delinquent principal, interest and escrow advances, or reduce the interest rate (even to below market). Foreclosure costs, late fees and other administrative expenses may not be capitalized. The modification must result in a fixed rate, fully amortizing loan and the modified principal balance may exceed 100% of loan-to-value ratio. A loan that is not delinquent, but in danger of default, can be modified.

Disposition Options

Pre-Foreclosure Sale. A pre-foreclosure sale allows a homeowner to satisfy the mortgage debt with the proceeds of a market sale, even if the proceeds of the sale are less than the amount owed. The homeowner must submit an application for this option. RHS requires that:

- The home's "as is" appraised value must be at least 63% of the total amount due on the mortgage;
- The net sales price must be at least 82% of the home's "as is" appraised value;
- The loan need only be 30 days in arrears; and
- The homeowner has ninety days to sell but this may be extended an additional thirty days if a sale is likely.

A pre-foreclosure sale will be reported to the national credit bureaus as a "short sale" and the lender is required to file Form 1099-A with the IRS and report any discharge of indebtedness, as described in Chapter 9, below.

Deed in Lieu. A deed in lieu allows the homeowner to voluntarily transfer the property in exchange for a release from obligations under the mortgage. Other loss mitigation options should be considered, including marketing the property through a pre-foreclosure sale process. There should be no junior liens on the property. Unlike HUD, RHS does not pay the homeowner an incentive for leaving the property. The homeowner, however, will not be pursued for a deficiency judgment by either the lender or the RHS. If the RHS forgives any indebtedness, there may be tax consequences for the homeowner. The counselor should consult the *Tax Consequences of Foreclosure, Deed in Lieu, Short Sales and Loan Workouts* section of this handbook for more information.

CHAPTER 9

Tax and Credit Rating Implications of a Workout

TAX CONSEQUENCES OF FORECLOSURE, DEEDS IN LIEU, SHORT SALES, AND LOAN WORKOUTS

A homeowner's federal tax situation is highly individualized, the tax laws are constantly changing, and tax advice is best left to experts. This book's authors are not tax experts and this chapter only identifies situations where there are significant and less significant tax implications to a foreclosure or workout. Homeowners should be urged to consult a qualified tax professional where it seems appropriate and to file a 1040 (long form) tax return.

Foreclosures and workouts have two potential types of tax consequences: capital gains and discharge of indebtedness (DOI). Roughly speaking, capital gains reflect the increased value of the home over its purchase price; discharge of indebtedness reflects the amount of debt forgiven.

Capital Gains

Capital gains may occur when a home is sold for more than its original sales price. The amount of capital gains is usually measured by the difference between the sale price and the purchase price (called the "basis"), after certain adjustments are made to both the sale and purchase price. Certain selling expenses may be deducted from the sales price, such as a realtor's commission. The original purchase price or basis is increased to the extent of certain home improvements. The basis may also be decreased to the extent to which the homeowner in past tax years claimed depreciation on the house because all or part of the home was rented to others.

If the net sale price is less than the basis, as adjusted, this is a capital loss. Our discussion will focus on a potential capital gain, where the house instead is sold for more than its basis, since that is what may cause a tax liability. If there is a gain, this does not mean there is a tax on that gain. The homeowner may qualify for an exclusion of up to $250,000 ($500,000 for a husband and wife filing a joint return). If the homeowner has lived in the property for less than two years, the $250,000 (or $500,000) amount is prorated. The amount not excluded is subject to tax, but that tax rate may be lower than the tax on the homeowner's other income.

Here is an example:		Here is another example. A single home-owner sells her home of many years:	
Purchase price:	$100,000	Purchase price:	$ 20,000
Certain improvements	$ 30,000	Certain improvements	$ 30,000
New Basis	$130,000	New Basis	$ 50,000
Sale Price	$160,000	Sale Price	$600,000
Sales Expenses	$ 9,000	Sales Expenses	$ 40,000
Net Sale Price	$151,000	Net Sale Price	$560,000
Capital Gain	$ 21,000	Capital Gain	$510,000
Exclusion	$250,000	Exclusion	$250,000
Taxable Gain	$ 0	Taxable Gain	$260,000
Capital Gains Tax	$ 0	Capital Gains Tax	$ 39,000
		(assuming a 15% rate)	

Applicability to Foreclosures and Workouts. Foreclosures, deeds in lieu, or short sales are all treated under the tax code as a sale. Thus whenever any of these events occur, a capital gain is possible where the sale price is greater than the house's basis, even if the sale price is less than outstanding mortgage amount. The capital gains calculation is essentially the same whether the sale is voluntary or pursuant to a foreclosure.

Sometimes with a deed in lieu or certain foreclosures, there is not a sale price. Instead there is a debt forgiven in exchange for the deed to the house. The amount of debt forgiven may be treated as the sale price, as long as it is no more than the home's fair market value. If cash is paid to the homeowner in addition to the debt forgiven, that amount should be included in calculating the sale price. Here is such an example:

Tom and Jane bought their home in 1970 for $50,000. They have just lost their home in foreclosure. They have made no qualifying home repairs. Their mortgage debt, at the time of the foreclosure, is $325,000. The fair market value, according to the appraisal done by the bank in the foreclosure, is $400,000. The bank paid Tom and Jane $5,000 in "cash for keys" to move. The sales price is $330,000 (forgiven mortgage debt plus cash for keys). They owe no capital gains tax because:

Basis:	$ 50,000
Sale Price	$330,000
Capital Gain	$280,000
Exclusion	$500,000
Taxable Gain	$ 0
Capital Gains Tax	$ 0

Note that the amount of debt forgiven is an alternative measure for a sale price *only if* the home's fair market value is at least as much as the debt forgiven. For capital gains analysis, the home's fair market value is used instead of the amount of debt forgiven, if the debt forgiven is higher than the home's fair market value, as in the following example:

Nancy bought her home in 1999 for $125,000. She has lost the home in foreclosure. She owes $132,000 on the mortgage, including the mortgagor's costs and fees and the home's fair market value is $80,000. Since the fair market value ($80,000) is less than the debt forgiven ($132,000), the capital gain is computed as the difference between the fair market value and the original purchase price. In this example, Nancy has a capital *loss* of $45,000 (the fair market value of $80,000 minus the purchase price of $125,000). Nancy does not owe any capital gains tax. [However, Nancy should review the discussion, below, of Discharge of Indebtedness Income to determine if she has taxable debt forgiveness income.]

Discharge of Indebtedness Income

The IRS considers that a taxpayer has income from discharge of indebtedness when a lender forgives some or all of a debt. This is because there is income to the borrower at the time money is borrowed, but it is not taxed then since it is offset by a duty to repay the debt. If the obligation to repay the debt is forgiven, then the government looks to see if that borrowed money now constitutes income to the borrower and, if so, how much. That income is taxable like any other income the homeowner receives. Nevertheless, as described below, there are a number of exceptions that may mean that discharge of indebtedness may produce no taxable income at all.

Examples of Discharge of Indebtedness. Almost any resolution of a foreclosure may create discharge of indebtedness income. For example, if there is a foreclosure and the homeowner is not liable for the deficiency, that forgiveness of the deficiency is discharge of indebtedness income. Another example is a short sale where the house sells for less than the debt and where the lender has agreed to forego any deficiency. The difference is again the amount of discharge of indebtedness income. A third example would be a loan modification in which the lender forgave the principal of the debt or wrote the debt down. The amount of forgiven debt would also be discharge of indebtedness income.

Relation of Capital Gains to Discharge of Indebtedness. These are two different concepts, and each must be analyzed separately. It is even possible that a foreclosure or short sale may result in both capital gains and discharge of indebtedness income. Consider this example:

A home is bought many years ago for $50,000, with no improvements since. The homeowner refinances the original mortgage loan into a new $210,000 mortgage loan. The lender later agrees to a short sale of $150,000, forgiving the remaining $60,000 of indebtedness. The capital gain from the $150,000 sale is $100,000 ($150,000 – $50,000) and the discharge of indebtedness income is $60,000 (the amount of debt forgiven). Since the capital gain is less than $250,000, the ex-homeowner typically will owe no capital gains tax.

IRS Form 1099C. The lender is required to report the discharge of indebtedness income to the IRS on Form 1099C. The borrower will also get a copy of this form. Lenders should not and need not report forgiven past-due interest and fees as discharge of indebtedness income, although some lenders do. If a lender does report amounts other than the principal as discharge of indebtedness income, the borrower should attach a statement to the tax return explaining the difference between the Form 1099C and the correct calculation of the amount, that is only the forgiven principal. Lenders are also likely to report the entire amount of the debt as forgiven; the borrower's tax preparer must do the correct calculation.

When Is Discharge of Indebtedness Income Not Taxable?

The income reported on a 1099C form may or may not actually be taxable. Many people and even some tax accountants assume that tax must always be paid on income which is reported on a 1099C form. That is incorrect. In many cases, taxpayers may exclude the discharge of indebtedness income from their taxable income.

Discharge of indebtedness income is not taxable in at least four situations, many of which commonly apply to borrowers facing foreclosure. The IRS will assume, however, that tax is due based on the 1099C form unless the homeowner establishes the entitlement to one of the exclusions. To do so, the homeowner must file Form 982 with Form 1040 and attach a detailed explanation of why the income is excluded. Borrowers must file a return, since the IRS often audits borrowers for whom the IRS received a 1099C without an accompanying return from the borrower. Discharge of indebtedness income is not taxable in at least the following four situations:

Forgiven Interest and Fees. Forgiven interest and fees are not even income, and thus are not taxable. When a workout plan reduces the interest rate or waives back-due interest and fees, this is not discharge of indebtedness income.

The Bankruptcy Exclusion. If the obligation to pay the debt has been discharged in the bankruptcy process, the discharge of indebtedness income is not taxable. The debt is not forgiven by the lender, but instead the obligation to pay it is discharged by the bankruptcy.

The timing of the bankruptcy filing is crucial. If the debt forgiveness agreement is reached *before* the filing of the bankruptcy, the taxable event has occurred and the tax is due. The tax obligation is unlikely to be discharged in a later bankruptcy. If the debt is forgiven *after* the bankruptcy is filed, then the bankruptcy exclusion applies.

If debt that the lender considers forgiven has been discharged in bankruptcy, the lender may file a 1099C in error. The homeowner should not ignore the 1099C, but rather should include a statement with the tax return that the debt had been discharged in bankruptcy with proof of the bankruptcy discharge.

The Insolvency Exclusion. The insolvency exclusion applies where the homeowner's liabilities exceeded assets at the time of the debt forgiveness. Lower income homeowners and those with high debt-loads are likely to be insolvent at the time indebtedness is forgiven, and thus may avoid all tax liability for this forgiveness.

The amount of the debt forgiveness income that is excluded depends on the amount of the insolvency. The amount by which the consumer's debts (including the amount to be forgiven) exceeds the consumer's assets equals the amount of the debt forgiveness income that is excluded.

> Consider, for example, a homeowner with assets valued at $120,000, including the house, and liabilities of $140,000, including the mortgage. This taxpayer is insolvent by $20,000. If $15,000 of the mortgage debt is forgiven, the debtor has $15,000 worth of income. The entire amount of this income would be excludable, however, because the amount of the income is less than the amount of the insolvency.

$120,000	total assets
– $140,000	total liabilities
– $ 20,000	extent of insolvency

If, on the other hand, $25,000 of the debt is forgiven, not all $25,000 of this income would be excludable. The debtor would have to include $5,000 of the income (the amount by which the discharge of debt exceeds the amount of the debtor's insolvency) as part of her overall gross income. The remaining $20,000 of the forgiven debt need not be included because that is the amount by which the debtor was initially insolvent.

As with the bankruptcy exclusion, a homeowner must explain when the income reported on a 1099C form is subject to the insolvency exclusion. Assets and liabilities establishing insolvency must be detailed on a separate statement filed with the homeowner's tax return, attached to Form 982.

Purchase Fraud/Disputed Debt Exclusion. In cases where the money was loaned to purchase property, and the sales price was inflated in the sale of the property, the amount of the debt forgiven in order to bring the loan into line with the value of the collateral is excludable from the borrower's income, provided that the borrower was not a party to the fraud and the forgiveness of the debt is clearly traceable to the fraud in the sale.[1] The borrower must file a statement explaining the facts and circumstances with her tax return. Similarly, if the amount of the debt is disputed, and a bona fide settlement results in a lower amount of debt, the amount forgiven is not income because the parties have agreed that the consumer never owed it.

What to Do When Taxes Are Paid in Error or the IRS Challenges the Amount Paid

For two years after the date the tax was paid in error, it is possible to file an amended return and seek a refund of the amount incorrectly paid. It is also possible, in response to an IRS notice of tax due, to explain the circumstances of the debt and why it should be excluded from income.

CREDIT RATING CONSEQUENCES OF LOAN WORKOUTS AND FORECLOSURE

There are no easy answers for homeowners who are worried about how workout agreements or foreclosure will affect their credit record. Moreover, there are no hard and fast rules about how any individual credit granting decision will be made based on a particular notation on a credit report. Each creditor evaluates credit reports differently. A notation that is fatal to an application for credit with one creditor may not preclude credit on reasonable terms from a different creditor. More information on this subject can be found in the *NCLC Guide to Surviving Debt*.

Here is some general information that may be useful to tell homeowners who are worried about their credit rating:

Concerns about future credit rating should rarely influence how homeowners address their current problem. A consumer cannot control how the credit report is evaluated by those who check credit reports. Any delinquency will usually mean "bad credit risk" to most creditors even if it is paid in full relatively quickly. On the other hand, with a foreclosure looming, the consumer will have many important concerns regarding putting a workout plan into operation, not the least of which is loss of the home. Credit reporting concerns should generally take a back seat to these other issues.

A foreclosure avoidance plan of any type is likely to look better on the credit report than a completed foreclosure. Any effort that prevents a foreclosure from being completed will show a creditor that the homeowner has made an effort. Repayment plans and loan modifications, if they cure the arrears, will show that the homeowners have gotten back on their feet.

A completed foreclosure is usually fatal to applications for new mortgages from reputable lenders for about two years. Bankruptcy is also usually fatal for at least two years. The completed foreclosure will be an important consideration for most lenders, even after two years has expired, until the notation is deleted from the credit record after seven years.

A deed in lieu of foreclosure is not a big improvement over foreclosure. One myth about credit reporting is that a deed in lieu of foreclosure is going to keep a borrower in good standing on their credit record. A deed in lieu of foreclosure is a strong black mark on a credit record; it is viewed only slightly less negatively than a foreclosure. A deed in lieu should be considered when appropriate, but it should not be seen as a "silver bullet" for future credit.

Unsecured credit, such as a credit card, is often available even to people with a recent foreclosure on their credit records. There is a great deal of competition in the credit card business. Companies even compete for borrowers with bad credit records. It is a good idea to shop around for reasonable terms, rather than simply accepting the first offer. Lower interest rates and fees may be available.

Adverse credit history cannot be reported after seven years, although bankruptcies can be reported for ten years.

Avoid credit repair scams. For-profit credit repair is almost always a scam. No one can clean a credit record entirely if there have been delinquencies on debts within the past seven years. Some credit repair companies recommend credit "fixes," which are illegal. Others charge a great deal of money to write letters to credit reporting agencies that a consumer can write just as easily for free.

Even when in a high risk credit pool, it is essential to shop around when applying for credit. Many finance companies and other "hard money" lenders prey on people's beliefs that they have no other potential source of credit. When offered credit only at high rates, a consumer should shop around. Use the APR (annual percentage rate) to compare one credit offer to another. Remember that home mortgages (other than the type one uses to buy the home) can be canceled within 3 business days from the date the homeowner signed the papers.

Chapter Notes

1. *See* IRS Rev. Rul. 92-99.

PART
III

Fighting the Foreclosure

CHAPTER 10

Legal Protections Against Foreclosure

CAN JOINTLY TITLED REAL PROPERTY BE FORECLOSED?

Many states have laws or rules that protect co-owners of property from seizure of the property for the debts owed by another co-owner. These general rules are described below, though they do not apply in all states.

Tenancy by the Entireties. Tenancy by the entireties is a form of joint ownership of property. It is only available to married couples and only when the property was acquired during the marriage. It is based on the legal fiction that the husband and wife are a single unit. In some states, it is presumed that married couples who own property jointly own it by the entireties. Other states require express mention of tenancy by the entireties in the deed (e.g., "Lucille Ball and Desi Arnez, as tenants by the entireties"). Upon divorce, this form of ownership reverts to "tenants in common" status. The interest of a deceased spouse automatically transfers to the surviving spouse, and the deceased's interest cannot be promised to anyone else—even if explicitly provided in the deceased's will.

Property that is owned by the entireties may not be partitioned, sold, or encumbered without the permission of both spouses. Likewise, judgment creditors of one party cannot enforce liens against the property while the tenancy by the entireties exists. In most states, only joint creditors of both the husband and the wife can attach and force a sale.

Joint Tenancy. Joint tenancy is another form of joint ownership of property. A joint tenancy exists when two or more co-owners, regardless of marital status, take identical interests by the same deed or other instrument. In contrast to tenancy by the entireties, if one of the owners in a joint tenancy owes a debt and the creditor wins a judgment against that owner, the creditor can foreclose on the property and reach that owner's share. A joint tenant has a right of automatic inheritance, known as "survivorship." In other words, when one owner dies, the deceased's interest automatically passes to the surviving owners. The deceased's interest cannot be promised to anyone else—even if explicitly provided in the deceased's will: Generally, to create a joint tenancy, all the prospective owners must take title at the same time, by the same document, and have an equal interest in the property including an undivided right to possession.

Tenancy in Common. Tenancy in common is the most common form of concurrent ownership. It is similar to joint tenancy except that there is no right of survivorship (automatic inheritance). Tenants in common each own a separate fractional share in undivided property. Each share of the property may be sold, mortgaged, or attached. Property held by tenants in common can be partitioned or encumbered by creditors. Individual and joint creditors can attach and force a sale. In most states, this is the presumed tenancy if no other form of tenancy is expressly provided for in the instrument.

Community Property States. In nine states, the property acquired during a marriage by either or both spouses is considered "community property" of both spouses, regardless of how the property is titled. These states are Arizona, California, Idaho, Louisiana, Nevada, New Mexico, Texas, Washington, and (to some extent) Wisconsin. In these states, the creditor of one spouse can attach the community property even if it is titled to the other spouse.

Tips for Counselors. Whenever co-owners of the home are married to each other, evaluate whether just one of them owes the debt on which foreclosure is threatened. If only one owes the debt, and the other spouse did not agree to the mortgage or lien, recommend that they consult a real estate attorney to determine whether the home is protected by the doctrine of tenancy by the entireties. Getting legal advice is particularly important if the debt is a court judgment arising out of a non-mortgage obligation, such as an automobile accident, a hospital bill, or a credit card bill, because there may be special legal steps that can help these homeowners.

SPECIAL PROTECTIONS FOR THE MILITARY: THE SERVICEMEMBERS CIVIL RELIEF ACT

The Servicemembers Civil Relief Act (SCRA)[1] provides special protections for military service personnel on *active duty* and their dependents, for debts incurred *before* the military service personnel went on active duty. Among the most significant protections are:

- Limitations on the foreclosure of real property owned by members on active duty;
- Restrictions on default judgments;
- Reduction of the interest rate on pre-active duty obligations to six percent;
- Limitations on eviction from residential property; and
- The right to terminate residential or vehicle leases.

The military is responsible for providing information to military personnel on the benefits available under the law. A number of states have similar laws, which are listed on pages 154–157 later in this chapter.

Who Is Protected by the Law?

The SCRA applies to members of the uniformed services on active duty. Persons entitled to the law's protections include:

- The armed forces (Army, Navy, Air Force, Marine Corps, and Coast Guard);
- The commissioned corps of both the National Oceanic and Atmospheric Administration and the Public Health Service;

- Members of the National Guard who are called to active service authorized by the President or Secretary of Defense for more than thirty consecutive days for the purpose of responding to a national emergency;
- Reservists ordered to report for military service, persons ordered to report for induction under the Military Selective Service Act; and
- United States citizens serving with allied forces.

Active Duty. Active duty includes full-time training, annual training duty, and attendance at a military school while in active military service. Active duty also includes periods of time that a member is absent from duty on account of sickness, wounds, leave, or other lawful cause, but not periods of time the member is AWOL or confined to military prison.

The dependents and co-obligors of servicemembers are entitled to many of the protections of the SCRA. However, in some cases the dependent or co-obligor must obtain a court order to get protections that are automatic for servicemembers.

Protections Against Foreclosure

The SCRA provides important protections for members of the military facing foreclosure while on active duty. The protections apply if the servicemember is obligated on mortgage, trust deed, or similar obligation (e.g., a land installment contract) that was originated before the servicemember began active duty servicemember.

The SCRA requires a court order prior to a foreclosure, sale, or seizure of property while the servicemember is on active duty or within ninety days after the end of active duty. This is especially helpful in non-judicial foreclosure states, where lenders are permitted to foreclose on mortgages without court action, as the foreclosure process tends to proceed swiftly. (Appendix E, below, summarizes state foreclosure laws and indicates whether the state allows non-judicial foreclosure.) If the lender forecloses without a court order, the sale is invalid and the lender may be subject to criminal prosecution. Even a threat to foreclose without a court order in violation of the SCRA is likely a violation of federal or state debt collection law.

Servicemembers may waive the prohibition against non-judicial foreclosure, but the waiver must be in writing and executed during or after the member's period of active duty. Assuming a foreclosure sale was properly performed, any state redemption period does not run while the servicemember is on active duty.

A court order is also required for tax sales of certain real property. The court must determine whether military service materially affected the servicemember's ability to pay the unpaid tax or assessment. The court may postpone a sale of the property or any proceeding to collect the unpaid tax during the period of active duty and for 180 days after active duty. If the property has already been sold, the law extends any state right to redeem the property until 180 days after the end of active duty. (If state law provides a longer redemption period, that period applies.)

In any court proceeding, whether for a foreclosure, a tax sale, or any other non-criminal matter, a servicemember who is on active duty has the right to ask the court to stay (postpone) the case. The servicemember can get an initial 90-day stay simply by requesting it in writing. The letter must explain why military duty requirements prevent the servicemember from appearing, and must say when he or she can appear. It must also include a letter or other communication from the servicemember's commanding officer, stating that military duty prevents the servicemember from appearing and that leave is not authorized. The servicemember can ask for a longer stay if necessary. If the court denies the stay, it must appoint a lawyer to represent the servicemember.

Other protections available under the law include the right to reopen a default foreclosure judgment issued during active duty or within sixty days after the end of active duty. The servicemember must seek to overturn the judgment no later than ninety days after release from active duty.

Interest Rate Reduction

The SCRA requires that creditors reduce the interest rate to 6% on any obligation entered into by a servicemember *before* active duty. The interest rate reduction lasts as long as the servicemember is on active duty. The interest rate reduction applies to all types of debt, including mortgages, car loans, credit cards, and business debts. The rate reduction even applies to the interest paid on obligations under a confirmed chapter 13 bankruptcy plan.

The interest rate reduction only applies to debts incurred *before* the servicemember entered active duty. It also does not apply to student loan debts, whether incurred before, during, or after active duty. A student loan debtor can, however, apply for a deferment due to military service, as described above in Chapter 4.

The interest over 6% must be forgiven, not just deferred. The amount of the monthly payment must be reduced to reflect the forgiven interest. Creditors cannot require that the servicemember continue to make the original regular monthly payment, even if they apply the extra portion of the payment to reduce the principal. When the servicemember and his or her spouse are jointly liable on an obligation, the law requires the interest rate to be reduced for both of them. The same is required if there are other co-obligors.

To take advantage of the interest rate reduction, the servicemember must give written notice to the creditor and a copy of the military orders calling him or her to active duty and any orders further extending active duty. This notice must be given no later than 180 days after the servicemember leaves active duty. The interest rate reduction is retroactive to the date the servicemember was called to active duty.

The law prohibits creditors from cutting off or changing the terms of credit because a servicemember exercises this or other rights under the SCRA. Denying credit or taking adverse actions such as acceleration, repossession, or a negative credit report is prohibited.

A separate law, passed in 2006, will cap interest rates at 36% for debts incurred while the servicemember is on active duty. This new law will be effective on October 1, 2007. It will not apply to residential mortgages or to debts that are secured by the items purchased.

Vehicle, Other Repossessions; Automobile Leases

The SCRA prohibits creditors from repossessing property such as cars or furniture without a court order if the servicemember paid a deposit or made an installment payment on the contract before entering active duty.

The SCRA gives the servicemember the option of terminating a vehicle lease upon entering active duty in certain circumstances. This right applies to any vehicle used or leased for use by the servicemember or a spouse or dependent.

The servicemember has the right to cancel the lease, if, after signing it, he or she enters active duty under a call or order for 180 days or more. Servicemembers may also terminate vehicle leases entered into *during* active duty upon receiving military orders for a permanent change of station outside the continental United States (or from Alaska, Hawaii, or a U.S. commonwealth, territory, or possession to a location in the continental U.S.) or to deploy with a military unit for 180 days or more.

To terminate a vehicle lease, the servicemember must give the lessor written notice with a copy of the military orders, and then return the vehicle within fifteen days. Termination of the lease is effective once these two steps are accomplished. The lessor is prohibited from imposing an early termination charge, but may charge for taxes, summonses, title and registration fees, and excess wear, use, or mileage. The lessor must refund any lease payments that the servicemember paid in advance.

As an alternative, if the servicemember does not want to return the car, the servicemember can ask a court to postpone the monthly payment under the lease during the period of active duty. Then, upon leaving the service, the servicemember will have a period equal to the period of active duty to make up the deferred payments, with no interest or penalties.

Tips for Counselors

The counselor should always inquire whether the homeowner is or was on active duty in the military or is a spouse or dependent of someone who is or was on active duty during any relevant time. If the homeowner is on active duty, the counselor should educate the homeowner about this law and suggest:

- That the person has requested interest rate reductions from *all* creditors—not just the mortgage creditor but any credit cards, car loans, business debts, and any other debts.
- That the mortgage holder and any creditor who might repossess the person's car or personal property know that the person is on active duty.
- If a foreclosure or tax sale is threatened, suggest that the homeowner notify all parties that he or she is on active duty.
- If a creditor files a foreclosure case or seeks a court order for a tax sale, suggest that the servicemember informs the court that he or she is on active duty. *See* the discussion above about the right of the servicemember to request a stay.
- Consider recommending that the person cancel the lease for any vehicle that is no longer needed for personal or family use (see above about when lease cancellation is allowed).

If the homeowner has recently been released from active duty, the counselor should:

- Suggest that the homeowner request interest rate reductions—this is allowed up to 180 days *after* the person has been released from active duty.
- If a foreclosure or tax sale has already occurred, evaluate whether the person can redeem (buy back) the property. A person recently released from active duty has a longer right to redeem the property than usual.

If the homeowner is a spouse or dependent of someone who is or was on active duty, the counselor should make sure the person in the military exercises all the rights listed above. A court can also prohibit a creditor from foreclosing or repossessing property from the spouse or dependent without a court order.

A Judge Advocate General (JAG) Corps attorney at a local military base may be able to help military members and their families with these rights.

States with Laws Protecting Military Servicemembers

Many states have laws similar to the SCRA. Some of these state laws provide protections beyond those provided by the federal law. Others have similar protections, but apply them to more people (e.g., National Guard members called into active duty by a governor). Many of these laws have been amended recently, and new states are adopting them, so the following list may not be complete. Key provisions of these laws that may relate to foreclosure are summarized below.

Alabama: Ala. Code §§ 31-12-1 to 31-12-10 preserves many servicemember rights and benefits during military service. It applies to National Guard and reserves called up to serve in armed conflict or state of emergency for 30 days or more.

Alaska: Alaska Stat. § 26.05.135 extends the protections of the federal act to National Guard and naval militia on active duty.

Arizona: Ariz. Rev. Stat. Ann. §§ 6-1260(L) restricts payday lending to servicemembers and spouses. It applies primarily to collection methods. Ariz. Rev. Stat. Ann. § 23-1390 tolls the six-month limitation period for filing unfair labor practice complaint for agricultural workers if service in the armed forces prevented the worker from filing the charge. Ariz. Rev. Stat. Ann. § 33-1413(F) excuses a mobile home park tenant who is member of armed forces from the requirement to give two weeks' notice before terminating a rental agreement requirement if he or she receives reassignment orders that do not allow such prior notification.

Arkansas: Ark. Code Ann. §§ 12-62-701 to 12-62-718 provides extensive protections, including: prohibition against termination of installment contracts for the purchase of real or personal property for any breach that occurs during military service; prohibition against self-help repossession; extension of the statute of limitations; reduction of the interest rate on pre-active duty obligations to 6%; restriction on eviction; and prohibition of non-judicial foreclosure. It applies to National Guard members called into active military service by the governor for more than 180 continuous days.

California: Cal. Mil. & Vet. Code §§ 400 to 409.13 (West) provides extensive protections, including stay of court actions; restrictions on eviction, foreclosure, and repossession; reduction of the interest rate on pre-active duty obligations to 6%; prohibition against non-judicial foreclosure; extension of redemption periods after foreclosure or tax sale; and tax deferral. These protections apply to National Guard members ordered into active state service by the governor or into active federal service by the President, and also to reservists called into federal active duty.

Connecticut: Conn. Gen. Stat. Ann. § 36a-737 provides the procedure to be used when a servicemember is called up while mortgage application is in progress.

Florida: Fla. Stat. §§ 250.5201 to 250.5205 prohibits termination of installment contracts for the purchase of real or personal property for any breach that occurs during military service; allows a court to order a stay of proceedings; restricts eviction; prohibits non-judicial foreclosure. These protections apply to persons called into state active duty by the governor for more than 17 days.

Georgia: Ga. Code Ann. § 46-5-8 provides the procedure for servicemembers to terminate their wireless telecommunication service contracts prior to the contract's expiration, i.e., when transferred, released from service, etc.

Hawaii: Haw. Rev. Stat. §§ 657D-1 to 657D-63 is a comprehensive law similar to the SCRA, including a prohibition against non-judicial foreclosure and a reduction of pre-active duty interest rates to 6%. It applies to persons called to state active duty.

Illinois: 330 Ill. Comp. Stat. § 60/5.1 allows a court to order a stay of proceedings if state or federal military service directly results in failure to meet pre-service obligations.

Iowa: Iowa Code § 29A.102 is similar to the SCRA. Among other things, it bars a creditor from self-help repossession for breach, before or during military service, of an installment contract to buy real or personal property entered into before entry into service; reduces interest rates to 6%; and prohibits non-judicial foreclosure. It applies to those in full-time state military service or state active duty.

Louisiana: La. Rev. Stat. Ann. § 9:3261 provides that servicemembers may terminate residential leases (in case of transfer, etc.). La. Rev. Stat. Ann. §§ 9:311 to 319 provides protections for servicemembers, covering , among other things, utilities, residential leases, motor vehicle leases, interest rates, and cell phone contracts. Note that a former statute on this subject (§§ 29:330 to 29:335) has been repealed. La. Rev. Stat. §§ 29:401 to 29:426 provides extensive provisions regarding servicemember health insurance, re-employment, occupational licenses, etc.

Maine: Me. Rev. Stat. Ann. tit. 37-B, § 387 provides servicemember protections against evictions; § 389-A provides servicemembers with the opportunity for stays of court proceedings, electronic testimony and evidence, expedited hearings, etc.; § 390 defers motor vehicle insurance coverage; § 390-A provides extensions of professional licenses.

Maryland: Md. Code Ann., Pub. Safety § 13-705 (West) applies the protections of the federal act to members of the National Guard or Maryland Defense when ordered into military duty under state law for 14 consecutive days or more. In addition, §§ 14-201 to 14-218 apply many SCRA-type protections to emergency management personnel during emergency periods and to people who suffer serious personal injury, family injury, or property damage during a declared emergency. These protections include stays of proceedings, and provisions concerning installment contracts, mortgages, evictions, and taxes.

Michigan: Mich. Comp. Laws § 32.517 applies to those in active state service. It exempts the servicemember's property from execution, seizure, or attachment for debts incurred prior to or during state service, provides for stays of proceedings, and restricts termination of heat, water, electricity, or gas for unpaid bills for the servicemember or his or her household during the first 90 days of service.

Minnesota: Minn. Stat. § 72A.20(8)(b) and (c) UNIP (Unfair Insurance Practices) statute provides protections regarding denial of life insurance and health insurance (or reinstatement after period of service) to servicemembers and their families (including National Guard).

Mississippi: Miss. Code Ann. § 75-24-5(2)(m) provides protections regarding reinstatement of motor vehicle insurance for returning servicemembers.

Missouri: Mo. Ann. Stat. § 41.944 (West) allows active duty service members to terminate residential leases, when transferred, released, etc.; § 430.140 protects servicemembers from chattel liens for small repair bills.

New Hampshire: N.H. Rev. Stat. Ann. § 540:11-a (West) provides protections regarding the termination of residential lease when the servicemember is transferred, called up, etc.

New Jersey: N.J. Stat. Ann. §§ 38:23C-1 to 38:23C-26 (West) is a comprehensive law similar to the SCRA. Among other things, it prohibits non-judicial foreclosure and provides that the period of military service is not included in any redemption period. It applies to those on federal active duty or in state military service pursuant to an order of the governor.

New York: N.Y. Mil. Law § 308 (McKinney) is a comprehensive law similar to the SCRA. It applies to those on federal active duty or those in the military service of the state pursuant to an order of the governor. Among other things, it prohibits non-judicial foreclosure and provides that the period of military service is not included in any redemption period.

Ohio: Ohio Rev. Code Ann. §§ 5919.29, 5923.12 (West) extends the protections of the SCRA to those ordered by the governor into National Guard active duty or training; § 317.322 exempts servicemembers from paying for a recording fee for a power of attorney; § 125.021 provides that the office of information technology may purchase bulk phone service for the use of active duty servicemembers and families; § 1343.031 addresses interest rates; § 1349.02 addresses motor vehicle leases; § 1349.03 addresses cell phone contracts; § 1923.062 addresses residential evictions, including mobile home; § 4933.12(F) addresses gas utility shutoffs; § 4933.121 addresses electricity utility shutoffs; § 323.122 extends amount of time to pay property tax; § 3770.07 provides that certain active duty personnel may make delayed claim for lottery prizes; § 3915.053 addresses insurance policies, providing that there is no lapse for non-payment during active duty; § 5747.026 extends period of time for filing income tax return or paying tax, for guard members and reservists called to active duty.

Oklahoma: Okla. Stat. Ann. tit. 44, § 208.1 (West) provides civil relief for National Guard members; adopts SCRA and Uniformed Services Employment and Reemployment Rights Act as state law and makes them applicable to guard.

Pennsylvania: 51 Pa. Cons. Stat. § 4105 makes National Guard members on active state service exempt from civil process, and suspends all presumptions arising from the lapse of time. 51 Pa. Cons. Stat. §§ 7301 to 7319 allows courts to stay proceedings; extends the redemption period after a tax sale; provides for the maximum interest rates and rescheduling of debt payments to account for reduced income during service period for National Guard on active federal or state duty of 30 or more consecutive days; restricts eviction; and includes other protections.

Tennessee: Tenn. Code Ann. § 26-1-111 addresses foreclosure of home mortgage or motor vehicle retail installment sales contract.

Texas: Tex. Civ. Prac. & Rem. Code § 16.022 (Vernon) tolls statute of limitations for actions to recover or defend title to real property for servicemembers on active duty in time of war. Tex. Fin. Code § 342.602 (Vernon) addresses payday loans. Tex. Govt. Code § 466.408 (Vernon) addresses claiming lottery prize. Tex. Labor Code § 101.116 (Vernon) addresses union dues. Tex. Prop. Code § 92.017 (Vernon) addresses residential leases and a tenant's right to terminate. Tex. Tax Code § 31.02(b) (Vernon) addresses extension of time to pay property taxes.

Utah: Utah Code Ann. §§ 39-7-101 to 39-7-119 applies to National Guard members called into active full-time service by the governor for at least 30 days. The provisions of this law include suspension of the statute of limitations; restrictions on termination of contracts and self-help repossession; and prohibition of non-judicial foreclosure.

Vermont: Vt. Stat. Ann. tit. 12, § 553 suspends the statute of limitations but does not provide other protections.

Virginia: Va. Code Ann. § 8.01-15.2 addresses default judgments and non-military affidavits; § 38.2-508.1 addresses life insurance; § 38.2-2205.1 addresses car insurance; § 55-248.21:1 addresses early termination of residential leases.

Washington: Wash. Rev. Code § 4.16.220 suspends the statute of limitations but does not provide other protections.

West Virginia: W. Va. Code § 11-21-61 extends time for filing and paying personal income taxes; § 21-1A-6 extends time for filing unfair labor practice complaints.

Wisconsin: Wis. Stat. Ann. § 21.75 (West) is a comprehensive law similar to the SCRA. It applies to member of the National Guard or a state defense force who are called into active state service by order of the governor, and also to some persons in federal service. Among other things, it limits interest rates; provides for stays of proceedings; and restricts foreclosure, actions to resume possession of personal property, and enforcement of storage liens.

Wyoming: Wyo. Stat. Ann. §§ 19-11-101 to 19-11-124 addresses employment and re-employment, benefits, insurance, professional licenses, etc. SCRA and Uniformed Services Employment and Reemployment Rights Act are made applicable to certain National Guard members.

SPECIAL PROTECTIONS AGAINST FORECLOSURE AVAILABLE IN CERTAIN STATES

Homeowners in a few states have special protections from foreclosure. These protections may involve a state program to provide temporary payments to help pay mortgages or may involve state laws that prohibit foreclosures in certain situations. These protections are relatively rare, but states are more likely to reinstitute such programs during economic recessions or after natural disasters.

State Mortgage Assistance Programs. Pennsylvania presently has a special mortgage assistance program that provides loans to homeowners who are threatened with foreclosure to help them get caught up on overdue payments and make some future payments. Other states such as Connecticut, Maryland, and New Jersey have had similar programs. You should make sure that homeowners apply for any assistance that is available through such programs.

Private Programs. There are also a variety of private programs for financial assistance with mortgage payments in different parts of the country.

State Bans on Foreclosure. During the economic depression of the 1930s, many states enacted moratorium laws postponing foreclosure sales of homes and farms. Where still in effect, these laws sometimes prevent foreclosures by requiring lenders to accept smaller payments during moratorium periods. For example, the Iowa foreclosure law provides general relief in cases of natural disasters and when the governor declares an economic emergency.

Occasionally, a state will declare a temporary local emergency and allow foreclosure relief in areas where plant closings have created widespread distress and depressed housing markets. This gives dislocated workers time to put their affairs in order. Most recently, Mississippi imposed a moratorium on foreclosure after Hurricane Katrina left many homes destroyed.

Disaster Assistance. A homeowner who defaults on the mortgage because of a natural disaster may be able to obtain state or federal disaster relief. The homeowner should contact local government or a local Federal Emergency Management Assistance (FEMA) office to find out what assistance is available.

MORTGAGES NOT USED TO PURCHASE THE HOME

Truth in Lending Act. The federal Truth in Lending Act requires lenders to disclose the most important terms of the credit transaction to consumers in clear, uniform language. It also gives consumers a three-day right to cancel certain mortgage loans—such as second mortgages, refinanced mortgages, debt consolidation loans involving mortgages, and home equity lines of credit—that are not used to purchase or build the home. If the lender fails to give the consumer the correct disclosures, or fails to inform the consumer properly of the right to cancel, the right to cancel can be extended for up to three years.

You should consider referring a homeowner to an attorney to evaluate a possible Truth in Lending cancellation claim if:

- The matter involves a non-purchase money mortgage loan;
- Less than three years have passed since loan closing; and
- There are irregularities in the transaction that raise red flags, e.g., the disclosed terms seem to be different from those imposed by the lender, the homeowner's copies of disclosure forms have blanks, the homeowner was given few or no papers, or given papers only some time after closing, or the homeowner was given contradictory documents about the loan terms or the right to cancel.

The Truth in Lending Act is complicated and technical. It will be difficult for a homeowner to assert a Truth in Lending claim without an attorney. You may be able to refer a low-income homeowner to a local legal services office. Legal services offices exist in all major cities and serve all rural regions of the country. For homeowners who are not eligible for representation by a legal services office, a good resource for a homeowner to locate a private consumer attorney is the website of the National Association of Consumer Advocates, www.naca.net. The "Find a Lawyer" feature allows users to search the organization's list of members by state or zip code and by type of case the attorney is willing to handle. In addition, most state bar associations and many local bar associations operate lawyer referral services.

High-Cost Mortgage Loans. The Home Ownership and Equity Protection Act (HOEPA) is an amendment to the Truth in Lending Act that was passed in 1994. It carves out a group of high-cost non-purchase money mortgage loans and subjects them to special restrictions and requirements. If the homeowner has a non-purchase money mortgage loan, and the interest rate, finance charge, or fees seem out of line, you should consider referring the homeowner to an attorney. If the lender violated certain of HOEPA's requirements, the homeowner has the right to cancel the loan up to three years after closing. As with Truth in Lending matters, you should try to find an attorney who has handled HOEPA matters before or is willing to spend a fair amount of time learning this complex and technical law.

Mortgages Resulting from Home Improvement Scams. A widespread and vicious scam is to pressure homeowners into home improvement contracts with unfavorable financing and a mortgage on the home. If the home improvement contractor never completes the work or the work is shoddy or wildly overpriced, the homeowner will then have legal claims against the home improvement contractor. A different company, often a finance company or a mortgage company, will nevertheless try to collect on the loan and foreclose when the homeowner refuses to pay or falls behind.

In almost all such situations, the homeowner can fight the foreclosure based on the misconduct of the home improvement contractor. That is, even though the contractor and lender are not the same company, there is enough of a connection between the two of them so that homeowner can raise the contractor's misconduct as a defense to repayment of the loan. A homeowner in this situation should be referred to an attorney.

MORTGAGES BASED ON UNFAIR AND OPPRESSIVE LOANS

Some lenders engage in outrageous loan conduct, and victimized borrowers should defend the foreclosure based on the lender's misconduct. Especially suspect are high-interest loans from home improvement contractors, finance companies, and mortgage companies.

There are many types of lender practices that may provide the homeowner with a defense to a foreclosure. The case study in Chapter 3, above, illustrates some of these practices. Other examples are:

- The lender misrepresented the nature of the document you signed, for example, saying, "this is just an application;"
- The lender made false statements about the basic loan terms, orally or in writing;
- The lender took advantage of the homeowner, for example by refinancing a low-rate loan or debt into a high-rate loan or making a loan that it was obvious the homeowner could not repay;
- The loan provided is different from what the lender promised;
- The lender has refinanced the loan repeatedly ("flipping");
- The interest rate exceeds the state maximum;
- The lender is not licensed to do business in your state;
- Illegal terms are included in the loan documents;
- The lender coerced the homeowner into signing the loan;
- The person who signed the mortgage was not the real owner of the mortgaged property (usually this involves forgery);
- The person who signed for the loan was not legally competent to do so (for example, children below a certain age or people who are mentally infirm).

If you spot any of these red flags, you should offer to refer the homeowner to a lawyer referral service or a legal services office. Likewise, if you suspect property flipping or a foreclosure rescue scam, discussed above in Chapter 3, you should also refer the homeowner to an attorney.

Chapter Note

1. 50 U.S.C. app. §§ 501–596.

CHAPTER 11

Answering Questions About Bankruptcy

Most of the homeowners you interview will have questions about bankruptcy. They are likely to have heard that bankruptcy is one way for them to deal with their financial problems.

You should not be in the business of giving legal advice about bankruptcy law. However, you may want to make sure that homeowners have accurate information so that they can make an informed choice. More information for non-lawyers about bankruptcy is contained in the book *NCLC Guide to Surviving Debt*.

Some homeowners may believe that the 2005 changes to the bankruptcy law will prevent them from filing bankruptcy. It is true that these changes have made the process more complicated. But the basic right to file bankruptcy and most of the benefits of bankruptcy remain the same for most consumers.

SOME KEY CONCEPTS YOU SHOULD KNOW

Automatic Stay. Filing a bankruptcy creates an "automatic stay" that temporarily prevents all creditors from taking any action to collect debts—including foreclosure. If the homeowner has filed other bankruptcy cases that were dismissed within the previous twelve months, however, there may be no automatic stay or it may only last for the first thirty days of the bankruptcy case. Even in this situation, the court can impose or extend the automatic stay if the consumer's current case has been filed in good faith.

"Fresh Start." The goal of any bankruptcy is to get help with existing debts and to get a second chance financially. There are two key elements to the bankruptcy "fresh start":

1. *Discharge.* A bankruptcy discharge eliminates the legal obligation to pay a debt. Not all debts are discharged in bankruptcy. Credit card debts, medical bills, and back utility debts normally are discharged. Child support, alimony, most student loans, court restitution orders, criminal fines, and most tax debts usually are not. Strictly speaking, the obligation to pay a mortgage, car loan, or other secured debt is eliminated by a bankruptcy discharge, but since the lien on the home or car is *not* eliminated the debtor must pay the debt in order to keep the home or car.
2. *Exemptions.* Exemption laws list property that the debtor can keep even after going through bankruptcy. Exemptions vary from state to state, but usually include some type of protection for equity in a home, auto, and household goods.

Chapter 13 Repayment Plans. A chapter 13 plan allows consumers to pay off their debts in whole or in part over time. Most importantly, it allows a homeowner with a mortgage default to get caught up over time, generally over a longer time period (often 3 to 5 years) than under a forbearance agreement.

Chapter 7 Liquidation. A chapter 7 case allows a consumer to discharge most unsecured debts without payment. Any property that is not protected by an exemption can be sold and the proceeds of the sale can be used to pay unsecured claims. In most consumer cases, all of the debtors' property is protected by exemptions, so none of it is sold. A chapter 7 case will not affect a mortgage lien. If the homeowner is behind on the mortgage when she files a chapter 7 bankruptcy and cannot get caught up, she can lose the house to foreclosure.

Reaffirmation Agreement. An agreement made during bankruptcy in which the consumer agrees to remain legally obligated on some or all of a debt that could otherwise have been eliminated. Consumers do not enter into reaffirmation agreements on mortgages in chapter 13 cases because the debt to the lender is not discharged. In chapter 7 cases, where consumers are current on the mortgage when they file and continue to make their mortgage payments, lenders often do not ask for a reaffirmation agreement even though the mortgage debt (not the lien) is discharged. Problems occasionally arise after bankruptcy, sometimes years later, if the consumer needs a workout agreement. Some lenders have been reluctant to provide loss mitigation options without a reaffirmation, out of concern they would be violating bankruptcy law. However, this should no longer be an issue because of a change made to the bankruptcy law in 2005 that protects the lender in this situation.

ELIGIBILITY TO FILE BANKRUPTCY

Credit Counseling. The homeowner must receive budget and credit counseling from an approved credit counseling agency within 180 days *before* a bankruptcy case is filed. Agencies are approved by the United States Trustee Program and are allowed to provide the counseling in-person, by telephone, or over the Internet. Homeowners should complete the counseling as soon as they think bankruptcy may be an option, especially if they may need to file to stop a foreclosure sale. To receive a discharge in a chapter 7 or 13 case, the homeowners must also submit proof to the court that they completed a course on financial management *after* filing bankruptcy.

"Means Test." There are few preconditions to a bankruptcy filing, although a judge can dismiss a chapter 7 case if the filing is an abuse of the bankruptcy system. This is rare but may occur if the consumer has substantial income to pay debts. A "means test" was added to the bankruptcy law in 2005 to make it more difficult for wealthy consumers to file a chapter 7 bankruptcy. For most homeowners considering bankruptcy, neither of these tests are important because homeowners typically file chapter 13 cases, not chapter 7.

Moreover, even most consumers who file chapter 7 cases are not affected by the means test. If the homeowner's income is below the median family income in your state (the national median family income for a family of 4 in 2006 was approximately $65,796—your state's figures may be higher or lower), the homeowner is protected by a "safe harbor" and not subject to the means test. The current state median family income figures are available on the United States Trustee Program's website, at www.usdoj.gov/ust/.

A consumer with income above the median must fill out a form that compares the consumer's monthly income with actual and assumed expenses in a variety of categories. If this form shows, based on standards in the law, that the consumer should have a certain amount left over to pay unsecured creditors, the bankruptcy court may decide that the consumer cannot file a chapter 7 case, unless there are special circumstances. If a chapter 7 case is not available, the homeowner can file a chapter 13 case.

Time Limits After Previous Bankruptcy. There are also time restrictions on filing bankruptcy. A person who has discharged debts in a chapter 7 bankruptcy in the past cannot get a discharge in another chapter 7 bankruptcy for eight years. Nor can such a person get a discharge in a chapter 13 case for four years. Significantly, the consumer can still file a chapter 13 case to cure a mortgage default during the four-year period, but cannot get a discharge of other debts.

MORTGAGE WORKOUT COMPARED TO CHAPTER 13 BANKRUPTCY

A chapter 13 bankruptcy can often be structured to give the homeowner a plan similar to a mortgage workout. But there are differences. Unlike a workout, a chapter 13 bankruptcy plan will generally not involve a change in the interest rate for the mortgage as a whole, and will not involve forgiveness of delinquent amounts. There are also expenses to file a bankruptcy and a portion of payments through the bankruptcy go to the bankruptcy trustee.

On the other hand, the plan may provide more time to catch up on the arrears than a workout plan, and the bankruptcy filing will stay most adverse actions against the homeowner, including foreclosure, giving the homeowner ample time to develop a repayment plan. The bankruptcy proceeding is also an excellent forum to raise legal claims against the lender or other parties.

The example on page 164 shows how, in a hypothetical case, a chapter 13 plan would compare to a mortgage workout. Both chapter 13 plans and mortgage workouts can be structured in nearly an infinite number of ways, however, so this comparison should be viewed just as one illustration of the possible differences.

CONSEQUENCES OF BANKRUPTCY FOR THE HOMEOWNER'S CREDIT RATING

Bankruptcy can stay on a consumer's credit record for ten years, rather than the normal seven years for other credit information. But bankruptcy usually does not make a person's credit record much worse than if there have already been numerous reports of defaults on debts.

Some creditors will lend to consumers who have recently completed bankruptcy since there is a good chance the loan will be repaid. They know that all or most of the consumer's past debts have been discharged and that the consumer cannot get a discharge in another chapter 7 case for a period of eight years. (There are also time restrictions on filing a chapter 13 bankruptcy after having received a chapter 7 discharge.)

Bankruptcy may pose a problem in getting approved for a conventional home mortgage. Even then, most mortgage lenders will not hold the bankruptcy against the consumer if the consumer has reestablished a good credit reputation for a period of two to four years after the discharge.

HYPOTHETICAL MORTGAGE WORKOUT/ BANKRUPTCY COMPARISON

Mr. and Mrs. P. have a 30-year first mortgage obtained ten years ago ($125,000 principal). The interest rate is 9.75% Monthly principal and interest payments are $1,073.94. Mr. P. lost his job in the middle of last year, was unemployed for nine months, and has generated arrears of $14,000 including foreclosure fees and costs. Mr. P. recently returned to work at a job which pays about 60% of his prior income.

Current Status

$ 95,000.00	remaining principal balance
$ 14,000.00	total arrears
$106,000.00	total current pay-off including unpaid interest and costs
$ 1,073.94	monthly payment (assume taxes and insurance are paid separately)

Fair market value of home: $175,000

Total Income: $2,000 monthly take-home

Most Likely Result in Addressing the Problem with Chapter 13 Bankruptcy

$1,073.94	ongoing monthly mortgage payment
$ 233.33	payment on arrears (assuming a cure over 60 months is permitted)
$ 57.28	interest on arrears payment each month
$ 32.25	trustee's fee each month[1]
$1,396.80	monthly to keep current and to cure the arrears (TOTAL)

With this chapter 13 plan, the homeowner will pay $1,396.80 for 60 months, which will cure the delinquency on the mortgage. After that, the homeowner will pay the regular mortgage payment of $1,073.94 for the remaining fifteen years of the 30-year loan.

Proposed Workout Plan Modifying the Mortgage

The homeowner proposes to extend the mortgage term, so that it has another 360 months to run, and to reduce the interest rate going forward to 8.5%, amortizing (i.e., capitalizing) the arrears of that period.

$106,000	principal balance
360	month term
8.5%	interest
$ 815.04	monthly payment (TOTAL)

With the loan modification, the homeowner will pay $815.04 a month for thirty years.

---

1. This figure for the trustee's fee is based on the assumption that the homeowner is allowed to make the regular monthly mortgage payment directly to the lender, rather than having to make the payment through the bankruptcy trustee. If the regular monthly mortgage payment is made through the trustee, the trustee's fee will be higher.

TIPS FOR COUNSELORS

A Chapter 13 Bankruptcy May Be an Option if a foreclosure sale of the homeowner's home has been scheduled, and a final workout agreement with the lender or servicer has not been reached. Refer the homeowner to an attorney who can advise of the advantages and disadvantages of filing bankruptcy.

Refer the Homeowner to a Credit Counseling Agency that is approved to provide pre-bankruptcy counseling. A list of agencies approved by the United States Trustee Program is available at: www.usdoj.gov/ust/.

Suggest Homeowners Review Their Credit Report if they filed a chapter 7 bankruptcy in the past, to make sure that all debts discharged in their bankruptcy are being reported as having a zero balance. This could be having a negative impact on their credit score and making it more difficult to get credit on good terms.

A History of a Chapter 7 Bankruptcy Is Not Grounds to Refuse a Workout, even where the homeowner never signed a reaffirmation agreement. Suggest that lenders or servicers refusing to enter into a workout agreement for that reason review the 2005 change in the law.

Give the Following Handout to Homeowners to help them understand bankruptcy. The handout is also available on the CD-Rom accompanying this handbook.

THIRTEEN IMPORTANT CONSIDERATIONS ABOUT BANKRUPTCY

1. **Bankruptcy may be the easiest and fastest way to deal with all types of debt problems.** Bankruptcy is a process under federal law designed to help people and businesses get protection from their creditors. Bankruptcy can be the right choice if you have no better way to deal with your debts. Although you may want to try other options first, you should not wait until the last minute to think about bankruptcy because some important bankruptcy rights may be lost by delay.

2. **Budget and credit counseling is required *before* filing bankruptcy.** You must receive budget and credit counseling from an approved credit counseling agency within 180 days before your bankruptcy case is filed. The counseling may take less than an hour to complete, but it is important to get this done as soon as you think bankruptcy may be an option, especially if you may need to file to stop a foreclosure sale or repossession. To find an approved credit counseling agency, go to www.usdoj.gov/ust.

3. **Most bankruptcy cases are complicated.** You should consider getting an attorney. Bankruptcy is a legal proceeding with complicated rules and forms. You probably need an attorney, especially if you hope to use bankruptcy to prevent foreclosure or repossession. Most bankruptcy attorneys will provide a free consultation to help you decide whether bankruptcy is the right choice.

4. **The most important short-term advantage of bankruptcy is that most creditors will be temporarily barred from continuing to collect debts from you except through the bankruptcy process.** This benefit is provided by the "automatic stay," which is created by filing the necessary paperwork at the beginning of a bankruptcy case. Foreclosures, repossessions,

utility shut-offs, lawsuits, and other creditor actions will be immediately (but perhaps only temporarily) stopped. There are exceptions, however, if you filed one or more bankruptcy cases that were dismissed within the previous twelve months.

5. **The most important long-term advantage of bankruptcy is that it can permanently wipe out your legal obligation to pay back many of your debts.** This benefit arises because of the bankruptcy "discharge" that you get for successfully completing a bankruptcy case.

6. **Bankruptcy will usually not wipe out certain types of debts such as alimony, child support, and most student loans.** This means that even if you file bankruptcy, you may remain legally obligated on these debts. If you want to deal with these kinds of debts in the bankruptcy process, you will need to propose a chapter 13 repayment plan, which will require you to make payments from your income over a period of three to five years.

7. **For most consumers, bankruptcy will not mean loss of property.** However, if you have certain types of very valuable property, the bankruptcy law may not allow you to keep it unless you pay its value to your creditors in a chapter 13 plan.

8. **The filing fee for bankruptcy is presently $274 under chapter 13 and $299 under chapter 7.** The fee can be paid in up to four installments over a period of 120 days (or up to 180 days with court permission). If you cannot afford to pay the filing fee in installments in a chapter 7 case, and your household income is below a certain amount (150% of the official poverty line), you can ask the bankruptcy court to waive the filing fee.

9. **If you file bankruptcy, you will need to attend a meeting with the bankruptcy trustee.** The trustee will ask you questions about your bankruptcy case and your finances. Creditors are invited to the meeting with the trustee and have the right to ask you questions, but they rarely attend. Occasionally there will also be hearings in the bankruptcy court that you will have to attend. If you receive a notice to go to court, it is important that you go.

10. **In order to receive your discharge, you must take a course in personal finances.** The typical course lasts approximately two hours. You can ask your attorney or the bankruptcy court for a list of organizations that provide approved courses.

11. **If you have had financial problems, bankruptcy will usually not make your credit record any worse.** However, the fact that you filed bankruptcy will remain on your credit record for 10 years. (Other negative information only stays on your record for 7 years.) Some creditors are willing to lend to people who recently filed bankruptcy.

12. **When you have completed bankruptcy, creditors may collect debts that are not discharged and you will have to pay any debt that arose after the bankruptcy case was started.** If a debt is not discharged, you may have to fall back on other strategies. The *NCLC Guide to Surviving Debt* is a good source of information on managing financial difficulties without filing bankruptcy. Even if you file bankruptcy, you may need to use other methods to deal with mortgage problems.

13. **Watch out for bankruptcy related scams.** There are many people and companies that advertise bankruptcy-related services in order to take advantage of vulnerable, financially distressed consumers. Some advertise help with foreclosure when all they really do is put you into bankruptcy without providing any advice on how this will help or assistance in getting through the process. Many of these businesses charge enormous fees. Others make promises which they cannot possibly keep. Do not pay money for debt counseling, foreclosure assistance, or bankruptcy without being sure you are dealing with a reputable business.

CHAPTER 12

Disputing the Amount Owed on the Mortgage: Loan Overcharges and Servicing Errors

The mortgage holder's calculation of the amount of the debt should not automatically be accepted as accurate. Sometimes servicers who work for the mortgage holder present the wrong amount as either the pay-off amount or the amount to cure a default. The debt balance should be scrutinized for excessive fees and overcharges. Fees that are not authorized by the loan note or by state law, or fees for services that were never provided, should not be included in the mortgage balance even if they are reasonable in amount. If the servicer has overcharged the homeowner, you need to address the error before the homeowner can cure the default or pay off the loan.

Improper and excessive fees can be a deal-breaker for a successful loss mitigation plan. Eliminating these fees may be a necessary step for the homeowner to obtain an effective workout. Some of the more common examples of overcharges are discussed below.

The first step in addressing servicing errors is to get the homeowner's payment records and examine them. How to do this is discussed in Chapter 5, above, along with general information about working with servicers. A sample "qualified written request" to get information from a servicer and dispute charges is also found in Chapter 5, above. The discussion that follows addresses how to spot servicing errors and what to do about them.

ESCROW ARREARAGES AND OVERCHARGES

Particularly some sub-prime lenders do not seek payments toward an escrow account for taxes and insurance—their motivation may be to mask the loan's high cost by making the homeowner's monthly payment appear smaller. These homeowners will be obliged to pay their taxes and insurance directly to the taxing authority and the insurance company. These homeowners will not face escrow arrearage errors, but you should make sure that the taxes and insurance payments are up-to-date, and should also make sure to include them when working out a budget for the homeowner.

On the other hand, most mortgages require the homeowner's monthly payment to include not only the principal and interest on the loan, but also amounts to be applied toward the taxes and insurance on the home. The servicer then holds the payments toward taxes and insurance in escrow. When the tax and insurance bills become due, the servicer pays them with the escrowed money.

Where the homeowner's payment includes taxes and insurance, problems can arise with the calculation of the consumer's monthly payment. In order to make sure that the right amount is escrowed, the servicer has to predict in advance how much the tax and insurance bills will be. Servicers sometimes make errors, either requiring the homeowner to pay too much or too little into escrow. In addition, insurance companies and taxing authorities often increase (and occasionally even decrease) what they require the homeowner to pay, so the servicer has to recalculate the amount the homeowner has to pay into escrow. This creates the possibility for additional errors. Other problems can arise if the servicer fails to pay the insurance or tax bills on time. Or the original servicer may fail to notify the consumer that a new servicer has taken over the loan, so the consumer's payments get lost between the old servicer and the new servicer.

Limits on the Allowed Escrow Amount

The federal Real Estate Settlement Procedures Act (RESPA) sets limits on how much the lender can require in escrow payments, and this should be examined to determine if the homeowner's default was at least partially caused by the lender taking more in escrow payments than it is legally allowed. The servicer cannot require a monthly escrow payment greater than $1/12$ of the total estimated escrow bills (taxes, insurance, etc.) that must be paid during the upcoming year.[1] The servicer may also require that the homeowner pay in an amount toward a "cushion," but this cushion should be no greater than an extra two months of escrow payments (which should not add more to the monthly escrow payment than two months of escrow payments divided by 12). For example, if the homeowner's tax and insurance payments total $3,384 per year, the total monthly escrow payment should be approximately $329, which would consist of a total tax and insurance monthly payment of $282 ($3,384 ÷ 12) plus a monthly cushion of $47 ($282 × 2 ÷ 12). The exact amount of the homeowner's escrow payment depends upon the time of the year when each of the escrow bills will need to be paid.

If the monthly escrow payment is significantly more than the total taxes and insurance divided by 12, you should review the most recent annual escrow statement, as described below. If necessary, request more information. This could mean that the servicer has made a mistake or is trying to collect improper fees or costs through the escrow payment.

The Annual Escrow Account Statement

RESPA requires the servicer to provide an annual escrow account statement (an example is reprinted in Appendix D of this handbook).[2] These statements must include the following information:

- The amount of the borrower's new monthly mortgage payment for the upcoming year and the portion of the monthly payment going into the escrow account;
- The amount of the past year's monthly mortgage payment and the portion of the monthly payment that went into the escrow account;
- The total amount paid into the escrow account during the past year;
- The total amount paid out of the account during the past year for taxes, insurance premiums, and other escrow bills;
- The current balance in the escrow account;

- An explanation of how any surplus is being handled by the servicer; and
- An explanation of how any shortage or deficiency is to be paid by the borrower.

The servicer is not required by RESPA to send an annual escrow statement if, at the time the yearly escrow analysis is done, the homeowner's mortgage payments are more than 30 days in arrears or the mortgage is in foreclosure. Information about the escrow account may still be obtained by making a "qualified written request." *See* Chapter 5, above. In addition, if the mortgage account is later reinstated or becomes current, the servicer must then send the annual escrow statement within 90 days.

Mistaken Demand for Immediate Payment of Escrow Arrearage

Errors sometimes occur when servicers fail to take into account changes in escrow bills from year to year. Most often this happens when there have been property tax bill adjustments based on reassessments or tax rate increases. When these changes are significant, the homeowner's monthly escrow payment may be set too low. As long as the homeowner's payments are current, however, RESPA requires the servicer to pay the escrow bills even if there is not enough money to cover them in the escrow account.[3]

When an escrow payment is set too low, the escrow account will be treated as in arrears. Such an arrearage will be shown on the next annual escrow statement as an escrow "shortage" (when the account has a balance smaller than expected) or "deficiency" (when the account has a negative balance because the servicer had to use its own funds to pay an escrow bill). The servicer is required to send a notice listing any shortage or deficiency amounts. This notice may be provided as part of the annual escrow statement or sent as a separate letter. It must also tell the homeowner how the servicer expects the amounts to be repaid.

If the escrow account has a shortage that is greater than one month's escrow payment, the servicer cannot demand full payment of the shortage in a lump sum, and must give the homeowner at least twelve months to pay it back as part of future escrow payments.[4] For example, if the account has a $315 shortage, the new escrow payment will increase by $26.25 per month for the next year ($315 ÷ 12).

If the account has a deficiency (negative balance), RESPA unfortunately is not that helpful. The servicer can require the homeowner to pay this back in as little as two months.[5] You should, however, ask for more time. There may good reason to ask for at least twelve months to repay the deficiency, especially if the servicer caused the deficiency by not updating its escrow records with correct amounts for the taxes and insurance. Some servicers have a "secret" policy to allow even longer repayment periods, but you will probably need to ask a supervisor in the escrow or collection department.

Double-Counting of Escrow Arrearage

Servicers may double-count escrow arrearages by including past-due escrow amounts in both the amount the borrower owes for future payments and the amount that the escrow account is in arrears. To determine if the escrow account has been overcharged, you must scrutinize both the amount of the escrow arrears and the amount of the default on principal and interest. Does the amount that the servicer claims is owing make sense in light of the number of months delinquent for both the arrears and the monthly payments? That is, do the escrow arrears roughly equal the amount of the monthly payment for taxes and insurance multiplied by the number of months the borrower is in default? Is the amount the borrower is alleged to be in default roughly equal to the monthly principal and interest payment, multiplied by the number of months delinquent? When the escrow arrears appear to be out of line, then more information should be requested.

Examples of Fee and Escrow Calculations

Example #1, forbearance agreement where foreclosure fees and escrow properly counted: The homeowner's total mortgage payment is $700 for principal and interest, plus a $250 escrow payment for taxes and insurance, and the homeowner is 6 months behind. The servicer's advance payment of attorney fees and other costs are $1,500. A forbearance agreement that spreads out the arrears over 12 months *without* double counting is as follows:

Arrearage:

$ 4,200	principal and interest arrearage ($700 × 6)
$ 1,500	escrow arrearage ($250 × 6)
$ 1,500	foreclosure fees and costs to date
$ 7,200	total arrearage

Monthly Repayment:

$ 600	monthly payment on arrearage ($7,200 ÷ 12)
$ 950	regular monthly payment including principal, interest, and escrow
$ 1,550	total monthly payment under forbearance agreement

Example #2, where foreclosure fees and costs are double-counted: The figures the servicer sends to the attorney for the total amount owed mistakenly include the foreclosure fees and costs to date *twice*, in the "escrow amount" owed and also listed separately.

Arrearage:

$ 4,200	principal and interest arrearage ($700 × 6)
$ 3,000	escrow due ($250 × 6 but also $1,500 foreclosure fees and costs to date)
$ 1,500	foreclosure fees and costs to date (included a second time)
$ 8,700	total amount due

In this example, the foreclosure fees and costs are double-counted. This gets even worse if the servicer then mistakenly includes the past-due escrow amount in both the amount the borrower owes for future escrow payments (as recovery of the shortage or deficiency) and the arrearage amount in a forbearance agreement.

Example #3, where BOTH foreclosure fees and escrow double-counted:

$ 8,700	payment arrearage subject to forebearance agreement (see Example #2)
$ 3,000	amount owed for future escrow payments ($1,500 escrow arrearage and $1,500 foreclosure costs as in example #2)
$ 11,700	total arrearage

Repayment:

$ 975	monthly payments persuant to both forebearance plan and escrow obligation ($11,700 ÷ 12)
<u>$ 950</u>	regular monthly payment including principal, interest, and escrow
$ 1,925	total monthly payments

This is a very costly error for the consumer. In this example, the error is $375 a month (the difference between $1925 and $1,550. Counselors may need a breakdown of the escrow figures to make sure double counting does not occur.

Miscalculation of Escrow Payment After a Workout Is Finalized

The problem of double counting described above can also occur *after* the servicer and homeowner agree on the terms of a repayment plan, sometimes weeks or months later when the annual escrow analysis is done. The servicer in computing the escrow payments due may not correct the escrow account to take the plan into consideration.

The escrow department is often different from the delinquency/loss mitigation/foreclosure departments with which you will ordinarily interact. What may happen is that the escrow department will continue to consider the escrow account delinquent even though the homeowner is repaying the back payments on the escrow through the repayment plan.

If the homeowner receives a notice or escrow statement from the servicer raising the total monthly payment because of an alleged escrow shortage or deficiency, this is a red flag. What the servicer should do is consider the escrow account current because the delinquent escrow amounts are being repaid in the plan. Especially after a workout, homeowners should be warned that a significant change to their payment amount should be evaluated to check for escrow overcharges.

Lender's Failure to Pay Escrow Bills on Time

If the homeowner's mortgage payments are not more than 30 days overdue, RESPA requires servicers to pay taxes, insurance, and other escrow bills in a timely manner as they become due.[6] This means that they should be paid before the deadline for penalties, such as interest or late fees. Failure to do so can cause borrowers to go into default, either because they are suddenly faced with a large tax bill or because the servicer adds late charges and interest to the escrow amount and the monthly payment jumps.

Counselors should always check that payments both in and out of escrow are being made in a timely way and in accord with the loan note. Homeowners should compare their tax and insurance bills with the actual escrow payouts shown on annual escrow statements. If these show that additional interest or late charges were paid, the homeowner should send the servicer a dispute letter and demand a refund. If something more drastic happens because the servicer did not make timely escrow payouts, such as a tax sale of the homeowner's home or a loss after insurance was canceled, you should refer the homeowner to an attorney. RESPA provides that the homeowner may be able to recover damages, costs, and attorney fees for this kind of violation.[7]

PROBLEMS RELATED TO SWITCHING SERVICERS

Consumer complaints about mortgage servicing show that many problems occur when servicing is transferred from one servicer to another. If the homeowner has a servicing problem, there is a good chance it began sometime around the time servicing was transferred.

The Required Transfer Notice. RESPA requires the current servicer to send the homeowner a notice at least 15 days before a new servicer takes over.[8] In addition, the new servicer must send a similar notice not more than 15 days after the transfer. These notices from the old and new servicer can be combined into one notice as long as it is sent at least fifteen days before the transfer.

The transfer notice must include the following information:

- The effective date of transfer;
- The name, address, and toll-free telephone number of the new servicer;
- A toll-free telephone number the homeowner can call for answers to questions;
- The date when the old servicer will stop accepting payments and the date when the new servicer will begin accepting payments;
- Information concerning the effect, if any, that the transfer may have upon the terms of mortgage life, disability, or other types of optional insurance; and
- What action, if any, the homeowner must take to maintain insurance coverage.[9]

Escrow Statements Where Servicer Is Changed. If the new servicer changes either the monthly payment amount for an escrow account or the accounting method used by the former servicer to calculate the escrow payment, the new servicer must also provide the borrower with an initial escrow account statement within sixty days of the date of servicing transfer.[10]

Payments Made During the Transition Period. If a homeowner mistakenly sends a timely payment during the 60-day period following the effective date of transfer to the old servicer, no late fee can be imposed and the payment cannot be treated as late for any other purposes.[11] This "safe harbor" period provides protection to the consumer not only if the homeowner sends payment to the wrong servicer but also if the old servicer fails to send the payment to the new servicer or sends it late.

MISAPPLIED PAYMENTS AND UNAUTHORIZED OR EXCESSIVE FEES AND COSTS

Servicers may make errors in their calculation of the amount due for principal and interest. Some of these errors result from miscalculation of interest or failure to credit the homeowner's payments. Other errors involve adding unjustified fees and charges to the balance. Errors of this sort are particularly common when a homeowner has fallen behind on mortgage payments. The discussion below focuses on how to spot these errors and what to do about them.

Misapplied Payments

Occasionally, a servicer will fail to credit payments or will credit payments incorrectly. This happens most often when servicing is transferred from one company to another, but it can happen even without a servicing transfer. You should compare whatever records of payments the borrower has with the payment history provided by the servicer and make sure that each payment is properly accounted for.

Sometimes the reason the servicer has not credited a homeowner's payment is that it has placed the payment in a "suspense" account because the payment was less than the full amount due. Most servicers will either return a partial payment to the borrower or hold it as "unapplied funds" in the suspense account until enough additional funds are received to equal a full monthly installment payment. But some servicers have a policy that partial payments are to be applied if they are short by only $25 or less.

If the borrower is making payments on time, the servicer should not charge late fees and past-due interest because the servicer has decided not to apply the payments. This is true even if the borrower has failed to include a late charge with the monthly payment.

There can also be problems caused by the order in which a servicer applies payments. In conventional mortgages, servicers apply the payments first to interest, then to principal, then to escrow payments due, and finally to late charges.[12] In contrast, some servicers of subprime loans will apply payments first to advances made (such as for force placed insurance or attorney fees), then to interest, then to late charges, and last to principal. This change in the order of the payment application can have very expensive long-term consequences for borrowers.

Interest Overcharges

Some lenders and servicers inappropriately claim unaccrued interest. Others calculate interest in ways not authorized by the contract. Some calculation methods are more disadvantageous to the homeowner than others.

Check to see if the lender is including interest associated with future payments. Make sure that interest is calculated at the rate and by the method required in the loan note. If the note is a variable rate loan, make sure that the rate has been adjusted correctly when the variable rate goes down, as well as up. A payment history for the account will almost always have a column that separately lists the portion of each payment that was applied to interest (and a column listing what was applied to principal).

Late Charges

Most loan notes have a provision governing late charges. The note will specify the amount, usually a fixed percent of the monthly payment for principal and interest, and the time when the payment is considered late, usually if the payment is not received by the end of 15 calendar days after it was due. Make sure that the lender has calculated the late charges correctly. Also make sure that the lender has charged only one late charge for each late payment. Borrowers should not be paying late charges on late charges.

Excessive Attorney Fees and Costs

Most standard mortgage contracts require the borrower to pay the lender's attorney fees in any action to enforce or collect sums due under the note. Generally, however, these fees must be reasonable and must be actually incurred by the lender. Sometimes the lender or servicer will charge a flat amount for attorney fees as soon as a case is referred to an attorney for foreclosure, even if the foreclosure is not completed or even commenced. (This charge is usually shown on a payment history as a "corporate advance.")

Other times, the fee is not based on a flat amount, but is still excessive for the amount of legal work performed. Since the lender is passing the attorney fees on to the borrower, the lender has little incentive to minimize them. Many foreclosure attorneys use a paralegal to generate form documents in as little as 15 minutes on a computer. A large fee for a small amount of work is unreasonable.

You should always ask to have the attorney fees waived. In many cases, it is possible to have the majority of the attorney fees waived in a workout, often because the lender has not actually incurred the fees.

A list of the foreclosure fees approved by HUD, Fannie Mae, and Freddie Mac is reproduced on page 175 and may also be found on the CD-Rom accompanying this handbook. These agencies regard the listed amounts as reasonable fees for a *completed* foreclosure. If the foreclosure is not completed, because there is a workout or for some other reason, the attorney is unlikely to have earned those fees. The unexpended fees should be returned and credited to the borrower's account.

Fees in excess of those listed for a simple uncontested foreclosure are likely not reasonable and should be challenged as such. On the other hand, if the foreclosure becomes contested, or there is a bankruptcy, the attorney may have earned more than the approved amounts. If there is a bankruptcy or the foreclosure is otherwise contested, the fees will need to be carefully scrutinized by detailed billing records.

Force Placed Insurance

If a homeowner's insurance policy is canceled, most servicers will buy a replacement policy and charge the premium to the borrower's account. This insurance often costs much more than the homeowner's own policy for much less coverage. Some serious problems have arisen in this area. Some lenders and servicers have:

- Bought force placed insurance even when the homeowner's own policy remains in force;
- Bought expensive force placed insurance when cancellation of the prior policy was the servicer's own fault (based on failure to pay premiums from the homeowner's escrow account); or
- Bought unnecessarily high-priced force placed insurance from their own subsidiaries or from independent insurance companies that pay large kickbacks.

When a servicer buys force placed to replace the homeowner's policy, it usually shows up as a major increase in the homeowner's escrow billing. If the mortgage does not have an escrow account, the servicer will either send the homeowner a demand for immediate payment of the force placed premium or set up an escrow account for payment of the insurance, often without the homeowner's authorization. Often an error or overcharge in this area causes a default because the homeowner is unable to make the higher payments. Resolving the insurance dispute in these cases can resolve the entire delinquency.

You should urge homeowners not to ignore major changes to their payment amount. Problems such as force placed insurance overcharges will compound if they are not addressed quickly. Most servicers have internal policies requiring notice to the homeowner before insurance is force-placed. For example, the Fannie Mae Servicing Guidelines states that force placed insurance coverage should only be obtained "after the servicer makes attempts to contact the borrower to obtain evidence of insurance."[13] If homeowners receive such a notice and have their own insurance, written proof of coverage (such as a certificate of insurance)

SCHEDULE OF STANDARD ATTORNEY FEES
APPROVED BY HUD, FANNIE, and FREDDIE[14]

State	Most Common Method of Foreclosure	HUD	Fannie Mae	Freddie Mac
Alabama	Non-judicial	$600	$550	$500
Alaska	Non-judicial	$1,250	$1,200	$1,000
Arkansas	Non-judicial	$650	$600	$500
Arizona	Non-judicial	$675	$625	$500
California	Non-judicial	$650	$600	$500
Colorado	Non-judicial	$850	$800	$700
Connecticut	Strict Foreclosure	$1,350	$1,200	$1,450
Delaware	Judicial	$1,000	$950	$900
District of Columbia	Non-judicial	$650	$600	$750
Florida	Judicial	$1,250	$1,200	$950
Georgia	Non-judicial	$650	$600	$550
Guam	Judicial	$1,250	$1,200	$1,200
Hawaii	Judicial	$1,900	$1,000	$1,200
Idaho	Non-judicial	$650	$600	$500
Illinois	Judicial	$1,150	$1,100	$900
Indiana	Judicial	$1,050	$1,000	$900
Iowa	Judicial	$900	$850	$750
Kansas	Judicial	$900	$850	$750
Kentucky	Judicial	$1,150	$1,100	$1,000
Louisiana	Judicial	$950	$900	$1,050
Maine	Judicial	$1,300	$1,250	$1,500
Maryland	Non-judicial	$850	$800	$800
Massachusetts	Non-judicial	$1,300	$1,250	$1,200
Michigan	Non-judicial	$700	$650	$500
Minnesota	Non-judicial	$700	$650	$500
Mississippi	Non-judicial	$600	$550	$500
Missouri	Non-judicial	$700	$650	$600
Montana	Non-judicial	$650	$600	$750
Nebraska	Judicial	$900	$850	$750
Nevada	Non-judicial	$650	$600	$800
New Hampshire	Non-judicial	$950	$900	
New Jersey	Judicial	$1,350	$1,300	$750
New Mexico	Judicial	$950	$900	$750
New York	Judicial	$1,300	$800	$900
North Carolina	Non-judicial	$600	$550	$650
North Dakota	Judicial	$950	$900	$800
Ohio	Judicial	$1,150	$1,100	$900
Oklahoma	Judicial	$950	$900	$700
Oregon	Non-judicial	$725	$675	$600
Pennsylvania	Judicial	$1,300	$1,250	$1,000
Puerto Rico	Judicial	$1,150	$1,100	$750
Rhode Island	Non-judicial	$950	$900	$800
South Carolina	Judicial	$850	$800	$750
South Dakota	Non-judicial	$600	$550	$700
Tennessee	Non-judicial	$600	$550	$550
Texas	Non-judicial	$600	$550	$500
Utah	Non-judicial	$600	$600	$500
Vermont	Strict Foreclosure	$1,000	$950	$700/$1300[15]
Virginia	Non-judicial	$650	$600	$550
Virgin Islands	Non-judicial	$1,150	$1,100	$800
Washington	Non-judicial	$725	$675	$600
West Virginia	Non-judicial	$600	$550	$500
Wisconsin	Judicial	$1,150	$1,100	$1,000
Wyoming	Non-judicial	$650	$600	$700

should be provided to the servicer along with a letter disputing the servicer's plan to buy force placed insurance. Some servicers, often due to slipshod procedures and incompetence, ignore the homeowner's proof of insurance. The homeowner should refuse to pay (or seek a refund of) any premiums for force placed insurance incurred due to the servicer's error. If the problem is not resolved after written proof of coverage and a dispute letter is provided, the homeowner should be referred to an attorney.

Unnecessary Private Mortgage Insurance Premiums

Private Mortgage Insurance (PMI), which protects the lender in the event of a default, is required on many purchase money mortgage loans where the borrower's down payment is less than 20% of the sale price. If there is a foreclosure and the foreclosure sale price is less than the balance due on the loan, PMI will pay the difference to the lender. Once the borrower has more than 20% equity in the property, there is no longer any need for the PMI and it should be canceled.

A 1998 law requires PMI policies to be automatically terminated as soon as the homeowner owes less than 78% of the value of the mortgaged property. The calculation is based on the value of the property at the time the mortgage was originated.[16] In addition, homeowners may request that the PMI be removed a little earlier—as soon as the principal loan balance is less than 80% of the value of the property at the time the mortgage was originated.

This right to cancel PMI, the exceptions to it, and details regarding the calculations are discussed in Chapter 4, above. Since PMI can make up a significant part of the homeowner's monthly payment, it is important to make sure that it is canceled as soon as possible. Canceling PMI alone can make the difference between an affordable and an unaffordable monthly payment.

Inspection Fees

Once an account goes into default, servicers will usually have an inspection of the property done to determine the current market value and the condition of the property, whether or not the property is occupied. This is done in order to determine whether a foreclosure is economically viable. The fees for this inspection are typically called property inspection fees, broker price opinions (BPOs), or appraisal fees, and are often shown on a payment history as a "corporate advance for property preservation." Sometimes it is the mortgage insurer or guarantor (i.e., Fannie Mae or Freddie Mac) that requires the servicer to do the inspection.

Some servicers charge these fees every month. Often, servicers charge hundreds of dollars for what is no more than a drive-by. In one case, a servicer charged several thousands of dollars for a helicopter inspection of a residential home owned by low-income borrowers!

Like all fees, it pays to scrutinize these fees for reasonableness. If the homeowner is in contact with the servicer soon after a default and is working to resolve the problem, property inspections and appraisals should be unnecessary. The Fannie Mae servicing guide states: "Generally, the servicer does not have to inspect a property that secures a delinquent mortgage if it has made contact with the borrower and is working with the borrower to resolve the delinquency (unless the mortgage insurer or guarantor requires a property inspection)."[17]

If the property is occupied, it is unlikely that a monthly inspection fee is reasonable. Certainly, repeated or inflated appraisal fees are not reasonable. At a minimum, these charges should stop once the homeowner has entered into a workout and is meeting the terms of the agreement.

Discharge or "Pay-Off Fees"

Some lenders charge the homeowner a fee for calculating the amount needed to pay off the loan in full when, for example, the homeowner is refinancing the loan or selling the home. These "pay-off" fees range from $25 to $100. Calculating the loan balance is a central task in servicing the loan. Charges for calculating the pay-off amount usually are not authorized by the loan note. Some state laws forbid this practice, even if it is authorized by the loan note.

WARNING SIGNS OF MORTGAGE SERVICING ABUSE

The following are warning signs of mortgage servicing abuse:

- Multiple demands for cure amounts that the servicer claims are insufficient after they have been paid by the borrower.
- Inconsistent demand letters.
- Unjustified and unreasonable late fees, interest charges, property inspection fees, property preservation fees, attorney fees, foreclosure expenses, etc.
- Unexplained "corporate advances" and "other fees."
- Unnecessary force placed insurance when homeowner has coverage.
- Excessive charges for force placed insurance.
- Returned payments.
- Improper posting of payments to a suspense account.
- Late posting and misapplication of payments.
- Failure to make timely payments out of escrow.
- Threatened foreclosure based on non-existent default.
- Failure to provide complete and accurate accounting of charges.
- Failure to provide timely and complete responses to qualified written requests from the homeowner.
- Failure to give the borrower timely notice of a transfer of servicing rights and to properly apply payments during the transfer period.
- Failure to reasonably exhaust loss mitigation options.
- Double-counting of fees in forbearance agreements.
- Failure to honor forbearance agreements.
- Inclusion of waiver of rights clauses in forbearance agreements.
- Unnecessary demands for electronic debit or wire transfers for payments.

CHALLENGING SERVICING ERRORS

Failure to Correct an Error After a Qualified Written Request

The federal Real Estate Settlement Procedures Act (RESPA) provides a mechanism for a homeowner to challenge servicing errors such as improper charges, improper calculation of interest, or failure to credit payments properly. The first step in such a challenge is to send the servicer a "qualified written request"—basically a letter that gives enough information so that the servicer can identify the borrower or the borrower's account, and that explains why the borrower believes the account is in error. A qualified written request can also be used to obtain information about the account. How to prepare and send a qualified written request is explained in Chapter 5, above.

Most lenders and servicers will correct errors if there is a legitimate dispute, after receiving a qualified written request. Sometimes, though, a servicer will not fix an error or eliminate a charge that the homeowner legitimately disputes. When that happens, the homeowner may have legal remedies.

A homeowner has a legal right of action under RESPA against a servicer who fails to respond properly to a qualified written request. Suit must be brought within three years of the date of the violation.[18] A homeowner may recover damages, costs, and reasonable attorney fees for "each such failure."[19] If the evidence also reveals a pattern or practice of noncompliance, the court may award additional damages for each violation up to $1,000. A servicer can, however, avoid liability by making the appropriate correction to the account within sixty days of discovering the error and before commencement of a court action.[20]

Other Legal Violations

The homeowner may have other claims as well. An overcharge is a breach of contract (the loan note) that can be challenged in a court proceeding. Unauthorized charges or improper servicing practices may give the homeowner grounds for legal claims under the state's unfair and deceptive acts and practices statute (UDAP), state debt collection laws, and state servicing laws.[21]

Servicers generally are excluded from coverage of the federal Fair Debt Collection Practices Act (FDCPA). However, a servicer may be subject to the FDCPA's requirements and possible claims by the homeowner for debt collection violations if the servicer acquired the right to service the mortgage after it went into default.

In some cases, a servicer may violate the Fair Credit Reporting Act if, for example, it makes a false report to a credit reporting agency that the account is in default and fails to correct the report after the homeowner disputes the information. Most overcharges are inadvertent. However, when an overcharge is deliberate (or when a creditor fails to correct an inadvertent overcharge after notice), or when a servicer wrongfully begins or refuses to stop a foreclosure sale, the servicer may violate a duty of good faith and fair dealing that your state law may impose on the parties to a contract.

Evaluating the Litigation Option

Pursuing litigation is not risk-free. If the lender will not correct the account, the homeowner must decide whether or not to pursue litigation, with the knowledge that doing so may make an amicable work-out plan impossible. Factors to consider include:

- The amount in dispute;
- The strength of potential legal claims;
- The strength of the homeowner's feelings about not repaying money she feels is not owed;
- The benefits of the workout package;
- The availability of cost-effective legal assistance; and
- The risk of passing up a workout in favor of uncertain litigation.

In some cases, it may be advantageous for the homeowner to challenge the amount owed under the mortgage even *after* a foreclosure. If money is to be returned to the homeowner based on the price at the sale, reduction of overcharges will increase the surplus proceeds paid to the homeowner. When the homeowner has a post-sale right to redeem the mortgage, a challenge to the claimed debt balance will reduce the amount the borrower must pay to redeem. If a deficiency judgment is sought, the homeowner also has an interest in reducing the total owed, and thereby reducing the amount of the deficiency. Finally, serious lender misconduct may give rise to independent claims that can result in significant damage awards to compensate the former homeowner.

SUMMARY: TIPS FOR COUNSELORS

1. Get a detailed breakdown of the amount claimed due, broken out at least by number and amount of principal and interest payments due, actual escrow advances and their purpose, and other fees. (See Chapter 5, above, for suggestions about how to get this information.)

2. Compare the records provided by the servicer with the amount claimed in the foreclosure and with the homeowner's own records. A simple spreadsheet or table with columns for each source of information is often helpful.

3. As soon as the homeowner believes there is an inaccuracy, suggest that the homeowner send a qualified written request (QWR) to the servicer, asking the servicer to investigate the discrepancy. A QWR is just a letter from the homeowner to the servicer, asking for information about the account and corrections of errors. It is helpful, but not necessary, to call it a "qualified written request" and to send it certified mail, return receipt requested. It must identify the loan account and be sent separately from any payments to the servicer. The servicer may, but need not, specify an address for QWRs. (See Chapter 5, above.) Once a QWR is sent, a servicer must respond or risk legal liability.

4. If the lender will not correct the balance, the homeowner must decide whether to pursue litigation or accede to the lender's charges. Making this decision requires a weighing of the benefits and risks of the workout plan offered by the lender and any possible legal claim.

5. Homeowners need to be especially vigilant after a workout has been completed to ensure that no fees or charges are added back in. Any unexpected increase in the payment or amount due should be scrutinized. Servicers commonly add forgiven charges back into the balance.

Chapter Notes

1. The escrow provisions of RESPA appear in 12 U.S.C. § 2609 and Regulation X, 24 C.F.R. § 3500.17.
2. 12 U.S.C. § 2609(c)(2).
3. Reg. X, 24 C.F.R. § 3500.17(k)(2).
4. Reg. X, 24 C.F.R. § 3500.17(f)(3)(ii).
5. Reg. X, 24 C.F.R. § 3500.17(f)(4)(ii).
6. The servicing provisions of RESPA appear in 12 U.S.C. § 2605 and Regulation X, 24 C.F.R. § 3500.21.
7. 12 U.S.C. § 2605(f). The statute of limitations is three years from the date of the violation. 12 U.S.C. § 2614.
8. 12 U.S.C. § 2605(b)(2)(A).
9. 12 U.S.C. § 2605(b)(3); Reg. X, 24 C.F.R. § 3500.21(d)(3).
10. Reg. X, 24 C.F.R. § 3500.17(e).
11. 12 U.S.C. § 2605(d); Reg. X, 24 C.F.R. § 3500.21(d)(5).
12. See Fannie Mae Single Family Servicer Guidelines, Part III, § 101.03: Payment Shortages (2002 and Supp.); General Freddie Mac Policies, Single Family Seller/Servicer Guide § 51.15(a) Accounting Methods (1989 and Supp.).

13. *See* Fannie Mae Single Family Servicer Guidelines, Part II, Chapter 6: Lender-Placed Property Insurance (Feb. 1, 2005).
14. Source: HUD Mortgagee Letter 05-30 and Fannie Mae and Freddie Mac servicing guides.
15. The higher attorney fee listed is for cases where there is equity in the property, thus requiring a foreclosure by judicial sale. Freddie Mac Single-Family Seller/Servicer Guide, vol. 2b, exh. 57a (Oct. 6, 2006).
16. 12 U.S.C. §§ 4901–4910.
17. Fannie Mae Single Family Servicer Guidelines, Part III, § 303: Properties Securing Delinquent Mortgages.
18. 12 U.S.C. § 2614.
19. 12 U.S.C. § 2605(f).
20. Remedies if the servicer simply fails to respond to the qualified written request are discussed in Chapter 6, above.
21. A summary of state servicing laws is contained in Appendix E of NCLC's *Foreclosures* (2d ed. 2007). While many of these statutes contain provisions similar to RESPA, some provide even greater rights to homeowners. State servicing laws that provide greater protections generally are not preempted.

CHAPTER 13

Homeowner Options After the Foreclosure Sale

All is not necessarily lost after the foreclosure sale of a home. Some issues remain and need the attention of the homeowner.

Buy-Back of the Home. The ex-homeowner may be able to buy back the home from the purchaser. This is more likely if the purchaser was also the lender. The ex-homeowner will generally need funding by a third party. However, if the house does not sell at the auction, the lender is occasionally willing to refinance with the homeowner, especially if the lender is a governmental entity.

Exercising the Right of Redemption Under State Law. In some states, homeowners have a "statutory right of redemption" after a foreclosure sale. This means that, for a set period of time after the foreclosure sale, the homeowner can get the home back by paying the total purchase price, plus interest and any allowable costs, to the foreclosure sale purchaser.

States that require judicial foreclosures are more likely to give the homeowner a right of redemption after the foreclosure sale than states that allow non-judicial foreclosure. The summary of state foreclosure law in Appendix E, which appears later in this handbook, includes a statement as to whether the state affords the homeowner a right of redemption after the foreclosure sale.

The right of redemption gives the homeowner a final window of opportunity to save the home, even after the foreclosure sale. It also gives the homeowner the opportunity to find a buyer for the home, which may enable the homeowner to realize some of the equity in the home. The buyer would pay the amount necessary to redeem the home and pay the homeowner the difference between the negotiated sale price and the redemption amount.

The deadlines and procedures for exercising the right of redemption vary from state to state. You should expect the deadlines and procedures to be enforced strictly. If a foreclosure sale has already occurred and the homeowner is trying to exercise the right of redemption, it is best to work closely with an attorney who is familiar with state foreclosure law and can make sure that all the deadlines and procedures are observed.

Bankruptcy Implications of the Right of Redemption. If the state gives the homeowner a right of redemption after the foreclosure sale, a bankruptcy filing may also help the homeowner save the home. Filing a bankruptcy case may give the homeowner a longer period of time to exercise the right of redemption.

A homeowner who wants to consider a bankruptcy filing after the foreclosure sale should be referred to a bankruptcy attorney immediately. Any bankruptcy case will have to be filed before the right to redeem expires, and that period can be very short. Such a bankruptcy will raise complicated issues and a homeowner is unlikely to succeed in the case without an attorney.

Redemption Period for Active Duty Military Personnel. Active duty military personnel are entitled to special protections. First, for any type of foreclosure sale, any period of time during which the owner was on active duty does not count against the redemption period. So, for example, if the state's law allows the homeowner to redeem the home for 60 days after the foreclosure sale, and the homeowner was on active duty during the first 45 days of that period, the 60-day redemption period would start to run only when the homeowner left active duty.

If the home was sold at a tax sale while the homeowner was on active duty, there is an additional extension of the right to redeem the home. Any redemption period given by state law is automatically extended until 180 days after the homeowner leaves active duty. (If the state law provides a *longer* period to redeem the property, however, that period applies.) The special protections for active duty military personnel are discussed in more detail in Chapter 10, below.

Asking a Court to Set Aside the Sale. In some circumstances, a court can set aside a foreclosure sale after it has occurred. For example, it may be possible to set aside the sale if the lender did not follow the proper procedure or if the property sold for an unconscionably low price. A few states have a post-sale judicial confirmation procedure whereby the homeowner can challenge the sale and raise defenses to the loan at that time. A homeowner who wants to explore whether the sale can be set aside should be referred immediately to an attorney experienced in these issues. The time period for asking the sale to be set aside may be very short. Very few sales are, however, set aside.

Obtaining Any Surpluses from the Sale. If there was equity in the home and the sale price was higher than the outstanding indebtedness due under the mortgage loan(s), then the homeowner may be entitled to the surplus. State or local law determines if there is a judicial procedure or formal way to make a claim for this money. If not, the homeowner should send a letter to the servicer and lender requesting an accounting and a return of any surplus. This letter should include the ex-homeowner's new address and telephone number. If the servicer or lender does not respond, a Qualified Written Request, as described above in Chapter 5, may be invoked to obtain this information. Finally, state law or the mortgage or deed of trust itself may provide for the refund of a surplus. Arguably, the lender has a fiduciary duty to refund any surplus.

> **Beware of Excessive Fees and Costs Charged That Eat Up the Surplus.** If the lender's fees and costs are excessive, these can be challenged.

Raising Legal Claims for Money Related to the Mortgage Loan. The homeowner may have a claim under contract law against the lender if any provision in the mortgage documents was breached. There may also be claims under the federal or state Fair Debt Collection Practices Act and the state Unfair and Deceptive Trade Practices Act against either the lender or the servicer or both. These and other claims for money may survive the sale, depending on state law. However, some legal claims are lost once the sale occurs.

PART
IV

Advanced Topics

CHAPTER 14

Securitization and MERS

UNDERSTANDING THE SECURITIZATION PROCESS

The capital underlying the residential mortgage market is increasingly coming from the financing mechanism known as "securitization." For example, subprime mortgage-backed securities grew from $18 billion issued in 1995 to more than $858 billion in 2005.

Securitization is the process by which lenders transform their loans into tradable securities. This occurs by pooling a large volume of loans and selling interests in the underlying cash flows to investors, often insurance companies, mutual funds, and other large financial institutions. The monthly payments made by the homeowners whose mortgage loans are in the pool of loans are used to pay the servicer, trustee, and investors.

The majority of mortgages in this country are packaged into pools that are sold to institutional and individual investors. For example, the "Ginnie Mae" mutual fund is simply a pool of mortgages from all over the country that produces a stream of income from the principal and interest paid by homeowners. Rather than buying a mortgage or a group of mortgages outright, investors in a mutual fund buy a share or shares of stock in all of the mortgages held in a particular Ginnie Mae pool, and are entitled to returns based on the income generated by that pool.

How to Tell If a Loan Is Securitized

In order to determine whether a loan has been securitized, it is necessary to know who is the true owner of the loan. The loan servicer, with whom the borrower has primary contact, is most often an agent for the owner of the loan. Under the Truth in Lending Act, the servicer is required, upon written request, to provide the homeowner with the name, address, and telephone number of the owner of the mortgage. The owner of the mortgage in a securitization transaction will generally be a bank or other financial institution acting as trustee for a particular loan trust.

For example:

Deutsche Bank National Trust Company, as trustee for Long Beach Mortgage Loan Trust 2003-2, or

Norwest Bank Minnesota, as trustee for the Amresco Residential Securities Mortgage Loan Trust 1998-2.

Common Securitization Terms

While securitizations can be structured in a number of different ways, the following players and other terms are common to many securitization transactions.

Lender. The originator of the loan, that is the mortgage holder (sometimes called the mortgagee) on the original loan documents.

Seller/Wholesale Lender. The seller is the party that sells the loans to the issuer (see below). The seller can be the original lender, or an affiliate of the original lender. Alternatively, the original lender can sell the loans to a wholesale lender who, in turn, becomes the seller of the loans to an issuer.

Issuer/Depositor. The seller transfers the notes to an issuer, also sometimes called a depositor. The issuer issues securities that represent undivided interests in the cash flows from a particular pool of loans. The issuer then sells the securities and transfers legal title in the loans to a trust entity.

Servicer. The entity that collects monthly payments from borrowers and passes on the required cash flows to the trustee. The servicer must advance to the trust payments due from delinquent borrowers, and also must advance the costs of foreclosure. The servicer retains a fee from borrower payments, usually .5%, and can also keep late charges, bad check charges, and other costs. In many securitized transactions the seller retains the right to service the loan, so the seller and the servicer may be the same entity.

Trustee. Usually a commercial bank, the trustee acts on behalf of the trust and investors. It is essentially an administrative function, to represent the trust, to monitor the effectiveness of the servicing, to manage and oversee the payments to the bondholders, and to administer any reserve accounts.

Custodian. The custodian may hold the notes and mortgages for safekeeping as an agent for the trust.

Underwriter. The Wall Street investment firm or firms that provide the initial capital to purchase the securities from the issuer and then, at a profit, sell them to its customers, institutional investors, and mutual funds. The underwriter plays a key role in structuring the entire transaction.

Rating Agency. The rating agency provides an evaluation of the credit quality of the securities. There are four rating agencies: Standard and Poor's; Moody's; Fitch; and Duff and Phelps. One of them has to rate the bonds as having an AAA quality in order for the transaction to be regarded as marketable. AAA bonds are the highest quality with the smallest risk of default and are considered stable and dependable.

Insurer. In order to achieve an AAA rating, mortgage pools have to be "credit enhanced." Often these enhancements come in the form of insurance.

Warehouse Lender/Facility. These financial entities provide the short-term cash a small lender needs to fund the mortgage initially, until the loans are securitized. Once the loans are purchased through the securitization process, there should be enough cash to repay the warehouse lender.

The Pooling and Servicing Agreement. The primary contractual document underlying a securitization transaction is the Pooling and Servicing Agreement (PSA). The PSA broadly governs the formation of the trust, the servicing of the loans in the trust, and the duties of various parties to the trust agreement. The PSA may also outline the loss mitigation or workout options available to the servicer and the scope of the servicer's authority to implement those options.

WHAT SECURITIZATION MEANS FOR THE HOMEOWNER

Servicers May Claim (Not Always Truthfully) That They Lack Authority to Modify a Securitized Loan. This often occurs when the homeowner is seeking permanent modification of the loan terms, such as a reduction in the interest rate, an extension of the loan payment period, or a reamortization with capitalization of arrears. Probing assertions that the servicer lacks authority to take some action may sometimes lead to the discovery that the option remains available, if the servicer takes an extra step. For the most part, pooling and servicing agreements (PSAs) permit loan modifications if the loan is in default or if the servicer determines that default is reasonably foreseeable. However, a few PSAs may limit the number of loan modifications to no more than 5% or 10% of the total loan pool. If the servicer has hit the cap, its hands may really be tied.

It may be worthwhile for counselors to review the PSA if they are having trouble coming to an agreement with a servicer. If the security was publicly sold, then the PSA is publicly available on the U.S. Securities and Exchange Commission's (SEC) website, www.sec.gov. However, searching SEC-filed documents requires the name of the actual loan trust in which the consumer's loan is contained. To do that digging, go to the CD-Rom accompanying this handbook and follow the instruction in "Finding Pooling and Servicing Agreements for Securitized Mortgage Loans." An actual agreement is included on the CD-Rom for your education.

The Securitization Process May Limit the Homeowner's Ability to Raise Defenses to Foreclosure. In some cases, obtaining loan paperwork or talking to the homeowner may uncover potential defenses to collection, such as Truth in Lending violations, usury, fraud, or unfair and deceptive practices. However, the purpose of securitization is, in part, to insulate investors from liability for the conduct of the originating lender. As a result, the question of whether a consumer can raise defenses and claims against the trust requires an extremely complex analysis.

One resource for the homeowner to find a private consumer attorney to assist in analyzing whether legal claims and defenses may be asserted against a mortgage loan trust is the website of the National Association of Consumer Advocates, www.naca.net. The "Find a Lawyer" feature allows users to search the organization's list of members by state or zip code and by the type of case the attorney is willing to handle. Most state bar associations, and many local bar associations as well, have lawyer referral services that may also be able to help. In addition, legal services offices exist in all major cities and serve all rural regions of the country. Referrals may be made to those offices for low-income clients.

MORTGAGE ELECTRONIC REGISTRATION SYSTEM (MERS)

The Mortgage Electronic Registration System (MERS) is an electronic registry and clearing-house established to track ownership and servicing rights in mortgages. Established in 1997, MERS was developed by the lending industry to reduce the costs associated with the bulk transfer of mortgage loans. Prior to MERS, each time a mortgage was transferred a document called an assignment was recorded in a public registry. Public registries typically charged a fee for this recording. MERS eliminates this expense as well as the costs of preparing the documents. Once a loan is assigned to MERS, all subsequent assignments will not be recorded in the public records. Instead, MERS remains the mortgage holder (mortgagee) of record. The system then internally tracks all changes of ownership, servicing rights, corporate names, and mergers.

MERS As Mortgagee (MOM). MERS can become the mortgagee of record in two ways. For a newly originated loan, a mortgage or deed of trust is prepared with MERS named on the mortgage as "nominee for the holder." Alternatively, a lender may execute an assignment to MERS after the loan closing. MERS, as mortgagee, claims no beneficial interest in the mortgage or the promissory note. That is, MERS does not claim to have a right to collect payments or control any litigation or settlement. MERS, however, often does assert the right to foreclose.

Using MERS to Identify the Servicer

The name of the current actual owner and servicer of the mortgage are shown in the MERS database. Homeowners may obtain the name of the current *servicer* by calling MERS' auto-mated system at 888-679-6377. The system does not provide any information regarding the actual owner of the loan.

When calling MERS to obtain information on a loan, homeowners and counselors should use the MIN number, a permanent 18-digit mortgage identification number assigned to every loan registered with MERS. The MIN number generally appears on the face of the mortgage or assignment and serves as the loan's identifier throughout the life of the loan, even if the ownership or servicing rights are transferred. If the original mortgage was registered with MERS, the MIN should appear on the mortgage or deed of trust.

If the mortgage loan was only registered with MIN after the loan was assigned, it will be more difficult to obtain the MIN. MERS claims that as an alternative the MERS website (www.mers-servicerid.org) allows identification using the borrower's name, property address, and/or Social Security Number. This identity can also be revealed by using the FHA or VA Case Number or Mortgage Insurance Certificate Number.

MERS Foreclosures and Getting MERS on the Same Page with the Servicer

While MERS has streamlined the bulk transfer of mortgages on the secondary market, it has also left many homeowners in a state of confusion. Most homeowners have never heard of MERS until they receive notices related to the foreclosure of their home. When homeowners then contact MERS (usually by calling its local attorney), MERS disclaims any ability to assist the homeowners. In some cases, MERS may refer the homeowner back to the servicer.

Adding to the confusion for consumers is the fact that the communication between MERS and the servicer is often poor. As a result, MERS may continue to press the foreclosure even when the servicer has indicated that it is not intending to foreclose. In such situations where MERS and the servicer seem to be at cross purposes, the counselor can facilitate a conference call among the parties to get everyone on the same page.

Legal Challenges to a MERS Foreclosure

Despite disclaiming any interest in the note or mortgage, MERS does assert that, as the lenders' "nominee," it has the right to initiate foreclosure actions in its own name. Several courts have questioned this assumption and some courts have even denied MERS the right to foreclose.

How the homeowner goes about such a legal challenge to a MERS foreclosure will depend on state foreclosure law. In approximately half the states (as listed below in Appendix E), mortgages are always foreclosed by judicial action: the lender must obtain a judicial decree authorizing a foreclosure sale. In these states, the consumer can raise the legal challenge in this proceeding. In non-judicial foreclosure states, mortgagees may conduct a sale of the property after giving notice as required by the terms of the mortgage or applicable state statute. The right of MERS to foreclose in these states is equally questionable. However, the homeowner must take affirmative action to stop the foreclosure sale before MERS' authority can be challenged.

Challenging MERS' right to foreclose is a means of temporarily delaying foreclosure proceedings. In some cases, a successful challenge may require the lender to begin the entire foreclosure process over again. This may give the homeowner enough additional time to arrange a workout, a refinancing, or a private sale.

If it appears that challenging MERS' right to foreclose would help the homeowners, they will benefit if they have an attorney present this defense for them. Legal services offices exist in all major cities and serve all rural regions of the country. Referrals may be made to those offices for low-income clients. A good resource for a homeowner to locate a private consumer attorney is the website of the National Association of Consumer Advocates, www.naca.net. The "Find a Lawyer" feature allows users to search the organization's list of members by state or zip code and by type of case the attorney is willing to handle. In addition, most state bar associations and many local bar associations operate lawyer referral services.

CHAPTER 15

Correcting Credit Reports and Other Consumer Dispute Rights

Financially distressed homeowners may appreciate information about their ability to dispute items in their credit report, to deal with identity theft, and to obtain information about a transaction or to require the business to investigate the consumer's dispute. During the pendency of such an investigation, these laws *may* (but not always) allow the consumer to withhold payment and to limit the business' right to furnish information to reporting agencies, engage in collection activities, add finance charges, or seize collateral.

CREDIT REPORTING RIGHTS IN A NUTSHELL

Virtually every homeowner has a credit reporting file that contains information about where the homeowner lives and works, how she pay her bills, or whether she has been sued, arrested, or has filed for bankruptcy. A credit bureau can only report the most accurate negative information for up seven (7) years and bankruptcy information for ten (10) years. However, there is no time limit on reporting information about criminal convictions.

Companies that gather and sell this information are called "consumer reporting agencies" or "credit bureaus." The information sold by credit bureaus to creditors, employers, insurers, and other businesses is called a "credit report." There are three major nationwide credit bureaus:

- Equifax, 800-685-1111, www.equifax.com;
- Experian, 888-EXPERIAN (888-397-3742), www.experian.com;
- TransUnion, 800-916-8800, www.transunion.com.

How to Obtain a Free Credit Report

Any consumer can get a free credit report once every 12 months from each of the three major credit bureaus. To order:

Go to www.annualcreditreport.com,
Call 877-322-8228, or
Complete the Annual Credit Report Request Form (available at www.ftc.gov/credit) and mail it to:

Annual Credit Report Request Service
P.O. Box 105281
Atlanta, GA 30348-5281.

Consumers should be warned NOT to contact the three credit bureaus individually for their free annual reports. The credit bureaus are only providing free annual credit reports through the centralized sources listed above. Using one of these centralized sources, the consumer may order free annual reports from all three credit bureaus at the same time, or they can order from only one bureau, saving their right to a free report from the other two until later in the year.

In order to get a free credit report, a consumer will need to provide her name, address, Social Security number, and date of birth. If the consumer has moved in the last two years, she may have to provide her previous address. To maintain the security of the credit files, each credit bureau may ask the consumer for some information that only the consumer would know, like the amount of her monthly mortgage payment. Each bureau might ask the consumer for different information.

Free credit reports are available in other circumstances as well. If an application is denied because of information from a credit bureau, and if the applicant requests a copy of his credit report within 60 days of receiving the denial notice, the applicant is entitled to the information without charge. One free report is available once in any 12 month period for consumers who certify in writing that they:

- Are unemployed and intend to apply for a job in the next 60 days;
- Are receiving public benefits assistance; or
- Believe that a credit report is wrong due to fraud.

In addition to the free credit report available under federal law, consumers also can get a free report under state law if they live in Colorado, Georgia, Maryland, Massachusetts, New Jersey, or Vermont. If none of the above circumstances apply, and the consumer wants a second report within a year, the credit bureaus may charge a fee, currently up to $10 for a copy of a credit report.

Credit Scores

It is important to realize, though, that free credit reports do not include a credit score, a number that summarizes a consumer's credit history, based on one of a number of different credit scoring systems. Moreover, many businesses, including mortgage lenders, credit card issuers, automobile lenders, and even insurance companies and utilities base their prices and decisions on the credit score, not the complete report.

While there are different credit scoring systems, scores typically range from 350 to 900. Anything over about 750 is generally considered to be a very good score. Some of the factors that can affect a score include:

- Payment history with many systems deducting points for late payments, accounts referred to collections, or bankruptcies.
- Amount of outstanding debt, with debt amounts that are close to the credit limit being likely to have a negative effect.
- Length of credit history, with more points given for a longer credit track record.
- Recent applications for credit can have a negative effect in some models. Nevertheless, many scoring models will not rate negatively inquiries by creditors who are

monitoring an account or looking at credit reports to make "prescreened" credit offers or inquiries by the consumer of her own report, and many models will not even treat credit applications as a negative factor. Consumers should not be afraid to shop for the best credit just because they are worried that too many inquiries will show up on their credit reports or lower their credit scores.

■ Number and types of credit accounts. Too many credit card accounts may have a negative effect on a score, as do certain types of credit, such as finance company loans. Instead, many models give more points to what they consider a healthy "mix."

To improve a credit score under most models, consumers should concentrate on paying bills on time, paying down outstanding balances, and not taking on new debt. It is likely to take some time to improve a score significantly. If there are any errors involving negative information, they should be disputed as discussed below.

How to Obtain a Consumer's Credit Score: Lenders who use credit scores in connection with a mortgage application must also provide the consumer, free of charge, that credit score and the associated key factors that adversely affected the score. In addition, credit bureaus are required to provide consumers with their credit scores upon request, and the charge for the score will be set by the Federal Trade Commission. Consumers are entitled to get from the credit bureaus:

■ Their current credit scores or most recent score that was calculated by the credit bureau relating to the extension of credit.

■ A statement indicating that the information and credit scoring model may be different from the credit score used by the lender.

■ The range of credit scores (lowest and highest) of the model used to generate the credit score so the consumer can check where her score fits into the range.

■ The key factors that adversely affected a credit score, listed in order of impact. The agency cannot list more than four (4) key factors, unless one of the factors is the number of inquiries, in which case that factor must be included.

■ The date on which the credit score was created.

■ The name of the provider of the credit score or the credit file used to generate the credit score.

How to Dispute Information in the Credit Report

Credit reports often contain inaccurate information. It is a good idea for consumers to check their credit reports regularly, even when they are not experiencing problems. The information in a credit report affects the consumers' credit scores and whether they can get a loan—and how much they will have to pay to borrow money. It is also helpful for consumers to make sure the information is accurate, complete, and up-to-date before they apply for a loan for a major purchase like a house or car, buy insurance, or apply for a job. Ordering a credit report can also help guard against identity theft.

If a consumer finds inaccurate or outdated information in his credit report, he has the right under the Fair Credit Reporting Act to dispute that information. Both the credit bureaus and the information provider have responsibilities to correct inaccurate or incomplete information in a credit report. The consumer can dispute information with both the credit bureau and the provider of information, i.e., the lender, collection agency, or other business, but it is essential to at least dispute the information with the credit bureau, or even with all three bureaus, if applicable.

The consumer should inform the credit bureau in writing what information is inaccurate. Although not required, it is prudent to put everything in writing and keep copies, and also contact the creditor at the same time. A letter is generally a better approach than using a credit bureau's website or even a printed form to report a dispute. The consumer may need to dispute information with all three of the national reporting agencies. The letter should be as specific as possible.

The credit bureau must investigate the items in question—usually within 30 days—unless they consider the consumer's dispute frivolous. It must also forward all relevant data provided about the dispute to the information provider. After the information provider receives notice of a dispute from the credit bureau, it must investigate, review all relevant information provided by the credit bureau, and report the results to the credit bureau. If the information provider finds the disputed information to be inaccurate, it must notify all nationwide credit bureaus so that they can correct this information in the consumer's file. Job applicants can have corrected reports sent to anyone who received a copy during the past two years.

When the investigation is complete, the credit bureau must give the consumer the written results, the name, address, and phone number of the information provider, and a free copy of the report, if the dispute results in a change. This free report does not count as the consumer's annual free report. If an item is changed or deleted, the credit bureau cannot put the disputed information back in the consumer's file unless the information provider verifies that it is accurate and complete. Nevertheless, even when information is deleted, the consumer should periodically check that the information has not been sent again to the agency.

If an investigation does not resolve a consumer's dispute with the credit bureau, the consumer can ask that a statement of the dispute be included in his file and in future reports, and be provided to anyone who received a copy of the report in the recent past. The consumer will probably have to pay a fee for this service If the consumer tells the information provider that he disputes an item, a notice of the dispute must be included any time the information provider reports the item to a credit bureau.

Who Can Get a Copy of a Homeowner's Credit Report

Only people with a legitimate business need, as recognized by the Fair Credit Reporting Act, can look at a credit report without the consumer's permission. For example, a company is allowed to get the report of an applicant for credit, insurance, employment, or to rent an apartment.

Employers can get a consumer's report only if the consumer says it is okay. A credit bureau may not give information about a consumer to an employer or prospective employer without the consumer's consent, unless the person is being investigated for suspected misconduct or compliance with federal, state, or local laws or preexisting written policies of the employer.

Identity Theft Claims

Disputing Fraudulent Charges. Consumers have a number of rights to dispute identity theft charges. Identity theft victims can get free copies of their credit report, over and above the one free report a year to which consumers are now entitled. The consumer, after reviewing the report, should request that the reporting agency delete any fraudulent information. The consumer must provide the agency with proof of the consumer's identity, a copy of an identity theft report (to the police or other agency), a description of what information in the report is fraudulent, and a statement that the thief, not the consumer, was involved in the transaction.

The reporting agency must then block that information within four business days and notify the creditor who furnished the information of the block. That creditor must then reinvestigate and take steps to prevent the information from being furnished to an agency again. Once an agency has notified a creditor of the identify theft, the creditor cannot sell or transfer the debt or send it out for collection.

The consumer can also provide a copy of an identity theft report to the creditor directly, and the creditor must then cease furnishing that information to reporting agencies, until it subsequently "knows" that the information in fact is correct. The consumer should contact the security or fraud department of each creditor involved in the theft, and follow up with a written notice, with a return receipt requested, to the address for billing inquiries (not the normal address). Finally, the consumer can ask for written confirmation when a creditor agrees that charges do not belong to the consumer.

A consumer can also seek information from any business that transacted with the thief in the victim's name. The consumer can gain access to the thief's application for credit and any business transaction records relating to the transaction. The consumer should make a written request to the business and must prove the consumer's identification and the validity of the identity theft claim, by providing information as requested by the business.

Similarly, if a consumer notifies a debt collector that a debt involves identity theft, the collector must provide the consumer with the same information about the debt that the consumer would have been entitled to receive had the consumer actually incurred the debt. This information is examined below under "Debt Collection Claims."

Heading Off New Identity Theft Charges. To protect against new fraudulent accounts being opened, the consumer can call a toll-free number for any of the three national credit reporting agencies to request that a fraud alert be placed in the consumer's file. The agency called must contact the other two national reporting agencies, and then, whenever new credit is sought in the consumer's name, a creditor contacting one of these agencies is told to take extra steps to verify the consumer's identity. This initial alert stays on the consumer's file for 90 days. The consumer can also file an identity theft report and seek an extended alert for seven years.

To find out if the identity thief has been passing bad checks in a consumer's name, call SCAN at 800-262-7771. To notify retailers not to accept checks drawn on a fraudulent account in the consumer's name, contact Telecheck, at 800-710-9898, and Certegy at 800-437-5120.

OTHER DISPUTE RIGHTS REGARDING SPECIFIC TYPES OF TRANSACTIONS

The law also provides other dispute rights, although these legal rights vary dramatically depending on the nature of the transaction, and some are of more practical use than others. Exercising rights to dispute debts and charges may result in the elimination of certain debts, allowing the homeowner to commit more of the household monthly income to the mortgage payment. In addition, the merchant's, lender's, or servicer's non-compliance with these statutes often provides the consumer with a claim for actual or statutory damages and attorney fees, so that there may be a viable legal remedy for a business' failure to cooperate, even if the litigation over the disputed amount itself is not practical. The counselor's role is to understand that these rights apply, to educate the consumer, and to make an appropriate referral to an attorney if the consumer cannot succeed on her own.

Mortgage Loans

Real Estate Settlement Procedures Act. The Real Estate Settlement Procedures Act (RESPA) provides consumers with important protections to dispute the amount due on a mortgage and to obtain information on the loan. In addition, RESPA does not preempt stronger state servicing laws, enacted in a number of states, that apply to a broader spectrum of loans or give greater consumer rights.[1]

To initiate RESPA protections, the consumer sends the servicer a "qualified written request," as described more fully above in Chapter 5, identifying the borrower and the account, and explaining the error or otherwise providing sufficient detail for the servicer to respond to the request.[2] Within 20 business days, the servicer must acknowledge receipt of the request, and, within 60 business days, either:

- Correct the account and notify the consumer;
- Conduct an investigation and state the reasons why the account is correct, with the name and phone number of a servicer employee who can provide further information; or
- Provide the information requested or explain why it is not available, plus provide the name and phone number of a servicer employee who can provide further information.

During this time, the servicer cannot report to a credit bureau as overdue any payment relating to the qualified written request. Nevertheless, HUD regulations allow the servicer to foreclose on the mortgage and pursue collection efforts. HUD regulations also state that the servicer need not respond if the request is sent more than a year after "the date of transfer of service" or the amount was paid in full. This clearly is meant to apply when an old servicer is no longer handling the loan or the loan is paid in full. Some servicers interpret this, however, as requiring the consumer to make the request within the first year that the servicer takes on a loan *and* within a year of the act or omission.

RESPA remedies include actual damages plus $1,000 additional statutory damages if there is a pattern or practice of non-compliance, plus attorney fees and costs. Particularly where violations lead eventually to foreclosure, damages, including emotional distress, can be significant.

TILA Right to Identify the Mortgage Holder. In this age of securitization, it is helpful to know who actually owns a loan. The Truth in Lending Act (TILA) gives consumers the right to make a written request of the entity receiving the consumer's payments. The servicer must provide the name, address, and telephone number of the owner of the obligation.[3] It appears that failure to provide this information does not lead to any TILA private remedies, however. This TILA right may be preferred over the RESPA approach because no time deadline is provided. Arguably, the servicer must respond faster than RESPA's 60 working days. On the other hand, there is no TILA private penalty for non-compliance.

Car Loans and Auto Title Pawns

The Right to an Accounting and to the Holder's Identity. Whenever an automobile or RV (or any other good) is taken as collateral on a loan, the Uniform Commercial Code (UCC)[4] § 9-210 provides consumers with the right to get information on the amount due. Where an auto title pawn takes a security interest in a vehicle, this UCC protection applies to that transaction as well. The consumer must send a request reasonably identifying the transaction and requesting an accounting of the amount still due. The creditor has 14 days to send an accounting of the amount due, identifying the components of the obligation in reasonable detail. Creditors who no longer hold the loan have 14 days to identify the assignee. The consumer is entitled to one free statement a year, and additional statements are capped at $25. Creditors failing to comply with any of these requirements without reasonable cause are liable for the consumer's actual damages plus up to $500.

As with mortgages, the TILA right to obtain the identity of the note holder still applies. For most car loans, the consumer also has the TILA right to receive, at no cost, the payoff figure within 5 days of any oral or written request. The response must be written if the consumer's request is written.[5] Failure to provide the payoff figure appears not to lead to any TILA private remedies.

Disputes Concerning the Vehicle. Where the dealer extends credit or arranges a car loan, UCC § 2-717 allows consumers, upon notifying the seller of their intent, to deduct damages resulting from a breach of contract from the next payments due. A related right is the consumer's ability to send a notice revoking acceptance of the vehicle, at which point the consumer's obligation to pay is eliminated. Both these rights typically continue against the note's assignee. The consumer should send notices to both the note holder and the dealer.

Deficiency Claims. When a creditor repossesses and sells the consumer's vehicle, if the sale price does not satisfy the obligation, the creditor is likely to seek the difference, called a deficiency. In that case, the creditor must provide the consumer with an explanation of the amount of the deficiency it is seeking. The consumer also has the right, at no charge, to obtain this explanation once every six months.[6] This is helpful if the consumer did not receive or retain the notice provided by the creditor, and also because the deficiency amount being sought may increase over time.

The creditor must send the explanation within 14 days of the consumer's request. The explanation contains much useful information, including how the deficiency was calculated, any rebates of unearned interest, the sale proceeds, and the types of expenses and total amount of expenses charged to the consumer. Remedies for non-compliance are actual damages plus, if the creditor's non-compliance is part of a pattern or a consistent practice of noncompliance, $500.

Mobile Home Loans

For loans used to purchase a new mobile home, the UCC § 9-210 rights described under "Car loans" apply. The consumer also has the RESPA rights set out above under "Mortgage Loans" to obtain information about the amount due and the identity of the holder of a mobile home mortgage loan. HUD regulations apply RESPA protections where the mortgage covers real property upon which a mobile home is located or will be located.[7] For all mobile home loans, the consumer has the TILA right to obtain information on the loan's true owner, as set out above under "Mortgage Loans."

Debt Collection Claims

When a third party is collecting on a debt, the consumer has a right under the Fair Debt Collection Practices Act (FDCPA) to dispute the debt or any portion of it and to determine the identity of the original creditor.[8] Collectors must inform consumers of this validation right, and, within 30 days of receiving this notice from the collector, the consumer may notify the debt collector in writing that all or part of the debt is disputed, and/or that the consumer is asking for the name and address of the original creditor.

The collector can take no collection action until it provides the requested information to the consumer. This has generally been interpreted as preventing the collector or creditor from initiating suit or making an adverse credit report. FDCPA remedies include statutory damages up to $1,000, plus any actual damages, and attorney fees.

Student Loans

The National Student Loan Data System (NSLDS) provides information on federal direct and guaranteed student loan obligations on-line at www.nslds.ed.gov. After ordering a PIN on-line, the student can check loan amounts, loan types, the loan's status, and disbursements. Alternatively, the student can call 1-800-4-FED-AID and speak to a person. In addition, the Department of Education has an ombudsman, who can be contacted at www.sfaheld.ed.gov or 877-577-2575, if attempts to resolve the matter with the lender fail.

Credit Cards

Credit card holders have three sets of rights to dispute a credit card charge under federal law. (These rights do not apply to debit card charges, which instead are subject to a different set of rights, discussed below.) In addition to these three federal rights, state law can help the consumer identify any collateral the credit card company may be claiming.

Unauthorized Use of a Credit Card. This protection shields the consumer against liability for unauthorized use of a credit card, when someone steals, borrows, or otherwise uses a card or card number without permission. Liability for unauthorized use of a credit card is limited to $50. If someone steals a card, for example, the credit card lender can charge you a maximum of $50 no matter how much the thief has charged on the card. Of course, the card issuer is not required to and frequently will not even charge this $50.

The situation may be trickier in cases where someone the consumer knows used the card, for example if the consumer gives a card to a son. The consumer may be liable for any charges the son runs up even if he is told to use the card for emergencies only. If the son took the card without the consumer's knowledge, the law limits the consumer's liability in the same way as if the card was lost or stolen, as long as the consumer is willing to take out a police report against the son.

As soon as a consumer knows of any type of unauthorized use of a credit card, call the lender to make a report. If the consumer calls before unauthorized charges are incurred, the consumer cannot be charged even $50, since the lender can take steps to cancel the card and send a new one.

If a charge unexpectedly appears on a bill for something the consumer did not authorize, the consumer can also use the billing error dispute right, as discussed below. Some credit card lenders have been telling consumers they can only report unauthorized use by sending a written billing error notice within 60 days of receiving the bill with the unauthorized charge. *This is not true.* Consumers can report unauthorized use over the telephone. They also are not required to do so within 60 days, although the sooner the report, the better.

After a report of an unauthorized charge, the credit card lender must conduct a "reasonable" investigation of the claim, unless it simply decides to take the charge off the account. A reasonable investigation might include analyzing the signature on the credit card slip, obtaining a copy of a police report, or comparing where a purchase was made versus where you live.

Billing Error Disputes. The second type of federal credit card protection involves disputes about a credit card bill, including merchant overcharges or charges for products never received. The Fair Credit Billing Act forces lenders to follow specific "billing error" procedures to resolve the dispute.

Under this law, the consumer must raise a dispute *in writing* to the credit card company, usually by sending a letter. The letter must be sent within sixty (60) days of the first bill with the improper charges. The letter must include the following information:

- Name and account number;
- The dollar amount of the dispute; and
- A statement of the reason for the dispute.

The letter of dispute must be sent to the address provided by the lender for this purpose. Information about this address and how to raise a dispute appears on the back of a credit card statement. An example of a dispute letter appears below. If appropriate, send backup documentation such as a letter explaining the problem to the merchant.

The law only permits the consumer to raise certain types of disputes using the billing error procedures. Some examples of reasons for dispute are:

- I did not authorize this charge (remember—you can raise the issue of unauthorized use by sending a written billing error notice, but you can report unauthorized use over the telephone, too);
- I did not receive the goods I ordered;
- I returned the goods I ordered because they were defective but did not get a credit;
- The merchant sent me the wrong goods;
- The merchant did not complete the services I contracted for or performed them incompletely;
- The merchant billed me for $100 when I agreed to pay $10;
- I canceled the contract with the merchant or contractor before work was performed;
- Although I agreed to buy something from this merchant, I did not authorize them to bill my account.

The consumer cannot raise a complaint about the quality of merchandise or services bought with a credit card in the form of a billing dispute. However, the consumer can withhold payment to the credit card lender for poor quality goods or services in many cases, which is the third type of credit card protection discussed below.

Once the consumer raises a dispute, the credit card company must investigate and report back in writing within two complete billing cycles or within 90 days, whichever comes first. In many cases, the charge will be canceled. Often a merchant will back off rather than risk losing the privilege of accepting business by credit card. Interest associated with a successfully disputed debt must also be canceled.

Until the dispute is resolved, the consumer does not need to pay the disputed portion of the bill. However, payment must be made to cover any undisputed amount. The credit card company cannot report the consumer as delinquent with respect to the disputed amount but may do so if part of the debt is undisputed and unpaid.

If the credit card company does not resolve the dispute in the consumer's favor, it must send a written explanation and give the consumer any supporting documentation upon request. It must allow a grace period normally permitted for the charge (unless the dispute was made after the grace period).

Sample Credit Card Billing Error Dispute Letter

June 15, 2007

Jane Consumer
101 Main Street
Anytown, USA 12345

Big Credit Card Co.
P.O. Box 666
Somewhere, DE 11111
[*The actual address you need to use appears on the back of the credit card bill you are disputing in a section called "Billing Rights Summary."*]

Dear Big Credit Card Co.:

My name is Jane Consumer. My account number is 123456789. I am disputing a charge on the bill you mailed on June 5, 2007. That bill includes a charge in the amount of $2,000.00 to Fix-It Garage. This amount is in error.

In April of this year I took my car to Fix-It Garage to be repaired. They estimated that the work would cost $400. I told them not to do any work in excess of $400. When they called to say the repairs were completed, they told me that the bill was $2,000. I did not agree to pay this amount and they have charged my account without my authorization.

I have contacted Fix-It Garage by telephone, in person, and by the enclosed letter in order to try to resolve the dispute. They have not agreed to withdraw the charge.

Please investigate this dispute and provide me with a written statement of the outcome. Thank you for your time and attention to this matter.

Very truly yours,

Jane Consumer

Stopping Payment on a Credit Card. The third important federal credit card dispute protection is the right to stop payment. This strategy can be used if the consumer: has a legitimate complaint about the quality of goods or services bought with the card; first makes a good faith effort to resolve the problem with the merchant directly; and meets the following two prerequisites:

- The goods or services must have cost more than $50; and
- Those goods or services must have been purchased in the consumer's home state or within 100 miles of the consumer's mailing address.

However, these last two limits do not apply if the credit card was issued by the seller (such as a department store card) or if the card issuer mailed an advertisement for the goods or services purchased.

After the consumer notifies the credit card company that payment is being withheld, the company cannot report the disputed amount as delinquent to a credit bureau until the dispute is settled or a court judgment is issued. The lender cannot treat the dispute as "settled" or take collection action against the consumer unless it has completed a reasonable investigation of the claim.

After its investigation, the card issuer may determine that the consumer must pay the amount on the credit card statement. In the typical case, however, the card issuer credits the amount to the consumer, charges that amount back to the merchant, and the merchant will have to come after the consumer for the disputed charge.

How to Enforce Credit Card Dispute Rights. In many cases, a credit card dispute will be resolved after contacting the credit card company. However, if the company does not respond to a dispute or the consumer is not satisfied with the results, there are additional steps to take:

Complain to OCC. Most credit card companies are national banks, which are regulated by a federal agency called the Office of the Comptroller of Currency (OCC). While the OCC's main mission is to protect the economic health of national banks, they do have a division that assists consumers. You can find out more information at the OCC's website at www.occ.treas.gov/customer.htm or call 800-613-6743. The consumer can file a complaint with the OCC at the following address:

> Office of the Comptroller of Currency
> Customer Assistance Group
> 1301 McKinney Street
> Suite 3450
> Houston, TX 77010
> FAX: 713-336-4301

A copy of the complaint should also be sent to the state Attorney General.

Sue the company or take them to arbitration. Federal law permits a consumer to sue the credit card company if it does not follow the dispute procedures discussed above or takes some action forbidden by law (such as reporting a disputed amount as delinquent to a credit bureau). The right to sue may be limited by a mandatory arbitration provision that most credit card companies have slipped into their contracts (probably one of those bill stuffers with tiny print that few consumers read), preventing the consumer from suing a credit card company in court. Instead, the consumer is required to use a private company to resolve the claim. If a consumer is forced to use the arbitration process, make sure to have the company agree to pay the costs, because arbitration can be very expensive, with the arbitrator often charging thousands of dollars a day.

Credit Cards Taking Security Interest in Items Purchased. Where a credit card affiliated with a merchant takes a security interest in the products being purchased, complicated issues can arise as to what collateral has been paid off and what items are still being held as security. The right to obtain a listing of this collateral is set out under "Small Loans" below.

Debit Cards and Check Payments

Error Resolution Rights Under the EFTA. The Electronic Fund Transfers Act (EFTA) provides consumer error correction rights applicable to debit card transactions, direct deposits, automatic bill payment plans, and other forms of electronic transfers withdrawn directly out of a consumer's bank account.[9] The consumer must send a notice within 60 days of receipt of a bank statement displaying the error, identifying the consumer and the bank account, and indicating the nature of the error. While this notice can be oral, the bank can require a confirming notice in writing.

If the bank does not credit the consumer's account immediately to correct the error, it must promptly institute an investigation, complete it within 10 business days, and send notice of the results to the consumer within three days. Any error must be fixed within one business day of its discovery. If the bank needs more time, it must first provisionally credit the consumer's account for the disputed amount, and then complete its investigation.

If the bank denies the consumer's claim, it must provide a written explanation and offer the consumer the opportunity to see the documents, in an "understandable form," upon which the bank relied. For certain forms of non-compliance with these error resolution requirements, the bank is liable for treble damages, and in any event is liable for actual damages plus statutory damages not less than $100 nor more than $1,000, plus attorney fees.

Applicability to Checks and Electronic Check Conversion. In an odd twist, consumers have significant statutory error resolution rights where they pay by credit or debit card or by a direct electronic transfer, but only have such rights in special cases where they pay by check. Where the consumer's check is deposited by the payee, the consumer has no special error resolution rights, except that the federal "Check 21" statute provides certain dispute rights where the problem is confined to the electronic imaging process for the consumer's check and is not related to the original paper check.

EFTA protections do apply to the increasingly common practice of merchants taking consumer checks not for deposit, but to use as a source document to initiate an electronic transfer. This can occur in two ways. The consumer may mail in a check (or drop it off at a lock box), and the merchant takes the routing and account information off the check, destroys the check, and initiates an electronic transfer out of the consumer's account in the amount of the check. Or, when the consumer presents a check at a store cash register, the store takes the information off the check, initiates an electronic transfer, and returns the canceled check to the consumer on the spot. The consumer's monthly statement should show these electronic check conversions as different transactions than those in which the consumer's check was actually negotiated.

Closed-End Small Loans

Many small loans take collateral in personal items, such as lawnmowers, stereos, and musical instruments, and these security interests trigger UCC § 9-210 rights described under "Car Loans." Significantly, in the case of some small loans, it may be unclear what collateral the creditor is presently claiming secures the loan. UCC § 9-210 allows the consumer to send a request reasonably identifying the consumer and the account number, and asking the creditor to approve or correct a list of collateral provided by the consumer. The creditor has 14 days to send a statement of the collateral. If the creditor does not respond, the creditor may be limited to the collateral listed by the consumer. The consumer is entitled to one free statement a year, and the price of additional statements is capped at $25. If the creditor fails to comply with section 9-210 without reasonable cause, the consumer has an action for actual damages plus $500.[10] The consumer also has the TILA rights to obtain the holder's identity, and the pay off figure, as described in the car loan discussion.

Telephone Charges

900-Number, Long-Distance, Other Unrelated Charges Found on Local Phone Bills. Today more and more types of charges are showing up on telephone bills sent by the local phone service, such as long-distance charges, 900-number charges, and even charges totally unrelated to telecommunications. A key question is whether refusal to pay disputed charges unrelated to local service can lead to disconnection of local phone service.

Phone companies cannot disconnect or interrupt a customer's local or long-distance service because of nonpayment of charges for any interstate pay-per-call 900-service.[11] The phone company collecting on a 900-number charge also has discretion to forgive, refund, or credit pay-per-call charges that violate federal law.[12]

Whether a local phone company can disconnect for nonpayment of a long-distance charge varies by state. A number of states also prohibit disconnection of phone service while a dispute is pending, and there is a general common law notion that utilities cannot disconnect based on collateral matters.

California is the first state to allow telephone companies to be billing agents for products unrelated to communications, such as newspapers or "take out" food. The state utility commission provides certain rights to dispute these charges. There can be no disconnection of basic telephone service for these other charges. If the customer is unable to get a billing problem resolved by contacting the vendor, the telephone company must investigate.[13]

Error Resolution Rights Under State PUC Regulations. Consumers disputing telephone charges have rights under state public utility commission (PUC) regulations. For a state-by-state analysis, see NCLC's *Access to Utility Service* Appendix A. Some PUC regulations are quite general, calling for utilities to provide a method by which customers may file complaints or mandating that utilities respond to complaints "fully and promptly." Other PUC regulations are more specific, setting forth the time period within which a utility must respond to complaints, whether such response must be in writing, and that the utility must inform its customers of their right to appeal a decision with the PUC.

Most state PUC regulations prohibit utilities from terminating service for nonpayment of disputed amounts, a prohibition which continues until the utility resolves the dispute or until the customer has exhausted all appeals. However, a minority of states' utility regulations permit utilities to require customers to put disputed amounts into escrow pending dispute resolution. In those states, failure to make a deposit during the course of a dispute investigation could result in termination of service.

Chapter Notes

1. A list of these state laws can be found in National Consumer Law Center, Foreclosures Appx. E (2d ed. 2007).
2. 24 C.F.R. § 3500.21(e).
3. 15 U.S.C. § 1641(f)(2).

4. The Uniform Commercial Code is adopted in almost a uniform manner in very state, with very few exceptions. Thus a state's law may have a different numbering than the UCC citations here, but a state is likely to have a provision as described here and elsewhere in this chapter.
5. 15 U.S.C. § 1615(c).
6. U.C.C. § 9-616.
7. 24 C.F.R. § 3500.2(b).
8. 15 U.S.C. § 1692(g)(b).
9. 15 U.S.C. § 1693; 12 C.F.R. § 205.
10. U.C.C. § 9-625(b), (f). Some states alter the $500 amount.
11. 47 U.S.C. § 228(c)(4); 47 C.F.R. § 64.1507.
12. 47 U.S.C. § 228(f); 47 C.F.R. § 64.1512.
13. Cal. Pub. Utility Code § 2890.

Bibliography and Helpful Websites

BIBLIOGRAPHY

NCLC Books & Brochures

National Consumer Law Center, *Foreclosures* (2d ed. 2007).

National Consumer Law Center, *Consumer Bankruptcy Law and Practice* (8th ed. 2006).

National Consumer Law Center, *Bankruptcy Basics* (2007).

National Consumer Law Center, *Student Loan Law* (3d. ed. 2006).

National Consumer Law Center, *Fair Credit Reporting* (6th ed. 2006).

The National Consumer Law Center Guide to Surviving Debt (2006).

The National Consumer Law Center Guide to the Rights of Utility Consumers (2006).

National Consumer Law Center, *Stop Predatory Lending* (2d ed. 2007).

The National Consumer Law Center Guide to Consumer Rights for Domestic Violence Survivors (2006).

The National Consumer Law Center Guide to Mobile Homes (2002).

Barron, Nancy, *Return to Sender: Getting a Refund or Replacement for Your Lemon Car* (2000).

National Consumer Law Center Consumer Education Brochures: NCLC has a wide array of brochures, some translated into other languages, that are available at www.consumerlaw.org.

National Consumer Law Publications can be ordered securely on-line at www.consumerlaw.org or from Publications, National Consumer Law Center, 77 Summer Street, 10th Floor, Boston, MA 02110, (617) 542-9595, FAX (617) 542-8028, publications@nclc.org.

Reports & Articles

Post-Purchase Counseling & Credit Counseling

Baker, Christi, *Report 1: Current State of Post-Purchase Programs, Chrysalis Consulting* (July 2004), *available at* http://content.knowledgeplex.org/kp2/cache/documents/42132.doc.

Capone, Charles A. and Albert Metz, *Mortgage Default and Default Resolutions: Their Impact on Communities,* (February 25, 2003), *available at* www.chicagofed.org/cedric/files/2003_conf_paper_session2_capone.pdf.

Collins, Michael and Rochelle Nawrocki Gorey, *Analyzing Elements of Leading Default Intervention Programs,* PolicyLab Consulting Group, L.L.C. (2005), *available at* http://content.knowledgeplex.org/kp2/cache/documents/94953.pdf.

Gorham, Lucy and Roberto Quercia, William Rohe, *Effective Practices in Post-Purchase Foreclosure Prevention and Sustainable Homeownership Programs,* Prepared for the Fannie Mae Foundation (April 2004), *available at* http://curs.unc.edu/curs-pdf-downloads/Publications/Roheeffectivepracticesfinalreport.pdf.

Hartarska, Valentina and Claudio Gonzalez-Vega, *Credit Counseling and the Incidence of Default on Housing Loans by Low-Income Households,* Rural Finance Program, Ohio State University (February 2002), *available at* http://aede.osu.edu/programs/RuralFinance/PDF%20Docs/Publications%20List/Papers/02P03.pdf.

Haurin, Donald R. and Stuart Rosenthal, *The Growth of Earnings of Low-Income Households and the Sensitivity of Their Homeownership Choices to Economic and Socio-Demographic Shocks,* U.S. Department of Housing and Urban Development (2005), *available at* www.huduser.org/Publications/pdf/EarningsOfLow-IncomeHouseholds.pdf.

Herbert, Christopher E. and Eric S. Belsky, *The Homeownership Experience of Low-Income and Minority Families: A Review and Synthesis of the Literature,* U.S. Department of Housing and Urban Development (2006), *available at* www.huduser.org/Publications/PDF/hisp_homeown9.pdf.

Hirad, Abdighani and Peter M. Zorn, *A Little Knowledge is a Good Thing: Empirical Evidence of the Effectiveness of Prepurchase Homeownership Counseling,* Working Paper, Joint Center for Housing Studies, Harvard University (2001), *available at* www.chicagofed.org/cedric/files/2003_conf_paper_session1_zorn.pdf.

Hornburg, Steven P., *Strengthening the Case For Homeownership Counseling: Moving Beyond "A Little Bit of Knowledge,"* Working Paper, Joint Center for Housing Studies, Harvard University (2004), *available at* www.jchs.harvard.edu/publications/homeownership/w04-12.pdf.

Housing Assistance Council, *Housing Counseling in Rural America* (January 1997), *available at* www.rural-home.org/pubs/counseling/tableofcon.htm.

McCarthy, George W. and Roberto G. Quercia, *Bridging the Gap Between Supply and Demand: The Evolution of the Homeownership, Education and Counseling Industry,* Research Institute for Housing America (2000), *available at* www.housingamerica.org/docs/RIHA00-01.pdf.

Neighborhood Housing Services of Chicago, *Midterm Report for the Chicago Homeownership Prevention Initiative* (2004), *available at* www.knowledgeplex.org/showdoc.html?id=90881.

Neighborhood Housing Services of Chicago, *Preserving Homeownership: Community-Development Implications of the New Mortgage Market* (March 25, 2004), *available at* www.nw.org/network/comstrat/foreclosure/documents/preservingHomeownershipRpt.pdf.

Quercia, Roberto and Susan Wachter, *Homeownership Counseling Performance: How Can It Be Measured?* Housing Policy Debate, Vol. 7, Issue 1, Fannie Mae Foundation (1996), *available at* www.fanniemaefoundation.org/programs/hpd/pdf/hpd_0701_quercia.pdf.

Quercia, Roberto and Spencer Cowan, Ana Moreno, *The Cost Effectiveness of Community Based Foreclosure Prevention,* Joint Center for Housing Studies at Harvard University (2004), *available at* www.jchs.harvard.edu/publications/finance/babc/babc_04-18.pdf.

Reid, Caroline Katz, *Achieving the American Dream? A Longitudinal Analysis of the Homeownership Experiences of Low-Income Households,* Center for Studies in Demography and Ecology (April 2004).

Wiranowski, Mark, *Sustaining Home Ownership Through Education and Counseling,* Joint Center for Housing Studies at Harvard University (2003), *available at* www.jchs.harvard.edu/publications/homeownership/w03-7_wiranowski.pdf.

Wong, Victoria & Norma Paz Garcia, *There's No Place Like Home: The Implications of Reverse Mortgages on Seniors in California,* Consumers Union (August 1999), *available at* http://64.224.99.117/finance/revinfowc899.htm.

Mortgage Lending

Bradford, Calvin, *Risk or Race: Racial Disparities and the Subprime Refinance Market,* Center for Community Change (May 2002), *available at* www.communitychange.org/default.asp.

Ernst, Keith, Farris, John & Stein, Eric, *North Carolina's Subprime Home Loan Market After Predatory Lending Reform,* Center for Responsible Lending (August 2002), *available at* www.responsiblelending.org.

Fishbein, Allen J., Patrick Woodall, *Exotic or Toxic? An Examination of the Non-Traditional Mortgage Market for Consumers and Lenders,* Consumer Federation of America (May 2006) *available at* www.consumerfed.org/pdfs/exotic_toxic_mortgage_report0506.pdf.

Li, Wei & Keith Ernst, *The Best Value in the Subprime Market,* Center for Responsible Lending (February 2006), *available at* www.responsiblelending.org/pdfs/rr010-State_Effects-0206.pdf.

Quercia, Roberto and Michael Stegman and Walter Davis, *The Impact of Predatory Loan Terms on Subprime Foreclosures* The University of North Carolina at Chapel Hill (January 2005), *available at* www.kenan-flagler.unc.edu/assets/documents/foreclosurepaper.pdf.

The Reinvestment Fund, *Predatory Lending: An Approach to Identifying and Understanding Predatory Lending* (2004).

Schloemer, Ellen, Wei Li, Keith Ernst, Kathleen Keest, *Losing Ground: Foreclosures in the Subprime Market and Their Cost to Homeowners*, Center for Responsible Lending (Dec. 2006) *available at* www.responsible lending.org/pdfs/CLR-foreclosure-rprt-1-8.pdf.

Stein, Eric, *Quantifying the Economic Cost of Predatory Lending*, Coalition for Responsible Lending (July 25, 2001), *available at* www.responsiblelending.org.

White, Alan M. & Mansfield, Cathy Lesser, *Subprime Mortgage Foreclosures: Mounting Defaults Draining Home Ownership*, Presentation at HUD-Treasury Predatory Lending Task Force Hearing in New York (2000), *available at* http://facstaff.law.drake.edu/cathy.mansfield/subprime.html.

Government Reports

U.S. General Accounting Office (GAO), *Single-Family Housing: Progress Made, but Opportunities Exist to Improve HUD's Oversight of FHA Lenders* (November 2004), *available at* www.gao.gov/new.items/d0513.pdf.

U.S. General Accounting Office (GAO), *Consumer Protection: Federal and State Agencies Face Challenges in Combating Predatory Lending* (February 24, 2004), *available at* www.gao.gov/new.items/d04280.pdf.

U.S. Department of Housing and Urban Development, Office of Policy Development & Research, *The Sustainability of Homeownership: Factors Affecting the Duration of Homeownership and Rental Spells* (December 2004), *available at* www.huduser.org/publications/affhsg/homeownsustainability.html.

National Predatory Lending Task Force, *Curbing Predatory Home Mortgage Lending: A Joint Report, U.S. Department of Housing and Urban Development and U.S. Department of Treasury* (June 2000), *available at* www.hud.gov:80/pressrel/treasrpt.pdf.

Mobile Homes

Jewell, Kevin, *Raising the Roof, Raising the Floor*, Consumers Union Southwest Regional Office, Public Policy Series, Vol. 6, No. 5 (May 2003), *available at* www.consumersunion.org/pdf/mh/raising.pdf.

Jewell, Kevin, *Paper Tiger; Missing Dragon: Poor Warranty Service and Worse Enforcement Leave Manufacture Home Owners in Lurch*, Consumers Union Southwest Regional Office, Public Policy Series, Vol. 5, No. 4 (November 2002), *available at* www.consumersunion.org/other/mh/paper-info.htm.

Mitchell, Kathy, *In Over Our Heads: Consumers Report Predatory Lending and Fraud in Manufactured Housing*, Consumers Union (February 2002), *available at* www.consumersunion.org/other/mh/overinfo.htm.

Other

Gross, Karen, *Financial Literacy Education: Panacea, Palliative, or Something Worse?*, 24 St. Louis U. Pub. L. Rev. 307 (2005).

Loonin, Deanne, *An Investigation of Debt Settlement Companies: An Unsettling Business for Consumers*, National Consumer Law Center (March 2005).

Loonin, Deanne, *Credit Counseling in Crisis: Poor Compliance and Weak Enforcement Undermine Laws Governing Credit Counseling Agencies*, National Consumer Law Center (November 2004).

Loonin, Deanne, Credit Counseling in Crisis: The Impact on Consumers of Funding Cuts, Higher Fees and Aggressive New Market Entrants, National Consumer Law Center (April 2003).

Tripoli, Steve and Elizabeth Renuart, *Dreams Foreclosed: The Rampant Theft of Americans' Homes Through Equity-Stripping Foreclosure "Rescue" Scams*, National Consumer Law Center (June 2005).

Furnham, Adrian & Argyle, Michael, The Psychology of Money (1998).

HELPFUL WEBSITES

[This list is not exhaustive, just illustrative.]

Mortgage Industry

Federal National Mortgage Association (Fannie Mae): www.allregs.com/efnma
   The Fannie Mae *Single-Family Servicing Guide* is available at this site.

Federal Home Loan Mortgage Corporation (Freddie Mac): www.freddiemac.com
   This site has the Bulletins and other notices that Freddie Mac issues to servicers.

Government National Mortgage Association (Ginnie Mae): www.ginniemae.gov
   A government corporation which guarantees mortgage-backed securities composed of FHA-insured or VA-guaranteed mortgage loans that are issued by private lenders.

PMI: www.pmigroup.com
   Private mortgage insurer.

MGIC: http://mgic.com
   A mortgage insurer.

U.S. Foreclosure Network (USFN): http://imis.usfn.org
   A national association of foreclosure attorneys.

Mortgage Bankers Association: www.mbaa.org
   A national association representing the real estate finance industry.

Current Mortgage Rates in the Prime Market: www.bankrate.com or www.mrate.com, to see what rates a homeowner might get in a refinancing.

Government Sites

U.S. Department of Housing and Urban Development: www.hud.gov
   This site includes HUDClips which has access to all mortgagee letters, handbooks and regulations.

U.S.D.A. Rural Housing Service: www.rurdev.usda.gov/rhs
   Information on the direct and guarantee loan programs.

U.S. Department of Veteran's Affairs: www.homeloans.va.gov/index.htm
   The Home Loan Guaranty Services website.

Federal Trade Commission: www.ftc.gov/bcp/menu-credit.htm
   FTC publications on consumer credit rights.

Internal Revenue Service: www.irs.gov
   An IRS site that is helpful in answering basic tax filing and other questions.

U.S. Department of Education: www.ed.gov
   Offers a number of very helpful free publications, including Student Guide, a guidebook for understanding student loans and grants. The publications are also available through ED Pubs, P.O. Box 1398, Jessup, MD, 27094-1398; (877) 4ED-PUBS (433-7827).

Credit Bureaus (and to order credit reports):

Equifax: www.equifax.com

Experian (formerly TRW): www.experian.com

TransUnion: www.transunion.com

To order free reports: www.annualcreditreport.com

General Consumer and Legal Sites

AARP: www.aarp.org

This website provides information about elder-related issues, including many consumer issues such as reverse mortgages and predatory lending.

AFFIL: www.affil.org

An organization designed to draw national attention to the problems with the lending industry in America.

American Bankruptcy Institute: www.abiworld.org

This website provides bankruptcy information for consumers and lawyers.

Better Business Bureau: www.bbb.org

You can check on a businesses' complaint record or file a complaint on-line.

Consumer Federation of America: www.consumerfed.org

A membership organization that advocates for consumers. The website also has educational information for consumers and all of the reports on different topics written by CFA staff.

Consumers Union: www.consumersunion.org

Consumers Union, publisher of *Consumer Reports*, is an independent, nonprofit testing and information organization serving consumers. The website includes information on a wide range of consumer topics.

National Association of Consumer Advocates: www.naca.net

Provides a listing of consumer attorney members throughout the country, divided by practice area. Also includes updated information on hot consumer topics and other events.

National Association of Consumer Bankruptcy Attorneys: www.nacba.org

Contains general information about consumer bankruptcy issues as well as referrals to bankruptcy attorneys nationwide.

National Consumer Law Center: www.consumerlaw.org

Updated to include information on key developments in consumer law, NCLC comments to regulatory and legislative proposals, and investigative reports on a variety of consumer credit topics. Also includes information on how to order NCLC publications, including books, periodicals and consumer education materials.

National Community Reinvestment Coalition: www.ncrc.org

The collective voice for its member organizations to Congress, bank regulatory agencies, the Executive branches of the federal government and the national press.

Penn State Dickinson School of Law Bankruptcy Pro Bono Directory: www.dsl.psu.edu

The "publications" section of this website contains a directory of national bankruptcy pro bono programs sorted by state.

Other

National Rural Housing Coalition: www.nrhcweb.org

Neighborhood Reinvestment Corporation: www.nw.org/network/home.asp

Fairbanks Settlement Information: www.consumerlaw.org/action_agenda/cocounseling/examples_litigation.shtml#fairbanks

Minnesota Mortgage Foreclosure Prevention Association: www.mmfpa.org

Sample Foreclosure Prevention Counseling Forms

Form 1: Foreclosure Prevention Intake Form

This form is designed to be filled in by a counselor based on information supplied by the homeowner. The form provides a complete overview of a homeowner's finances in order to help a counselor determine which foreclosure prevention strategies are possible. The form is also available on the CD-Rom accompanying this handbook.

Form 2: Foreclosure Prevention Counseling Checklist

The purpose of this case-tracking checklist for default and delinquency counseling is to keep track of deadlines and actions necessary to achieve a successful mortgage loan workout. This form is also available on the CD-Rom accompanying this handbook.

Form 3: Sample Authorization to Release Information

In order to present a client's full range of foreclosure prevention options, a counselor generally must obtain information about the amount of money the loan servicer claims due. Due to valid privacy concerns for borrowers, very few servicers will release information to a counselor without written authorization from the borrower. This appendix contains a sample client authorization form. Generally, a form of this type is sent by facsimile to the loan servicer with Form 4, below, requesting necessary information. Both forms are found on the CD-Rom accompanying this handbook.

Form 4: Sample Request for Information from Loan Servicer

This sample form is useful for obtaining necessary information from a loan servicer about the status of a client's loan. The information provided on this form helps determine the amounts that the servicer believes are needed to cure or pay-off the loan. In some cases, obtaining this information will crystallize a dispute the borrower may have concerning the amount due on the loan. This form is also available on the CD-Rom accompanying this handbook.

Form 5: Sample Qualified Written Request Under RESPA

This is a sample "qualified written request" for information under the Real Estate Settlement Procedures Act (RESPA). A section of RESPA, 12 U.S.C. § 2605, provides a procedure and a remedy to obtain information from a loan servicer that fails to provide it under a more informal request. This sample is also found on the CD-Rom accompanying this handbook.

Form 6: Homeowner's Checklist for Avoiding Foreclosure

This is a checklist for homeowners in financial distress. It provides general suggestions and ideas on how to prepare for and work through tough times. This is also available on the CD-Rom accompanying this handbook.

You may not be having financial trouble now, but many people do have money problems at some point in their lives. The best way to avoid foreclosure is to make your mortgage the first bill that you pay each month. However, that is not always possible. The following pages provide general suggestions and ideas as to how you can prepare for and work through tough times. **NOTE:** This checklist is not comprehensive and is not intended to provide legal advice. If you need legal advice, you should speak with a lawyer.

Appx. A ■ SAMPLE FORECLOSURE PREVENTION COUNSELING FORMS **213**

A

Appx.

FORM 1: FORECLOSURE PREVENTION INTAKE FORM

I. CLIENT INFORMATION

Date: _____

Name(s) _____

Address _____

Home Phone _____

Work Phone _____

Best Times to Reach _____

Marital Status _____

Spouse (if any) _____

Children (names and ages) _____

Others in Household: _____

II. INFORMATION ABOUT HOME BEING FORECLOSED

Address of Property (if different from above) _____

Names of all Co-owners w/ Address (if different) _____

Year Purchased _____

Original Purchase Price _____

Estimate of Current Value _____

Number of Rooms _____

Owner Occupant?
    At purchase?   Yes ___   No ___
    Now?   Yes ___   No ___

Multi-Family Home?   Yes ___   No ___
    Name of tenants   _____
    Rent received   _____

Condition   Exc ___   Good ___   Fair ___   Poor ___

Major repairs needed

Describe: _____

_____

_____

Number of Mortgages _____

Other Liens _____

Notes:

III. MORTGAGE

Please note: some information about the mortgage may be obtained after a review of the client's records.

Type of Mortgage Purchase Money ___
        Refinance ___
        Home Equity Loan ___
        Debt Consolidation ___
        Other ___

Year of Mortgage _____

Original Amount _____

Has client brought original loan papers Yes ___ No ___

Current Lender or Servicer _____

Address of Current Lender or Servicer _____
  Phone: _____
  Fax: _____
  Contact Person _____

Loan Account Number _____

Investor/Insurer FHA Insured ___
      VA ___
      RHS ___
      Fannie Mae ___
      Freddie Mac ___
      PMI _____
      Other _____

Term of mortgage (in months) _____

Interest Rate _____

Principal and Interest Payment (monthly) _____

Tax and Insurance Payment (monthly) _____

Total Monthly Payment _____

Months Behind _____

Total Arrears Including Costs _____

Current Principal Balance _____

Payoff Amount _____

Is Client in Default? Yes ___   No ___

Status/Amount of Monthly Payment

Reason for Default

Client's Statement of Objectives and Plan

Appx. A ▪ SAMPLE FORECLOSURE PREVENTION COUNSELING FORMS **215**

Appx. A

Other Mortgages and Liens   Yes ___   No ___
    Describe

Notes:

IMPORTANT NOTE: If there are other mortgages, obtain information for each using the questions on the form above.

IV. HOUSEHOLD FINANCIAL INFORMATION

INCOME BUDGET FOR HOUSEHOLD

SOURCE OF INCOME	LAST MO. ACTUAL	THIS MO. EXPECTED	THIS MO. ACTUAL	ADJUSTED MONTHLY
Employment	$	$	$	$
Overtime				
Child Support/Alimony				
Pension				
Interest				
Public Benefits				
Dividends				
Trust Payments				
Royalties				
Rents Received				
Other (List)				
TOTAL (MONTHLY)	$	$	$	$

NOTES/ANTICIPATED CHANGES:

EXPENSE BUDGET FOR HOUSEHOLD

TYPE OF EXPENSE	LAST MO. ACTUAL	THIS MO. EXPECTED	THIS MO. ACTUAL	ADJUSTED MONTHLY
Payroll Deductions	$	$	$	$
Income Tax Withheld				
Social Security				
FICA				
Wage Garnishments				
Credit Union				
Other				
Home Related Expenses				
Mortgage or Rent				
Second Mortgage				
Third Mortgage				
Real Estate Taxes				
Insurance				
Condo Fees & Assessments				
Mobile Home Lot Rent				
Home Maintenance/Upkeep				
Utilities				
Gas				
Electric				
Oil				
Water/Sewer				
Telephone:				
Land Line				
Cell				
Cable TV				
Internet				
Other				
Food				
Eating Out				
Groceries				
Clothing				
Laundry and Cleaning				
Medical				
Current Needs				
Prescriptions				

Appx. A ■ SAMPLE FORECLOSURE PREVENTION COUNSELING FORMS **217**

Appx. A

TYPE OF EXPENSE	LAST MO. ACTUAL	THIS MO. EXPECTED	THIS MO. ACTUAL	ADJUSTED MONTHLY
Medical (cont'd.)				
Dental				
Insurance Co-Payments or Premiums				
Other				
Transportation				
Auto Payments				
Car Insurance				
Gas and Maintenance				
Public Transportation				
Life Insurance				
Alimony or Support Paid				
School Expenses				
Student Loan Payments				
Entertainment				
Newspapers/Magazines				
Charity/Church				
Pet Expenses				
Amounts Owed on Debts				
Credit Card _____				
Credit Card _____				
Credit Card _____				
Medical Bill _____				
Medical Bill _____				
Other Back Bills (List)				
Cosigned Debts				
Business Debts (List)				
Other Expenses (List)				
Miscellaneous				
TOTAL				

Other Important Debt Issues:

Wage Garnishments	Yes___	No___
Pending Court Cases	Yes___	No___
Pending Utility Shut-offs	Yes___	No___
Car Loan Defaults or Repossessions Tax Debts	Yes___	No___
Student Loan Debts	Yes___	No___

Other:

Notes/Anticipated Changes:

Describe Assets and Other Resources:

Savings	Yes___	No___	Amount $_____
Court Cases Pending Against Others	Yes___	No___	Value $_____
Anticipated Tax Refunds	Yes___	No___	Amount $_____
Assets Which Can Be Sold	Yes___	No___	Value $_____
Pension or Retirement Funds	Yes___	No___	Value $_____

Other Assets and Notes:

INCOME AND EXPENSE TOTALS

	Last Mo. Actual	This Mo. Expected	This Mo. Actual	Adjusted Expected
A. Total Projected Monthly Income				
B. Total Projected Monthly Expenses				
Excess Income or Shortfall (A minus B)				

Notes:

Appx. A ■ SAMPLE FORECLOSURE PREVENTION COUNSELING FORMS **219**

Appx. A

V. OTHER INFORMATION

1. Have client(s) made an effort to arrange a workout on their own? What result?

2. Has the client filed bankruptcy? If so when? Current status of case if still pending? If bankruptcy is over, what result?

3. Other issues which came up during interview.

4. Questions and open issues that must be resolved.

FORM 2: FORECLOSURE PREVENTION COUNSELING CHECKLIST

Client(s)Name _____

Counselor _____

	TASK DATE	**COMMENTS**
File Opened		
Initial Interview		
Foreclosure Status Sale Date (if scheduled) Other Deadlines Pending		
Release Form Signed		
Request Info. from Servicer		
Receive Info. from Servicer		
Budget Complete		
Pay Stubs Received		
Supporting Document Rcvd.		
Hardship Letter		
Options Counseling Complete		
Workout Package Comp.		
Workout Package Mailed		
Init. Resp. from Servicer		
Final Response		___ Approved ___ Denied
Workout Papers Signed		
Case Closed		

Appx. A ■ SAMPLE FORECLOSURE PREVENTION COUNSELING FORMS   **221**

Appx. A

FORM 3: SAMPLE AUTHORIZATION TO RELEASE INFORMATION

TO: Handout Mortgage Co
           [Address]
           Attention: Loss Mitigation Department

RE: Account No: 1234567
           Borrowers: Sam and Sally Consumer
           Prop. Address: [Address]

AUTHORIZATION TO RELEASE INFORMATION

Dear Sir or Madam:

We are working with the Neighborhood House Counseling Service (a HUD certified counseling agency) on a plan to resolve our mortgage delinquency. We hereby authorize you to release any and all information concerning our account to the Neighborhood House Counseling Service at their request.

We further authorize you to discuss our case with Barry Booth or Beverly Bonder. They are working to help us address our financial problems and to propose a loss mitigation plan which is within your guidelines.

At present, we request that you fill out the request for loan information which accompanies this letter. Please return it to Beverly Bonder by fax (555-345-8768) no later than Friday, February 28, 2006. You may release additional information to the Neighborhood House Counseling Service in the future without further authorization.

Thank you taking the time to deal with this request.

Very truly yours,

Sam and Sally Consumer
Phone: [Phone Number]

FORM 4: SAMPLE REQUEST FOR INFORMATION FROM LOAN SERVICER

Borrower(s) _____ Loan #: _____

Address _____

Pursuant to the attached authorization by the borrower, please supply the following information about the above referenced account. The information will be used to help the borrower propose a loss mitigation plan, if possible.

Mortgage Investor: _____

Investor Loan #: _____

Mortgage Insurance Company: _____

Loan Payment Info:

Current Interest Rate: _____ _____%

Monthly Principal & Interest Payment: _____ _____

Monthly Escrow Payment: _____ _____

Total Monthly Mortgage Payment: _____ _____

Amount of Arrears:

Due for (Earliest unpaid installment): _____ _____

Late Charges Due: _____ _____

Foreclosure Fees & Costs Due: (itemize all charges) ____ _____

Other Unpaid Charges: _____ _____

Balance in Suspense Account: _____ _____

TOTAL ARREARS (as of _____) _____ $_____

Total Balance Due on Loan:

Unpaid Principal Balance: _____ _____

Past Due Interest: _____ _____

Unpaid Escrow: _____ _____

TOTAL AMOUNT DUE ON LOAN (PAY-OFF) (as of _____) $_____

Per Diem Interest: _____ _____

Date of Most Recent BPO/Appraisal: _____   Value: _____

Other Comments:

FORECLOSURE STATUS: _____

SALE DATE (IF SCHEDULED): _____

Appx. A ■ SAMPLE FORECLOSURE PREVENTION COUNSELING FORMS **223**

Appx. A

FORM 5: SAMPLE QUALIFIED WRITTEN REQUEST UNDER RESPA

Joe & Sally Consumer

[Address]

January 1, 2006

VIA CERTIFIED MAIL
USA Federal Bank, FSB
[Address]

Attn: Mortgage Loan Accounting Department

Re: Loan # 99999999
Joe and Sally Consumer
[Address]

Dear Sir or Madam:

USA Federal Bank, FSB is the servicer of our mortgage loan at the above address. We dispute the amount that is owed according to the Monthly Billing Statement and request that you send us information about the fees, costs and escrow accounting on our loan. This is a "qualified written request" pursuant to the Real Estate Settlement and Procedures Act (section 2605(e)).

Specifically, we are requesting an itemization of the following:

1. A complete payment history, including but not limited to the dates and amounts of all the payments we have made on the loan to date;
2. A breakdown of the amount of claimed arrears or delinquencies, including an itemization of all fees charged to the account;
3. An explanation of how the amount due on the Monthly Billing Statement ($1,000) was calculated and a explanation of why this amount was increased to $2,000 on August 1, 2005;
4. The payment dates, purpose of payment and recipient of any and all foreclosure fees and costs that have been charged to our account;
5. The payment dates, purpose of payment and recipient of all escrow items charged to our account since [date USA Federal Bank took over the servicing];
6. A breakdown of the current escrow charge showing how it is calculated and the reasons for any increase within the last 24 months; and
7. A copy of any annual escrow statements and notices of a shortage, deficiency or surplus, sent to us within the last three (3) years.

Thank you for taking the time to acknowledge and answer this request as required by the Real Estate Settlement and Procedures Act (section 2605(e)).

Very truly yours,

Joe & Sally Consumer

FORM 6: HOMEOWNER'S CHECKLIST FOR AVOIDING FORECLOSURE

Before Trouble Starts

Start a file, in a safe place, for records relating to your home
- Purchase and sale agreement
- Mortgage application
- Closing documents
- Property tax bills
- Property insurance information
- Letters you receive from **and** copies of letters you mail to the bank

Use checks or money orders to pay bills
- Do not send cash
- Do not use credit cards
- Keep a record of all payments (date paid and check number)
- Correct errors quickly

Pay high priority bills first
- Food
- Mortgage
- Utilities (heat, hot water, electricity, gas)
- Do not pay credit cards or other unsecured debts **before** the mortgage

When Things Start to Feel Tight

Where is the money going?
- Create a budget that shows your current income and expenses
- Review every item on your budget
- Prepare a revised, realistic budget that you can live with until your circumstances improve

Increase your income
- Collect federal and state benefits if you are eligible
- Claim the earned income tax credit if you are eligible
- Stop all voluntary deductions being taken out of your paycheck
- Consider selling unnecessary property to raise money

Reduce your expenses
- Review every expense for potential savings—reduce or eliminate unnecessary expenses
- Pay only for the type of phone service you need
- Cancel cable television service temporarily
- Identify ways to conserve on energy and other utilities
- Participate in a home weatherization program
- Review your homeowner's and auto insurance policies and shop around
- Claim the owner-occupant property tax exemption and others for which you are eligible

Other Considerations
- Contact your mortgage servicer at the first sign of trouble
- Ask your utility company for budget billing so you can pay the same amount each month
- If you are behind on your utility bills, start an affordable repayment plan

Appx. A ■ SAMPLE FORECLOSURE PREVENTION COUNSELING FORMS   **225**

A
Appx.

After Falling Behind

Identify the problem
- What caused your current situation (job loss, illness, divorce, decreased income)
- How long do you expect your difficulty to last
- What specific type of help do you need
- How much can you afford to pay toward your mortgage

Communicate
- Speak with your bank's delinquent loan or loss mitigation specialist
- Explain your situation
- Ask for a mortgage workout package
- Keep a phone log that shows the date and time of your call, who you spoke to, the person's phone number, and what was said
- Follow up your phone call with a letter and keep a copy for yourself
- Send all letters by certified mail and keep the receipt

Pay what you can and save the rest
- Send to the bank as much of the mortgage payment as possible
- If the bank returns your payment, save the money and **do not spend it** on other bills

Know your options
There are many ways the bank can help you if you fall behind on your mortgage. Which one you choose/need and what the bank allows will depend on your individual situation.

Reinstatement: You give the bank all of the back payments you owe and start making your regular monthly payment. With a *partial reinstatement* you pay at least one-half of the back-payments first and agree to a repayment plan for the rest of what you owe.

Repayment Plan: You make the regular mortgage payment plus an additional amount toward the back-payments until you are caught up (usually no longer than 12 months). If the bank sets up a repayment plan for you, make sure it is reasonable. Do not agree to a plan that will not work for you.

Forbearance: The bank agrees that for a limited period of time it will accept a lower monthly payment or no monthly payment. At the end of the forbearance agreement you must bring the account current.

Modification: The bank agrees to change one or more terms of the mortgage. Possible changes include: reducing the interest rate; extending the term of the mortgage; and adding the arrears to the unpaid principal balance of your loan.

Short Sale: The bank may let you sell the home even if you owe more than the property is worth and agree to accept the lesser amount as payment in full. You must have a buyer and a signed purchase and sale agreement. Anyone else who has a lien on the property and the private mortgage insurer, if there is one, must also agree to the short sale.

Refinance: You take out a new mortgage to pay off the old mortgage. Sometimes it makes sense to refinance. You should contact a legitimate lender and proceed carefully. Beware of large fees and high interest rates.

Deed in Lieu: You cannot afford to keep the home and you give the house back to the bank. **Do not** ask for a deed in lieu when you have equity in the property or when a short sale is possible. The bank will not accept a deed in lieu if there are other mortgages or liens on the property.

Documentation for a workout (requirements may vary from bank to bank)
- Signed and dated letter that **briefly** explains what happened
- Documentation of your hardship (doctor's letters, etc.)
- One month worth of pay stubs or other proof of income
- Two most recent signed federal tax returns and W2s (3 years if self-employed)
- An accurate budget showing all of your monthly income and expenses
- A list of your assets (cars, bank accounts, etc.)
- A list of your liabilities (mortgages, loans, liens, other outstanding debts)
- This package must be complete before the bank will review it
- Keep copies for your file

Other Things to Know

Talk to a lawyer or counselor experienced in *default and delinquency counseling*
- If you cannot reach a solution with your bank
- If you disagree with the amount the bank says you owe
- If you wish to consider filing bankruptcy

Foreclosures move very quickly
- Keep track of deadlines
- Do not wait until the last minute to get help
- Your rights will be cut off once the foreclosure sale takes place

Foreclosures are public
- Foreclosure notices appear in newspapers and court records
- Some people may try to take advantage of you by offering a "quick fix"
- Carefully review offers to refinance or consolidate your credit card debts with your mortgage as this may make matters worse
- Avoid "deals" with high interest rates and large fees
- Do not agree to sell your home to someone who claims they will lease it back to you
- Talk to a lawyer or counselor **before you sign anything**

Where to go for help
- Your local non-profit housing organization
- Your mortgage company
- The U.S. Department of Housing and Urban Development (HUD)

Resource List

Name and phone number of housing agency

(To locate a HUD certified counseling agency near you, search **www.hudhcc.org/agencies.html.** Or try the main HUD site at **www.hud.gov.** Or call HUD at 1-800-569-4287)

Contact Name and phone number at mortgage lender

The book *NCLC Guide to Surviving Debt* is available from National Consumer Law Center, 77 Summer Street, 10th Floor, Boston, MA 02110 or 617-542-9595 for the publications department, order on-line at www.consumerlaw.org, or ask at your local bookstore. This book covers practical strategies for managing debt problems, preventing foreclosures, and other consumer credit issues. Additional useful information may be found at www.consumerlaw.org.

Consumer Information About Taking on a New Credit Card

This handout is also available on the CD-Rom accompanying this handbook.

EIGHT THINGS TO THINK ABOUT BEFORE YOU TAKE A NEW CARD

More than five billion credit card offers are mailed to consumers each year. Most of us get several offers for new credit cards every week. In addition, credit cards are advertised everywhere. We see advertisements on television, the Internet, at sporting events, in restaurants, and increasingly on college campuses and even in high schools.

In the past, you rarely got new credit card offers if you had credit problems. Lenders reviewed credit reports and chose not to offer credit to consumers they considered bad risks. More recently, lenders buy huge mailing lists and offer credit to everyone on the list without an individual evaluation of their credit history. They offer credit cards to anyone with an adequate credit score, whether or not you can afford the credit or are already over-extended.

Credit card offers can be very enticing. Nearly every offer promises some special benefit with a new card. In some cases, the offer is for a low rate. In others, no annual fee is promised. Still others advertise free goods or services, low minimum payments, frequent flyer miles, cash back, special member privileges, and contributions to schools or favorite charities. These offers, however, never discuss the downside of a new card or the potential risks.

1. **Avoid accepting too many offers.** There is rarely a good reason to carry more than one or two credit cards. You should be very selective about choosing cards that are best for you. Having too much credit can lead to bad decisions and unmanageable debts. Opening too many new credit card accounts can also lower your credit score.

2. **Beware of subprime credit cards.** Instead of turning you down because of bad credit, some lenders will offer you subprime credit cards. These cards generally come with very high interest rates, other expensive fees, and low credit limits. You may also be charged for unnecessary products such as "credit protection." Some lenders will actually issue cards with low credit limits, and then add so many fees that you cannot charge any purchases to the card because you will already be maxed out when you receive it! Other lenders use subprime credit cards as a trick to revive old debts from other credit card companies. They buy up your old debts, and then offer you a new credit card. When the account is opened, the new lender slaps the old debt on the new credit card account.

3. **Watch out for bait-and-switch offers.** Some credit card lenders will send you an offer advertising an attractive, low-interest credit card with a high limit, but include—in the fine print—the statement that the lender can substitute a less attractive, more expensive card if you do not qualify. The substituted card often has a higher interest rate, more expensive fees, and/or a lower credit limit.

4. **Look carefully at the interest rate.** You should always know the interest rate on your cards and should try to keep the rate as low as possible. It is often hard to do this, because the terms are so confusing and sometimes misleading. Credit card lenders usually have several interest rates for a credit card. They also constantly change their rates. Some important terms to understand are:

   ■ *APR.* This is the interest rate expressed as an annual figure. Most cards have different APRs for purchases versus cash advances versus balance transfers and other types of transactions.

   ■ *Variable rates.* Most credit cards use variable rates, which change with the rise or fall of a common index rate (an example of a variable rate might be "U.S. Prime Rate plus 5%"). If your rate is variable, you need to understand when and how it may change. Variable interest rates can be very confusing. And even "fixed" rates can be variable—your credit card lender usually has the right to change your interest rate with just 15-days notice.

   ■ *"Teaser" rates.* A teaser rate is an artificially low initial rate that lasts only for a limited time, such as six months or less. After that, the rate automatically goes up. If you build up a balance while a teaser rate is in effect, you will end up repaying the debt at a much higher permanent rate.

   ■ *Penalty rates.* Many credit card contracts, including those that advertise low permanent rates, provide in the small print that your interest rate increases if you make even a single late payment. Some lenders will increase your rate even if you are never late on their credit card, but are late with a payment to any other creditor or if your credit score drops too low. The penalty rate may be on top of late charges or other fees. You should review your contract to see if such terms apply. If you are having financial problems, late charges and penalty interest rates will put you further into debt. Even if you are not having financial problems, these terms are important if you make a late payment by accident.

5. **Fees, fees, fees.** Other terms of credit may be just as important as interest rates. Credit card companies now impose a number of different fees—late payment fees, fees for exceeding a credit limit, annual fees, membership fees, cash advance fees, balance transfer fees, even fees for buying lottery tickets with a card—and keep raising these fees every year. These fees significantly increase the cost of a credit card, so that a card that appears cheaper with a low APR could end up being much more expensive.

6. **Look for the grace period.** Most credit cards offer a "grace period" or "free ride period," the amount of time in which you can pay off purchases without incurring finance charges (cash advances usually do not have a grace period). Without a grace period, finance charges begin accruing immediately, and a low rate may actually be higher than it looks. If you intend to pay off the balance in full each month, the terms of the grace period are especially important. Many credit cards have reduced their grace period. They have also reduced the time between when they send a bill

Appx. B ■ CONSUMER INFORMATION ABOUT TAKING ON A NEW CREDIT CARD   **229**

Appx. B

and when the payment is due, increasing the risk that you will go past the grace period and pay both interest charges and a late fee.

7. **Always read both the disclosures and the credit contract.** You will find disclosures about the terms of a credit card offer in a box, usually on the reverse side of or accompanying the credit card application. Review these carefully. If the disclosure box is on the reverse side of the application, make a copy before you return it to the lender. However, the law does not require that all relevant information be disclosed in this box. For this reason, you must also read your credit contract, which comes with the card. If you do not understand these terms, call the lender for an explanation.

8. **If you do take a credit card and discover terms you do not like: Cancel!** You can always cancel any credit card at any time. Although you will be responsible for any balance due at the time of cancellation, you should not keep using a card after you discover that its terms are unfavorable. You should also cancel the card if the lender changes the terms of your agreement and you do not like the new terms. Otherwise, you will be stuck with the new (and probably unfavorable) terms.

Avoiding Credit Card Problems

Credit card debts can spiral out of control. Here are some ways to protect yourself from getting in over your head.

Do not use credit cards to finance an unaffordable lifestyle. If you are constantly using your card without the ability to pay the resulting bill in full each month, consider whether you are using your cards to make an unreasonable budget plan work. No one can live forever by borrowing without a plan to pay off the resulting debts.

If you get into financial trouble, do not make it worse by using credit cards to make ends meet. Finance charges and other fees will add to your debt burden. However, using a credit card in a period of financial difficulty is preferable to taking out a home equity loan and putting your home on the line.

Do not get hooked on minimum payments. If you pay only the minimum, chances are that you will not be paying down your debt, or that you will be paying it off very slowly. For example, a $1,000 balance with an 18% annual percentage rate will take nearly 20 years to pay off if you make a minimum payment of 2% of the monthly balance. Also, lenders reserve the right to increase the minimum payment at their option. This means that you can budget for a $50 minimum payment only to find out that the new minimum payment of $100 applies.

Do not run up the balance in reliance on a temporary "teaser" interest rate. Money borrowed during a temporary rate period of 6%, is likely to be paid back at a much higher permanent rate of 15% percent or more.

If you can afford to do so consistently with your budget plan, make your credit card payments on time. Avoid late payment charges and penalty rates if you can do so without endangering your ability to keep up with higher priority debts. Bad problems get worse fast when you have a new higher interest rate and late charge to pay during a time of financial difficulty. Many lenders will waive a late payment charge or default rates of interest one time only. It is worth calling to ask for a waiver if you make a late payment accidentally or with a good excuse.

Avoid the special services, programs, and goods which credit card lenders offer to bill to their cards. Most of the special services such as credit card fraud protection plans, credit record protection, travel clubs, life insurance, and other similar offers are a bad deal or are overpriced.

Beware of unsolicited increases by a credit card lender to your credit card limit. Some lenders increase your credit limit even when you have not asked for more credit. Do not assume that this means that the lender thinks you can afford more credit. Lenders generally increase the limit for consumers that they think will carry a bigger balance and pay more interest.

Avoid cashed check loans. Another credit offer to avoid takes the form of a check mailed to your home, usually by your credit card lender. When you cash the check, you not only accept high interest rate credit, but also get stuck with a big balance on a new account right from the start.

Consumer Information on the Earned Income Tax Credit

The Earned Income Credit: A Powerful Benefit for People Who Work

What is the Earned Income Credit?

The EIC is a special tax benefit for working people who earn low or moderate incomes. It has several important purposes: to reduce the tax burden on these workers, to supplement wages, and to provide a work incentive.

Workers who qualify for the EIC and file a federal tax return can get back some or all of the federal income tax that was taken out of their pay during the year. They may also get extra cash back from the IRS. Even workers whose earnings are too small to owe income tax can get the EIC. What's more, the EIC offsets any additional taxes workers may owe, such as payroll taxes.

Who can get the EIC and how much is it worth?

Single or married people who worked full-time or part-time at some point in 2006 can qualify for the EIC, depending on their income.

• Workers who were raising one child in their home and had income of less than $32,001 (or $34,001 for married workers) in 2006 can get an EIC of up to **$2,747**.

• Workers who were raising more than one child in their home and had income of less than $36,348 (or $38,348 for married workers) in 2006 can get an EIC of up to **$4,536**.

• Workers who were not raising children in their home, were between ages 25 and 64 on December 31, 2006, and had income below $12,120 (or $14,120 for married workers) can get an EIC up to **$412**.

Workers with *investment income* exceeding $2,800 in 2006 may not claim the EIC.

How does the EIC work?

• **Eligible workers can pay less in taxes and get a check from the IRS.** Mr. and Mrs. Johnson have two children, ages 20 and 21, in college. They earned $29,000 in 2006 and owe the IRS $550 in income tax, none of which was

---

Who is a "Qualifying Child" for the EIC?

• Sons, daughters, stepchildren, grandchildren and adopted children
• Brothers, sisters, stepbrothers, or stepsisters — as well as descendants of such relatives
• Foster children who are placed with the worker by an authorized government or private placement agency

"Qualifying children" must live with the worker for more than half of the year. They must be under age 19, or under age 24 if they are full-time students. Children of any age who have total and permanent disabilities also may be qualifying children. Valid Social Security numbers are required for qualifying children born before December 31, 2006.

Reprinted with permission from The Center on Budget and Policy Priorities, 820 First Street, NE, Suite 510, Washington, DC 20002, 202-408-1080, Fax 202-408-1056, center@center.cbpp.org, www.cbpp.org.

withheld from their pay during the year. Their income makes them eligible for an EIC of $1,936. So, the EIC eliminates their $550 income tax — now they don't owe IRS anything — and gives them a refund of $1,386.

- **Eligible workers can get a check from the IRS.** Marlene Rogers is raising two children and earned $10,000 in 2006. Her Social Security and Medicare payroll tax was $765. She is eligible for an EIC of $4,000, which pays her back her payroll tax and gives her an EIC refund of $3,235.

- **Eligible workers who aren't raising children can get a check.** Joe Smith has no children. He worked part-time in 2006 and earned $5,300. Because of his low earnings he had no income tax taken out of his paycheck and owes nothing to the IRS. His earnings entitle him to an EIC check for $405, offsetting most of the payroll taxes that were withheld from his pay.

How do you get the EIC?

- Workers raising a "qualifying child" in their home in 2006 must file either Form 1040 or 1040A and *must* fill out and attach Schedule EIC. Workers with children cannot get the EIC if they file Form 1040EZ or do not attach Schedule EIC. Married workers must file a joint return to get the EIC.

- Workers who were not raising a "qualifying child" in their home in 2006 can file any tax form — including the 1040EZ. These workers write "EIC" (or the dollar amount of their credit) on the Earned Income Credit line on the tax form. They do **not** file Schedule EIC.

- A correct name and Social Security number must be provided for every person listed on the tax return and Schedule EIC. If this information is incorrect or missing, the IRS will delay the refund.

- Workers don't have to calculate their own EIC; if they choose, the IRS will do it for them!

Workers raising children can get the EIC in their paychecks! Workers who are raising children can get part of their EIC in their paychecks throughout the year and part in a check from the IRS after they file their tax return. This is called the Advance EIC payment option. *For more information, see "Get the EIC in Your Paychecks! The Advance EIC" on p. 9 of this booklet.*

Workers can get FREE help filing their tax forms

Many families that apply for the EIC pay someone to complete their tax forms. This can often cost between $55 and $100, or can be more. Getting a "quick tax refund" that comes back in a few days costs even more. Paying for tax preparation takes away from the value of the EIC. But low-income workers can get free help with tax preparation through a program called VITA (Volunteer Income Tax Assistance). *For more information, see the booklet in this kit, "Free Tax Help and Asset Development."*

Does the EIC affect eligibility for other public benefits?

The EIC does not count as income in determining eligibility for benefits like cash assistance ("welfare"), Medicaid, food stamps, SSI or public housing. Some benefit programs count the EIC as a resource under certain circumstances. *For more information, see "Need Answers? Q&A on the EIC and CTC," on p. 13 of this booklet.*

Can immigrant workers get the EIC?

Many immigrants who are legally authorized to work can qualify for the EIC, as long as they meet the other eligibility requirements.

The materials in this kit should answer many questions about the EIC. *For more information, call the IRS at 1-800-TAX-1040.*

The Child Tax Credit: An Extra Tax Break for Working Families!

What is the Child Tax Credit?

The Child Tax Credit (CTC) is a federal tax credit worth up to $1,000 in 2006 for each qualifying child under age 17 claimed on the worker's tax return. While the CTC has been in effect since 1998, Congress changed the credit in 2001 to make it available to millions more low- and moderate-income working families and provided many families a larger CTC than they could have received in the past. This "Additional CTC" is refundable, meaning some families can get the credit even if they owe no income tax. (This kit refers to the "Additional CTC" as the "CTC refund.") Eligible families can receive the CTC refund in a check from the IRS.

Who Can Claim the Child Tax Credit Refund?

To be eligible for the CTC refund, a single or married worker must:

• have a qualifying child under age 17;
• have taxable earned income above $11,300; and

• have either a Social Security number (SSN) or an Individual Taxpayer Identification Number (ITIN). ITINs are issued by the IRS to individuals who are unable to obtain a Social Security number. *Immigrant workers with either type of number may be able to claim the CTC refund. For more information on ITINs, see p. 28 in the booklet in this kit, "Free Tax Help and Asset Development."*

Can a working family get both the Child Tax Credit refund and the Earned Income Credit?

Yes!! Most low-wage working families that qualify for the CTC refund will also be eligible for the EIC. For many families that qualify for both credits, the EIC will be larger, but the CTC still will provide a significant income boost. Despite the overlap in eligible families, there are important differences in the eligibility rules for the two credits and in the procedures for claiming them. *For a comparison of the two sets of rules, see the table on the inside back cover of this booklet.*

Who is a "Qualifying Child" for the CTC?

• Sons, daughters, stepchildren, grandchildren and adopted children
• Brothers, sisters, stepbrothers, or stepsisters — as well as descendants of such relatives
• Foster children who are placed with the worker by an authorized government or private placement agency

A child claimed for the CTC must be under age 17 at the end of 2006. The child must live with the worker for more than half of the year in the U.S. and must be either a citizen or a resident alien. The child must have either a valid Social Security number or an Individual Taxpayer Identification Number (ITIN).

Note:

- a child may not be claimed for the CTC if the child provides over one-half of his or her own support.
- a non-custodial parent who is allowed to claim his or her child as a dependent by a divorce or separation agreement is the parent entitled to claim the child for the CTC. *For more information, see p. 18 in this booklet.*

How do families get the Child Tax Credit refund?

1. File a federal income tax return — Form 1040 or 1040A, but not 1040EZ. The instructions and worksheet included in the IRS tax form packet will help tax filers figure their income tax and calculate their maximum possible CTC. The CTC is first used to reduce or eliminate any income tax a tax filer owes. If any of the CTC is remaining after the income tax has been eliminated (i.e. if the family's income tax was less than its maximum CTC), the tax filer moves on to the next step in the process — Form 8812.

2. File Form 8812. Form 8812, "Additional Child Tax Credit," is used to find out if the family qualifies for a CTC refund and, if so, the amount of the refund. This form must be attached to the tax return for a family to receive the CTC refund.

How does the CTC work?

- Eligible families can get up to $1,000 for each qualifying child under age 17 claimed on their tax return. (For example, a parent with two such children can claim a CTC of up to $2,000 — 2 children x $1,000.) The CTC first is used to reduce or eliminate a family's income tax liability. Families may be able to get all or part of any remaining CTC as a refund.

- The CTC refund is based on the amount by which the earned income of a worker (and spouse, if married) exceeds $11,300. Families with any CTC remaining after their income tax liability has been eliminated may receive a refund in the lesser of two amounts: (1) the amount of the family's CTC that remains, or (2) 15 percent of the family's earned income over $11,300. (For example, if a family earns $16,000, 15 percent of its income above $11,300 is $705: ($16,000 - $11,300 = $4,700; 15 percent of $4,700 is $705.)

How can a family benefit?

- Maxine is a single parent with a 15-year-old child. She earned $16,000 in 2006 and had $185 in income tax withheld from her pay. Her maximum CTC of $1,000 is first used to eliminate her $185 income tax, leaving $815 of her CTC remaining ($1,000 - $185 = $815). Fifteen percent (15%) of Maxine's earnings over $11,300 is $705. Since the remaining CTC of $815 is more than $705, Maxine is eligible to receive a CTC refund for the lower amount — $705. (She gets back the $185 in income tax she paid, receives an additional CTC refund of $705, and also is eligible for an EIC of $2,557, bringing her total refund to $3,447!)

Does the CTC affect public benefits?

The CTC refund does not count as income in determining eligibility for any federal, state or local program benefits, such as food stamps, SSI, or child care, financed even in part by federal funds. Some benefit programs count the EIC as a resource under certain circumstances. *For more information, see "Need Answers? Q&A on the EIC and CTC," on p. 13 of this booklet.*

Not Living With Children?
You May Qualify for the EIC

Very low-income workers who are not raising children in their home are eligible for a small Earned Income Credit. The credit is available to people who worked full- or part-time in 2006 and:

- were at least age 25 and under age 65 on December 31, 2006;

- had earnings of less than $12,120 (or $14,120 for married workers);

- did not have a "qualifying child" for the EIC in 2006 *(See p. 3 of this booklet)*; and

- were *not* the dependent or qualifying child for the EIC of another taxpayer in 2006.

The credit for workers not raising children is worth up to $412 for tax year 2006 — the average is expected to be about $230. This credit works the same way as the EIC for families: it gives back some or all of the federal taxes taken out of a worker's pay during the year. Even workers whose earnings are too small to have paid federal income tax can get the credit.

Why is the EIC important for workers not raising children?

It provides a financial boost to those who work at very low wages or are only able to find part-time work. This includes many day laborers, migrant workers, temporary employees, people who are homeless and general assistance recipients who worked part of the year.

How do you get this credit?

Eligible workers not raising children get the EIC by filing a federal income tax return. They can use Form 1040, 1040A, or 1040EZ. On the "Earned Income Credit" line they simply fill in the amount of their credit or write "EIC" and the IRS will calculate the amount of the credit for them. Married workers must file a joint return to claim this credit.

What do we know about the workers eligible for this credit?

In tax year 2005, more than 4 million such workers received credits worth over $970 million.

Population statistics tell us about workers likely to qualify for this credit.

- The average annual earnings for these workers are about $6,050. Half (51 percent) of them work in service industries. About 21 percent work full-time, year round.

- Almost 80 percent of these workers have at least a high school diploma.

- The majority of these workers — approximately 60 percent — are non-Hispanic white. About 17 percent are African American and about 15 percent are Latino.

- About 16 percent are married. About 45 percent are single men and 39 percent are single women.

What are the special outreach challenges?

- For some, the EIC may seem too small to make filing a tax return worthwhile.
- Some may fear entering the tax system either because they haven't filed taxes in a long time or because they owe child support.
- Very low-income workers may be skeptical of information about programs from government agencies such as the IRS. Your outreach materials should contain the name and number of a contact organization that is trusted by low-income workers in your community.

For more ideas on reaching workers not raising children likely to be eligible for the EIC, and those who might be able to claim the CTC, see p. 22 in the booklet, "Outreach Strategies," in this kit.

Extra Credit for Some Non-custodial Parents

Lower-income workers whose children do not live with them may also qualify for the Child Tax Credit (CTC): a non-custodial parent who is permitted by a divorce or separation agreement to claim a child as a dependent on his or her tax return and earned more than $11,300 in 2006 may be eligible for a CTC of up to $1,000 per child under age 17. Outreach messages that target this group of parents and highlight the CTC as an extra opportunity are critical. *For more details on the CTC, see the fact sheet "The Child Tax Credit: An Extra Tax Break for Working Families!" on p. 5 of this booklet.*

Sample Loan and Other Documents

This appendix contains:
- A sample mortgage
- A sample promissory note (fixed)
- A sample promissory note (adjustable)
- A sample Change Rate Notice for ARM
- A Sample Annual Escrow Account Statement

SAMPLE MORTGAGE

MORTGAGE

DEFINITIONS
Words used in multiple sections of this document are defined below and other words are defined in Sections 3, 11, 13, 18, 20 and 21. Certain rules regarding the usage of words used in this document are also provided in Section 16.

(A) "Security Instrument" means this document, which is dated _____, _____, together with all Riders to this document.

(B) "Borrower" is _____. Borrower is the mortgagor under this Security Instrument.

(C) "Lender" is _____. Lender is a _____ organized and existing under the laws of _____. Lender's address is _____ _____. Lender is the mortgagee under this Security Instrument.

(D) "Note" means the promissory note signed by Borrower and dated _____, _____. The Note states that Borrower owes Lender _____ Dollars (U.S. $ _____) plus interest. Borrower has promised to pay this debt in regular Periodic Payments and to pay the debt in full not later than _____.

(E) "Property" means the property that is described below under the heading "Transfer of Rights in the Property."

(F) "Loan" means the debt evidenced by the Note, plus interest, any prepayment charges and late charges due under the Note, and all sums due under this Security Instrument, plus interest.

(G) "Riders" means all Riders to this Security Instrument that are executed by Borrower. The following Riders are to be executed by Borrower [check box as applicable]:

☐ Adjustable Rate Rider   ☐ Planned Unit
☐ Condominium Rider   Development Rider
☐ Second Home Rider   ☐ Other(s) [specify]
☐ Balloon Rider   _____
☐ 1–4 Family Rider   ☐ Biweekly Payment Rider

(H) "Applicable Law" means all controlling applicable federal, state and local statutes, regulations, ordinances and administrative rules and orders (that have the effect of law) as well as all applicable final, non-appealable judicial opinions.

(I) "Community Association Dues, Fees, and Assessments" means all dues, fees, assessments and other charges that are imposed on Borrower or the Property by a condominium association, homeowners association or similar organization.

(J) "Electronic Funds Transfer" means any transfer of funds, other than a transaction originated by check, draft, or similar paper instrument, which is initiated through an electronic terminal, telephonic instrument, computer, or magnetic tape so as to order, instruct, or authorize a financial institution to debit or credit an account. Such term includes, but is not limited to, point-of-sale transfers, automated teller machine transactions, transfers initiated by telephone, wire transfers, and automated clearinghouse transfers.

(K) "Escrow Items" means those items that are described in Section 3.

(L) "Miscellaneous Proceeds" means any compensation, settlement, award of damages, or proceeds paid by any third party (other than insurance proceeds paid under the coverages described in Section 5) for: (i) damage to, or destruction of, the Property; (ii) condemnation or other taking of all or any part of the Property; (iii) conveyance in lieu of condemnation; or (iv) misrepresentations of, or omissions as to, the value and/or condition of the Property.

(M) "Mortgage Insurance" means insurance protecting Lender against the nonpayment of, or default on, the Loan.

(N) "Periodic Payment" means the regularly scheduled amount due for (i) principal and interest under the Note, plus (ii) any amounts under Section 3 of this Security Instrument.

(O) "RESPA" means the Real Estate Settlement Procedures Act (12 U.S.C. § 2601 et seq.) and its implementing regulation, Regulation X (24 C.F.R. Part 3500), as they might be amended from time to time, or any additional or successor legislation or regulation that governs the same subject matter. As used in this Security Instrument, "RESPA" refers to all requirements and restrictions that are imposed in regard to a "federally related mortgage loan" even if the Loan does not qualify as a "federally related mortgage loan" under RESPA.

(P) "Successor in Interest of Borrower" means any party that has taken title to the Property, whether or not that party has assumed Borrower's obligations under the Note and/or this Security Instrument.

TRANSFER OF RIGHTS IN THE PROPERTY
This Security Instrument secures to Lender: (i) the repayment of the Loan, and all renewals, extensions and modifications of the Note; and (ii) the performance of Borrower's covenants and agreements under this Security Instrument and the Note. For this purpose, Borrower does hereby mortgage, grant and convey to Lender and Lender's successors and assigns, with power of sale, the following described property located in the _____ [Type of Recording Jurisdiction] of _____ _____ [Name of Recording Jurisdiction] which currently has the address of _____ [Street] _____ [City], Massachusetts _____ [Zip Code] ("Property Address"):

TOGETHER WITH all the improvements now or hereafter erected on the property, and all easements, appurtenances, and fixtures now or hereafter a part of the property. All replacements and additions shall also be covered by this Security Instrument. All of the foregoing is referred to in this Security Instrument as the "Property."

BORROWER COVENANTS that Borrower is lawfully seised of the estate hereby conveyed and has the right to mortgage, grant and convey the Property and that the Property is unencumbered, except for encumbrances of record. Borrower warrants and will defend generally the title to the Property against all claims and demands, subject to any encumbrances of record.

THIS SECURITY INSTRUMENT combines uniform covenants for national use and non-uniform covenants with limited variations by jurisdiction to constitute a uniform security instrument covering real property.

UNIFORM COVENANTS. Borrower and Lender covenant and agree as follows:

1. Payment of Principal, Interest, Escrow Items, Prepayment Charges, and Late Charges. Borrower shall pay when due the principal of, and interest on, the debt evidenced by the Note and any prepayment charges and late charges due under the Note. Borrower shall also pay funds for Escrow Items pursuant to Section 3. Payments due under the Note and this Security Instrument shall be made in U.S. currency. However, if any check or other instrument received by Lender as payment under the Note or this Security Instrument is returned to Lender unpaid, Lender may require that any or all subsequent payments due under the Note and this Security Instrument be made in one or more of the following forms, as selected by Lender: (a) cash; (b) money order; (c) certified check, bank check, treasurer's check or cashier's check, provided any such check is drawn upon an institution whose deposits are insured by a federal agency, instrumentality, or entity; or (d) Electronic Funds Transfer.

Payments are deemed received by Lender when received at the location designated in the Note or at such other location as may be designated by Lender in accordance with the notice provisions in Section 15. Lender may return any payment or partial payment if the payment or partial payments are insufficient to bring the Loan current. Lender may accept any payment or partial payment insufficient to bring the Loan current, without waiver of any rights hereunder or prejudice to its rights to refuse such payment or partial payments in the future, but Lender is not obligated to apply such payments at the time such payments are accepted. If each Periodic Payment is applied as of its scheduled due date, then Lender need not pay interest on unapplied funds. Lender may hold such unapplied funds until Borrower makes payment to bring the Loan current. If Borrower does not do so within a reasonable period of time, Lender shall either apply such funds or return them to Borrower. If not applied earlier, such funds will be applied to the outstanding principal balance under the Note immediately prior to foreclosure. No offset or claim which Borrower might have now or in the future against Lender shall relieve Borrower from making payments due under the Note and this Security Instrument or performing the covenants and agreements secured by this Security Instrument.

2. Application of Payments or Proceeds. Except as otherwise described in this Section 2, all payments accepted and applied by Lender shall be applied in the following order of priority: (a) interest due under the Note; (b) principal due under the Note; (c) amounts due under Section 3. Such payments shall be applied to each Periodic Payment in the order in which it became due. Any remaining amounts shall be applied first to late charges, second to any other amounts due under this Security Instrument, and then to reduce the principal balance of the Note.

If Lender receives a payment from Borrower for a delinquent Periodic Payment which includes a sufficient amount to pay any late charge due, the payment may be applied to the delinquent payment and the late charge. If more than one Periodic Payment is outstanding, Lender may apply any payment received from Borrower to the repayment of the Periodic Payments if, and to the extent that, each payment can be paid in full. To the extent that any excess exists after the payment is applied to the full payment of one or more Periodic Payments, such excess may be applied to any late charges due. Voluntary prepayments shall be applied first to any prepayment charges and then as described in the Note.

Any application of payments, insurance proceeds, or Miscellaneous Proceeds to principal due under the Note shall not extend or postpone the due date, or change the amount, of the Periodic Payments.

3. Funds for Escrow Items. Borrower shall pay to Lender on the day Periodic Payments are due under the Note, until the Note is paid in full, a sum (the "Funds") to provide for payment of amounts due for: (a) taxes and assessments and other items which can attain priority over this Security Instrument as a lien or encumbrance on the Property; (b) leasehold payments or ground rents on the Property, if any; (c) premiums for any and all insurance required by Lender under Section 5; and (d) Mortgage Insurance premiums, if any, or any sums payable by Borrower to Lender in lieu of the payment of Mortgage Insurance premiums in accordance with the provisions of Section 10. These items are called "Escrow Items." At origination or at any time during the term of the Loan, Lender may require that Community Association Dues, Fees, and Assessments, if any, be escrowed by Borrower, and such dues, fees and assessments shall be an Escrow Item. Borrower shall promptly furnish to Lender all notices of amounts to be paid under this Section. Borrower shall pay Lender the Funds for Escrow Items unless Lender waives Borrower's obligation to pay the Funds for any or all Escrow Items. Lender may waive Borrower's obligation to pay to Lender Funds for any or all Escrow Items at any time. Any such waiver may only be in writing. In the event of such waiver, Borrower shall pay directly, when and where payable, the amounts due for any Escrow Items for which payment of Funds has been waived by Lender and, if Lender requires, shall furnish to Lender receipts evidencing such payment within such time period as Lender may require. Borrower's obligation to make such payments and to provide receipts shall for all purposes be deemed to be a covenant and agreement contained in this Security Instrument, as the phrase "covenant and agreement" is used in Section 9. If Borrower is obligated to pay Escrow Items directly, pursuant to a waiver, and Borrower fails to pay the amount due for an Escrow Item, Lender may exercise its rights under Section 9 and pay such amount and Borrower shall then be obligated under Section 9 to repay to Lender any such amount. Lender may revoke the waiver as to any or all Escrow Items at any time by a notice given in accordance with Section 15 and, upon such revocation, Borrower shall pay to Lender all Funds, and in such amounts, that are then required under this Section 3.

Lender may, at any time, collect and hold Funds in an amount (a) sufficient to permit Lender to apply the Funds at the time specified under RESPA, and (b) not to exceed the maximum amount a lender can require under RESPA. Lender shall estimate the amount of Funds due on the basis of current data and reasonable estimates of expenditures of future Escrow Items or otherwise in accordance with Applicable Law.

The Funds shall be held in an institution whose deposits are insured by a federal agency, instrumentality, or entity (including Lender, if Lender is an institution whose deposits are so insured) or in any Federal Home Loan Bank. Lender shall apply the Funds to pay the Escrow Items no later than the time specified under RESPA. Lender shall not charge Borrower for holding and applying the Funds, annually analyzing the escrow account, or verifying the Escrow Items, unless Lender pays Borrower interest on the Funds and Applicable Law permits Lender to make such a charge. Unless an agreement is made in writing or Applicable Law requires interest to be paid on the Funds, Lender shall not be required to pay Borrower any interest or earnings on the Funds. Borrower and Lender can agree in writing, however, that interest shall be paid on the Funds. Lender shall give to Borrower, without charge, an annual accounting of the Funds as required by RESPA.

If there is a surplus of Funds held in escrow, as defined under RESPA, Lender shall account to Borrower for the excess funds in accordance with RESPA. If there is a shortage of Funds held in escrow, as defined under RESPA, Lender shall notify Borrower as required by RESPA, and Borrower shall pay to Lender the amount necessary to make up the shortage in accordance with RESPA, but in no more than 12 monthly payments. If there is a deficiency of Funds held in escrow, as defined under RESPA, Lender shall notify Borrower as required by RESPA, and Borrower shall pay to Lender the amount necessary to make up the deficiency in accordance with RESPA, but in no more than 12 monthly payments.

Upon payment in full of all sums secured by this Security Instrument, Lender shall promptly refund to Borrower any Funds held by Lender.

4. Charges; Liens. Borrower shall pay all taxes, assessments, charges, fines, and impositions attributable to the Property which can attain priority over this Security Instrument, leasehold payments or ground rents on the Property, if any, and Community Association Dues, Fees, and Assessments, if any. To the extent that these items are Escrow Items, Borrower shall pay them in the manner provided in Section 3.

Borrower shall promptly discharge any lien which has priority over this Security Instrument unless Borrower: (a) agrees in writing to the payment of the obligation secured by the lien in a manner acceptable to Lender, but only so long as Borrower is performing such agreement; (b) contests the lien in good faith by, or defends against enforcement of the lien in, legal proceedings which in Lender's opinion operate to prevent the enforcement of the lien while those proceedings are pending, but only until such proceedings are concluded; or (c) secures from the holder of the lien an agreement satisfactory to Lender subordinating the lien to this Security Instrument. If Lender determines that any part of the Property is subject to a lien which can attain priority over this Security Instrument, Lender may give Borrower a notice identifying the lien. Within 10 days of the date on which that notice is given, Borrower shall satisfy the lien or take one or more of the actions set forth above in this Section 4.

Lender may require Borrower to pay a one-time charge for a real estate tax verification and/or reporting service used by Lender in connection with this Loan.

5. Property Insurance. Borrower shall keep the improvements now existing or hereafter erected on the Property insured against loss by fire, hazards included within the term "extended coverage," and any other hazards including, but not limited to, earthquakes and floods, for which Lender requires insurance. This insurance shall be maintained in the amounts (including deductible levels) and for the periods that Lender requires. What Lender requires pursuant to the preceding sentences can change during the term of the Loan. The insurance carrier providing the insurance shall be chosen by Borrower subject to Lender's right to disapprove Borrower's choice, which right shall not be exercised unreasonably. Lender may require Borrower to pay, in connection with this Loan, either: (a) a one-time charge for flood zone determination, certification and tracking services; or (b) a one-time charge for flood zone determination and certification services and subsequent charges each time remappings or similar changes occur which reasonably might affect such determination or certification. Borrower shall also be responsible for the payment of any fees imposed by the Federal Emergency Management Agency in connection with the review of any flood zone determination resulting from an objection by Borrower.

If Borrower fails to maintain any of the coverages described above, Lender may obtain insurance coverage, at Lender's option and Borrower's expense. Lender is under no obligation to purchase any particular type or amount of coverage. Therefore, such coverage shall cover Lender, but might or might not protect Borrower, Borrower's equity in the Property, or the contents of the Property, against any risk, hazard or liability and might provide greater or lesser coverage than was previously in effect. Borrower acknowledges that the cost of the insurance coverage so obtained might significantly exceed the cost of insurance that Borrower could have obtained. Any amounts disbursed by Lender under this Section 5 shall become additional debt of Borrower secured by this Security Instrument. These amounts shall bear interest at the Note rate from the date of disbursement and shall be payable, with such interest, upon notice from Lender to Borrower requesting payment.

All insurance policies required by Lender and renewals of such policies shall be subject to Lender's right to disapprove such policies, shall include a standard mortgage clause, and shall name Lender as mortgagee and/or as an additional loss payee. Lender shall have the right to hold the policies and renewal certificates. If Lender requires, Borrower shall promptly give to Lender all receipts of paid premiums and renewal notices. If Borrower obtains any form of insurance coverage, not otherwise required by Lender, for damage to, or destruction of, the Property, such policy shall include a standard mortgage clause and shall name Lender as mortgagee and/or as an additional loss payee.

In the event of loss, Borrower shall give prompt notice to the insurance carrier and Lender. Lender may make proof of loss if not made promptly by Borrower. Unless Lender and Borrower otherwise agree in writing, any insurance proceeds, whether or not the underlying insurance was required by Lender, shall be applied to restoration or repair of the Property, if the restoration or repair is economically feasible and Lender's security is not lessened. During such repair and restoration period, Lender shall have the right to hold such insurance proceeds until Lender has had an opportunity to inspect such Property to ensure the work has been completed to Lender's satisfaction, provided that such inspection shall be undertaken promptly. Lender may disburse proceeds for the repairs and restoration in a single payment or in a series of progress payments as the work is completed. Unless an agreement is made in writing or Applicable Law requires interest to be paid on such insurance proceeds, Lender shall not be required to pay Borrower any interest or earnings on such proceeds. Fees for public adjusters, or other third parties, retained by Borrower shall not be paid out of the insurance proceeds and shall be the sole obligation of Borrower. If the restoration or repair is not economically feasible or Lender's security would be lessened, the insurance proceeds shall be applied to the sums secured by this Security Instrument, whether or not then due, with the excess, if any, paid to Borrower. Such insurance proceeds shall be applied in the order provided for in Section 2.

If Borrower abandons the Property, Lender may file, negotiate and settle any available insurance claim and related matters. If Borrower does not respond within 30 days to a notice from Lender that the insurance carrier has offered to settle a claim, then Lender may negotiate and settle the claim. The 30-day period will begin when the notice is given. In either event, or if Lender acquires the Property under Section 22 or otherwise, Borrower hereby assigns to Lender (a) Borrower's rights to any insurance proceeds in an amount not to exceed the amounts unpaid under the Note or this Security Instrument, and (b) any other of Borrower's rights (other than the right to any refund of unearned premiums paid by Borrower) under all insurance policies covering the Property, insofar as such rights are applicable to the coverage of the Property. Lender may use the insurance proceeds either to repair or restore the Property or to pay amounts unpaid under the Note or this Security Instrument, whether or not then due.

6. Occupancy. Borrower shall occupy, establish, and use the Property as Borrower's principal residence within 60 days after the execution of this Security Instrument and shall continue to occupy the Property as Borrower's principal residence for at least one year after the date of occupancy, unless Lender otherwise agrees in writing, which consent shall not be unreasonably withheld, or unless extenuating circumstances exist which are beyond Borrower's control.

7. Preservation, Maintenance and Protection of the Property; Inspections. Borrower shall not destroy, damage or impair the Property, allow the Property to deteriorate or commit waste on the Property. Whether or not Borrower is residing in the Property, Borrower shall maintain the Property in order to prevent the Property from deteriorating or decreasing in value due to its condition. Unless it is determined pursuant to Section 5 that repair or restoration is not economically feasible, Borrower shall promptly repair the Property if damaged to avoid further deterioration or damage. If insurance or condemnation proceeds are paid in connection with damage to, or the taking of, the Property, Borrower shall be responsible for repairing or restoring the Property only if Lender has released proceeds for such purposes. Lender may disburse proceeds for the repairs and restoration in a single payment or in a series of progress payments as the work is completed. If the insurance or condemnation proceeds are not sufficient to repair or restore the Property, Borrower is not relieved of Borrower's obligation for the completion of such repair or restoration.

Lender or its agent may make reasonable entries upon and inspections of the Property. If it has reasonable cause, Lender may inspect the interior of the improvements on the Property. Lender shall give Borrower notice at the time of or prior to such an interior inspection specifying such reasonable cause.

8. Borrower's Loan Application. Borrower shall be in default if, during the Loan application process, Borrower or any persons or entities acting at the direction of Borrower or with Borrower's knowledge or consent gave materially false, misleading, or inaccurate information or statements to Lender (or failed to provide Lender with material information) in connection with the Loan. Material representations include, but are not limited to, representations concerning Borrower's occupancy of the Property as Borrower's principal residence.

9. Protection of Lender's Interest in the Property and Rights Under this Security Instrument. If (a) Borrower fails to perform the covenants and agreements contained in this Security Instrument, (b) there is a legal proceeding that might significantly affect Lender's interest in the Property and/or rights under this Security Instrument (such as a proceeding in bankruptcy, probate, for condemnation or forfeiture, for enforcement of a lien which may attain priority over this Security Instrument or to enforce laws or regulations), or (c) Borrower has abandoned the Property, then Lender may do and pay for whatever is reasonable or appropriate to protect Lender's interest in the Property and rights under this Security Instrument, including protecting and/or assessing the value of the Property, and securing and/or repairing the Property. Lender's actions can include, but are not limited to: (a) paying any sums secured by a lien which has priority over this Security Instrument; (b) appearing in court; and (c) paying reasonable attorneys' fees to protect its interest in the Property and/or rights under this Security Instrument, including its secured position in a bankruptcy proceeding. Securing the Property includes, but is not limited to, entering the Property to make repairs, change locks, replace or board up doors and windows, drain water from pipes, eliminate building or other code violations or dangerous conditions, and have utilities turned on or off. Although Lender may take action under this Section 9, Lender does not have to do so and is not under any duty or obligation to do so. It is agreed that Lender incurs no liability for not taking any or all actions authorized under this Section 9.

Any amounts disbursed by Lender under this Section 9 shall become additional debt of Borrower secured by this Security Instrument. These amounts shall bear interest at the Note rate from the date of disbursement and shall be payable, with such interest, upon notice from Lender to Borrower requesting payment.

If this Security Instrument is on a leasehold, Borrower shall comply with all the provisions of the lease. If Borrower acquires fee title to the Property, the leasehold and the fee title shall not merge unless Lender agrees to the merger in writing.

10. Mortgage Insurance. If Lender required Mortgage Insurance as a condition of making the Loan, Borrower shall pay the premiums required to maintain the Mortgage Insurance in effect. If, for any reason, the Mortgage Insurance coverage required by Lender ceases to be available from the mortgage insurer that previously provided such insurance and Borrower was required to make separately designated payments toward the premiums for Mortgage Insurance, Borrower shall pay the premiums required to obtain coverage substantially equivalent to the Mortgage Insurance previously in effect, at a cost substantially equivalent to the cost to Borrower of the Mortgage Insurance previously in effect, from an alternate mortgage insurer selected by Lender. If substantially equivalent Mortgage Insurance coverage is not available, Borrower shall continue to pay to Lender the amount of the separately designated payments that were due when the insurance coverage ceased to be in effect. Lender will accept, use and retain these payments as a non-refundable loss reserve in lieu of Mortgage Insurance. Such loss reserve shall be non-refundable, notwithstanding the fact that the Loan is ultimately paid in full, and Lender shall not be required to pay Borrower any interest or earnings on such loss reserve. Lender can no longer require loss reserve payments if Mortgage Insurance coverage (in the amount and for the period that Lender requires) provided by an insurer selected by Lender again becomes available, is obtained, and Lender requires separately designated payments toward the premiums for Mortgage Insurance. If Lender required Mortgage Insurance as a condition of making the Loan and Borrower was required to make separately designated payments toward the premiums for Mortgage Insurance, Borrower shall pay the premiums required to maintain Mortgage Insurance in effect, or to provide a non-refundable loss reserve, until Lender's requirement for Mortgage Insurance ends in accordance with any written agreement between Borrower and Lender providing for such termination or until termination is required by Applicable Law. Nothing in this Section 10 affects Borrower's obligation to pay interest at the rate provided in the Note.

Mortgage Insurance reimburses Lender (or any entity that purchases the Note) for certain losses it may incur if Borrower does not repay the Loan as agreed. Borrower is not a party to the Mortgage Insurance.

Mortgage insurers evaluate their total risk on all such insurance in force from time to time, and may enter into agreements with other parties that share or modify their risk, or reduce losses. These agreements are on terms and conditions that are satisfactory to the mortgage insurer and the other party (or parties) to these agreements. These agreements may require the mortgage insurer to make payments using any source of funds that the mortgage insurer may have available (which may include funds obtained from Mortgage Insurance premiums).

As a result of these agreements, Lender, any purchaser of the Note, another insurer, any reinsurer, any other entity, or any affiliate of any of the foregoing, may receive (directly or indirectly) amounts that derive from (or might be characterized as) a portion of Borrower's payments for Mortgage Insurance, in exchange for sharing or modifying the mortgage insurer's risk, or reducing losses. If such agreement provides that an affiliate of Lender takes a share of the insurer's risk in exchange for a share of the premiums paid to the insurer, the arrangement is often termed "captive reinsurance." Further:

(a) Any such agreements will not affect the amounts that Borrower has agreed to pay for Mortgage Insurance, or any other terms of the Loan. Such agreements will not increase the amount Borrower will owe for Mortgage Insurance, and they will not entitle Borrower to any refund.

(b) Any such agreements will not affect the rights Borrower has—if any—with respect to the Mortgage Insurance under the Homeowners Protection Act of 1998 or any other law. These rights may include the right to receive certain disclosures, to request and obtain cancellation of the Mortgage Insurance, to have the Mortgage Insurance terminated automatically, and/or to receive a refund of any Mortgage Insurance premiums that were unearned at the time of such cancellation or termination.

11. Assignment of Miscellaneous Proceeds; Forfeiture. All Miscellaneous Proceeds are hereby assigned to and shall be paid to Lender.

If the Property is damaged, such Miscellaneous Proceeds shall be applied to restoration or repair of the Property, if the restoration or repair is economically feasible and Lender's security is not lessened. During such repair and restoration period, Lender shall have the right to hold such Miscellaneous Proceeds until Lender has had an opportunity to inspect such Property to ensure the work has been completed to Lender's satisfaction, provided that such inspection shall be undertaken promptly. Lender may pay for the repairs and restoration in a single disbursement or in a series of progress payments as the work is completed. Unless an agreement is made in writing or Applicable Law requires interest to be paid on such Miscellaneous Proceeds, Lender shall not be required to pay Borrower any interest or earnings on such Miscellaneous Proceeds. If the restoration or repair is not economically feasible or Lender's security would be lessened, the Miscellaneous Proceeds shall be applied to the sums secured by this Security Instrument, whether or not then due, with the excess, if any, paid to Borrower. Such Miscellaneous Proceeds shall be applied in the order provided for in Section 2.

In the event of a total taking, destruction, or loss in value of the Property, the Miscellaneous Proceeds shall be applied to the sums secured by this Security Instrument, whether or not then due, with the excess, if any, paid to Borrower.

In the event of a partial taking, destruction, or loss in value of the Property in which the fair market value of the Property immediately before the partial taking, destruction, or loss in value is equal to or greater than the amount of the sums secured by this Security Instrument immediately before the partial taking, destruction, or loss in value, unless Borrower and Lender otherwise agree in writing, the sums secured by this Security Instrument shall be reduced by the amount of the Miscellaneous Proceeds multiplied by the following fraction: (a) the total amount of the sums secured immediately before the partial taking, destruction, or loss in value divided by (b) the fair market value of the Property immediately before the partial taking, destruction, or loss in value. Any balance shall be paid to Borrower.

In the event of a partial taking, destruction, or loss in value of the Property in which the fair market value of the Property immediately before the partial taking, destruction, or loss in value is less than the amount of the sums secured immediately before the partial taking, destruction, or loss in value, unless Borrower and Lender otherwise agree in writing, the Miscellaneous Proceeds shall be applied to the sums secured by this Security Instrument whether or not the sums are then due.

If the Property is abandoned by Borrower, or if, after notice by Lender to Borrower that the Opposing Party (as defined in the next sentence) offers to make an award to settle a claim for damages, Borrower fails to respond to Lender within 30 days after the date the notice is given, Lender is authorized to collect and apply the Miscellaneous Proceeds either to restoration or repair of the Property or to the sums secured by this Security Instrument, whether or not then due. "Opposing Party" means the third party that owes Borrower Miscellaneous Proceeds or the party against whom Borrower has a right of action in regard to Miscellaneous Proceeds.

Borrower shall be in default if any action or proceeding, whether civil or criminal, is begun that, in Lender's judgment, could result in forfeiture of the Property or other material impairment of Lender's interest in the Property or rights under this Security Instrument. Borrower can cure such a default and, if acceleration has occurred, reinstate as provided in Section 19, by causing the action or proceeding to be dismissed with a ruling that, in Lender's judgment, precludes forfeiture of the Property or other material impairment of Lender's interest in the Property or rights under this Security Instrument. The proceeds of any award or claim for damages that are attributable to the impairment of Lender's interest in the Property are hereby assigned and shall be paid to Lender.

All Miscellaneous Proceeds that are not applied to restoration or repair of the Property shall be applied in the order provided for in Section 2.

12. Borrower Not Released; Forbearance By Lender Not a Waiver. Extension of the time for payment or modification of amortization of the sums secured by this Security Instrument granted by Lender to Borrower or any Successor in Interest of Borrower shall not operate to release the liability of Borrower or any Successors in Interest of Borrower. Lender shall not be required to commence proceedings against any Successor in Interest of Borrower or to refuse to extend time for payment or otherwise modify amortization of the sums secured by this Security Instrument by reason of any demand made by the original Borrower or any Successors in Interest of Borrower. Any forbearance by Lender in exercising any right or remedy including, without limitation, Lender's acceptance of payments from third persons, entities or Successors in Interest of Borrower or in amounts less than the amount then due, shall not be a waiver of or preclude the exercise of any right or remedy.

13. Joint and Several Liability; Co-signers; Successors and Assigns Bound. Borrower covenants and agrees that Borrower's obligations and liability shall be joint and several. However, any Borrower who co-signs this Security Instrument but does not execute the Note (a "co-signer"): (a) is co-signing this Security Instrument only to mortgage, grant and convey the co-signer's interest in the Property under the terms of this Security Instrument; (b) is not personally obligated to pay the sums secured by this Security Instrument; and (c) agrees that Lender and any other Borrower can agree to extend, modify, forbear or make any accommodations with regard to the terms of this Security Instrument or the Note without the co-signer's consent.

Subject to the provisions of Section 18, any Successor in Interest of Borrower who assumes Borrower's obligations under this Security Instrument in writing, and is approved by Lender, shall obtain all of Borrower's rights and benefits under this Security Instrument. Borrower shall not be released from Borrower's obligations and liability under this Security Instrument unless Lender agrees to such release in writing. The covenants and agreements of this Security Instrument shall bind (except as provided in Section 20) and benefit the successors and assigns of Lender.

14. Loan Charges. Lender may charge Borrower fees for services performed in connection with Borrower's default, for the purpose of protecting Lender's interest in the Property and rights under this Security Instrument, including, but not limited to, attorneys' fees, property inspection and valuation fees. In regard to any other fees, the absence of express authority in this Security Instrument to charge a specific fee to Borrower shall not be construed as a prohibition on the charging of such fee. Lender may not charge fees that are expressly prohibited by this Security Instrument or by Applicable Law.

If the Loan is subject to a law which sets maximum loan charges, and that law is finally interpreted so that the interest or other loan charges collected or to be collected in connection with the Loan exceed the permitted limits, then: (a) any such loan charge shall be reduced by the amount necessary to reduce the charge to the permitted limit; and (b) any sums already collected from Borrower which exceeded permitted limits will be refunded to Borrower. Lender may choose to make this refund by reducing the principal owed under the Note or by making a direct payment to Borrower. If a refund reduces principal, the reduction will be treated as a partial prepayment without any prepayment charge (whether or not a prepayment charge is provided for under the Note). Borrower's acceptance of any such refund made by direct payment to Borrower will constitute a waiver of any right of action Borrower might have arising out of such overcharge.

15. Notices. All notices given by Borrower or Lender in connection with this Security Instrument must be in writing. Any notice to Borrower in connection with this Security Instrument shall be deemed to have been given to Borrower when mailed by first class mail or when actually delivered to Borrower's notice address if sent by other means. Notice to any one Borrower shall constitute notice to all Borrowers unless Applicable Law expressly requires otherwise. The notice address shall be the Property Address unless Borrower has designated a substitute notice address by notice to Lender. Borrower shall promptly notify Lender of Borrower's change of address. If Lender specifies a procedure for reporting Borrower's change of address, then Borrower shall only report a change of address through that specified procedure. There may be only one designated notice address under this Security Instrument at any one time. Any notice to Lender shall be given by delivering it or by mailing it by first class mail to Lender's address stated herein unless Lender has designated another address by notice to Borrower. Any notice in connection with this Security Instrument shall not be deemed to have been given to Lender until actually received by Lender. If any notice required by this Security Instrument is also required under Applicable Law, the Applicable Law requirement will satisfy the corresponding requirement under this Security Instrument.

16. Governing Law; Severability; Rules of Construction. This Security Instrument shall be governed by federal law and the law of the jurisdiction in which the Property is located. All rights and obligations contained in this Security Instrument are subject to any requirements and limitations of Applicable Law. Applicable Law might explicitly or implicitly allow the parties to agree by contract or it might be silent, but such silence shall not be construed as a prohibition against agreement by contract. In the event that any provision or clause of this Security Instrument or the Note conflicts with Applicable Law, such conflict shall not affect other provisions of this Security Instrument or the Note which can be given effect without the conflicting provision.

As used in this Security Instrument: (a) words of the masculine gender shall mean and include corresponding neuter words or words of the feminine gender; (b) words in the singular shall mean and include the plural and vice versa; and (c) the word "may" gives sole discretion without any obligation to take any action.

17. Borrower's Copy. Borrower shall be given one copy of the Note and of this Security Instrument.

18. Transfer of the Property or a Beneficial Interest in Borrower. As used in this Section 18, "Interest in the Property" means any legal or beneficial interest in the Property, including, but not limited to, those beneficial interests transferred in a bond for deed, contract for deed, installment sales contract or escrow agreement, the intent of which is the transfer of title by Borrower at a future date to a purchaser.

If all or any part of the Property or any Interest in the Property is sold or transferred (or if Borrower is not a natural person and a beneficial interest in Borrower is sold or transferred) without Lender's prior written consent, Lender may require immediate payment in full of all sums secured by this Security Instrument. However, this option shall not be exercised by Lender if such exercise is prohibited by Applicable Law.

If Lender exercises this option, Lender shall give Borrower notice of acceleration. The notice shall provide a period of not less than 30 days from the date the notice is given in accordance with Section 15 within which Borrower must pay all sums secured by this Security Instrument. If Borrower fails to pay these sums prior to the expiration of this period, Lender may invoke any remedies permitted by this Security Instrument without further notice or demand on Borrower.

19. Borrower's Right to Reinstate After Acceleration. If Borrower meets certain conditions, Borrower shall have the right to have enforcement of this Security Instrument discontinued at any time prior to the earliest of: (a) five days before sale of the Property pursuant to any power of sale contained in this Security Instrument; (b) such other period as Applicable Law might specify for the termination of Borrower's right to reinstate; or (c) entry of a judgment enforcing this Security Instrument. Those conditions are that Borrower: (a) pays Lender all sums which then would be due under this Security Instrument and the Note as if no acceleration had occurred; (b) cures any default of any other covenants or agreements; (c) pays all expenses incurred in enforcing this Security Instrument, including, but not limited to, reasonable attorneys' fees, property inspection and valuation fees, and other fees incurred for the purpose of protecting Lender's interest in the Property and rights under this Security Instrument; and (d) takes such action as Lender may reasonably require to assure that Lender's interest in the Property and rights under this Security Instrument, and Borrower's obligation to pay the sums secured by this Security Instrument, shall continue unchanged. Lender may require that Borrower pay such reinstatement sums and expenses in one or more of the following forms, as selected by Lender: (a) cash; (b) money order; (c) certified check, bank check, treasurer's check or cashier's check, provided any such check is drawn upon an institution whose deposits are insured by a federal agency, instrumentality or entity; or (d) Electronic Funds Transfer. Upon reinstatement by Borrower, this Security Instrument and obligations secured hereby shall remain fully effective as if no acceleration had occurred. However, this right to reinstate shall not apply in the case of acceleration under Section 18.

20. Sale of Note; Change of Loan Servicer; Notice of Grievance. The Note or a partial interest in the Note (together with this Security Instrument) can be sold one or more times without prior notice to Borrower. A sale might result in a change in the entity (known as the "Loan Servicer") that collects Periodic Payments due under the Note and this Security Instrument and performs other mortgage loan servicing obligations under the Note, this Security Instrument, and Applicable Law. There also might be one or more changes of the Loan Servicer unrelated to a sale of the Note. If there is a change of the Loan Servicer, Borrower will be given written notice of the change which will state the name and address of the new Loan Servicer, the address to which payments should be made and any other information RESPA requires in connection with a notice of transfer of servicing. If the Note is sold and thereafter the Loan is serviced by a Loan Servicer other than the purchaser of the Note, the mortgage loan servicing obligations to Borrower will remain with the Loan Servicer or be transferred to a successor Loan Servicer and are not assumed by the Note purchaser unless otherwise provided by the Note purchaser.

Neither Borrower nor Lender may commence, join, or be joined to any judicial action (as either an individual litigant or the member of a class) that arises from the other party's actions pursuant to this Security Instrument or that alleges that the other party has breached any provision of, or any duty owed by reason of, this Security Instrument, until such Borrower or Lender has notified the other party (with such notice given in compliance with the requirements of Section 15) of such alleged breach and afforded the other party hereto a reasonable period after the giving of such notice to take corrective action. If Applicable Law provides a time period which must elapse before certain action can be taken, that time period will be deemed to be reasonable for purposes of this paragraph. The notice of acceleration and opportunity to cure given to Borrower pursuant to Section 22 and the notice of acceleration given to Borrower pursuant to Section 18 shall be deemed to satisfy the notice and opportunity to take corrective action provisions of this Section 20.

21. Hazardous Substances. As used in this Section 21: (a) "Hazardous Substances" are those substances defined as toxic or hazardous substances, pollutants, or wastes by Environmental Law and the following substances: gasoline, kerosene, other flammable or toxic petroleum products, toxic pesticides and herbicides, volatile solvents, materials containing asbestos or formaldehyde, and radioactive materials; (b) "Environmental Law" means federal laws and laws of the jurisdiction where the Property is located that relate to health, safety or environmental protection; (c) "Environmental Cleanup" includes any response action, remedial action, or removal action, as defined in Environmental Law; and (d) an "Environmental Condition" means a condition that can cause, contribute to, or otherwise trigger an Environmental Cleanup.

Borrower shall not cause or permit the presence, use, disposal, storage, or release of any Hazardous Substances, or threaten to release any Hazardous Substances, on or in the Property. Borrower shall not do, nor allow anyone else to do, anything affecting the Property (a) that is in violation of any Environmental Law, (b) which creates an Environmental Condition, or (c) which, due to the presence, use, or release of a Hazardous Substance, creates a condition that adversely affects the value of the Property. The preceding two sentences shall not apply to the presence, use, or storage on the Property of small quantities of Hazardous Substances that are generally recognized to be appropriate to normal residential uses and to maintenance of the Property (including, but not limited to, hazardous substances in consumer products).

Borrower shall promptly give Lender written notice of (a) any investigation, claim, demand, lawsuit or other action by any governmental or regulatory agency or private party involving the Property and any Hazardous Substance or Environmental Law of which Borrower has actual knowledge, (b) any Environmental Condition, including but not limited to, any spilling, leaking, discharge, release or threat of release of any Hazardous Substance, and (c) any condition caused by the presence, use or release of a Hazardous Substance which adversely affects the value of the Property. If Borrower learns, or is notified by any governmental or regulatory authority, or any private party, that any removal or other remediation of any Hazardous Substance affecting the Property is necessary, Borrower shall promptly take all necessary remedial actions in accordance with Environmental Law. Nothing herein shall create any obligation on Lender for an Environmental Cleanup.

NON-UNIFORM COVENANTS. Borrower and Lender further covenant and agree as follows:

22. Acceleration; Remedies. Lender shall give notice to Borrower prior to acceleration following Borrower's breach of any covenant or agreement in this Security Instrument (but not prior to acceleration under Section 18 unless Applicable Law provides otherwise). The notice shall specify: (a) the default; (b) the action required to cure the default; (c) a date, not less than 30 days from the date the notice is given to Borrower, by which the default must be cured; and (d) that failure to cure the default on or before the date specified in the notice may result in acceleration of the sums secured by this Security Instrument and sale of the Property. The notice shall further inform Borrower of the right to reinstate after acceleration and the right to bring a court action to assert the non-existence of a default or any other defense of Borrower to acceleration and sale. If the default is not cured on or before the date specified in the notice, Lender at its option may require immediate payment in full of all sums secured by this Security Instrument without further demand and may invoke the STATUTORY POWER OF SALE and any other remedies permitted by Applicable Law. Lender shall be entitled to collect all expenses incurred in pursuing the remedies provided in this Section 22, including, but not limited to, reasonable attorneys' fees and costs of title evidence.

If Lender invokes the STATUTORY POWER OF SALE, Lender shall mail a copy of a notice of sale to Borrower, and to other persons prescribed by Applicable Law, in the manner provided by Applicable Law. Lender shall publish the notice of sale, and the Property shall be sold in the manner prescribed by Applicable Law. Lender or its designee may purchase the Property at any sale. The proceeds of the sale shall be applied in the following order: (a) to all expenses of the sale, including, but not limited to, reasonable attorneys' fees; (b) to all sums secured by this Security Instrument; and (c) any excess to the person or persons legally entitled to it.

23. Release. Upon payment of all sums secured by this Security Instrument, Lender shall discharge this Security Instrument. Borrower shall pay any recordation costs. Lender may charge Borrower a fee for releasing this Security Instrument, but only if the fee is paid to a third party for services rendered and the charging of the fee is permitted under Applicable Law.

24. Waivers. Borrower waives all rights of homestead exemption in the Property and relinquishes all rights of curtesy and dower in the Property.

BY SIGNING BELOW, Borrower accepts and agrees to the terms and covenants contained in this Security Instrument and in any Rider executed by Borrower and recorded with it.
Witnesses:

SAMPLE PROMISSORY NOTE (FIXED)

NOTE

1. BORROWER'S PROMISE TO PAY

In return for a loan that I have received, I promise to pay U.S. $_____ (this amount is called "Principal"), plus interest, to the order of the Lender. The Lender is _____. I will make all payments under this Note in the form of cash, check or money order.

I understand that the Lender may transfer this Note. The Lender or anyone who takes this Note by transfer and who is entitled to receive payments under this Note is called the "Note Holder."

2. INTEREST

Interest will be charged on unpaid principal until the full amount of Principal has been paid. I will pay interest at a yearly rate of _____%.

The interest rate required by this Section 2 is the rate I will pay both before and after any default described in Section 6(B) of this Note.

3. PAYMENTS

(A) Time and Place of Payments

I will pay principal and interest by making a payment every month.

I will make my monthly payment on the _____ day of each month beginning on _____, _____. I will make these payments every month until I have paid all of the principal and interest and any other charges described below that I may owe under this Note. Each monthly payment will be applied as of its scheduled due date and will be applied to interest before Principal. If, on _____, 20___, I still owe amounts under this Note, I will pay those amounts in full on that date, which is called the "Maturity Date."

I will make my monthly payments at _____ _____ or at a different place if required by the Note Holder.

(B) Amount of Monthly Payments

My monthly payment will be in the amount of U.S. $_____.

4. BORROWER'S RIGHT TO PREPAY

I have the right to make payments of Principal at any time before they are due. A payment of Principal only is known as a "Prepayment." When I make a Prepayment, I will tell the Note Holder in writing that I am doing so. I may not designate a payment as a Prepayment if I have not made all the monthly payments due under the Note.

I may make a full Prepayment or partial Prepayments without paying a Prepayment charge. The Note Holder will use my Prepayments to reduce the amount of Principal that I owe under this Note. However, the Note Holder may apply my Prepayment to the accrued and unpaid interest on the Prepayment amount, before applying my Prepayment to reduce the Principal amount of the Note. If I make a partial Prepayment, there will be no changes in the due date or in the amount of my monthly payment unless the Note Holder agrees in writing to those changes.

5. LOAN CHARGES

If a law, which applies to this loan and which sets maximum loan charges, is finally interpreted so that the interest or other loan charges collected or to be collected in connection with this loan exceed the permitted limits, then: (a) any such loan charge shall be reduced by the amount necessary to reduce the charge to the permitted limit; and (b) any sums already collected from me which exceeded permitted limits will be refunded to me. The Note Holder may choose to make this refund by reducing the Principal I owe under this Note or by making a direct payment to me. If a refund reduces Principal, the reduction will be treated as a partial Prepayment.

6. BORROWER'S FAILURE TO PAY AS REQUIRED

(A) Late Charge for Overdue Payments

If the Note Holder has not received the full amount of any monthly payment by the end of _____ calendar days after the date it is due, I will pay a late charge to the Note Holder. The amount of the charge will be _____% of my overdue payment of principal and interest. I will pay this late charge promptly but only once on each late payment.

(B) Default

If I do not pay the full amount of each monthly payment on the date it is due, I will be in default.

(C) Notice of Default

If I am in default, the Note Holder may send me a written notice telling me that if I do not pay the overdue amount by a certain date, the Note Holder may require me to pay immediately the full amount of Principal which has not been paid and all the interest that I owe on that amount. That date must be at least 30 days after the date on which the notice is mailed to me or delivered by other means.

(D) No Waiver By Note Holder

Even if, at a time when I am in default, the Note Holder does not require me to pay immediately in full as described above, the Note Holder will still have the right to do so if I am in default at a later time.

(E) Payment of Note Holder's Costs and Expenses

If the Note Holder has required me to pay immediately in full as described above, the Note Holder will have the right to be paid back by me for all of its costs and expenses in enforcing this Note to the extent not prohibited by applicable law. Those expenses include, for example, reasonable attorneys' fees.

7. GIVING OF NOTICES

Unless applicable law requires a different method, any notice that must be given to me under this Note will be given by delivering it or by mailing it by first class mail to me at the Property Address above or at a different address if I give the Note Holder a notice of my different address.

Any notice that must be given to the Note Holder under this Note will be given by delivering it or by mailing it by first class mail to the Note Holder at the address stated in Section 3(A) above or at a different address if I am given a notice of that different address.

8. OBLIGATIONS OF PERSONS UNDER THIS NOTE

If more than one person signs this Note, each person is fully and personally obligated to keep all of the promises made in this Note, including the promise to pay the full amount owed. Any person who is a guarantor, surety or endorser of this Note is also obligated to do these things. Any person who takes over these obligations, including the obligations of a guarantor, surety or endorser of this Note, is also obligated to keep all of the promises made in this Note. The Note Holder may enforce its rights under this Note against each person individually or against all of us together. This means that any one of us may be required to pay all of the amounts owed under this Note.

9. WAIVERS

I and any other person who has obligations under this Note waive the rights of Presentment and Notice of Dishonor. "Presentment" means the right to require the Note Holder to demand payment of amounts due. "Notice of Dishonor" means the right to require the Note Holder to give notice to other persons that amounts due have not been paid.

10. UNIFORM SECURED NOTE

This Note is a uniform instrument with limited variations in some jurisdictions. In addition to the protections given to the Note Holder under this Note, a Mortgage, Deed of Trust, or Security Deed (the "Security Instrument"), dated the same date as this Note, protects the Note Holder from possible losses which might result if I do not keep the promises which I make in this Note. That Security Instrument describes how and under what conditions I may be required to make immediate payment in full of all amounts I owe under this Note. Some of those conditions are described as follows:

If all or any part of the Property or any Interest in the Property is sold or transferred (or if Borrower is not a natural person and a beneficial interest in Borrower is sold or transferred) without Lender's prior written consent, Lender may require immediate payment in full of all sums secured by this Security Instrument. However, this option shall not be exercised by Lender if such exercise is prohibited by Applicable Law.

If Lender exercises this option, Lender shall give Borrower notice of acceleration. The notice shall provide a period of not less than 30 days from the date the notice is given in accordance with Section 15 within which Borrower must pay all sums secured by this Security Instrument. If Borrower fails to pay these sums prior to the expiration of this period, Lender may invoke any remedies permitted by this Security Instrument without further notice or demand on Borrower.

WITNESS THE HAND(S) AND SEAL(S) OF THE UNDERSIGNED.

SAMPLE PROMISSORY NOTE (ADJUSTABLE)

ADJUSTABLE RATE NOTE

(1 Year Treasury Index—Rate Caps)

THIS NOTE CONTAINS PROVISIONS ALLOWING FOR CHANGES IN MY INTEREST RATE AND MY MONTHLY PAYMENT. THIS NOTE LIMITS THE AMOUNT MY INTEREST RATE CAN CHANGE AT ANY ONE TIME AND THE MAXIMUM RATE I MUST PAY.

1. BORROWER'S PROMISE TO PAY

In return for a loan that I have received, I promise to pay U.S. $ _____ (this amount is called "Principal"), plus interest, to the order of the Lender. The Lender is _____. I will make all payments under this Note in the form of cash, check or money order.

I understand that the Lender may transfer this Note. The Lender or anyone who takes this Note by transfer and who is entitled to receive payments under this Note is called the "Note Holder."

2. INTEREST

Interest will be charged on unpaid principal until the full amount of Principal has been paid. I will pay interest at a yearly rate of _____%. The interest rate I will pay will change in accordance with Section 4 of this Note. The interest rate required by this Section 2 and Section 4 of this Note is the rate I will pay both before and after any default described in Section 7(B) of this Note.

3. PAYMENTS

(A) Time and Place of Payments

I will pay principal and interest by making a payment every month.

I will make my monthly payment on the first day of each month beginning on _____, _____. I will make these payments every month until I have paid all of the principal and interest and any other charges described below that I may owe under this Note. Each monthly payment will be applied as of its scheduled due date and will be applied to interest before Principal. If, on _____, 20_____, I still owe amounts under this Note, I will pay those amounts in full on that date, which is called the "Maturity Date."

I will make my monthly payments at _____ _____ or at a different place if required by the Note Holder.

(B) Amount of My Initial Monthly Payments

Each of my initial monthly payments will be in the amount of U.S. $_____. This amount may change.

(C) Monthly Payment Changes

Changes in my monthly payment will reflect changes in the unpaid principal of my loan and in the interest rate that I must pay. The Note Holder will determine my new interest rate and the changed amount of my monthly payment in accordance with Section 4 of this Note.

4. INTEREST RATE AND MONTHLY PAYMENT CHANGES

(A) Change Dates

The interest rate I will pay may change on the first day of _____, _____, and on that day every 12th month thereafter. Each date on which my interest rate could change is called a "Change Date."

(B) The Index

Beginning with the first Change Date, my interest rate will be based on an Index. The "Index" is the weekly average yield on United States Treasury securities adjusted to a constant maturity of one year, as made available by the Federal Reserve Board. The most recent Index figure available as of the date 45 days before each Change Date is called the "Current Index."

If the Index is no longer available, the Note Holder will choose a new index which is based upon comparable information. The Note Holder will give me notice of this choice.

(C) Calculation of Changes

Before each Change Date, the Note Holder will calculate my new interest rate by adding _____ percentage points (_____ %) to the Current Index. The Note Holder will then round the result of this addition to the nearest one-eighth of one percentage point (0.125%). Subject to the limits stated in Section 4(D) below, this rounded amount will be my new interest rate until the next Change Date.

The Note Holder will then determine the amount of the monthly payment that would be sufficient to repay the unpaid principal that I am expected to owe at the Change Date in full on the Maturity Date at my new interest rate in substantially equal payments. The result of this calculation will be the new amount of my monthly payment.

(D) Limits on Interest Rate Changes

The interest rate I am required to pay at the first Change Date will not be greater than _____% or less than _____%. Thereafter, my interest rate will never be increased or decreased on any single Change Date by more than one percentage point (1.0%) from the rate of interest I have been paying for the preceding 12 months. My interest rate will never be greater than _____%.

(E) Effective Date of Changes

My new interest rate will become effective on each Change Date. I will pay the amount of my new monthly payment beginning on the first monthly payment date after the Change Date until the amount of my monthly payment changes again.

(F) Notice of Changes

The Note Holder will deliver or mail to me a notice of any changes in my interest rate and the amount of my monthly payment before the effective date of any change. The notice will include information required by law to be given to me and also the title and telephone number of a person who will answer any question I may have regarding the notice.

5. BORROWER'S RIGHT TO PREPAY

I have the right to make payments of Principal at any time before they are due. A payment of Principal only is known as a "Prepayment." When I make a Prepayment, I will tell the Note Holder in writing that I am doing so. I may not designate a payment as a Prepayment if I have not made all the monthly payments due under the Note.

I may make a full Prepayment or partial Prepayments without paying a Prepayment charge. The Note Holder will use my Prepayments to reduce the amount of Principal that I owe under this Note. However, the Note Holder may apply my Prepayment to the accrued and unpaid interest on the Prepayment amount, before applying my Prepayment to reduce the Principal amount of the Note. If I make a partial Prepayment, there will be no changes in the due dates of my monthly payment unless the Note Holder agrees in writing to those changes. My partial Prepayment may reduce the amount of my monthly payments after the first Change Date following my partial Prepayment. However, any reduction due to my partial Prepayment may be offset by an interest rate increase.

6. LOAN CHARGES

If a law, which applies to this loan and which sets maximum loan charges, is finally interpreted so that the interest or other loan charges collected or to be collected in connection with this loan exceed the permitted limits, then: (a) any such loan charge shall be reduced by the amount necessary to reduce the charge to the permitted limit; and (b) any sums already collected from me which exceeded permitted limits will be refunded to me. The Note Holder may choose to make this refund by reducing the Principal I owe under this Note or by making a direct payment to me. If a refund reduces Principal, the reduction will be treated as a partial Prepayment.

7. BORROWER'S FAILURE TO PAY AS REQUIRED

(A) Late Charges for Overdue Payments

If the Note Holder has not received the full amount of any monthly payment by the end of _____ calendar days after the date it is due, I will pay a late charge to the Note Holder. The amount of the charge will be _____% of my overdue payment of principal and interest. I will pay this late charge promptly but only once on each late payment.

(B) Default

If I do not pay the full amount of each monthly payment on the date it is due, I will be in default.

(C) Notice of Default

If I am in default, the Note Holder may send me a written notice telling me that if I do not pay the overdue amount by a certain date, the Note Holder may require me to pay immediately the full amount of Principal which has not been paid and all the interest that I owe on that amount. That date must be at least 30 days after the date on which the notice is mailed to me or delivered by other means.

(D) No Waiver By Note Holder

Even if, at a time when I am in default, the Note Holder does not require me to pay immediately in full as described above, the Note Holder will still have the right to do so if I am in default at a later time.

(E) Payment of Note Holder's Costs and Expenses

If the Note Holder has required me to pay immediately in full as described above, the Note Holder will have the right to be paid back by me for all of its costs and expenses in enforcing this Note to the extent not prohibited by applicable law. Those expenses include, for example, reasonable attorneys' fees.

8. GIVING OF NOTICES

Unless applicable law requires a different method, any notice that must be given to me under this Note will be given by delivering it or by mailing it by first class mail to me at the Property Address above or at a different address if I give the Note Holder a notice of my different address.

Any notice that must be given to the Note Holder under this Note will be given by delivering it or by mailing it by first class mail to the Note Holder at the address stated in Section 3(A) above or at a different address if I am given a notice of that different address.

9. OBLIGATIONS OF PERSONS UNDER THIS NOTE

If more than one person signs this Note, each person is fully and personally obligated to keep all of the promises made in this Note, including the promise to pay the full amount owed. Any person who is a guarantor, surety or endorser of this Note is also obligated to do these things. Any person who takes over these obligations, including the obligations of a guarantor, surety or endorser of this Note, is also obligated to keep all of the promises made in this Note. The Note Holder may enforce its rights under this Note against each person individually or against all of us together. This means that any one of us may be required to pay all of the amounts owed under this Note.

10. WAIVERS

I and any other person who has obligations under this Note waive the rights of Presentment and Notice of Dishonor. "Presentment" means the right to require the Note Holder to demand payment of amounts due. "Notice of Dishonor" means the right to require the Note Holder to give notice to other persons that amounts due have not been paid.

11. UNIFORM SECURED NOTE

This Note is a uniform instrument with limited variations in some jurisdictions. In addition to the protections given to the Note Holder under this Note, a Mortgage, Deed of Trust, or Security Deed (the "Security Instrument"), dated the same date as this Note, protects the Note Holder from possible losses which might result if I do not keep the promises which I make in this Note. That Security Instrument describes how and under what conditions I may be required to make immediate payment in full of all amounts I owe under this Note. Some of those conditions are described as follows:

If all or any part of the Property or any Interest in the Property is sold or transferred (or if Borrower is not a natural person and a beneficial interest in Borrower is sold or transferred) without Lender's prior written consent, Lender may require immediate payment in full of all sums secured by this Security Instrument. However, this option shall not be exercised by Lender if such exercise is prohibited by Applicable Law. Lender also shall not exercise this option if: (a) Borrower causes to be submitted to Lender information required by Lender to evaluate the intended transferee as if a new loan were being made to the transferee; and (b) Lender reasonably determines that Lender's security will not be impaired by the loan assumption and that the risk of a breach of any covenant or agreement in this Security Instrument is acceptable to Lender.

To the extent permitted by Applicable Law, Lender may charge a reasonable fee as a condition to Lender's consent to the loan assumption. Lender may also require the transferee to sign an assumption agreement that is acceptable to Lender and that obligates the transferee to keep all the promises and agreements made in the Note and in this Security Instrument. Borrower will continue to be obligated under the Note and this Security Instrument unless Lender releases Borrower in writing.

If Lender exercises the option to require immediate payment in full, Lender shall give Borrower notice of acceleration. The notice shall provide a period of not less than 30 days from the date the notice is given in accordance with Section 15 within which Borrower must pay' all sums secured by this Security Instrument. If Borrower fails to pay these sums prior to the expiration of this period, Lender may invoke any remedies permitted by this Security Instrument without further notice or demand on Borrower.

WITNESS THE HAND(S) AND SEAL(S) OF THE UNDERSIGNED.

SAMPLE CHANGE RATE NOTICE FOR ARM

[Mortgage Company]

January 17, 2003
Loan: [NUMBER]

Dear: [NAME]

Effective with your 03-01-03 payment the interest rate on your mortgage loan will be adjusted, as required by your Mortgage Mote. Please refer to your Note for details on how we are required to compute your new rate, or call our Customer service Department at 1-800-555-5555.

Your current interest rate of 11.10000% was based on the index rate of 1.98375%. Your new interest rate of 11.10000% is based on the new index of 1.43000%, then added to your margin of 5.95000%. The result was then rounded as specified in your Note.

In conjunction with the interest rate change, your Principal and Interest payment will also be adjusted as specified by your Note. Your Principal and Interest payment will be $ 459.97 effective with your 03-01-03 payment. Your new total payment, including your monthly escrow deposit, will be $530.55. Your new Principal and Interest amount was based on a projected principal balance of $47,209.37.

These changes will be reflected on your Monthly Statement when the 03-01-03 payment is due. If you have any questions regarding this change, please Contact our Customer Service Department, toll-free, at 1-800-555-5555.

Sincerely,

[Mortgage Company]

SAMPLE ANNUAL ESCROW ACCOUNT STATEMENT

[Bank Name]
Customer Service:
Toll free 1.800.555.5555 Se habla espanol
TDD Dial 7-1-1 for relay assistance
Annual Escrow
Account Statement
Statement Date: November 08, 2006
Review Period: January 2006 to December 2006
Your Loan Number:

What is an escrow account?
A portion of each of your monthly home loan payments goes into an escrow account. This money is used to pay items such as your property taxes and insurance premiums when they are due.
In accordance with federal guidelines, we review your Escrow Account at least one time each year to ensure that we are collecting enough money to make all required payments. This document is a review of your Escrow Account activity since your last analysis.

Monthly Home Loan Payment			
	Current	New Payment (effective 01/01/07) if you select Option A below	New Payment (effective 01/01/07) if you select Option B below
Principal & Interest	1,337.13	1.337.13	1,337.13
Escrow Account Deposit	247.86	324.45*	324.45*
Plus: Account Balancer/ Shortage	0.00	0.00	146.79**
Total Payment Amount	1,584.99	1,661.58	1,808.37

Your new total payment includes an updated monthly escrow deposit, based on projected amounts to be paid from your Escrow Account, of $324.45* and, if applicable, an amount needed to repay the escrow shortage of $146.79**.

Please review the detailed information provided on the back of this page.

Here are your shortage repayment options. You may select one of the following options:

Option A: Pay Entire Shortage Now* Pay the entire $1,761.47 escrow account shortage using the Escrow Account Balancer Payment Coupon below for a new total payment of $1,661.58. **See chart above.**

*Pay a portion of your shortage—every $12 paid reduces your total payment by $1.

*NOTE: The new payment amount will be effective the month after the shortage amount is received. Any remaining increase in the escrow payment is to cover the projected increase in your bills for the upcoming years.

Option B: Pay Shortage Over 12 Months

Pay the $1,761.47 escrow account shortage in 12 Account Balancer payments of $146.79 each. To choose this option, no action is required. The 12 payments will be automatically added to your home loan payment for January 2007 through December 2007.

If you select this option, your new monthly home loan payment (effective 01/01/07) will be $1,808.37. See chart above.

ANTICIPATED ESCROW ACCOUNT PAYMENTS

This section reflects the escrow activity that is expected to occur in the next 12 months. The *Total Tax and Insurance Monthly Payment Amount* at the bottom of this chart is your new monthly escrow deposit, as listed on Page 1 of this statement.

TAX

Item	Annual Expense	Anticipated Date(s) of Payment
COUNTY TAX	$ 2,909.37	DECEMBER 07

INSURANCE

Item	Annual Expense	Anticipated Date(s) of Payment
FIRE/HOMEOWN	$ 984.00	MARCH 07

TOTAL TAX AND INSURANCE MONTHLY PAYMENT AMOUNT = $ 324.45

Balancing Your Escrow Account

The front of this statement shows that you have an Escrow Account Shortage of $1,761.47. How was this determined?

Your previous year's activity is used to estimate the deposit and disbursement activity in your Escrow Account and project your *lowest account balance* for the year ahead. Your projected *lowest account balance* is compared to your *minimum required balance* as shown in the *Escrow Account Balancer* below these paragraphs. This determines the amount required to bring your Escrow Account into balance.

Since taxes and insurance premiums often go up, we require that you maintain a *minimum required balance* in your account at all times to prevent a negative balance in your account.

As shown in the information in the box and graph below, you will reach your *lowest account balance* of -$1,112.57 in March 07. This is subtracted from your *minimum required balance* of $648.90 resulting in an Escrow Account Shortage of $1,761.47.

In order to pay your Escrow Account Shortage and bring your account into balance, you may pay the $1,761.47 shortage in full (Option A on front) or pay the shortage over 12 months (Option B on front). It's your choice.

Escrow Account Balancer

Minimum Required Balance	$648.90
Less: Lowest Account Balance (Mar 07)	-$1,112.57
Annual Account Balancer/Shortage	$1,765.47
Monthly Account Balancer/Shortage	146.79

Projected Escrow Account Balance

The graph below shows your projected Escrow Account Balance for the next 12 months with your new monthly Escrow Account Deposit of $324.45 and the "Anticipated Escrow Account Payments" chart shown on the next page. Your projected beginning escrow balance of -$1,101.92 is based on anticipated deposits and disbursements. (See chart at the top of page 249.)

Escrow Account History for the Prior Payment Period

The following is a comparison of the anticipated and actual Escrow Account activity for the previous payment period. Anticipated amounts are taken from your last analysis. Your most recent monthly payment during the past year was $1,584.99, of which $1,337.13 was for principal and interest and $247.86 went into your Escrow Account.

At the time of your last analysis, your anticipated lowest balance was $495.72. In reviewing your account activity, your actual low escrow balance was -$1,101.92.

NOTE: An asterisk (*) in the chart below indicates a difference between what actually occurred and what was anticipated. This difference may be due to a change in Escrow items such as an increase in your insurance premium or a change in the due date of your property tax. Insurance and Tax payments may be disbursed before their due dates to allow for more mail and posting time at the insurance company or tax office. An "E" in the chart below indicates expected activity. (See chart at the bottom of page 249.)

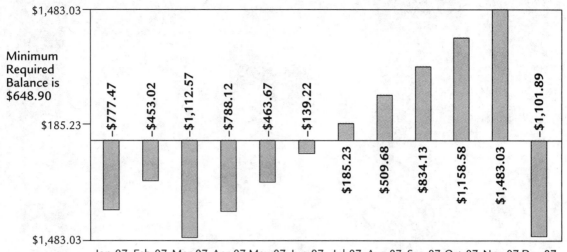

Minimum Required Balance is $648.90

$1,483.03

$185.23

$1,483.03

Jan-07 Feb-07 Mar-07 Apr-07 May-07 Jun-07 Jul-07 Aug-07 Sep-07 Oct-07 Nov-07 Dec-07

Bar values: −$777.47, −$453.02, −$1,112.57, −$788.12, −$463.67, −$139.22, $185.23, $509.68, $834.13, $1,158.58, $1,483.03, −$1,101.89

↑ Lowest Account Balance is −$1,112.57 which is $1,761.47 short of Minimum Required Balance

Month	Deposits to Escrow (credits to Escrow) Anticipated	Actual	Payments from Escrow (debits from Escrow) Anticipated	Actual	Description	Escrow Balance Projected	Actual
Jan 06	247.86	247.86				611.14	−182.87
Feb 06	247.86	247.86				859.00	64.99
Mar 06	247.86	247.86	859.00	984.00*	FIRE/HOMEOWN	1,106.86	312.85
Apr 06	247.86	247.86				495.72	423.29
May 06	247.86	247.86				743.58	−175.43
Jun 06	247.86	247.86				991.44	72.43
Jul 06	247.86	247.86				1,239.30	320.29
Aug 06	247.86	247.86				1,487.16	568.15
Sep 06	247.86	247.86				1,735.02	816.01
Oct 06	247.86	247.86				1,982.88	1,063.87
Nov 06	247.86	247.86				2,230.74	1,311.73
Dec 06	247.86	247.86E	2,115.36	2,909.37	COUNTY TAX	2,478.60	1,559.59
						611.10	−1,101.92
Total	**2,974.32**	**2,974.32**	**2,974.36**	**3,893.37**			

Summary of State Foreclosure Laws

This appendix contains a summary of state foreclosure laws. With respect to the HUD-time frames, HUD regulations require that a mortgagee exercise reasonable diligence in prosecuting foreclosures. Failure to complete a foreclosure within the time period specified is considered a failure to comply with the regulation, unless the delay is caused by reasons beyond the mortgagee's control. The expected time frames given for Fannie Mae (FNMA) represent the optimum time period within which FNMA expects a foreclosure to be completed. When foreclosure is initiated, time frames for individual cases may be shorter than either the FNMA or HUD guidelines. They are unlikely to be longer.

A note on the categories within each summary: The "preforeclosure notice" category refers generally to the notice of sale and notice of default, if required. It does not refer to notice of the commencement of a court action, though such notice would always be required under court rules governing service of process. The "number of notices" category refers to whether the state requires a separate notice of default in addition to a notice of sale.

Foreclosure law can be complicated and may change as amendments to the laws are passed. It is important that you obtain further information on these issues and the likely time frames from someone in your state with experience in foreclosures or foreclosure defense.

ALABAMA

Ala. Code §§ 35-10-1 to 35-10-30, §§ 6-5-247 to 6-5-256
Most Common Method of Foreclosure: Power of Sale.
Preforeclosure Notice:
  Number of Notices: One: Notice of Sale.
  Amount of Notice Required: Thirty days prior to sale.
  Content of Notice: Time, place, and terms of sale.
  Method of Service: By publication once a week for three consecutive weeks.
Redemption: Within one year after foreclosure by paying the purchase price to the buyer plus interest and costs, but borrower loses the right to redeem unless he or she surrenders possession within ten days after foreclosure sale.
Deficiency: A deficiency judgment is obtainable.

ALASKA

Alaska Stat. § 34.20.070 (Michie)

Most Common Method of Foreclosure: Power of Sale for deeds of trust.

Preforeclosure Notice:

> *Number of Notices:* One: Notice of Default and Sale.
>
> *Amount of Notice Required:* Notice is to be served not less than thirty days after default and not less than three months before sale.
>
> *Content of Notice:* a) Name of trustor; b) book and page where trust deed is recorded, or the serial number assigned to the trust deed by the recorder; c) description of the property, including property's street address if there is one; d) statement that breach has occurred; e) nature of the breach; f) sum owing; and g) date, time, and place of sale.
>
> *Method of Service:* By certified mail on the borrower and occupant.

Right to Cure Default/Reinstate: Can cure any time before the sale, but the lender can refuse to accept payment if two prior Notices of Default and Sale have been recorded.

Redemption: No right of redemption after sale if a nonjudicial foreclosure. § 34.20.090.

Deficiency: No deficiency judgment after a foreclosure by power of sale. § 34.20.100.

ARIZONA

Ariz. Rev. Stat. §§ 33-741 to 33-749, 33-801 to 33-821

Most Common Method of Foreclosure: Power of sale for deeds of trust; judicial foreclosure for mortgages.

Foreclosure by Power of Sale Permitted?: On deeds of trust only. § 33-807.

Judicial Foreclosure Procedure: After expiration of the forfeiture period, the mortgagee must bring action in Superior Court in the county where the property is located.

Preforeclosure Notice:

> *Number of Notices:* For a power of sale, one notice: Notice of Sale. A power of sale cannot be exercised before the expiration of ninety days from the recording of the Notice of Sale. § 33-807. For a judicial foreclosure, one notice: Notice of Election to Forfeit.
>
> *Amount of Notice Required:* If judicial foreclosure, notice must be recorded twenty days before forfeiture. The mortgagee can only enforce forfeiture after the expiration of the following periods after the date monies are due: thirty days if less than twenty percent of the purchase price is paid; sixty days if greater than or equal to twenty percent and less than thirty percent of the purchase price is paid; 120 days if greater than or equal to thirty percent and less than fifty percent or more of the purchase price is paid; nine months if fifty percent or more of the purchase price is paid. § 33-742.
>
> *Content of Notice:* See Statutory forms §§ 33-743(B) and 33-808. Must state how to reinstate and the deadline for reinstatement. § 33-743(F).
>
> *Method of Service:* For a power of sale, the foreclosure notice must be recorded in the applicable count recorder's office, published in a newspaper at least once a week for four consecutive weeks, posted twenty days before the sale on the property, and mailed by registered or certified mail to the owner of record or other person who has recorded a request for notice prior to the recording of the notice of sale. §§ 33-808, 33-809. For a judicial foreclosure, by in-hand delivery or by first class mail. § 33-743.

Right to Cure Default/Reinstate: For a power of sale foreclosure, up to 5:00 p.m. on the last day, other than a Saturday or legal holiday, before the sale date or the filing of an action to foreclose the trust deed. § 33-813. For a judicial foreclosure, up to twenty days after service of the Notice of Intent to Forfeit.

Redemption: For a judicial foreclosure, can redeem judgment prior to the sale if the property is not abandoned.[1] § 33-726.

Deficiency: For purchase money mortgages for a one- to two-family home on less than two and one-half acres no deficiency, unless the court finds that the mortgagor committed waste. §§ 33-729, 33-814(G).

ARKANSAS

Ark. Code §§ 18-49-101 to 18-49-106, §§ 18-50-101 to 18-50-116 (Michie)

Most Common Method of Foreclosure: Power of Sale (except for agricultural land).

Judicial Foreclosure Procedure: See §§ 18-49-101 to 18-49-106.

Preforeclosure Notice:

   Number of Notices: One: Notice of Default and Intention to Sell; must be recorded.

   Amount of Notice Required: Notice must be mailed, by certified and first class mail, within thirty days of recording (§ 18-50-104) and published once a week for four weeks prior to date of sale. Notice must also be posted in the courthouse and on the Internet. § 18-50-105. Trustee must also file affidavit of mailing with recorder of deeds prior to or on date of sale. § 18-50-106. If judicial foreclosure, single notice must be published once at least ten days prior to sale. § 18-49-104.

   Content of Notice: a) Names of parties; b) description of the property; c) book and page where mortgage is recorded; d) default; e) amount owing; f) statement that you may lose your property if you do not take immediate action; and g) time, date, and place of sale. § 18-50-104.

   Method of Service: By mail and by publication.

Right to Cure Default/Reinstate: Up to the time of the sale. § 18-50-114.

Redemption: If a judicial foreclosure, within one year by payment of the purchase price plus interest and the costs of the sale. Right of redemption may be waived in mortgage. § 18-49-106. No redemption if foreclosed by power of sale.

Post-Sale Provisions Regarding Proceeds: Proceeds are applied to the expenses of the sale, mortgage debt, and other recorded liens, with any surplus to the mortgagor. § 18-50-109.

Deficiency: No bids for less than two-thirds of entire indebtedness can be accepted. § 18-50-107. A deficiency judgment is limited to the lesser of the indebtedness minus the fair market value or the indebtedness minus the sale price of the property. § 18-50-112. Action for a deficiency after a non-judicial foreclosure must be brought within one year of date of sale.

High-Cost Home Loans: Intentional violation of the Arkansas Home Loan Protection Act, Ark. Code Ann. §§ 23-53-101 through 106, renders the loan agreement void. The creditor may not collect any principal, interest or other fees, and the borrower can recover payments made. Ark. Code Ann. § 23-53-106. A borrower may raise violations of the Act against an assignee (unless the assignee can show that it took certain precautions to avoid accepting assignments of high-cost home loans) as a defense by recoupment or setoff in a collection action, or to obtain possession of the home. § 23-53-105. TILA right of rescission and other remedies provided by the Act are available to the borrower by way of recoupment against a party foreclosing, at any time during life of the loan. Ark. Code Ann. § 23-53-106.

CALIFORNIA

Cal. Civ. Code §§ 2924 to 2924*l* (West)

Most Common Method of Foreclosure: Power of Sale.

Judicial Foreclosure Procedure: See Cal. Civ. Proc. Code, §§ 725a to 730.5 (West).

Preforeclosure Notice:
   Number of Notices: Two: Notice of Default and Notice of Sale.
   Amount of Notice Required: For a Notice of Default, three months. For a Notice of Sale,
      twenty days.
   Content of Notice: Notice of Default: a) identify the mortgage; b) nature of the breach;
      c) election to sell to satisfy obligation; and d) if curable. Notice must be filed in the
      county where the mortgaged property is located. *Notice of Sale:* a) time and place of
      sale; and b) total amount due plus a reasonable estimate of costs and expenses.
      § 2924c. Name, instate street address and toll-free or instate telephone number of the
      trustee or its agent. Street address or legal description of property. If personal property
      or fixtures are to be sold, these must be described. § 2924f.
   Method of Service: By certified or registered mail, and by regular first class mail and by
      publication once a week for three weeks, beginning twenty days before the sale, in a
      newspaper of general circulation, and posting in a public place and in a conspicuous
      place on the property. Notice of sale must also be recorded. § 2924b.
Right to Cure Default/Reinstate: Can cure within five days before the sale. § 2924c.
Redemption: None, if foreclosed by a power of sale and a deficiency judgment is waived or
   prohibited. Right of redemption if foreclosed by judicial procedure unless deficiency judgment is waived or prohibited.
Post-Sale Provisions Regarding Proceeds: Within thirty days of sale, the trustee must give notice of
   any surplus to anyone who may have a claim on the proceeds. Claims are to be sent to the trustee
   to determine priority. If the trustee cannot resolve the claims, then the court will. § 2924j.
Deficiency: No deficiency under a judicial foreclosure judgment unless there is a right to redemption. No deficiency judgment under a power of sale foreclosure.
High-Cost Home Loans: A provision in a loan agreement that violates enumerated subsections of
   the high-cost home loan act is unenforceable against borrower. The listed subsections forbid,
   inter alia, call provisions and balloon payments. The court may reform the loan terms to
   conform to the statute. Cal. Fin. Code §§ 4973, 4978 (West).
Miscellaneous: Special notice is required under the Unruh Act for deeds of trust, where the security interest is a single-family owner-occupied residence and it secures the obligation
   under the Unruh Retail Installment Sales Act (§§ 1801 to 1812.20). § 2924f.

COLORADO

Colo. Rev. Stat. §§ 38-38-100.3 to 38-38-114
Most Common Method of Foreclosure: Power of Sale by a public trustee.
Preforeclosure Notice:
   Number of Notices: One—a combined notice of sale, right to cure, and right to redeem—but
      it is to be mailed twice, once within 20 days after recording the notice of election and
      demand, and once 45 to 60 days before the first scheduled date of sale. (§ 38-38-103).
   Amount of Notice Required: By mail, within 20 days after recording notice of election and
      demand, and between 45 and 60 days before first scheduled sale date. It must also be
      published once a week for four weeks between 60 and 45 days prior to first scheduled
      sale date. (§ 38-38-103).
   Content of Notice: Notice of Election and Demand: names of grantors, beneficiaries or
      grantees, and holder; date of deed of trust; information about recordation of deed of
      trust; original principal balance; current principal balance; description of the prop-
      erty; statement whether holder is foreclosing on all or part of the property; statement

of the violation of the note or deed of trust on which the foreclosure is based; and name, address, and bar number of holder's attorney (§ 38-38-101); plus supporting documents. Notice to homeowner: All of the above, plus a statement about deadline for notice of intent to cure and notice of intent to redeem; the name, address, and telephone number of each attorney for holder; the date and place of sale; and a statement that the lien being foreclosed may not be a first lien. (§ 38-38-103).

Method of Service: By publication and by mail.

Right to Cure Default/Reinstate: Up to noon of the day before the sale, but must give 15 day prior notice of intent to cure. § 38-38-104.

Redemption: By lienholders only within specified periods. § 38-38-302.

Post-Sale Provisions Regarding Proceeds: Excess proceeds go to creditors in order of priority, with any balance to the mortgagor. § 38-38-111.

Deficiency: § 38-38-106 states that owner may raise as defense that successful bid was less than fair market value of property.

CONNECTICUT

Conn. Gen. Stat. §§ 49-1 to 49-31j

Most Common Method of Foreclosure: Strict foreclosure (no sale). If the strict foreclosure process is used, the court gives the mortgagor a period of time to pay the debt; if the mortgagor does not do so within the specified period of time, title vests in mortgagee. § 49-24. The court may also order foreclosure by sale. See § 49-25 for sale procedure.

Judicial Foreclosure Procedure: Strict foreclosure is commenced by filing of Writ, Summons, and Complaint, as in any other civil action. Must serve all junior lienholders. Lender must provide Notice to homeowner of statutory protections from foreclosure at time the action commences. § 49-31e.

Redemption: If the court orders foreclosure by sale, the redemption period is set by the court. § 49-19. An encumbrancer can redeem.

Deficiency: A deficiency judgment is obtainable within thirty days after the redemption period expires (§ 49-14), and after a court hearing.

Miscellaneous: The mortgagor, if underemployed or unemployed, can apply for protection from foreclosure and the court can restructure the debt. But the mortgagor cannot raise a defense to foreclosure and file for protection. § 49-31f. *See* § 8-265dd ("Emergency Mortgage Assistance Program").

DELAWARE

Del. Code Ann. tit. 10, § 5061

Most Common Method of Foreclosure: Judicial.

Foreclosure by Power of Sale Permitted?: No.

Judicial Foreclosure Procedure: Scire facias/Order to show cause why the mortgaged premises should not be seized upon breach of a condition. Writ served like a summons. Twenty days to answer.

Preforeclosure Notice:

    Number of Notices: One.

    Amount of Notice Required: Ten days pre-sale.

    Content of Notice: a) Day, hour, and place of sale; b) what land and tenements are to be sold; and c) where they lie.

Method of Service: By posting in ten places and delivery by the sheriff to the defendant, or by publication in a newspaper two weeks prior to sale. Del. Code Ann. tit. 10, § 4973.

Right to Cure Default/Reinstate: None.

Redemption: Once the sale is confirmed by the court, no redemption.

Post-Sale Provisions Regarding Proceeds: Surplus goes to the mortgagor/owner. Del. Code Ann. tit. 10, § 5067.

Deficiency: To obtain a deficiency judgment, must file suit on the note. No deficiency in *scire facias* action.

Miscellaneous: Sale must be confirmed by the court. Once confirmed, no redemption. No counterclaims or set-offs allowed in *scire facias* action.

DISTRICT OF COLUMBIA

D.C. Code Ann. § 42-815

Most Common Method of Foreclosure: Power of Sale.

Preforeclosure Notice:

   Number of Notices: One.

   Amount of Notice Required: Thirty days prior to sale.

   Content of Notice: Amount of loan and amount of default, and date, time, and place of sale and such other information as required by D.C. regulations.

   Method of Service: By registered or certified mail.

Right to Cure Default/Reinstate: Up to five days before the sale, once in two consecutive years. § 42-815.01.

Redemption: None after a power of sale foreclosure.

Deficiency: A deficiency judgment is obtainable. § 42-816.

FLORIDA

Fla. Stat. Ann. §§ 702.01, 45.031 (West)

Most Common Method of Foreclosure: Judicial action. The mortgagee can request the issuance of an order to show cause to the mortgagor why final judgment of foreclosure should not be entered. § 702.10.

Foreclosure by Power of Sale Permitted?: No.

Judicial Foreclosure Procedure: File complaint in equity. If a show cause order is requested, a hearing may be held twenty-one days after in-hand service or thirty-one days after the first publication date. Defendant may file a defensive motion but no answer is valid unless it is verified. Sale is made by the clerk no less than twenty days after the final decree. After the sale, the clerk must file a certification of sale indicating the highest bidder and amount of the bid. If there are no objections within ten days, the clerk files the certificate of title. § 45-031.

Preforeclosure Notice:

   Number of Notices: One.

   Amount of Notice Required: Notice must be published in a newspaper for two consecutive weeks with the second publication at least five days before the sale date. §§ 45-031, 702.035.

   Content of Notice: a) Description of the property; b) time and place of sale; and c) statement that sale will be made pursuant to decree of foreclosure, giving the docket number of the case, name of the case, where pending and name of the clerk making the sale.

   Method of Service: By publication.

Redemption: Up to the date the clerk files the certificate of sale.

Post-Sale Provisions Regarding Proceeds: Disbursed by the clerk according to the final decree. Must file a report after disbursement. § 45-031.

Deficiency: Can include a deficiency action in a foreclosure action, but must have in-hand service on the defendant to pursue a deficiency. The court has discretion as to a deficiency decree. §§ 702.06, 45-031(8). Even if a default judgment is entered on the foreclosure, the defendant is entitled, by case law, to a jury trial on the amount of the deficiency.

High-Cost Home Loans: Under the Florida Fair Lending Act, Fla. Stat. Ann. §§ 494.0078 to 494.00797, the lender must mail a notice of the right to cure default 45 days before filing a foreclosure action. If the amount necessary to cure the default will change during the 45-day period, the notice must include information sufficient to calculate the amount during that period. The notice must also include the date by which payment must be made (not less than 45 days from the notice), the name, address and telephone number of a contact to pay or dispute the defaulted amount, and the consequences of failure to cure. § 494.00794

GEORGIA

Ga. Code Ann. §§ 44-14-160 to 44-14-191

Most Common Method of Foreclosure: Power of Sale.

Preforeclosure Notice:

    Number of Notices: One: Notice of Sale.

    Amount of Notice Required: By mail, fifteen days prior to sale. Additional notice by advertising may be required.

    Method of Service: By registered or certified mail or statutory overnight delivery.

Post-Sale Provisions Regarding Proceeds: After the foreclosing mortgagee is paid, surplus goes to the mortgagor.

Deficiency: No default judgment unless the mortgagee makes a report of the sale to the court within thirty days after the sale for confirmation of sale, and the sale is confirmed. The court will not confirm the sale unless it is satisfied that the property brought its true market value.

High-Cost Home Loans: Loans covered by the Georgia Fair Lending Act, Ga. Code Ann. §§ 7-6A-1 to 7-6A-11, require additional notices. Notice of intent to foreclose must be provided fourteen days prior to publication of advertisement required by § 44-14-162. Before foreclosure action is filed, lender must send notice of right to cure. Borrower can cure the default and reinstate up until the time of sale. The Act limits the fees, including attorney fees, that can be charged to reinstate the loan. § 7-6A-5. In an action to enjoin foreclosure or to keep or regain possession of the home, assignees of high-cost home loans are subject to all affirmative claims and any defenses with respect to the loan that the borrower could assert against the creditor of the loan, unless the assignee exercised reasonable diligence at the time of the purchase of the loan to avoid purchasing or taking assignment of high-cost home loans. The borrower may assert against the creditor all claims and defenses that the borrower may have against the seller or home improvement contractor. § 7-6A-6.

GUAM

7 Guam Code Ann. §§ 24101, 24104 to 24105, 24107, 23113, 23124

Most Common Method of Foreclosure: Judicial foreclosure.

Judicial Foreclosure Procedure: All foreclosures must be brought in Superior Court.

Preforeclosure Notice:

    Number of Notices: Notice of Sale.

Amount of Notice Required: Twenty days prior to the sale.

Content of Notice: Time, place of sale, description of the property and terms of the sale.

Method of Service: By posting in three public places in city or town where property located and publication once a week for a period of at least twenty days prior to sale.

Redemption: Within one year after foreclosure by paying the purchase price, plus interest of one percent per month and any taxes, improvements and costs arising since foreclosure.

Post-Sale Provisions Regarding Proceeds: Surplus, if any, goes to mortgagor. § 24105.

Deficiency: Deficiency judgment is available. § 24107.

HAWAII

Haw. Rev. Stat. §§ 667-1 to 667-42

Most Common Method of Foreclosure: Judicial.

Foreclosure by Power of Sale Permitted?: Yes; two alternative processes are available. *See* §§ 667-5, 667-21 to 667-42.

Judicial Foreclosure Procedure: Complaint is filed in circuit court.

Preforeclosure Notice:

Number of Notices: Notice of Sale. § 667-5.

Amount of Notice Required: If by publication, once per week for three consecutive weeks, the last publication to be not less than fourteen days before the sale. If by posting, on the property at least twenty-one days before the sale.

Content of Notice: Description of the property, and time and place of sale. § 667-7.

Method of Service: For a judicial foreclosure, the officer conducting the sale must post notice in three conspicuous places for thirty days prior to the sale, or if on Oahu, advertise at least three times in a newspaper. § 651-43.

Redemption: None.

Post-Sale Provisions Regarding Proceeds: Proceeds are applied to liens in order of priority. § 667-3. An affidavit of sale must be recorded within thirty days after the sale.

IDAHO

Idaho Code §§ 45-1505 to 45-1515 (Michie)

Most Common Method of Foreclosure: Power of Sale.

Preforeclosure Notice:

Number of Notices: One: Notice of Default Sale.

Amount of Notice Required: One hundred twenty days prior to sale.

Content of Notice: a) Set forth default; b) names of parties to the deed of trust; c) description of the property; d) book and page number of recorded deed; e) sum owing; f) default; and g) date, time, and place of sale.

Method of Service: By registered or certified mail to the owner; by in-hand service on the occupant 120 days prior to the sale; and by publication four times with the final publication at least thirty days prior to the sale.

Right to Cure Default/Reinstate: Can cure within 115 days of the filing of Notice of Default and Sale.

Post-Sale Provisions Regarding Proceeds: Proceeds are applied to the sale expenses, the debt of the foreclosing creditor, other liens, and then any surplus goes to the debtor. § 45-1507.

Deficiency: Amount of a deficiency judgment is limited by the fair market value at the date of sale, as found by the court. § 45-1512. Action must be brought within three months after the sale.

ILLINOIS

735 Ill. Comp. Stat. §§ 5/15-1501 to 5/15-1512

Most Common Method of Foreclosure: Judicial.

Foreclosure by Power of Sale Permitted?: No. 735 Ill. Comp. Stat. § 5/15-1405.

Judicial Foreclosure Procedure: Initiated by complaint or counterclaim which meets requirements of § 5/15-1504. Must record notice of foreclosure, which must include information regarding the pending foreclosure, like a *lis pendens.* § 5/15-1503. After judgment, the sale is conducted by a judge or sheriff.

Preforeclosure Notice:

   Number of Notices: One: Notice of Sale.

   Amount of Notice Required: Not more than forty-five days and not less than seven days pre-sale. § 5/15-1507.

   Content of Notice of Sale: a) Name, address, and phone number of person to contact for information; b) common address and description of the property; c) legal description of the property; d) description of improvements; e) times for inspection; f) time and place of sale; g) terms of sale; h) the case title, case number, and court in which foreclosure was filed; and i) such other information as ordered by the court. § 5/15-1507.

   Method of Service: By publication for three consecutive weeks, once per week, with the first notice published not more than forty-five days prior to the sale and last notice not less than seven days pre-sale.

Right to Cure Default/Reinstate: Ninety days from the date of service of the complaint. 735 Ill. Comp. Stat. § 5/15-1602.

Redemption: Generally, until the latter of seven months after service of complaint or three months after the entry of judgment of foreclosure. *See* 735 Ill. Comp. Stat. §§ 5/15-1603 to 5/15-1604.

Post-Sale Provisions Regarding Proceeds: The person conducting the sale must file a report of sale with the court. The court then conducts a hearing to confirm the sale.

Deficiency: A deficiency judgment is obtainable. Surplus is held by a person appointed by the court until the court orders distribution.

High-Cost Home Loans: Under the High Risk Home Loan Act, 815 Ill. Comp. Stat. §§ 137/1 to 137/175, lender must send credit counseling notice to borrower who has been delinquent more than 30 days. If the lender is notified in writing by an approved credit counselor within 15 days after mailing that the borrower is seeking approved credit counseling, the lender may not initiate foreclosure action until 30 days after the date of such notice, unless the parties have otherwise entered into a written debt management plan within the 30-day period. § 137/100. Lender of a high risk loan with legal right of foreclosure must use judicial foreclosure proceedings. Before filing foreclosure action, lender must give at least 30-day notice of right to cure default, including sufficient information for borrower to calculate amount necessary to cure default if amount will change during 30-day period due to permitted late fees or daily interest. The notice must also include deadline for curing default (not less than 30 days), consequences of failure to cure, and the names, addresses and telephone numbers of persons to contact to pay or dispute the default. § 137/105. If a provision of a loan agreement violates the Act, that provision is unenforceable against the borrower. (The statute forbids, inter alia, call provisions and balloon payments.) Borrower may raise violations of Act against assignee (unless the assignee exercises due diligence and takes other precautions to avoid accepting assignment of high-cost home loans) as claims or defenses in foreclosure or collection actions, or in actions to enjoin foreclosure or regain possession. § 137/135.

INDIANA

Ind. Code §§ 32-30-10-1 to 32-30-10-14; 32-29-1-1 to 32-29-1-11; 32-29-7-1 to 32-29-7-14
Most Common Method of Foreclosure: Judicial.
Foreclosure by Power of Sale Permitted?: No. § 32-29-1-3.
Judicial Foreclosure Procedure: "One action" state. The complaint is filed in equity in the circuit court where the property is located. The sale is conducted by a sheriff, or by an auctioneer if the court orders. Waiting periods between filing and sale: three months for mortgages signed on or after July 1, 1975; six months for mortgages signed after Dec. 30, 1957 but before July 1, 1975; twelve months for mortgages signed before Jan. 1, 1958. Waiting periods can be waived, but if waived, no deficiency judgment.
Preforeclosure Notice:
  Number of Notices: One.
  Amount of Notice Required: Publication once per week for three consecutive weeks, with the first advertisement at least thirty days prior to the sale and copy served on borrower at time of first advertisement.
  Content of Notice: Location of property, and common description. § 32-29-7-3.
  Method of Service: By advertisement, by posting in three public places, and by service upon the owner in accordance with Indiana Rules of Procedure governing service of process.
Redemption: None after the sale.
Post-Sale Provisions Regarding Proceeds: Proceeds applied to sale expenses, taxes, amount of redemption where certificate of sale outstanding, payment of principal, interest, residue secured by mortgage and not due, surplus to debtor, heirs, or assigns per court. § 32-30-10-14.
Deficiency: A deficiency judgment is obtainable if there is a written agreement, and if the applicable waiting period is not waived.
High-Cost Home Loans: Borrower may cure default by tendering amount or performance required by mortgage at any time before transfer of title pursuant to foreclosure, judicial proceeding and sale, or otherwise. § 24-9-5-2. Lender with right to foreclose must use the judicial foreclosure procedure of the state in which the property securing the loan is located. § 24-9-5-3. Borrower in foreclosure may raise violations of high-cost home loan statute against lender or subsequent holder or assignee as claim, counterclaim or defense, or in an action to enjoin foreclosure or preserve or regain possession. Ind. Code § 24-9-5-1.

IOWA

Iowa Code §§ 654.1 to 654.26
Most Common Method of Foreclosure: Judicial.
Foreclosure by Power of Sale Permitted?: No (§ 654.1), except as provided in § 654.18 ("Alternative Nonjudicial Voluntary Foreclosure Procedure") or § 655A (Nonjudicial Foreclosure of Nonagricultural Mortgages). The mortgagee waives the deficiency if an alternative procedure is used.
Judicial Foreclosure Procedure: The complaint is filed in equity; "one action" state.
Preforeclosure Notice:
  Number of Notices: One.
  Amount of Notice Required: Four weeks prior to the sale.
  Content of Notice: Time and place of sale.
  Method of Service: By posting in three public places, and by publication in a newspaper.
Right to Cure Default/Reinstate: As to agricultural land, once in twelve months, up to forty-five

days after the Notice of Default is given. As to nonagricultural land, the borrower has thirty days to cure the default.

Redemption: Waived if an alternative procedure is used. (§ 654.18) One year if a judicial foreclosure.

Post-Sale Provisions Regarding Proceeds: Surplus is paid to the mortgagor. § 654.7.

Deficiency: Limited in certain cases by § 654.26. No deficiency if nonjudicial foreclosure procedure is used under § 655A.

Miscellaneous: An agricultural land mortgagor has a right of first refusal after recording of the sheriff's deed. § 654.16A. See § 654.16 for other special protections for farms. In a foreclosure of non-agricultural land without redemption, the mortgagee can elect foreclosure without redemption, but the mortgagor can request a delay of the sale if it is a primary residence. § 654.20. A mortgagor can apply for a continuance if default is admitted and the default is due to climatic conditions, or if the governor declares a state of economic emergency. The moratorium can last one to two years (Moratorium Statute § 654.15). See §§ 654.2A to 654.2D for special rules relating to agricultural property, and §§ 654A.1 to 654A.16 for Farm Mediation Program.

KANSAS

Kan. Stat. Ann. § 60-2410

Most Common Method of Foreclosure: Judicial.

Foreclosure by Power of Sale Permitted?: No.

Judicial Foreclosure Procedure: Complaint filed in local district court. If personal service, mortgagor has twenty days to respond. If service by publication, mortgagor has forty-one days.

Preforeclosure Notice of Sale: An officer gives public notice of the time and place of the sale once a week for three weeks by advertisement, with the last publication not less than seven days and not more than fourteen days prior to the sale. The sale must be confirmed by the court.

Redemption: An owner can redeem within twelve months of the sale or less if the property was abandoned, or three months if less than one-third of original debt has been paid; twelve months if all mortgages on property total less than one-third of market value of property for the amount paid by the purchaser and interest, costs, and taxes. § 60-2414. The three month redemption period may be extended for another three months if owner loses primary source of income after foreclosure.

Deficiency: The court can deny confirmation of sale for an inadequate price, or set an upset price. § 60-2415.

KENTUCKY

Ky. Rev. Stat. Ann. §§ 426.525 to 426.720 (Michie)

Most Common Method of Foreclosure: Judicial.

Foreclosure by Power of Sale Permitted?: No. § 426.525.

Judicial Foreclosure Procedure: Complaint filed in Circuit Court. Defendants have twenty days to respond from date of service.

Preforeclosure Notice:

   Number of Notices: One.

   Amount of Notice Required: If by advertisement, once per week for three consecutive weeks. If by posting, fifteen days preceding the sale.

   Content of Notice: Time, place, and terms of sale, and description of the property.

   Method of Service: By posting on the courthouse door and three other places.

Redemption: Within one year, if the sale does not bring at least two-thirds of the property's appraised value. To redeem, must pay original purchase money and ten percent interest. §§ 426.530, 426.220.

Post-Sale Provisions Regarding Proceeds: Surplus goes to the defendant. § 426.500.

Deficiency: A deficiency judgment is obtainable if the borrower is served in-hand or fails to answer.

High-Cost Home Loans: Lenders must provide notice of default and right to cure thirty days prior to initiation of foreclosure for loans covered by Ky. Rev. Stat. Ann. § 360.100. The notice should contain the amount needed to cure the default, the date payment is due and, if amount needed to cure will change, information sufficient to enable borrower to calculate daily change.

Miscellaneous: The commissioner or officer who makes the sale must report the sale price to the court and the sale must be confirmed by the court. § 426.540. Land must be appraised before the sale.

LOUISIANA

La. Code Civ. Proc. Ann. arts. 3721 to 3753, 2631 to 2772 (West)

Most Common Method of Foreclosure: Judicial.

Judicial Foreclosure Procedure: By "Executory Proceeding" (arts. 2631 to 2724) or "Ordinary Proceeding" (art. 3722). Nearly all foreclosures are by executory proceeding. Under executory process, the mortgagor confesses judgment in the mortgage in the event he does not make required payments. Upon the filing of a petition, with the mortgage attached, the court can order issuance of Writ of Seizure of Sale. Art. 2638. Defenses may be raised through an injunction, or suspensive appeal.

Preforeclosure Notice: Notice of Sale is contained in the petition for Executory Process which is posted on the property. Notice of Seizure must be published at least twice, and not less than three days after the debtor has been served with written notice of seizure.

Redemption: No right of redemption.

Deficiency: A deficiency judgment is only obtainable in an ordinary proceeding or in an executory proceeding if the property has been appraised in accordance with Art. 2723.

Miscellaneous: See Patrick S. Ottinger, *Enforcement of Real Mortgages by Executory Process*, 51 La. L. Rev. 87 (1990), for more information on executory process.

MAINE

Me. Rev. Stat. Ann. tit. 14, §§ 6101 to 6325 (West)

Most Common Method of Foreclosure: Judicial/strict foreclosure.

Foreclosure by Power of Sale Permitted?: No, except against a corporation or partnership or limited liability company. § 6203-A.

Judicial Foreclosure Procedure: File complaint in Superior Court. The court must determine after a hearing whether a breach has occurred. Process is to be served in accordance with Maine Rules of Civil Procedure.

Preforeclosure Notice: Sale follows the expiration of the period of redemption.

    Number of Notices: One.

    Amount of Notice Required: By publication once per week for three consecutive weeks, with the first publication not more than ninety days after the expiration of the period of redemption, and by mail thirty days before sale for foreclosures after Jan. 1, 1995. Sale shall be held not less than thirty days and not more than forty-five days after the date of the first publication. § 6323.

Method of Service: By publication.

Right to Cure/Reinstate: Within thirty days of notice of default. Amount required to cure can include reasonable attorney fees. § 6111.

Redemption: Within one year after the service of a foreclosure notice unless mortgage provides for a shorter period. §§ 6202, 6204.

Post-Sale Provisions Regarding Proceeds: The mortgagee must distribute proceeds per the judgment and must file a report with the court and mail a copy to the mortgagor. Any surplus is paid to the mortgagor. § 6324.

Deficiency: Limited to the amount established as of the date of the sale (§ 6323), and by the fair market value as of the date of the sale if the mortgagee is the purchaser. § 6324.

MARYLAND

Md. Code Ann., Real Prop. § 7-105

Most Common Method of Foreclosure: Power of Sale with court supervision.

Preforeclosure Notice:

    Number of Notices: Two: Notice of Action and Notice of Sale.

    Amount of Notice Required: Notice of Action: No later than two days after action is docketed. § 7-105(a-1)(2). Notice of Sale: By mail, not earlier than thirty days and not later than ten days prior to the sale. § 7-105(b)(1)(ii). By publication, at least once per week for three consecutive weeks with the last publication not more than one week prior to the sale. Rule 14-206.

    Content of Notice: Notice of action: docketing of action, intended foreclosure sale, and mandatory notice regarding availability of organization or agency for assistance. Notice of Sale: time, place, and terms of sale.

    Method of Service: By regular and certified mail to the record owner and junior lienholders, and by publication.

Redemption: Equitable redemption is permitted.

Deficiency: A deficiency judgment may be obtained by motion after sale. (Rule 14-208) Report of the sale to the court and an audit are required.

Miscellaneous: Right of record owner to file an action for failure to make sale in compliance with statute expires three years from ratification of sale. § 7-105(b)(4).

MASSACHUSETTS

Mass. Gen. Laws ch. 244, § 14

Most Common Method of Foreclosure: Power of Sale.

Preforeclosure Notice:

    Number of Notices: One: Notice of Sale to owner no later than fourteen days before sale date and by publication three successive weeks.

    Content of Notice: a) Date, time, place, and terms of sale; b) name of mortgagor; and c) description of the property.

    Method of Service: By registered or certified mail, or by publication.

Right to Cure Default/Reinstate: None.

Redemption: None after the sale if sold pursuant to power of sale in mortgage deed or if buyer in possession of land for three years.

Deficiency: A deficiency judgment is obtainable. Notice of intent to seek a deficiency must be given with the Notice of Sale. Notice of Sale must be served twenty-one days prior to the sale if a deficiency judgment is to be sought.

High-Cost Home Loans: Under the Predatory Home Loan Practices Act, Mass. Gen. Laws ch. 183C, §§ 1–19, before accelerating loan for default a lender must notify the consumer in writing and offer a reasonable opportunity to pay outstanding balance. 183C, § 9. High-cost home loan made without compliance with counseling requirements is unenforceable. 183C, § 3. Court that finds violation of home loan statute has power to rescind high-cost home loan, bar lender from collecting, enjoin judicial or non-judicial foreclosure or other lender action, reform the terms of a high-cost home mortgage, enjoin other prohibited conduct, and provide other relief. 183C, § 18. Borrower in foreclosure may raise violations of the statute against assignee (unless the assignee exercises due diligence and takes other precautions to avoid accepting assignment of high-cost home loans) as a defense or counterclaim, or in an action to enjoin foreclosure or preserve or regain possession. 183C, § 15.

Miscellaneous: Notice of postponement of the sale, if any, is not required. Most foreclosure sales are held after a judicial process in Land Court to determine that the mortgagor is not a soldier or sailor on active duty overseas. No other defenses may be raised in this judicial proceeding.

MICHIGAN

Mich. Comp. Laws §§ 600.3101 to 600.3180, 600.3201 to 600.3280

Most Common Method of Foreclosure: Power of Sale.

Preforeclosure Notice:

   Number of Notices: One.

   Amount of Notice Required: If by publication, once per week for four consecutive weeks. If by posting, within fifteen days of the first advertisement.

   Content of Notice: a) Names of mortgagor, mortgagee, and assignee if any; b) date of mortgage and date recorded; c) amount due; d) description of the premises; and e) length of redemption period.

   Method of Service: By publication and by posting.

Redemption: Redemption periods are determined by the number of units, number of acres, and percentage of original loan outstanding and whether property is abandoned. *See* § 600.3240.

Deficiency: A written agreement that personally obligates the borrower is required. Judgment is limited by the true value of the property, unless foreclosure is by court action.

MINNESOTA

Minn. Stat. §§ 580.01 to 580.30

Most Common Method of Foreclosure: Power of Sale.

Preforeclosure Notice:

   Number of Notices: Two: Notice of Sale and Foreclosure Advice Notice, but the latter is to be delivered with the former

   Amount of Notice Required: Four weeks prior to the sale for service on the occupant. Published notice must be published six weeks before the sale. The Foreclosure Advice Notice must be delivered with the Notice of Sale and with each subsequent written communication regarding the foreclosure up to the day of redemption.

Content of Notice: Notice of Sale: a) Name of mortgagor and mortgagee and original amount of mortgage; b) date of mortgage, when and where recorded; c) amount due; d) description of the premises; e) time and place of sale; f) time for redemption; and g) the mortgagee's right to reduce the redemption period under the statute. The Foreclosure Advice Notice (expires Dec. 31, 2009) advises mortgagors to call the Minnesota Housing Finance Agency for more assistance.

Method of Service: By service on the occupant like a summons, or by publication in a newspaper.

Right to Cure/Reinstate: Borrower has the right to reinstate prior to foreclosure by bringing the loan current including foreclosure fees and costs. § 580.30.

Redemption: Twelve months or six months, depending on date of mortgage, whether property is agricultural, and number of acres. § 580.23. Borrower is entitled to possession during the redemption period.

Deficiency: Limited by the fair market value which is determined by a jury. No deficiency is available if nonjudicial foreclosure is used and six month redemption period is applicable.

MISSISSIPPI

Miss. Code Ann. §§ 89-1-55 to 89-1-59

Most Common Method of Foreclosure: Power of Sale.

Preforeclosure Notice:

    Number of Notices: One: Notice of Sale.

    Amount of Notice Required: If by advertisement, three consecutive weeks before the sale.

    Content of Notice: Name of the original mortgagor, terms and place of sale.

    Method of Service: By advertisement, and by posting on the courthouse door.

Right to Cure Default/Reinstate: Up to the date of the sale.

Redemption: None.

Post-Sale Provisions Regarding Proceeds: Surplus goes to the mortgagor after junior lienholders are paid.

Deficiency: May be obtained in proceeding filed within one year from sale date. If mortgagee is high bidder at sale, deficiency may be denied if bid at sale is not reasonable.

Miscellaneous: The governor can declare a disaster and impose a moratorium on foreclosures for up to two years. § 89-1-301.

MISSOURI

Mo. Rev. Stat. §§ 443.290 to 443.453

Most Common Method of Foreclosure: Power of Sale.

Preforeclosure Notice:

    Number of Notices: One.

    Amount of Notice Required: Twenty days.

    Content of Notice: a) Date, book, and page of record of mortgage; b) grantor; c) date, time, terms, and place of sale; and d) description of the property. § 443.320.

    Method of Service: By publication, and by registered or certified mail to the record owner. § 443.325.

Redemption: Foreclosure under a power of sale forecloses equity of redemption unless the lender is the purchaser. If the lender is the purchaser, can redeem up to one year after the sale if notice of intent to redeem is given within ten days before the sale, or at the sale if a bond is posted. §§ 443.410, 443.420.

Deficiency: May be obtained by mortgagee.

MONTANA

Mont. Code Ann. §§ 71-1-222 to 71-1-235 and §§ 71-1-301 to 71-1-321 (Small Tract Financing Act)

Most Common Method of Foreclosure: Power of Sale.

Preforeclosure Notice:

    Number of Notices: One: Notice of Sale.

    Amount of Notice Required: Thirty days. § 71-1-224. 120 days for Small Tract Financing Act. § 71-1-315.

    Content of Notice: Not indicated. See § 71-1-313 for Small Tract Financing Act content requirements.

    Method of Service: By advertisement thirty days prior to the sale; by posting in five conspicuous places; or by in-person service thirty days pre-sale on the occupant, mortgagor, and persons claiming interest of record. § 71-1-224. See § 71-1-315 for Small Tract Financing Act requirements.

Right to Cure Default/Reinstate: Under the Small Tract Financing Act, may cure at any time prior to the sale; applies to deeds of trust on property of less than forty acres.

Redemption: One year after the sale by paying the amount of the purchase and costs. The mortgagor retains possession during the redemption period if the property is a home. *See* §§ 25-13-802, 25-13-821.

Post-Sale Provisions Regarding Proceeds: Surplus is deposited with the court. The court directs distribution. § 71-1-225.

Deficiency: A deficiency judgment is not allowed on a foreclosure of a purchase price mortgage unless judicial foreclosure process is used. §§ 71-1-232, 71-1-317.

NEBRASKA

Neb. Rev. Stat. §§ 25-2137 to 25-2155

Most Common Method of Foreclosure: Judicial.

Foreclosure by Power of Sale Permitted?: No.

Judicial Foreclosure Procedure: File petition in the district court where the property is located. The sale is made by the sheriff.

Preforeclosure Notice:

    Number of Notices: One.

    Amount of Notice Required: If by publication, once per week for four consecutive weeks.

    Content of Notice: Time and place of sale. § 25-1529.

    Method of Service: By publication, and by posting on the courthouse door and five other public places in the county. Sales made without such notice shall be set aside on motion. § 25-1529.

Right to Cure Default/Reinstate: Defendant can pay installments due while the suit is pending. Upon such payment, the petition shall be dismissed. § 25-2148. If the defendant pays after the decree is issued, the decree remains in effect but is stayed and can be executed if the defendant defaults again.

Redemption: Before the sale is confirmed.

Post-Sale Provisions Regarding Proceeds: Surplus goes to the defendant, after being brought into court. § 25-2146.

Deficiency: May be obtained by filing a separate action after sale. § 25-2140.

Miscellaneous: The debtor must be given notice of the homestead exemption before confirmation of sale. § 25-1531.

NEVADA

Nev. Rev. Stat. § 107.080
Most Common Method of Foreclosure: Power of Sale for deeds of trust.
Preforeclosure Notice:
   Number of Notices: Two: Notice of Default (Breach) and Election to Sell; and Notice of Sale.
   Amount of Notice Required: For Notice of Default (Breach), three months. For Notice of Sale, three weeks.
   Content of Notice: Notice of Default: must describe default and may contain notice of intent to accelerate entire unpaid balance if permitted by secured obligation. Notice of Default also must be recorded. *Notice of Sale:* must state time and place of sale and must be published once per week for three weeks.
   Method of Service: Notice of Default: By mail to the grantor and owner on the date the Notice is recorded, and within ten days of recording of Notice, by mail to each person who filed a request for a copy and to each "person with an interest" subordinate to the deed of trust. *Notice of Sale:* By mail within twenty days before the date of sale set forth in the Notice of Sale.
Right to Cure Default/Reinstate: Thirty-five days from recording and mailing to grantor and owner of Notice of Default.
Redemption: None for nonjudicial foreclosures.
Deficiency: Limited to the lesser of (i) the amount by which the amount of the secured debt exceeds the fair market value of the property as determined by the court, or (ii) the difference between the amount for which the property was sold and the amount of the secured debt, with interest from the date of sale.
High-Cost Home Loans: Power of sale under trust agreement entered into on or after October 1, 2003, and subject to § 152 of the Home Ownership and Equity Protection Act of 1994 and applicable federal regulations, requires additional notice at least 60 days before date of sale. The notice, which must be personally served unless otherwise directed by a court, must include applicable telephone numbers and addresses for offices of consumer credit counseling, attorney general, division of financial institutions, legal services, and lender. Date of sale may not be less than 30 days after date of most recently filed action, if any, claiming unfair lending practice in connection with the trust agreement. §§ 107.080, 107.085. Court that finds violation of high-cost home loan statute (Nev. Rev. Stat. §§ 598D.010 through 598D.150) has power to award equitable remedy and may cure any existing default and cancel a pending foreclosure sale, trustee's sale or other sale to enforce the agreement. If damages are awarded (statute allows three times actual damages) borrower has a defense against the unpaid obligation up to the amount of the damages. Nev. Rev. Stat. § 598D.110.

NEW HAMPSHIRE

N.H. Rev. Stat. Ann. § 479:25
Most Common Method of Foreclosure: Power of Sale.
Preforeclosure Notice:
   Number of Notices: One.[2]
   Amount of Notice Required: If to the mortgagor, in hand or by certified or registered mail twenty-five days before the sale. If by publication, once per week for three consecutive

weeks with the first publication not less than twenty days prior to the sale. Also, any grantee with an interest in the property recorded at least thirty days prior to the sale must get twenty-five days notice.

Content of Notice: a) Date, time, and place of sale; b) location of the property; c) date of mortgage; d) volume and page number where mortgage is recorded; e) terms of sale; f) that the mortgagor has the right to petition the court, with notice to the mortgagee and posting of bonds as the court may require, to enjoin the sale; and g) that failure to take action will bar any action based on the validity of the foreclosure.

Method of Service: By hand or by registered or certified mail, and by publication in a newspaper of general circulation published in the county where the town is located.

Redemption: Up to the time of sale, by paying the full amount due plus costs. § 479:18.

Post-Sale Provisions Regarding Proceeds: The seller must record the deed and affidavit of compliance within sixty days of the sale. § 479:26.

Deficiency: May be obtained in action filed after sale.

Miscellaneous: The mortgagee has a duty of good faith and due diligence in the conduct of the sale. If the duty is violated, the borrower may be able to get damages equal to the difference between the sale price and the fair market value. Murphy v. Fin. Dev. Co., 126 N.H. 536 (1985).

NEW JERSEY

N.J. Stat. Ann. §§ 2A:50-1 to 2A:50-21 (West)

Most Common Method of Foreclosure: Suit in equity.

Foreclosure by Power of Sale Permitted?: No, in most circumstances (§§ 2A:50-2.2, 2A:50-2.3) (can waive the right to a judicial foreclosure if the property is non-residential; is not one-, two-, three-, or four-family in which the borrower lives; is a second mortgage; and if the lender is a bank).

Judicial Foreclosure Procedure: Can get judgment to foreclose in whole or in part. Set-offs allowed. Sale is by the sheriff (§ 2A:50-19); the sheriff must make a report of the sale. The court must confirm the sale. The mortgagor has ten days after the sale to object. Rule 4:65-5.

Preforeclosure Notice:

   Number of Notices: One.

   Amount of Notice Required: Thirty days before taking any legal action, by registered or certified mail, return receipt requested. § 2A:50-56 (residential mortgages only).

   Content of Notice: Include obligation, nature of default, right to cure, how to cure, time to cure, that the lender intends to foreclose if default is not cured, advise the mortgagor to seek legal counsel, the availability of financial assistance programs, the lender's address and telephone number, description of the property.

   Method of Service: By posting on the property and in the county office four times for four weeks, or by advertisement in two newspapers and mailed to the mortgagor and other parties. Record *lis pendens*.

Right to Cure Default/Reinstate: Up to date of final judgment by tendering amount due before default, perform any obligations necessary, pay costs, and contractual late charges. May reinstate only once in eighteen months. § 2A:50-57 (residential mortgages only). Final judgment of foreclosure of residential mortgage may be delayed if debtor certifies that there is a reasonable likelihood that debtor will be able to provide payment necessary to cure the default within forty-five days. § 2A:50-58.

Redemption: Six months after the entry of judgment.

Post-Sale Provisions Regarding Proceeds: Surplus is deposited with the court and paid to persons entitled to it as determined by the court. § 2A:50-37.

Deficiency: No personal deficiency judgment in foreclosure actions or execution thereon for balance due. Deficiency judgment is obtainable in an action after foreclosure. Judgment is limited by the fair market value. Action for a deficiency judgment must be brought within three months. § 2A:50-1.

High-Cost Home Loans: High-cost home loans covered under the Home Ownership Security Act, N.J. Stat. Ann. §§ 46:10B-22 to 10B-35 (West), must use judicial foreclosure procedures. N.J. Stat. Ann. § 46:10B-26(k) (West).

NEW MEXICO

N.M. Stat. Ann. §§ 48-7-1 to 48-7-24, 39-5-1 to 39-5-23 (Michie)
Most Common Method of Foreclosure: Judicial.

Foreclosure by Power of Sale Permitted?: With limitations. See §§ 48-7-7 and 48-10-10 for commercial property or certain loans to benefit low income households, including loans by qualified non-profits to low income households, and loans to finance low income housing projects. § 48-10-3.

Judicial Foreclosure Procedure: Sale may not take place until thirty days after judgment. The sale is conducted by the sheriff. Before the sale, the sheriff must have the property appraised. The property cannot sell for less than two-thirds of its appraised value. § 39-5-5. See also § 39-5-14 regarding "reoffer of unsold property."

Preforeclosure Notice:

Number of Notices: One: Notice of Sale.

Amount of Notice Required: If by publication, for four weeks preceding the sale.

Content of Notice: a) Title of the case in which foreclosure judgment is obtained; b) date of judgment; c) amount of judgment; d) description of the property; and e) time and conditions of sale. Notice may be in English or Spanish; the sheriff must determine which will be most effective to give the most extensive notice. § 39-5-1.

Method of Service: By publication, or by posting in six of the most public places in the county.

Redemption: Within nine months of the sale by paying the purchaser the purchase price and ten percent interest, or by paying same amount into the court. § 39-5-21. The redemption period may be shortened by the parties to not less than one month. §§ 39-5-19, 39-5-18.

Deficiency: No provision regarding deficiency upon judicial foreclosure. No deficiency judgment after power of sale foreclosure on property occupied by low income household. § 48-10-17.

High-Cost Home Loans: The Home Loan Protection Act, N.M. Stat. Ann. §§ 58-21A-1 to 58-21A-14, requires lenders to provide notice of right to cure prior to filing a foreclosure action for loans covered by the Act. The notice should contain the amount needed to cure the default and, if amount needed to cure will change, information sufficient to enable borrower to calculate daily change. Borrowers are given thirty days from delivery of notice to cure the default. Lenders must use judicial foreclosure procedures. Borrower in foreclosure may raise violations of the Act against an assignee (unless the assignee exercises due diligence and takes other precautions to avoid accepting assignment of high-cost home loans) as counterclaim or defense, or in action to enjoin foreclosure or preserve or retain possession of the home. N.M. Stat. § 58-21A-11.

Miscellaneous: A deed of trust can be foreclosed by a power of sale under the Deeds of Trust Act, but the Act only applies to commercial deeds of trust of $500,000 or more. §§ 48-10-1 to 48-10-21. Prepayment penalty prohibited. § 48-7-19.

NEW YORK

N.Y. Real Prop. Acts. Law §§ 1301 to 1391 (McKinney)

Most Common Method of Foreclosure: Judicial.

Foreclosure by Power of Sale Permitted?: Yes.

Judicial Foreclosure Procedure: Must name all the parties with an interest in the property or a lien. § 1311. *Lis pendens* also must be filed.

Preforeclosure Notice:

   Method of Service: By advertisement.

Right to Cure Default/Reinstate: Can pay the amount due into the court any time before the final judgment and the case will be dismissed; after judgment, but before the sale, the proceedings shall be stayed upon payment of arrearages.[3] § 1341.

Redemption: None after the sale.

Post-Sale Provisions Regarding Proceeds: An officer must make a report to the court, and surplus must be paid to the court within five days of receipt. The sale must be confirmed by the court. § 1354.

Deficiency: A deficiency judgment is obtainable if the defendant was served in-hand or appears in the action. Limited by the market value of the property. § 1371.

High-Cost Home Loans: Foreclosure complaint of high-cost home loan must contain, and lender must prove, allegation that plaintiff lender has complied with law relating to such loans, N.Y. Banking Law § 6-*l*, and to lenders of such loans, N.Y. Banking Law § 595-a; Real Prop. Acts. Law § 1302. An intentional violation of the high-cost home loan statute voids the transaction, and bars the lender from collecting. N.Y. Banking Law § 6-*l*. The loan may be rescinded for a violation of the law, whether the violation is raised as an affirmative claim or a defense. Rescission is available as a defense without time limitation. A borrower in foreclosure may raise against assignee any claim to recoupment or defenses to payment, based on violation of this statute, that could be raised against the original lender. N.Y. Banking Law § 6-*l*(10)–(12); Real Prop. Acts. Law § 1302.

NORTH CAROLINA

N.C. Gen. Stat. §§ 45-21.1 to 45-21.33

Most Common Method of Foreclosure: Power of Sale with prior hearing before clerk.

Preforeclosure Notice:

   Number of Notices: Three: Notice of Default, Notice of Hearing and Notice of Sale.

   Amount of Notice Required: For Notice of Default, thirty days before notice of hearing. For Notice of Hearing, ten days before the hearing. For Notice of Sale, twenty days before the sale for service on the debtor. § 45-21.16.

   Content of Notice: Notice of Default: Amount of principal and interest due, the interest rate, and any other sums claimed to be due. § 45-21.16. *Notice of Hearing:* a) description of the property, date and original amount of mortgage, and the book and page where recorded; b) name and address of holder; c) nature of default; d) whether mortgage has been accelerated; e) any right to cure; f) right of debtor to appear before the clerk to show cause why foreclosure should not be allowed; g) that if foreclosure is consummated, debtor will be evicted; and h) other miscellaneous information. § 45-21.16. Must confirm that notice of default mailed. *Notice of Sale:* a) description of instrument (mortgage); b) date, time, and place of sale; c) description of the property; and d) terms of sale. § 45-21.16A.

   Method of Service: For a Notice of Hearing, by service on the debtor like a summons. For a Notice of Sale, by posting fifteen days prior to the sale; by publishing in a newspaper once per week for two consecutive weeks, with the date of the last publication not less than ten days before the sale; or by regular mail to the debtor. § 45-21.17.

Redemption: By payment in full, plus expenses of sale or proposed sale, before sale or within ten days thereafter. §§ 45-21.20, 45-21.27.

Post-Sale Provisions Regarding Proceeds: Final report of the sale must be filed with the clerk within thirty days of the receipt of sale proceeds. The report must include proof of notice. § 45-21.33. Surplus proceeds go to the person entitled to them, if known; if not known, the proceeds are paid to the court clerk for determination. § 45-21.31.

Deficiency: The mortgagor can show the fair market value of the property as a defense in a deficiency action. § 45-21.36. No deficiency judgment on foreclosure by power of sale of purchase money mortgage. § 45-21.38.

Miscellaneous: See § 45-21.34 for enjoining a mortgage sale or confirmation thereof. Upset bids are allowed. Note that issues at clerk's hearing are limited to whether there was a valid debt; whether a default has occurred; whether holder has right to foreclose and whether proper notice was given. Other defenses must be raised in action to enjoin foreclosure.

NORTH DAKOTA

N.D. Cent. Code §§ 32-19-01 to 32-19-41

Most Common Method of Foreclosure: Judicial.

Foreclosure by Power of Sale Permitted?: No, except mortgages held by the state which contain a power of sale. § 35-22-01.

Judicial Foreclosure Procedure: Action is brought in district court. The complaint must state whether the plaintiff will seek a deficiency judgment. Notice of Intent to Foreclose must be served on the owner of record at least thirty days, but not more than ninety days, prior to commencement of an action. § 32-19-20. The notice must state the amount due and that if the amount due is not paid within thirty days, foreclosure will be commenced. Notice is to be served by registered or certified mail, or in-hand. The sale is made by the sheriff.

Preforeclosure Notice:

> *Number of Notices:* One.

> *Amount of Notice Required:* If by advertisement, once per week for three consecutive weeks with the last publication to be at least ten days prior to the sale.

> *Method of Service:* By advertisement, if a newspaper is printed in the county, otherwise by posting on the courthouse door and five other places. A sale made without the required notice must be set aside. § 28-23-04.

Right to Cure Default/Reinstate: After judgment but before the sale, the defendant can bring into court the amount due and the proceedings will be stayed, but the court can enforce the judgment if the defendant subsequently defaults in payments.[4] Can cure default within thirty days of notice of intent to foreclose. § 32-19-28.

Redemption: Within 60 days, but one year for agricultural land. The period of redemption begins at the time of the filing of the foreclosure action or at the time of first publication of the foreclosure notice. §§ 32-19-18, 28-24-02.

Post-Sale Provisions Regarding Proceeds: Any surplus after payment of the debt and costs shall be brought into court for the defendant, subject to the order of the court.

Deficiency: No deficiency for foreclosure of residential property of four or fewer units up to forty contiguous acres; may obtain deficiency judgment for agricultural land of more than 40 acres but must be based on fair market value; for other properties, deficiency judgments may be based on appraised value. § 32-19-03.

Miscellaneous: § 15-07-10: authorizes original mortgagor to repurchase non-grant lands following foreclosure by matching highest bid within one hour after sale.

OHIO

Ohio Rev. Code Ann. §§ 2323.07, 5301.39, 5721.18 (West)
Most Common Method of Foreclosure: Judicial.
Foreclosure by Power of Sale Permitted?: No. *See* Etna Coal & Iron v. Marting, 14 O.F.D 325.
Judicial Foreclosure Procedure: The lender must sue the borrower in the county where the property is located to obtain a foreclosure order. Must have the property appraised and the property must be offered for sale at not less than two-thirds the appraised value. The sale is conducted by the sheriff.
Preforeclosure Notice:
  Number of Notices: One.
  Amount of Notice Required: Thirty days by advertisement, once per week for three consecutive weeks.
Redemption: Up to the confirmation of sale by paying the full amount of the judgment and costs.
Post-Sale Provisions Regarding Proceeds: Sale must be confirmed by the court.
Deficiency: A deficiency judgment is allowed, but void after two years from the confirmation of sale. § 2329.08.

OKLAHOMA

Okla. Stat. tit. 12, §§ 686, 764 to 765, 773; Okla. Stat. tit. 46, §§ 41 to 49
Most Common Method of Foreclosure: Judicial.
Foreclosure by Power of Sale Permitted?: Yes, but may not be used against a homestead, if the homeowner chooses to require judicial foreclosure, nor may it be used to foreclose a lien for an extension of credit primarily for agricultural purposes. Judgment is required. Okla. Stat. tit. 12, § 686.
Judicial Foreclosure Procedure: "One action" state. Complaint is filed in equity.
Preforeclosure Notice: Executed by the sheriff. Okla. Stat. tit. 12, § 764. But see Okla. Stat. tit. 46, §§ 40 to 49 (Power of Sale Act), although the Act does not apply to a homestead if the mortgagor elects judicial foreclosure pursuant to Okla. Stat. tit. 46, § 43A(2)(b).
  Number of Notices: One.
  Amount of Notice Required: If by mailing, at least ten days prior to the sale. If by publication, beginning thirty days prior to the sale.
  Content of Notice: Legal description of the property, and time and place of sale.
  Method of Service: By first class mail to the judgment debtor and other lienholders. By publication of notice for two consecutive weeks, beginning thirty days prior to the sale.
Right to Cure Default/Reinstate: If a power of sale is used, can cure within thirty-five days of notice of intent to foreclose, but not more than three times in twenty-four months. Okla. Stat. tit. 46, § 44.
Redemption: Up to the confirmation of sale. Okla. Stat. tit. 42, §§ 18 to 20.
Post-Sale Provisions Regarding Proceeds: Any surplus must be paid to the defendant on demand. Okla. Stat. tit. 12, § 773.
Deficiency: A deficiency judgment is limited by the market value of the property on the date of sale. Okla. Stat. tit. 12, § 686. After the sale, notice of the confirmation hearing must be

given to all persons who received the Notice of Sale. Objections may be filed. Okla. Stat. tit. 12, § 765. The mortgagee must move for a deficiency judgment within ninety days of sale. Okla. Stat. tit. 12, § 686. If the debtor allows the foreclosure to proceed under power of sale, and gives timely notice that the property is homestead and that he or she elects against a deficiency judgment, then no deficiency judgment. Okla. Stat. tit. 46, §§ 41 to 49.

OREGON

Or. Rev. Stat. §§ 86.735 to 86.795

Most Common Method of Foreclosure: Power of Sale for deeds of trust.

Preforeclosure Notice:

   Number of Notices: Two: Notice of Default and Notice of Sale. Notice of Default must be recorded.

   Amount of Notice Required: For Notice of Sale, 120 days prior to sale. For publication, once per week for four consecutive weeks with the last publication more than twenty days pre-sale.

   Content of Notice: a) Names of parties; b) description of the property; c) where deed of trust is recorded; d) nature of default; e) sum owing; f) election to sell; g) date, time, and place of sale; and h) right to reinstatement up to five days before sale by curing default.

   Method of Service: By publication, and by both first class and certified mail to the grantor and occupant.

Right to Cure Default/Reinstate: Up to five days before the sale. Limits on costs for a residential mortgage. § 86.753.

Post-Sale Provisions Regarding Proceeds: Any surplus proceeds go to the grantor. § 86.765.

PENNSYLVANIA

Pa. Stat. Ann. tit. 35, §§ 1680.402c to 1680.409c (West); Pa. Stat. Ann. tit. 41, §§ 403 to 404 (West); Pa. R. Civ. P. 1141 to 1150

Most Common Method of Foreclosure: Judicial.

Judicial Foreclosure Procedure: Action commenced by filing a complaint in Court of Common Pleas. Must serve the owner as well as the occupant of the property.

Preforeclosure Notice: See Pa. Stat. Ann. tit. 41, § 403.

   Number of Notices: Two: 1) Notice of right to apply to Pennsylvania Housing Finance Agency for Assistance. Pa. Stat. Ann. tit. 35, § 1680.403c. 2) Notice of Intention to Foreclose. Pa. Stat. Ann. tit. 41, § 403. For form of notice, see 10 Pa. Code § 7.4.

   Amount of Notice Required: Thirty days.

   Content of Notice: a) Particular obligation or real estate security interest; b) nature of claimed default; c) right to cure default and how to cure; d) time to cure; e) method by which debtor's ownership or possession may be terminated; and f) right of debtor to sell or refinance. § 403(c).

   Method of Service: By certified or registered mail to the owner's last known address and to the property.

Right to Cure Default/Reinstate: Up to one hour before the bidding, but not more than three times in one year, by paying the amount due and costs. Pa. Stat. Ann. tit. 41, § 404.

Redemption: None after the sale.

Deficiency: A deficiency judgment is allowed in a separate action filed after completion of sale.

PUERTO RICO

30 P.R. Laws Ann. §§ 2701 to 2725

Most Common Method of Foreclosure: Summary Procedure (§ 2701) or Judicial Action (P.R. R. Civ. P. 51.8).

Preforeclosure Notice: Debtor must be given twenty days to cure default before the procedure can be initiated. § 2703. Demand made by certified mail. Cure amount does not include attorney fees.

Foreclosure Process: Foreclosure procedure initiated by filing a brief which meets requirements of § 2706. It then gives debtor thirty days to pay off any claims plus fees and costs. § 2710.

Debtor can submit deposition of objections within first twenty days of the thirty days of demand for payment. § 2706. Court can hold hearing on defenses within ten days of service thereof.

After thirty days pass and objections resolved—property can be sold at auction by marshall. § 2719. Marshall must issue edict of date, time, place of auction. §§ 2720, 2721.

Sale must then be confirmed by court. § 2725.

RHODE ISLAND

R.I. Gen. Laws §§ 34-27-1 to 34-27-5

Most Common Method of Foreclosure: Power of Sale.

Preforeclosure Notice:

    Number of Notices: One.

    Amount of Notice Required: If by mail, thirty days prior to the first publication. If by publication, twenty-one days and must publish three times. § 34-27-4.

    Content of Notice: Date, time, and place of sale. § 34-11-22.

    Method of Service: By certified mail and by publication.

Redemption: Up to three years after the sale by filing a lawsuit. § 34-23-3.

Deficiency: A deficiency judgment is obtainable.

SOUTH CAROLINA

S.C. Code Ann. §§ 15-39-610, 29-3-630 to 29-3-790 (Law. Co-op.)

Most Common Method of Foreclosure: Judicial.

Judicial Foreclosure Procedure: In any action, the plaintiff must establish the amount of the debt. Notice is given as in any civil action.

Notice of Sale:

    Number of Notices: One.

    Amount of Notice Required: If by advertisement, for three weeks prior to the sale.

    Content of Notice: a) Property to be sold; b) time and place of sale; and c) name of plaintiff and defendant.

    Method of Service: By advertisement in a newspaper, and by posting in three public places.

Redemption: None after foreclosure.

Deficiency: Upset bids are accepted within thirty days of sale. § 15-39-720. Deficiency judgments are allowed (§ 29-3-660), but the defendant can ask the court for an order of appraisal within thirty days of the sale.

High-Cost Home Loans: If, before the maturity date of the debt, the court finds a violation of the high-cost home loans statute, S.C. Code Ann. §§ 37-23-10 through 37-23-85, it may refuse to enforce the agreement, or the term or part that was unlawful, or rewrite the agreement to eliminate the unlawful part. S.C. Code Ann. § 37-23-50. In an action to collect the debt, borrower may raise a violation of this statute as a matter of defense by recoupment or setoff. S.C. Code Ann. § 37-23-50.

SOUTH DAKOTA

S.D. Codified Laws §§ 21-48-1 to 21-48-26 (Michie)
Most Common Method of Foreclosure: Power of Sale. See §§ 21-47-1 to 21-47-25 for the judicial foreclosure procedure; see also §§ 21-48A-1 to 21-48A-5 for nonjudicial voluntary foreclosure.
Preforeclosure Notice:
  Number of Notices: One.
  Amount of Notice Required: By publication, four weeks. Written notice to be served twenty-one days prior to sale. § 21-48-6.1.
  Content of Notice: a) Names of mortgagor and mortgagee; b) date of mortgage; c) amount due; d) description of the property; and e) time and place of sale; f) debtor's right to apply for judicial foreclosure action; g) description of default; and h) names and addresses of all persons claiming a recorded interest in the property. § 21-48-6.
  Method of Service: By publication once per week for four consecutive weeks.
Redemption: None after a power of sale foreclosure. But see §§ 21-49-11 to 21-49-40 for "Short Term Redemption Mortgages."
Deficiency: A deficiency judgment is limited by the true market value of the property if mortgagee, payee or other holder purchases the property directly or indirectly. § 21-48-14.
Miscellaneous: After commencement of foreclosure by a power of sale, the mortgagor can require a mortgagee to foreclose by action by making an application to the court. No reasons need be given. § 21-48-9.

TENNESSEE

Tenn. Code Ann. §§ 35-5-101 to 35-5-111, 66-8-101 to 66-8-102
Most Common Method of Foreclosure: Power of Sale.
Preforeclosure Notice:
  Number of Notices: One: Notice of Sale.
  Amount of Notice Required: Notice to be sent to debtor by registered mail, return receipt requested, 30 days prior to publication date. § 35-5-101(e). If by publication, twenty days. If by posting, thirty days. Must publish three times with the first notice at least twenty days prior to the sale.
  Content of Notice: a) Names of parties; b) description of the land; c) time and place of sale; and d) identification of any federal or state liens. § 35-5-104.
  Method of Service: By publication or by posting.
Redemption: Up to two years. §§ 66-8-101, 66-8-102.
Deficiency: A deficiency judgment is obtainable.
Miscellaneous: The sale is not voidable nor void if the notice provisions are not complied with. The trustee could be guilty of misdemeanor, however. §§ 35-5-106, 35-5-107.

TEXAS

Tex. Prop. Code Ann. § 51.002 (Vernon)
Most Common Method of Foreclosure: Power of Sale.

Preforeclosure Notice:

   Number of Notices: Two: Notice of Default (with twenty days to cure) and Notice of Sale (for residential mortgage foreclosures only).

   Amount of Notice Required: Twenty-one days prior to sale.

   Content of Notice: Earliest time of sale, and place of sale.

   Method of Service: By certified mail and by posting on the courthouse door.

Right to Cure Default/Reinstate: Can cure within twenty days of the Notice of Default. § 51.002(d).

Redemption: No right of redemption.

Deficiency: A deficiency action must be brought within two years of the sale. The borrower can ask the court to determine the fair market value. If the court determines that the fair market value is greater than the sale price, the borrower is entitled to an offset. § 51.003.

Miscellaneous: Note special provision regarding deed-in-lieu. § 51.006. Foreclosure of certain loans secured by a lien on a homestead is prohibited by Tex. Const. art. 16, § 50, except when certain requirements are met. These requirements include foreclosure only by court order. Tex. Const. art. 16, § 50(a)(6).

UTAH

Utah Code Ann. §§ 57-1-19, 78-37-1; Utah R. Civ. P. 69(i),(j)

Most Common Method of Foreclosure: Power of sale.

Preforeclosure Notice:

   Number of Notices: Two: Notice of Default and Notice of Sale.

   Amount of Notice Required: Notice of Default: Must be recorded at least three months prior to sale. Must be mailed to mortgagor by certified or registered mail within ten days after recording. *Nonjudicial Foreclosure Procedure:* Notice of Sale describing the property and time and place of sale must be published three times and last date of publication must be at least ten days prior to sale.

Right to Cure Default/Reinstate: Within three months of the filing of the Notice of Default. § 57-1-31.

Post-Sale Provisions Regarding Proceeds: Court may direct that any surplus be deposited in the court, to be distributed as the court directs. § 78-37-4.

Deficiency: A deficiency judgment is obtainable. § 78-37-2.

VERMONT

Vt. Stat. Ann. tit. 12, § 4526 (strict foreclosure); Vt. Stat. Ann. tit. 12, §§ 4531, 4532 (power of sale)

Most Common Method of Foreclosure: Strict foreclosure.

Foreclosure by Power of Sale Permitted?: Yes, if a power of sale is contained in the mortgage or the court orders the sale. Vt. Stat. Ann. tit. 12, § 4531a; *see* Vt. Stat. Ann. tit. 12, § 4532.

Judicial Foreclosure Procedure: Filing of complaint complying with Vt. R. Civ. P. 80.1. Complaint is served in accordance with Vt. R. Civ. P. 4. Accounting must be submitted to the court; the court makes a finding as to principal, interest, and costs due. The court then issues a writ of possession to the mortgagee and the mortgagee takes the property free and clear of the interests of any named defendants.

Preforeclosure Notice:

   Number of Notices: Two: Notice of Intent to Foreclose and Notice of Sale (power of sale foreclosure).

Amount of Notice: Notice of Intent: Thirty days prior to notice of sale. *Notice of Sale:* Sixty days prior to sale.

Content of Notice: Notice of Intent: the mortgage to be foreclosed, the condition claimed to have been breached, whether debt has been accelerated, amount to be paid or other action necessary to cure, and time to cure, intention to foreclose by power of sale, right to notice of sale. *Notice of Sale:* Legal description of premises, terms of sale, right to redeem, right to redemption, time and place of sale.

Method of Service: Registered or certified mail. Notice of Sale must also be recorded, and must be published once a week for three weeks in newspaper of general circulation.

Redemption: Six months from the date of judgment of foreclosure. Vt. Stat. Ann. tit. 12, § 4528.

Post-Sale Provisions Regarding Proceeds: If foreclosure is by power of sale, any surplus shall be paid to other parties in order of priority of their liens and to the defendant mortgagor.

Deficiency: The plaintiff must request a deficiency in the complaint; if the mortgagee is the purchaser, the deficiency judgment is limited by the fair market value. Vt. R. Civ. P. 80.1(j)(2).

Miscellaneous: With a power of sale foreclosure, the sale cannot take place within seven months of the complaint if the property is a dwelling house of two units or less. Vt. Stat. Ann. tit. 12, § 4531a; *see* Vt. Stat. Ann. tit. 12, § 4531) (which states that a lien held by a federal agency which cannot be foreclosed by strict foreclosure may be foreclosed by sale).

VIRGINIA

Va. Code Ann. §§ 55-59 to 55-66.6 (Michie)
Most Common Method of Foreclosure: Power of Sale.
Preforeclosure Notice:
 Number of Notices: One.
 Amount of Notice Required: For service by mail, fourteen days. For publication, four weeks. §§ 55-59.2, 55-59.1.
 Content of Notice: a) Time, date, and place of sale; b) terms of sale; and c) names of trustees. § 55-59.3.
 Method of Service: By in-hand delivery, or by mail and publication.
Redemption: No right of redemption for a nonjudicial foreclosure.
Deficiency: A deficiency judgment is obtainable.

VIRGIN ISLANDS

5 V.I. Code Ann. §§ 484, 492 to 496; 28 V.I. Code Ann. §§ 535, 538
Most Common Method of Foreclosure: Power of Sale.
Preforeclosure Notice:
 Number of Notices: Notice of Sale.
 Amount of Notice Required: Written or printed notice, posted in a public place or near office of court clerk and published once a week for four weeks prior to the sale in a newspaper in the judicial division in which the sale is to take place.
 Content of Notice: Time, place of sale, and description of the property.
 Method of Service: Publication.
Right to Cure Default/Reinstate: Up to time of sale.
Redemption: Within six months after the order of confirmation of sale by payment of the purchase amount plus interest at the legal rate and any taxes that the purchaser may have paid.

WASHINGTON

Wash. Rev. Code §§ 61.24.020 to 61.24.140
Most Common Method of Foreclosure: Power of Sale on deed of trust.[5]
Preforeclosure Notice:
  Number of Notices: Two: Notice of Default and Notice of Sale. § 61.24.030.
  Amount of Notice Required: For a Notice of default, thirty days. For a Notice of Sale, ninety days.
  Content of Notice: Notice of Default: a) description of the property; b) where instrument is recorded; c) nature of default; d) itemized account of arrears; e) itemized account of other charges; f) total amount necessary to reinstate; g) that failure to cure within thirty days will result in foreclosure sale in 120 days; h) effect of foreclosure; i) that mortgagor has recourse to courts. *Notice of Sale:* a) description of property; b) time, date, and place of sale; c) where deed of trust is recorded; d) amount in arrears; e) total sum owing; f) terms of sale; g) effect of foreclosure; h) that mortgagor can file court action; and i) reinstatement rights.
  Method of Service: For a Notice of Default, by registered or certified mail and first class mail, by posting, or by personal service. For a Notice of Sale, by registered or certified mail and first class mail, by posting on a conspicuous place, or by in-person service on the occupant.
Right to Cure Default/Reinstate: Up to eleven days before the sale. § 61.24.040.
Post-Sale Provisions Regarding Proceeds: The trustee deposits notice of proceeds with the clerk and the court determines distribution.
Deficiency: No deficiency decree if the foreclosure is by power of sale. § 61.24.100. A deficiency may be obtained in the event of judicial foreclosure.

WEST VIRGINIA

W. Va. Code §§ 38-1-3 to 38-1-15
Most Common Method of Foreclosure: Power of Sale.
Preforeclosure Notice:
  Number of Notices: One.
  Amount of Notice Required: If to the mortgagor, within a reasonable time before the sale. If to any subordinate lienholder, at least twenty days prior to the sale.
  Content of Notice: a) Time and place of sale; b) names of parties to the deed; c) date of the deed; d) office and book in which it is recorded; e) description of the property; and f) terms of sale.
  Method of Service: By publication, and by certified mail return receipt requested.
Right to Cure Default/Reinstate: For ten days after the notice of right to cure is served; the notice of right to cure can be served five days after the default. No right to cure if in default and notice is served three or more times. § 46A-2-106.
Redemption: None if the sale is confirmed.
Deficiency: Surplus sale proceeds go to the mortgagor. § 38-1-7. Return of account must be made within two months after the sale or the trustee forfeits its commission. § 38-1-8.
Miscellaneous: See § 38-1-14 for special provisions regarding foreclosure of a credit line for a deed of trust.

WISCONSIN

Wis. Stat. §§ 846.01 to 846.25

Most Common Method of Foreclosure: Judicial.

Judicial Foreclosure Procedure: The court enters judgment and orders the sale. The sale cannot take place for one year after judgment (§ 846.10), unless the mortgagee waives the right to a deficiency judgment on a property of less than twenty acres, in which case the property can be sold six months after judgment. § 846.101. If the property is abandoned, it can be sold two months after judgment. § 846.102.

Preforeclosure Notice: Given by the sheriff or referee making the sale. § 846.16.

    Number of Notices: One.

    Amount of Notice Required: If by publication, six weeks. If by posting, three weeks. § 815.31.

    Content of Notice: Time and place of sale, and description of the property.

    Method of Service: If by publication, once per week for six weeks. If by posting, in three places three weeks prior to the sale. § 815.31.

Right to Cure Default/Reinstate: Can cure by bringing the amount due into the court before judgment and the case will be dismissed. After judgment, can bring amount due into the court and the proceedings will be stayed, but the court may enforce judgment upon subsequent default. § 846.05.

Redemption: Can redeem any time before the sale. § 846.13.

Deficiency: A deficiency judgment is obtainable and must be pled in foreclosure action. § 846.04.

WYOMING

Wyo. Stat. Ann. §§ 34-4-101 to 34-4-113 (power of sale); §§ 1-18-101 to 1-18-114 (judicial sale) (Michie)

Most Common Method of Foreclosure: Power of Sale.

Preforeclosure Notice:

    Number of Notices: Two: Notice of Intent to Foreclose, and Notice of Sale.

    Amount of Notice Required: Notice of Intent to Foreclose must be served by certified mail ten days before beginning publication. § 34-4-103. Notice of Sale must be published four weeks prior to the sale. Prior to the first publication, a copy of the Notice of Sale must be served by certified mail upon the record owner, the person in possession if different than the record owner, and holders of recorded mortgages and liens which appear of record at least 25 days before the sale date. § 34-4-104.

    Content of Notice: a) Name of mortgagor and mortgagee; b) date of mortgage and when recorded; c) amount due under mortgage; d) description of the property; e) terms of sale; and f) a statement that "The property being foreclosed upon may be subject to other liens and encumbrances that will not be extinguished at the sale and any prospective purchaser should research the status of title before submitting a bid." § 34-4-105. *Cf.* § 1-18-101(b).

    Method of Service: By publication, and by certified mail with return receipt requested. Must also serve notice on the person in possession of the property if different than the record owner.

Redemption: Within three months from date of sale. § 1-18-103.

Post-Sale Provisions Regarding Proceeds: Surplus goes to the mortgagor on demand. For foreclosures and execution sales commenced on or after July 1, 2005, proceeds are paid in the following order: a) reasonable collection and enforcement expenses, and mortgagee's attorney fees and legal expenses to the extent provided by law, b) satisfaction of the obligations secured by the mortgage being foreclosed; c) satisfaction of subordinate or junior mortgages or liens; and d) surplus proceeds to the mortgagor. §§ 34-4-113, 1-18-113.

Deficiency: A deficiency judgment is obtainable if a separate written agreement obligates the mortgagor.

Appendix Notes

1. *But see* Ariz. Rev. Stat. § 12-1285 (post-judgment redemption requires payment of purchase price plus interest at 8%, plus any assessments or taxes paid with interest).
2. If the mortgage is a second mortgage, the borrower must be served with a Notice of Intent to Foreclose fifteen days before commencement of the foreclosure proceedings. N.H. Rev. Stat. Ann. § 397-A:16-a.
3. However, upon subsequent default by the defendant, the court can order enforcement of the judgment. *But see* Fed. Nat'l Mortgage Ass'n v. Miller, 123 Misc. 2d 431, 473 N.Y.S.2d 743 (Sup. Ct. 1984) (effect of acceleration clause).
4. *But see* Metro. Bld'g & Loan Ass'n v. Weinberger, 67 N.D. 627, 275 N.W. 638 (1937) (section does not apply to mortgages which have been accelerated).
5. Power of sale foreclosure is not available for agricultural or farm land. Wash. Rev. Code § 61.24.030.

APPENDIX **F**

Summary of State Real Estate Tax Abatement Laws

Every state has enacted special property tax abatement schemes or exemptions which relieve at least some taxpayers of a portion of their property tax liability by virtue of age, disability, income level, or personal status. All states have approved tax relief for older homeowners, and some states extend this relief to older renters as well. The abatements provided by these programs can be significant, and should be thoroughly explored for every homeowner. Their benefits are not automatic, however. Most abatement programs require that the homeowner apply for and submit proof of eligibility for an abatement or an exemption. Application must usually be made within a short period after the issuance of the tax bill. These time periods are generally not extendable, if an application is not timely made, the right to the abatement will be lost. Often homeowners who stand to benefit most are not even aware of these existing programs and so pay more than necessary.

This appendix summarizes and abridges state tax abatement laws. Refer to the statutory citations for more information. Careful research may turn up additional laws which apply on a state or local basis. In addition, in some communities, there may be formal or informal policies to negate or postpone tax enforcement proceedings for older taxpayers or taxpayers experiencing a hardship. Check for this possibility by contacting the taxing authorities directly.

ALABAMA

Ala. Code §§ 40-9-1 to 40-9-33

Elder and Disabled Exemption: The principal residence, plus up to 160 acres adjacent thereto, of any person who is age sixty-five or older, with a net income of $7,500 or less is exempt from local property taxes. § 40-9-21.

Homestead: Homestead is exempt up to $4,000 in assessed value if owner is not sixty-five or older. § 40-9-19(a). Homestead of elder (over sixty-five) or disabled or blind person entitled to exemption of up to $2,000 in assessed value, but localities can enact higher exemption up to $4,000. Elder (over sixty-five) with income of less than $12,000, or blind or disabled persons entitled to exemption up to $5,000. These exemptions do not apply to county-wide and school district taxes levied for school purposes. Municipalities may, however, allow an exemption from school district taxes for elder and disabled homeowners. § 40-9-19.1

Veterans: Home of veteran (purchased pursuant to 38 U.S.C. § 701 and Chapter 12) is exempt from all *ad valorem* property taxes as long as home is occupied by veteran or surviving spouse. § 40-9-20.

Appx. F

ALASKA

Alaska Stat. §§ 29.45.030, 29.45.040, 09.38.010 (Michie) [end bold]

Elder and Disabled Veterans Exemption: The principal residence of a resident sixty-five or older, a disabled person, or a resident at least sixty years old who is the widow or widower of either is exempt from local property taxes on the first $150,000 of the assessed value of the real property. § 29.45.030(e). By ordinance approved by the voters, a municipality may exempt from taxation the assessed value of such property exceeding $150,000. § 29.45.050(i).

Elder and Disabled Veterans Tax Equivalency Payment: A resident sixty-five or older, a disabled person, or a resident at least sixty years old who is the widow or widower of either and who rents a permanent place of abode is eligible to apply for a tax equivalency payment. § 29.45.040.

Homestead: A person is entitled to a homestead exemption not exceeding $54,000 of the value of the principal residence of that person or that person's dependents. § 09.38.010.

ARIZONA

Ariz. Rev. Stat. §§ 43-1072, 42-11111, 42-17301 to 42-17313

Elder: Residents, who are at least sixty-five, who have a sufficiently low income and paid property taxes or rent, are entitled to an income tax credit. § 43-1072. Property tax deferral is available for residents who are at least seventy, who are low income, own no other real property, meet certain residency requirements, and whose home is valued at not more than $150,000. §§ 42-17301 to 42-17313.

Disabled: Property of qualified disabled persons exempt from tax. Ariz. Const. art. 9, § 2.2; Ariz. Rev. Stat. § 42-11111.

Veterans: Property of qualified honorably discharged veterans and widows exempt from taxes. Ariz. Const. art. 9, §§ 2, 2.1.

ARKANSAS

Ark. Code Ann. §§ 26-3-301 to 26-3-310 (Michie)

Disabled Veterans and Their Surviving Spouses and Minor Dependent Children: Disabled veteran is exempt from all state taxes on his homestead. § 26-3-306(a)(1)(A). Upon the death of the veteran, his surviving spouse and minor children are entitled to the exemption. § 26-3-306(a)(1)(B)(i). The surviving spouse and minor dependent children of a member of the armed forces killed within the scope of military duties is entitled to the exemption. Protects spouse until he or she remarries. The surviving spouse of a service member killed while on active duty may reinstate the property tax exemption if his or her subsequent marriage terminates. Protects children until they reach the age of majority.

CALIFORNIA

Cal. Const. art. XIII, § 3(k); Cal. Rev. & Tax. Code § 218 (West)

Homestead: $7,000 of the full value of a resident's principal residence is exempt from taxation. Cal. Const. art. XIII, § 3(k); Cal. Rev. & Tax. Code § 218.

Elder: Owners and renters who are at least sixty-two, and who have a gross household income below $35,251, are eligible for property tax assistance on those taxes paid on the first $34,000 in assessed value. Cal. Rev. & Tax. Code §§ 20501–20564. There is also a provision for property tax postponement. Cal. Rev. & Tax. Code §§ 20581–20622. The income limitation is adjusted annually for inflation.

Disabled: Disabled are eligible for the same property tax assistance as elders (Cal. Rev. & Tax. Code §§ 20501–20564), as well as property tax postponement (Cal. Rev. & Tax. Code §§ 20581–20622).

Veterans: Principal residences of disabled veterans and those who died while on active duty are exempt from taxation up to a dollar amount which depends on a variety of factors. Cal. Rev. & Tax. Code § 205.5. Surviving spouses of disabled veterans are eligible for the same exemptions. Cal. Rev. & Tax. Code § 205.5.

COLORADO

Colo. Rev. Stat. §§ 39-31-101 to 39-31-104

Elder: Residents who are at least sixty-five, and meet other criteria, are eligible for a grant to assist with real property taxes. §§ 39-31-101 to 39-31-104. Also, residents at least sixty-five may be eligible to defer taxes on their homestead. §§ 39-3.5-101 to 39-3.5-117. The Colorado legislature has also provided for the creation of Property Tax Work-off Programs for elders. §§ 39-3.7-101 to 39-3.7-102.

CONNECTICUT

Conn. Gen. Stat. §§ 12-1 to 12-170dd

General: All residents are eligible for an income tax credit for a portion of the amount of their property tax paid on their primary residence. § 12-704c. A municipality may abate the property taxes on any residence which exceed eight percent of the resident's income. § 12-124a. Also, § 12-62d provided that a municipality may provide for property tax relief following tax rate evaluations which raise the tax rate to at least 1.5% of the market value of residences but in 2006 this section was repealed "effective July 1, 2006, and applicable to assessment years commenting on or after October 1, 2010."

Elder: Homeowners who are at least sixty-five, and meet certain other qualifications, are eligible for property tax relief. §§ 12-170aa to 12-170dd. A number of other statutes provide for further property tax relief for elders. §§ 12-129b, 12-129.

Disabled: Disabled persons are eligible for the same property tax relief as elders. §§ 12-170aa to 12-170dd. Disabled persons who meet certain other criteria are eligible for other exemptions. §§ 12-81(17), 12-81(20) (disabled veterans), 12-81(21) (disabled veterans), 12-81(55), 12-81i, 12-81j, 12-83 (disabled veterans over sixty-five).

Veterans: Veterans and their surviving spouses, children, and parents may be eligible for property tax exemptions. §§ 12-81(19) to 12-81(26), 12-81f, 12-81g, 12-82, 12-93a.

DELAWARE

Del. Code Ann. tit. 9, §§ 8131 to 8141, 8363

Elder: Elder (sixty-five and over) homeowners with income of not more than $3,000 per year are entitled to an exemption from taxation of $5,000 of assessed value. [Note: statute states it does not apply to property taxes levied by a municipality.] This exemption also provides relief from mobile home taxes.

DISTRICT OF COLUMBIA

D.C. Code Ann. §§ 47-849 to 47-850.04

General: For single family residential property and property with not more than five dwelling units, which includes the principal dwelling place of the owner, $63,000 is deducted from the estimated market value in calculating tax. § 47-850(a).

Elder: All "Class 1" property owners sixty-five and older whose annual household income is less than $100,000 shall be eligible for a fifty percent decrease in property tax liability. § 47-863. Class 1 property is property occupied by the owner and contains not more than five dwelling units.

FLORIDA

Fla. Stat. Ann. §§ 196.001 to 196.32 (West)

Homesteads: Homesteads exempted from all taxation up to a certain amount in assessed value. § 196.031. Residents eligible for homestead exemptions may also be eligible to defer property taxes on their residence. §§ 197.242 to 197.262.

Elder: Amount of assessed value eligible for homestead exemption expanded for residents sixty-five or older. § 196.031(3)(a).

Disabled: Amount of assessed value eligible for homestead exemption expanded for totally and permanently disabled residents. §§ 196.031(3)(b), 196.101. Surviving spouses of disabled veterans are eligible for the same homestead exemptions as their deceased spouses. §§ 196.081, 196.091.

GEORGIA

Ga. Code Ann. §§ 48-5-40 to 48-5-56

Homestead: Homestead exemption allowed up to $2,000 in assessed value. § 48-5-44.

Elder: There are a number of provisions for homestead exemptions for elders (§§ 48-5-47, 48-5-47.1, 48-5-48.3 (effective Jan. 1, 2007), 48-5-52), as well as deferrals. §§ 48-5-72, 48-5-72.1.

Disabled: Homestead exemptions for qualified disabled veterans. Ga. Code Ann. § 48-5-48.

GUAM

11 Guam Code Ann. §§ 24110, 24402 to 24404

Elder: Elder persons (55 years or older) receive eighty percent abatement of tax on principal residence owned for five consecutive years or more. Property valuation frozen at amount assessed in first year of eligibility. §§ 24110, 24113.

Homestead Exemption: For purposes of assessing real property, homeowner entitled to exemption on the first $50,000 of the appraised value of improvements. Exemption limited to one home for any one owner. §§ 24402, 24404.

Disabled: Permanently disabled receive 80% abatement for principal residence of 5 year duration. §§ 24112, 24113.

HAWAII

Haw. Rev. Stat. §§ 246-1 to 246-63

General: Principal residence exempt from property taxes for up to $ 12,000 in assessed value. § 246-26.

Elder: Homes of residents aged sixty to sixty-nine are entitled to double the exemption (up to $24,000), and homes of residents seventy and over are entitled to two and one-half times the exemption ($30,000). § 246-26(d).

Disabled: Disabled persons, are entitled to real property tax exemptions up to a taxable value of $15,000. § 246-31. Qualified disabled veterans are exempted from all property taxes. § 246-29.

Miscellaneous: Eligible low-income renters are eligible for an income tax credit. § 235-55.7.

IDAHO

Idaho Code §§ 55-1001 to 55-1011, 63-602AA, 63-602G (Michie)

Homestead: The dwelling house or mobile home in which the owner resides or intends to reside, or unimproved land regardless of size and owned with the intent of placing such a residence thereon, is exempt from taxation but the exemption amount shall not exceed the lesser of the (i) total net value of the land, mobile home and improvements, or (ii) $100,000. §§ 55-1001, 55-1003.

Residential Improvements: The lesser of the first $75,000 (amount to be adjusted to reflect cost-of-living fluctuations) or fifty percent of the market value for assessment purposes of residential improvements to an owner-occupied residence is exempt from property taxation. § 63-602G.

Undue Hardship: Persons owning real property may be relieved from paying all or a part of their property tax upon a showing of undue hardship. § 63-602AA.

ILLINOIS

320 Ill. Comp. Stat. §§ 25/1 to 25/13, 30/1 to 30/8

Tax Relief: (320 Ill. Comp. Stat. § 25/4): Persons sixty-five and over and disabled persons within statutory income limitations (e.g., $35,740 for a three person household in grant year 2000) are entitled to a "grant" in the amount by which their property taxes for the year exceed 3.5% of their household income. Maximum amount of grant is $700, less 4.5% of household income.

Tax Deferral: (320 Ill. Comp. Stat. §§ 30/1 to 30/8): Taxpayers sixty-five years or older with an income of not more than $40,000 ($50,00 for 2006 and after) can apply for deferral of all or part of the property taxes on their residence. Deferral claimed plus interest cannot exceed eighty percent of the taxpayer's equity in the property. If the taxes deferred equal eighty percent, the taxpayer must pay interest each year at six percent. Upon the death of the taxpayer, taxes plus interest become due from the taxpayer's heirs, unless the heir is a surviving spouse. If the heir is the surviving spouse, the deferral can be continued. Otherwise, the heirs must pay the taxes. If the taxes are not paid, then the town can foreclose.

INDIANA

Ind. Code §§ 6-1.1-12-1 to 6-1.1-12-42

Elder: Persons over age sixty-five with income not more than $25,000, and whose home is valued at not more than $144,000, are entitled to a deduction of the lesser of half the assessed value or $12,400. Explicitly applies to mobile homes. Surviving spouse covered if age sixty or over. § 6-1.1-12-9.

Blind and Disabled Persons: Persons with income of not more than $17,000, are entitled to a deduction from the assessed value of $12,480. § 6-1.1-12-11.

Disabled Veterans or Surviving Spouses: If totally disabled (§ 6-1.1-12-14) are entitled to a $12,480 deduction unless value of property exceeds $113,000. This deduction can be used with any other deductions which the taxpayer may be eligible for, except the deduction for World War I veterans. (Must be at least ten percent disabled and 62 or older, or must be totally disabled.) § 6-1.1-12-14.

Surviving Spouses of World War I Veterans: Entitled to deduction of $18,720. § 6-1.1-12-16.

World War I Veterans: Entitled to a $18,720 deduction if the value of their property does not exceed $163,000. §§ 6-1.1-12-17.4, 6-1.1-12-16 (spouses).

Partially Disabled Veterans and Surviving Spouses: Entitled to $24,960 exemption where individual with service-connected disability, served in a war and at least 10% disabled. § 6-1.1-12-13.

IOWA

Iowa Code §§ 425.1 to 425.40

Homestead: Homeowners are entitled to a credit against the actual levy (tax) on the first $4,850 of actual value for the homestead. § 425.1.

Elder and Disabled: In addition to the homestead exemption, older persons (sixty-five and over) and totally disabled persons are entitled to a credit or reimbursement for taxes paid based on the income schedule contained in § 425.23. Example of credit: if income is $0 to $8,499.99, credit is one-hundred percent of taxes paid; if income is $8,500 to $9,499.99, credit is eighty-five percent of taxes paid. These amounts are adjusted for inflation. §§ 425.16 to 425.40.

KANSAS

Kan. Stat. Ann. § 79-4501

Homestead: Persons 55 or older, disabled, or having dependent children are entitled to tax refund (on income taxes) for property taxes paid according to the schedule contained in § 79-4508 to be adjusted for cost-of living increases annually. The maximum refund is $600. § 79-4509.

KENTUCKY

Ky. Rev. Stat. Ann. § 132.810 (Michie)

Elder and Disabled: Homeowners age sixty-five or older, or persons who are totally disabled are entitled to a $6,500 exemption on their personal residence, based on purchasing power of 1972 dollar. § 132.810. Per statute, amount of exemption is to be adjusted for increases in the cost-of-living.

LOUISIANA

La. Rev. Stat. Ann. § 47:1703 (West)

Homestead: Pursuant to Section 20 of Article VII of the La. Constitution, $7,500 of the assessed value of a homestead is exempt.

MAINE

Me. Rev. Stat. Ann. tit. 36, §§ 841, 6251 (West)

Infirmity or Poverty: An assessor may grant an abatement based on his judgment, either on his own knowledge or on written application. Assessor must notify persons who have expressed an inability to pay their taxes of the right to request an abatement within three years of the imposition of the tax.

Widows and Children of Veterans: Unremarried widows and children of veterans may be granted such abatement as the assessor deems proper, within one year of the imposition of the tax.

Homestead: Elders may be eligible for deferral of property taxes based upon income. § 6251.

MARYLAND

Md. Code Ann., Tax-Prop. §§ 9-101, 9-104, 9-105

Elder and Disabled Veterans: (§ 9-104): Persons over age seventy and disabled veterans are entitled to a credit against their property tax, the amount of which is a percentage of their income. The percentage is graduated by income level, see § 9-104(g)(2) for table of percentages. No credits for property owners with income greater than $200,000. Surviving spouse of disabled veteran is entitled to credit up until spouse remarries.

General/Homestead: (§ 9-105): For all homesteads, owner is entitled to a tax credit against property tax which is calculated as follows:

For the State Property Tax: 1) multiplying the prior year's assessment by 110%; 2) subtracting that amount from the current year's assessment; 3) if the difference is a positive number, multiplying the difference by the applicable state tax rate for the current year.

For the County or Municipal Property Tax: 1) multiplying the current year's assessment by the percentage established by the county or municipality; 2) subtracting that amount from the current year's assessment; 3) if the difference is a positive number, multiplying the difference by the applicable county or municipal tax rate for the current year.

MASSACHUSETTS

Mass. Gen. Laws ch. 59, § 5

Aged, Widowed or Orphaned Taxpayers: Entitled to exemption, either to the extent of $2,000 in property value or $175 in tax, if the household income is less than $20,000. (clause 17). These amounts are adjusted annually according to the consumer price index. (clause 17E). Assessors may provide additional abatements to those taxpayers who by reason of age, infirmity, poverty, or hardship relating to a change to active military status, the assessors judge are "unable to contribute fully." Tax deferral also available for persons over sixty-five. (clauses 41 to 41D).

Blind: Entitled to exemption to the extent of $5,000 value or $437.50 in tax. (clause 37).

Elder with Limited Income: Entitled to an exemption of $4,000 or a $350 credit.

Veterans: Disabled (ten percent or more) or recipient of Purple Heart. Surviving spouses. Parents of soldiers or sailors killed in wartime service. Certain surviving spouses of World War I veterans. Greater of $2,000 in valuation or $400 in tax. For veterans with certain injuries, or certain medal recipients, exemptions of $4,000 or $750, or $8,000 or $1,250. Disabled veterans in "specially adapted housing": $10,000 or $950. One-hundred percent disabled veterans: $10,000 or $1,500. (clauses 22 to 22E).

Miscellaneous: Surviving spouses of firefighters and police killed in the line of duty are entitled to an abatement. Mass. Gen. Laws ch. 59, § 5 cl. 42.

MICHIGAN

Mich. Comp. Laws §§ 211.1 to 211.7ff

Low Income: Homestead is eligible for exemption from taxation in whole or in part, based on guidelines developed by local assessing unit. § 211.7u. Local guidelines may not set income limitations below the federal poverty line.

Disabled Veterans and Their Surviving Spouses: Disabled veterans living in housing specially adapted with the aid of certain federal financial assistance are exempt from all taxation on their homestead. Upon the death of the veteran, a surviving spouse is entitled to the exemption until remarriage. § 211.7b.

MINNESOTA

Minn. Stat. § 290A.04

General Property Tax Relief: Taxpayers are allowed a refund of property taxes paid in the amount by which the property taxes exceed a specified percentage of income. The percentage varies by income level. Income limit is $77,520 per year. In addition, if property taxes increase in one year more than twelve percent or $100, the owner is entitled to an additional refund on the increase over the greater of twelve percent or $100. Maximum refund is $1,000.

MISSISSIPPI

Miss. Code Ann. §§ 27-33-3; 27-33-67 to 27-33-79

Homestead: Taxpayers under sixty-five are entitled to an exemption on their homestead based on assessed value, up to a maximum exemption of $300 for those counties which have completed their update of *ad valorem* taxation, and $240 for counties without completed updates.

Elder Homestead: Taxpayers over age sixty-five, and certain totally disabled persons, are entitled to an exemption to the extent of $7,500 of assessed value in those counties which have completed their update of *ad valorem* taxation, and $6,000 in counties without completed updates.

MISSOURI

Mo. Rev. Stat. §§ 135.010 to 135.035

Elder: Persons sixty-five and over, with income of $25,000 or less, are entitled to a tax credit for income taxes based on the amount by which their total property tax exceeds a certain percentage of their income. Refer to tables at § 135.030 for percentages and credit amounts. Eligibility described in § 135.010(1), (2).

MONTANA

Mont. Code Ann. § 15-6-211

Low-Income Disabled Veterans: Exemption for survivors of veterans killed on duty or veterans with one-hundred percent service-connected disability. Must also be low-income as defined in § 15-6-211(a)(iii). Also applies to unmarried surviving spouses.

NEBRASKA

Neb. Rev. Stat. §§ 77-3501 to 77-3530

Homestead: Exempt amount for homestead is the lesser of (a) the taxable value of the homestead or (b) eighty percent of the average assessed value of single family residential property in the homeowner's county of residence, or $40,000 for low income, and $50,000 for disabled and veterans, whichever is greater. § 77-3501.01. Percentage of exempt amount homeowner is entitled to claim is based on income. For example, if income is between $0 and $19,200 for a single claimant or $22,500 for a married or closely related claimant, homeowner is entitled to claim one-hundred percent of the exempt amount. § 77-3507.

Disabled: Disabled persons and veterans, entitled to exemption based on income and subject to maximum exempt amount. §§ 77-3508, 77-3509. Exemption reduced if homestead value exceeds certain amounts. § 77-3506.03

NEVADA

Nev. Rev. Stat. §§ 361.080 to 361.159

Widows: Exemption not to exceed $1,000, the amount to be adjusted annually based on CPI percentage increase. § 361.080.

Blind: Exemption not to exceed $3,000, the amount to be adjusted annually based on CPI percentage increase. Medical verification is required. § 361.085.

Veterans: Exemption of $2,000, the amount to be adjusted annually based on CPI percentage increase. Does not extend to family of veterans. § 361.090.

Disabled Veterans: Exemption for veterans with service-connected permanent disabilities and unremarried surviving spouses. Amount of exemption varies based on percentage of disability. Maximum of $20,000, adjusted each year starting with fiscal year 2005–2006 to reflect CPI increases. § 361.091.

NEW HAMPSHIRE

N.H. Rev. Stat. Ann. § 76:16

General: Selectmen or assessors may abate any tax assessed for good cause shown. Any person aggrieved by the assessment of a tax may apply in writing for abatement by March 1 of the year following the notice of the imposition of the tax. Poverty or inability to pay is good cause. *See* Brigg's Petition, 29 N.H. 547 (1854). Tax deferral is available for those over sixty-five or disabled, who have owned home for at least five years, if assessors believe that tax would cause undue hardship or possible loss of property. N.H. Rev. Stat. Ann. § 72:38-a.

NEW JERSEY

N.J. Stat. Ann. §§ 54:4-3.30, 54:4-8.11, 54:4-8.57 to 54:4-8.63 (West)

General: Formerly two kinds of exemption were provided, homestead and N.J. Saver, but the latter was folded into the former in 2004. Homestead rebate allowed for amount by which property taxes exceed 5% of gross income, but within annually-adjusted income-based ranges. §§ 54:4-8.57 to 8.75.

Senior Citizens, Blind or Disabled: Entitled to $250 deduction. § 54:4-8.59.

Veterans: Property of certain totally disabled veterans and surviving spouses, and spouses of veterans killed on active service, is exempt from taxation. § 54:4-3.30 (§ 54:4-3.30 was recognized as unconstitutional in *Hennefield v. Town of Montclair*, 22 N.J. Tax 166 (Mar. 15, 2005); legislation proposed 2006).

NEW MEXICO

N.M. Const. art. VIII, §§ 5, 11; N.M. Stat. Ann. §§ 7-37-4 to 7-37-5.1, 42-10-9 to 42-10-13 (Michie)

Head of Family and Veteran Exemptions: Up to $2,000 of the taxable value of the residential real property of the head of the family is exempt from property tax. "Head of the family" includes one spouse in a joint household, a widow or widower, a head of household providing more than fifty percent support to any related person, a single person, or a condominium association member or like entity paying property tax through the association. N.M. Const. art. VIII, § 5; N.M. Stat. Ann. § 7-37-4. Veterans or their surviving unmarried spouses who are New Mexico residents or who hold the property in a grantor trust established under Internal Revenue Code §§ 671–677 are entitled to an exemption of $3,000 for 2004, $3,500 for 2005, and $4,000 for 2006 and later. N.M. Const. art. VIII, § 5; N.M. Stat. Ann. § 7-37-5.

Property of totally disabled veteran is completely exempt if it has been especially adapted for the veteran's disability using a federal grant for adapted housing, because of the service connected disability. Property exempt under this section remains exempt if occupied by veteran's unremarried surviving spouse. § 7-37-5.1.

NEW YORK

N.Y. Real Prop. Tax Law §§ 458 to 460, 466 to 467 (McKinney)

Elder: (sixty-five and older) Property is exempt from taxation to the extent of fifty percent of the assessed value, provided that the governing board of the municipality adopts a local law enacting exemption. Exemption is subject to income limitations, see § 467(b)(1). Municipality must send notice of the exemption to residents. § 467(4).

Veterans: Property of disabled veteran which has been adapted using federal grant for that purpose is totally exempt. Certain other property of veterans is exempt up to $5,000. § 458. Alternative exemptions for veterans, with amount varying according to whether veteran served in combat, and whether disabled (rate of exemption tied to percentage of disability). Municipalities may, within limits, increase or decrease the amount of these exemptions, or refuse to grant them. § 458-a.

Disabled: Municipalities may grant exemptions for improvements to property necessary to accommodate disabled resident. § 459. Property of disabled persons with limited income is fifty percent exempt from municipal taxation, including taxation by other taxing entities (counties, school districts, etc.). § 459-c.

Volunteer Firefighters or Ambulance Workers: Certain counties may allow exemptions of up to ten percent to certain volunteer firefighters or ambulance workers. § 466-b.

Physically Disabled Crime Victims: Any improvements to real property used to facilitate and accommodate the use of such real property by physically disabled victims of crime are exempt from taxation. § 459-b.

Clergy: Any real property owned by clergy engaged in work assigned by the church or denomination of which he is a member is exempt to the extent of $1,500 of value. § 460.

NORTH CAROLINA

N.C. Gen. Stat. § 105-277.1

Elder or Disabled: For persons over sixty-five or disabled, with an income of $18,000 per year or less through July 1, 2003 (subject to cost of living adjustments in subsequent years), the greater of $20,000 or fifty percent of the appraised value of permanent residence is excluded from taxation.

NORTH DAKOTA

N.D. Cent. Code § 57-02-08.1

Elder with Limited Income: Persons sixty-five and older, unless property value exceeds $50,000, or permanently disabled with income of $14,500 or less receive a reduction in the assessment of the taxable value of their homestead. Reduction is based on income. For example, if income is less than $8,500, then reduction is one-hundred percent of taxable valuation, up to a maximum of $3,038 of taxable valuation. See provision for percentages.

OHIO

Ohio Rev. Code Ann. §§ 323.151 to 323.159 (West)

Disabled, Elder, and Surviving Spouse of Disabled or Elder Person: Homestead exemption allowed up to a taxable value of $5,000 (or seventy-five percent) according to a schedule based on total income. § 323.152.

OKLAHOMA

Okla. Stat. tit. 68, §§ 2904 to 2906, 2888 to 2890; Okla. Stat. tit. 31, § 2.

Elder and Disabled Persons: A person sixty-five years or older or a totally disabled person who is also a head of household, a resident of the state during the entire preceding year, and whose gross household income does not exceed $12,000 may file for relief from property tax. Okla. Stat. tit. 68, §§ 2904–2906.

Rural and Urban Homesteads: Any single person of legal age, a married couple and their minor child or children, or the minor child or children of a deceased person (residing together or separated), or a surviving spouse is entitled to a homestead exemption from *ad valorem* taxes of $1,000 of assessed value. Heads of households whose gross household income did not exceed $20,000 in the preceding year are entitled to an additional $1,000 exemption. A rural homestead may not exceed 160 acres of land and improvements, and an urban homestead may not exceed one acre. If more than twenty-five percent of the square footage of the improved property claimed as an urban homestead is used for business purposes, the homestead exemption is limited to $5,000. Okla. Stat. tit. 31, § 2; Okla. Stat. tit. 68, §§ 2888–2890.

OREGON

Or. Rev. Stat. § 307.250

Disabled Veterans: Exemption not to exceed $15,000 for certain disabled veterans and unremarried surviving spouses. Exemption is $18,000 if disability is service-connected. Since July 1, 2000, exemption each year is 103% of previous year's exemption.

PENNSYLVANIA

Pa. Stat. Ann. tit. 72, §§ 4751-21 to 4751-26 (West)

Elder: Persons age sixty-five or over are entitled to a tax rebate for property taxes paid, according to a schedule which is based on income and amount paid. Schedule at § 4751-24.

PUERTO RICO

29 P.R. Laws Ann. § 814

Veterans: Property tax exemption of up to $5,000 of assessed value of property for period of ten years. Subject to certain restrictions, injured veterans' primary residence exempt from property tax. Subject to certain restrictions, property tax exemption on the first $50,000 of the appraised value of the property for disabled veterans who receive disability compensation of fifty percent or more from the Veterans Administration.

RHODE ISLAND

R.I. Gen. Laws §§ 44-3-12 to 44-3-52

Totally Disabled: City or town council may freeze tax rate and valuation for totally disabled persons. Applicant must meet established income requirements of the locality. §§ 44-3-15, 44-3-16.

Visually Impaired: Exemption of $6,000 for the visually impaired, with some variations as to the amount of the exemption by town. § 44-3-12. Towns may increase this exemption up to $22,500. If a town does not increase exemption over $6,000, exemption must increase, whenever town increases tax rate, by the same percentage as the tax rate.

Elder: Towns and municipalities may by local ordinance provide for the freezing of the rate and valuation of taxes of persons age sixty-five and older subject to income requirements set by towns. § 44-3-16. Some towns have exemptions of varying amounts rather than a freeze. Advocates should check the statute for particular towns.

SOUTH CAROLINA

S.C. Code Ann. §§ 12-37-210 to 12-37-450 (Law. Co-op.)

Elder or Disabled: The first $50,000 of the fair market value of the dwelling place of a person who is sixty-five or older or disabled or blind is exempt. Explicitly includes mobile home on property of another. § 12-37-250.

Veterans Exemptions: If one-hundred percent disabled, dwelling house and one acre of land totally exempt. Also protects surviving spouses of totally disabled veterans or veterans killed in action. Same exemption for police and firefighters suffering total service-connected disability and for any veteran who received Medal of Honor or was a prisoner of war during WWI, WWII, Korea, or Vietnam. Same exemption for paraplegic or hemiplegic persons. § 12-37-220.

SOUTH DAKOTA

S.D. Codified Laws §§ 10-6B-1 to 10-6B-15 (Michie)

Elder and Disabled: (if adopted by local tax board) Elder and disabled persons are entitled to a property tax reduction based on income. For example, if a family's household income is between $0 and $5,640, then property taxes are reduced by fifty-five percent; if income is between $5,641 and $5,758, then taxes are reduced by fifty-three percent. Maximum income is $7,765 for family, $5,758 for single person. Certain low income seniors and low income disabled persons are eligible for a freeze of their tax assessments (owners of single family homes, with income of $14,000 or less for single person, $17,500 for family). These figures are adjusted annually for change in the consumer price index.

TENNESSEE

Tenn. Code Ann. §§ 67-5-701 to 67-5-705

Elder Low-Income: Low-income elder homeowners pay no taxes on the first $25,000 of value, subject to income limitations. Income limit $20,000 (2007). § 67-5-702. Income limitation will be adjusted according to the cost of living increases for Social Security.

Disabled: Disabled persons pay no taxes on the first $25,000 of value, subject to income limitations. Income limit for 1996 was $20,000. § 67-5-703. Income limitation will be adjusted according to the cost of living increases for Social Security.

Disabled Veteran: Disabled veterans pay no taxes on the first $175,000 of fair market value of property. § 67-5-704.

Maximum Tax for Elder: Towns may adopt a resolution which sets the maximum tax for an elder person (over sixty-five), unless income is more than $12,000 per year, at the 1979 level, or the year in which they purchased the property, or the year in which they reached age sixty-five, whichever is later. The maximum tax may be increased if improvements to the property increase its value. § 67-5-705.

TEXAS

Tex. Tax Code Ann. § 11.13 (Vernon)

Homestead: Owner is entitled to exemption from county taxation of $3,000 of the assessed value of residence, and exemption of $15,000 of appraised value from school district taxation.

Elder and Disabled: Entitled to an additional $10,000 exemption from school district taxation. (Exemption amount may be increased by the governing tax body.) Certain surviving spouses are also covered.

UTAH

Utah Code Ann. §§ 59-2-1104 to 59-2-1220

Disabled Veterans: The first $200,000 of taxable value of property is exempt for veterans who are one-hundred percent disabled due to a service-related injury. For lesser disabilities, the exemption will be the same percentage of $200,000, that is, a fifty percent disability confers an exemption of $100,000. Also applies to unremarried surviving spouses and minor orphans. § 59-2-1104.

Blind Persons: Tax exemption for the first $11,500 of property owned by blind persons. Also applies to unremarried surviving spouses and minor orphans. Must file application for exemption each year with verification by doctor. § 59-2-1106.

Low Income: Counties have discretion to remit or abate taxes of any low-income person in an amount not to exceed the amount of the homeowner's credit for the lowest household income bracket under § 59-2-1208 or not more than fifty percent of total tax assessed for that year, whichever is less. § 59-2-1107. Individuals under sixty-five qualify only if disabled or can show extreme hardship. § 59-2-109. Counties may also defer taxes for low-income persons. Deferred taxes continue to accumulate with interest as lien against property. Individuals under age sixty-five qualify only if disabled or can show extreme hardship. §§ 59-2-1108, 59-2-1109.

VERMONT

Vt. Stat. Ann. tit. 24, § 1535

General: The board of assessors may abate in whole or in part the taxes of persons who are unable to pay. § 1535(a).

VIRGIN ISLANDS

33 V.I. Code Ann. § 2305

Homestead: Exemption from real property taxes for principal residence up to the first $20,000 of the assessed value.

Elder: For residents sixty and older whose gross income does not exceed $10,500, exemption is up to the first $30,000 of the assessed value of the property.

Veterans: Veterans and widows of veterans are exempt from property tax up to the first $25,000 of the assessed value of the property. Subject to certain restrictions, veterans who have permanent and total disability due to certain injuries completely exempt from property taxes.

Appx. F

VIRGINIA

Va. Code Ann. §§ 58.1-3200 to 58.1-3228 (Michie)

Elder or Disabled: Localities may by ordinance provide for exemptions from, deferral of, or combination program of exemptions from taxation of real estate of persons at least sixty-five years of age or disabled. § 58.1-3210. Or exemptions may be provided for value of property that represents the increase in value from the year such person reached age sixty-five or the ordinance became effective, whichever is later.

Restrictions: Applies to persons whose income is less than $50,000 per year or the income limit for the family to qualify for federal housing assistance as published by HUD. § 58.1-3211. Up to $10,000 in income may be excluded if the owner is permanently disabled. Also, financial worth (excluding value of the property) cannot exceed $200,000. § 58.1-3211(2). Listed towns can increase the income and financial worth limits to $72,000 per year, and $340,000.

Other Exemptions: Localities may adopt partial exemptions for substantial rehabilitation, renovation or replacement of property in certain areas. § 58.1-3220. Or for the abatement of taxes on buildings that were razed or destroyed or damaged by circumstances beyond the owner's control. § 58.1-3222.

WASHINGTON

Wash. Rev. Code Ann. § 84.36.381 (West)

Seniors and Veterans: Exemption for sixty-one or older and veterans with 100% service-connected disability. Surviving spouse if fifty-seven or older and spouse was receiving exemption at time of death. Amount of exemption is based on income.

Disabled: Exemption for persons retired due to disability, and surviving spouses. Amount of exemption varies depending on income.

WEST VIRGINIA

W. Va. Code §§ 11-6B-1 to 11-6B-12

Elder or Disabled: First $20,000 of value exempt from homestead when owner is sixty-five or older, or is disabled, and has been resident of West Virginia for two years. § 11-6B-3.

WISCONSIN

Wis. Stat. §§ 234.621 to 234.625

Elder: Persons sixty and older with income of not more than $20,000, may apply for loans to pay for property taxes and special assessments in the amount of the property taxes at prime plus one percent. The loan is due upon the death of the taxpayer or transfer of the property. The loan creates a lien on the property for the amount of the loan. §§ 234.622 to 234.625.

WYOMING

Wyo. Stat. Ann. §§ 39-11-105, 39-13-105, 39-13-109 (Michie)

Veteran Exemption: Veterans who are bona fide residents for at least three years at the time of claiming the exemption are entitled to an annual exemption from property tax of $2,000 of the assessed value, not to exceed a total tax benefit of $800. §§ 39-11-105(a)(xxiv), 39-13-105. A surviving spouse is entitled to the same exemption so long as she is unmarried. § 39-13-

105(a)(v). Veterans with a service-related disability are entitled to up to a $2,000 additional exemption, depending upon the percentage of disability.

Improvements for Handicapped Access: Any improvement to residential property making an entrance to or common facilities within the property accessible to a handicapped person is exempt from property tax. § 39-11-105(a)(xxxii).

Homestead Tax Credit: Persons occupying a homestead as a principal residence are entitled to a specified property tax credit depending on the size of the property, the assessed value, and whether the land upon which the dwelling is located
is owned by the same person owning the dwelling. §§ 39-13-109(d)(i)(A), (E) & (F).

Property Tax Relief Program: Low-income property owners may apply for a property tax refund. § 39-13-109(c)(iii). Note that this statute is repealed effective January 1, 2008. § 39-13-109(c)(iii)(G).

Answer Sheet to Chapter 3 Questions

CHECKLIST: IDENTIFYING A PREDATORY MORTGAGE LOAN

#	Indicator	Check if included
Marketing & Sales		
1	Aggressive telephone or mail solicitations to targeted neighborhoods	✔
2	Door-to-door solicitation by home improvement contractor	
3	Kickbacks to mortgage brokers	✔
4	Steering to high rate lenders	✔
5	Promising specific terms, e.g., a fixed rate loan; switching at closing	✔
6	Property flipping	
The Application		
7	Structuring loans with payments borrowers can't afford	✔
8	Falsifying loan applications (particularly regarding income level)	
9	Adding "insincere" co-signers	
10	Making loans to mentally incapacitated homeowners	
11	Forging signatures on loan documents (i.e., required disclosures)	
12	Paying off subsidized mortgages or lower interest rate loans	
13	Shifting unsecured debt into mortgages	
14	Loans in excess of 100% LTV	
15	Falsifying appraisals	
The Loan		
16	High annual percentage rate	
17	High points or padded closing costs	✔
18	ARM sold to borrower with limited/no ability to pay higher payments	✔
19	Balloon payments	
20	Negative amortization	
21	Bogus broker fees	
22	Requiring credit insurance	
23	Falsely identifying loans as lines of credit or open-end mortgages	
24	Mandatory arbitration clauses	
25	Excessive prepayment penalties	✔
26	Rushed loan closing	
27	Back-dating documents, esp. the notice of right to cancel	
28	Failing to give copies of documents to homeowner at closing	

#	Indicator	Check if included
After Closing		
29	Loan flipping (repeated refinancing, often after high-pressure sales tactics)	✔
30	Excessive late fees (including daily interest)	
31	Deliberately posting payments late	
32	Abusive collection practices	
33	Incomplete or shoddy work by home improvement contractor	
34	Shoddy installation of mobile home/damaged mobile home	
35	Failure to pay off debts as promised	
36	Foreclosure "rescue" scams	

Additional red flags illustrated by the case study that are not specifically listed in this checklist include: unfair or deceptive practice to fail to advise the homeowners regarding the escrow; lying to them about whether the new loan escrows for taxes and insurance; and payment of high broker fees to a broker when none should have been involved because the lender contacted the homeowners to refinance its own loan, not the broker.

Glossary

(This glossary is provided with the complements of AFFIL partners: Center for Responsible Lending and the National Consumer Law Center.)

Bold words are separately defined in this glossary.

Acceleration. When a **creditor** claims the total balance of a loan is due immediately. This can not usually occur unless you have fallen behind on payments. In the case of a home mortgage, receipt of a letter stating that a loan has been "accelerated" is normally an important warning sign of foreclosure.

Accord and Satisfaction. This is the legal term which applies when you make clear that you consider your payment the full and final resolution of a disputed debt. If the creditor accepts the payment, the law treats that acceptance as the final payment of the debt.

Adjustable Rate Mortgage (ARM). A mortgage in which the interest rate can be adjusted at specified intervals by a given formula using an index and margin.

Amortize. This means to pay off a loan with regular payments. Part of each payment is applied to principal and to interest. At the end of the term, the loan is paid in full. There is no balloon payment.

Amount Financed. The amount of money you are getting in a loan, calculated under rules required by federal law. This is the amount of money you are borrowing after deduction of certain loan charges that the **Truth in Lending Act** defines as **finance charges**, i.e., **principal** minus finance charges. You should think of the amount financed as the real amount you are borrowing. You will find the amount financed for a loan on the **disclosure statement** that is given to you when the loan papers are signed.

Annual Percentage Rate. The interest rate on a loan expressed under rules required by federal law. It is more accurate to look at the annual percentage rate (as opposed to the stated interest rate) to determine the true cost of a loan, because it tells you the full cost of the loan including many of the lender's fees. You will find the annual percentage rate for a loan on the **disclosure statement** that is given to you when the loan papers are signed.

Answer. In a lawsuit, this is a legal document that the **defendant** must file to respond to the claims being raised. There are often short time deadlines to file an answer. Failure to file an answer can result in a **default judgment**.

Appraisal. An estimate of the value of property made by a qualified professional called an "appraiser." Appraisals vary in price depending upon whether it contains a full report with a market analysis involving comparable sales or a simple "drive by."

Arbitration. See **mandatory arbitration**.

Arrears. The total amount you are behind on a debt. Usually the amount of all back payments plus any collection costs.

Assignment. The transfer of a mortgage or deed of trust to another party usually evidenced by a document showing that the current mortgage holder (assignor) assigned its rights to the new holder (assignee).

Assignee. When a mortgage is transferred from one party to another (usually because the loan is purchased for investment purposes), the party that assumes ownership of the mortgage, as well as the rights and responsibilities attached to that mortgage, is known as the "assignee." An assignee may receive all or part of a security interest.

Assignee Liability. A legal term that means that the purchaser of a loan may be held liable for legal claims against the original lender. Typically, the original lenders sell loans in the secondary market after the loan closes. If a predatory lending claim arises, assignee liability ensures that the borrower can pursue legal action. Assignee liability also encourages loan purchasers to conduct thorough due diligence.

Attachment. A legal process that allows a creditor to "attach" a **lien** to property that you own. Depending on state law, almost any kind of property may be subject to attachment, including your home, automobile, bank accounts, and wages. Once a **lien** is attached to the property, you may face further collection action on that property, including **execution, garnishment** or **foreclosure**.

Automatic Stay. An automatic end to creditor collection activity. Filing bankruptcy is the only way to get this protection. If the **debtor** filed other bankruptcy cases that were dismissed within the previous twelve months, however, she may not get an automatic stay or it may only last for the first thirty days of the bankruptcy case.

Auto/Car Title Loan. A short term loan secured by a borrower's car title. A typical car title loan has a triple-digit annual interest rate, requires repayment within one month, and is made for much less than the value of the car. Many borrowers who cannot afford to pay off their loans repeatedly extend them for additional fees. In some states, lenders are allowed to keep the surplus from the sale of the car if the borrower defaults on payment.

Balloon Payment. A large lump-sum **payment** that is due as the last payment on a loan. Often used by lenders as a way to make monthly payments artificially low.

Bank. A financial institution that accepts deposits, makes loans, and performs other services for its customers. According to Robert Frost, "a bank is a place where they lend you an umbrella in fair weather and ask you for it back when it begins to rain."

Bankruptcy. A legal process available in all states that allows you to address your debt problems according to a set of special rules while getting protection from continued collection activity. See also **liquidation** and **reorganization**.

Bond. Amounts required by a court order to protect a party to a lawsuit while the case proceeds. A bond may be required in some circumstances to pursue an appeal.

Bounce Loans. A short-term loan granted by a bank to cover an overdraft incurred by using either paper check or debit cards. Banks charge high penalty fees for each overdraft, ranging from $20 to $35 per overdraft plus a per-day fee of $2 to $5 at some banks until the account is brought to a positive balance. With "bounce loan" programs, banks pay themselves back the amount of the overdraft and fees out of the next deposit. See **overdraft loan**.

Broker's Price Opinion. An evaluation of property value typically based on a drive-by exterior examination, public data sources, and recent comparable sales, that is obtained by a

servicer as an alternative to a full appraisal after a loan is in default or when the loan is being modified.

Cap. A ceiling that limits how much the interest rate on the loan may be adjusted. There are periodic caps, which limit how much the interest may be adjusted per period, and a lifetime cap, which limits how much the interest rate may be adjusted over the life of the loan.

Capitalization. Capitalization occurs when items owed on a loan are treated as part of a new principal balance. When **arrears** are "capitalized," the amount of the arrears is included in the principal before the interest rate is applied. Often, capitalization and **reamortization** go hand in hand. If the arrears are "capitalized" and the loan is "reamortized," your lender will recalculate your payment using the existing interest rate and the new principal balance.

Chapter 7 Bankruptcy. See **liquidation**.

Chapter 13 Bankruptcy. See **reorganization**.

Check Cashing. Service offered by alternative financial institutions to people who do not have access to mainstream banking services. Although the fees can be high (typically 3% of the check value), unlike predatory payday lending, the practice generally does not encourage a cycle of debt.

Closed-end Loan. A loan with a fixed term.

Closing. The process of signing loan papers which obligate the borrower to repay a loan. This term is associated with the signing of a mortgage loan. It is also called the settlement.

Closing Agent. The mortgage closing or settlement is usually conducted by an agent for the lender. This person is called the closing agent. Often this agent is an attorney.

Closing Costs. These are costs related to the financing and title transfer of real estate. They include expenses such as points, taxes, title insurance, mortgage insurance, commissions, and fees.

Collateral. Property put up to secure a loan. If you have given a creditor collateral, that creditor can normally take and sell the collateral if you are not able to repay the loan. A creditor with collateral is normally known as a "**secured creditor.**"

Commitment. An agreement, often in writing, between a lender and a borrower to loan money at a future date subject to the completion of paperwork or compliance with stated conditions. The commitment may guarantee an interest rate or other terms until a future date. See **lock**.

Complaint. A document beginning a lawsuit. A complaint normally includes a statement of all of the claims being raised by the person bringing the lawsuit.

Conventional Loan. A loan issued to a borrower with an excellent or very good credit rating. Conventional loans do not include those insured by the federal government, such as the Federal Housing or Veterans Administrations, or subprime loans.

Cosigner. A person who agrees to be responsible for someone else's debt. A cosigner is normally responsible for paying back a debt just as if he or she had received the money.

Counterclaim. A response to a lawsuit in which the person being sued raises legal claims against the person (or business) which started the case. For example, if you are sued by an automobile seller who claims you did not pay for a car, you might counterclaim that the car was a "lemon."

Credit Bureau. Also called consumer reporting agency or credit reporting agency. This is a company that receives information about a consumer's credit history and keeps records that are available to those seeking data about that consumer.

Credit Insurance. Insurance designed to pay off a borrower's mortgage debt if the borrower dies or is otherwise incapable of meeting the loan obligation. When sold in a "single premium" or "lump sum," all premiums are charged in advance and typically added to the loan balance, increasing the overall cost by requiring the borrower to pay interest on the premiums over the life of the loan. Since single-premium credit insurance has fallen into disfavor, lenders have introduced analogous products such as "debt cancellation" contracts.

Credit Report. Also called a consumer report or a credit record. A report documenting the credit history and current status of a borrower's monthly payment obligations and containing public information such as bankruptcies, court **judgments**, and tax liens.

Credit Score. A credit score (sometimes called a "FICO" score) is a number that summarizes your credit history. The score is based on a number of factors, including how well debts have been paid off, current levels of debt, types of credit, and length of credit history. Lenders use credit scores to decide who qualifies for a loan and how much the loan should cost. Scores generally range from 350 to 900; most lenders consider a score over 660 to be very good.

Creditor. Also called a lender. Any person or business to whom you owe money.

Cure a Default. If you have defaulted on a debt, this is a process for correcting the **default**. Most often, a "cure" refers to getting caught up on missed payments (paying the **arrears**). A cure may also be called **reinstatement**.

Debt Collector. The most common use of this term applies to anyone who collects debts. However, under the federal **Fair Debt Collection Practices Act** "FDCPA," the term "debt collector" only applies to collection agencies and lawyers (or their employees) that are collecting debts for others. State laws may cover other types of collectors.

Debt Consolidation. Refinancing debt into a new loan. In the mortgage lending context, relatively short-term, unsecured debt often is rolled into long-term mortgage loans, putting the home at greater risk.

Debt-to-Income Ratio. The relationship between the consumer's monthly debt payments and the monthly income, expressed as a ratio. Lenders will often set a maximum debt-to-income ratio and usually do not make loans to consumers whose ratios exceed the lender's standard.

Debt Management Plan. Debt management plans are offered by many credit counseling agencies. Through debt management plans (DMPs), consumers send the credit counseling agency a monthly payment, which the agency then distributes to the consumer's creditors. In return, the consumer is supposed to get a break, usually in the form of creditor agreements to waive fees and to lower interest rates.

Debtor. Any person who owes money to another. In **bankruptcy**, the term "debtor" refers to the person who begins a bankruptcy case.

Debtor's Examination. Also known as "post-judgment process," "asset examination," and "supplementary process." This is normally a court ordered proceeding in which a debtor must appear in court or in an attorney's office to answer questions about current income and assets from which a **judgment** may be collected. In many states, failure to appear at a debtor's examination can result in an arrest warrant.

Debt Settlement. Negotiation and settlement services are different from debt management services (see **debt management plan**) mainly because the debt settlement agencies do not send regular monthly payments to creditors. Instead, these agencies generally maintain a consumer's funds in separate accounts, holding the money until the agency believes it can settle a consumer's debts for less than the full amount owed.

Deed. A deed is an instrument that transfers ownership from the seller to the buyer upon the closing of the sale.

Deed-in-Lieu. An agreement to turn real estate over to a lender as an alternative to **foreclosure**.

Deed of Trust. In some states, this is the term used for a pledge of real estate as **collateral**. It is similar to a **mortgage**.

Default. Failing to meet the requirements of an agreement. Most defaults involve failure to make required payments. However, other types of defaults are possible, including failure to maintain necessary insurance and failure to keep **collateral** in proper condition.

Default Judgment. A **judgment** in a lawsuit against a party who did not meet legal requirements in connection with the case. The most common reason for a default judgment is failing to file an **answer** or other necessary papers before deadlines specified by law.

Default Rate. The interest rate the creditor will charge once the borrower defaults on the loan. If a default interest rate is listed in a loan contract, it is always higher than the contract interest rate.

Defendant. In a lawsuit, this is the person or business that is being sued.

Defense. A legal reason why a court should not award any or all of what is requested in a lawsuit. For example, a statement that the money is not owed is a defense to a collection lawsuit.

Deficiency. The amount a debtor owes a creditor on a debt after the creditor seizes and sells the **collateral**. A deficiency arises when the collateral is sold for less than the amount of the debt. Normally, a creditor must bring a lawsuit to collect a deficiency.

Deposition. A proceeding in a legal case in which a person is asked questions about relevant facts (usually in a lawyer's office) and gives sworn answers under oath. Your deposition may be required if you start a lawsuit or if one is filed against you. Your lawyer may require depositions of others. Depositions are a normal part of the **discovery** process used to prepare for a court trial.

Deregulation. The process started in the 1980s of loosening or eliminating regulation of the lending industry. Deregulation resulted, in part, in the removal of usury caps and borrower protections. Since then, abusive lending practices have increased.

Discharge. A document that ends a debtor's legally enforceable obligation to pay a debt. It is common to get a discharge of a mortgage debt after the mortgage is fully paid off. In addition, most bankruptcies result in a discharge at the end of the case that applies to many debts.

Disclosure Statement. This term is commonly used to refer to the document that explains loan terms according to the **Truth in Lending Act**.

Discovery. This term covers a variety of legal processes by which the parties to a lawsuit obtain information from each other and documents related to the case.

Discount Fee. See **points**.

Downpayment. Money paid to make up the difference between the purchase price and the mortgage amount. Down payments are usually 20% of the sale price on **conventional loans**.

Equity. Your equity in property is the amount of cash you would keep if you sold property and paid off all of the liens on that property. For example, if you own a house worth $100,000, but you owe $60,000 on your original mortgage and $10,000 on a second mortgage, you have $30,000 in equity. The same principle applies to cars and other types of property.

Equity Stripping. Loan terms on mortgages (usually refinances) designed to maximize the lender's revenues by increasing the borrower's loan balance; this practice reduces the borrower's equity in the home. Equity stripping may occur in various ways, but the most common is charging excessive fees that are financed as part of the new loan.

Escrow. Amounts set aside for a particular purpose. A formal escrow usually requires a legal agreement that covers permissible usage of the escrow and how and where the money is to be kept. One type of escrow is money you pay to your mortgage company to cover taxes and insurance. Escrow is also used when you have a dispute with a creditor. You may choose to set up an escrow to pay the debt in the event you lose the dispute.

Escrow Closing or Settlement. The occasion where the purchase of a home is financed or a non-purchase money loan (see **home equity loan**) and **mortgage** is signed, the buyer pays the mortgage, and closing costs are paid.

Eviction. A legal process terminating the right to occupy a home, apartment or business property. State law eviction proceedings are required before putting someone out.

Execution. The process of enforcing a court judgment by taking property from the **defendant**. Execution of a judgment of **eviction**, for example, involves the sheriff or a public official putting the tenants out. Execution of a **judgment lien** involves seizing and selling the property subject to the lien.

Exempt Property. Property that the law allows you to keep when you are being faced with collection on an **unsecured debt**. In **bankruptcy**, exempt property is protected from sale to satisfy the claims of creditors. Your exemption applies to your **equity** in the property after deduction for the amounts you owe to pay **liens** on that property.

Exemptions. These are laws that give you the right to keep your **exempt property**.

Exploding ARM (adjustable rate mortgage). A common type of "hybrid" ARM in the subprime market that includes both a fixed- and adjustable-interest rate component. A "2/28" hybrid ARM comes with an initial short-term fixed interest rate for two years, followed by rate adjustments, generally in six-month increments for the remainder of the loan's term. Typically the introductory rate is artificially low, giving homeowners a dramatic increase in housing costs after the introductory period expires.

Fair Credit Reporting Act. A federal (national) law that regulates **credit bureaus** and the use of credit reports.

Fair Debt Collection Practices Act. A federal (national) law that governs the conduct of debt collectors and that prevents many abusive collection tactics.

Fannie Mae. See **Federal National Mortgage Association**.

Federal Deposit Insurance Corporation (FDIC). An independent agency created by Congress in 1933 to maintain financial stability and public confidence in the nation's banking system. The FDIC insures deposits in banks and thrift institutions for up to $100,000. The agency also directly examines and supervises about 5,300 banks and savings banks, more than half of the institutions in the U.S. banking system.

Federal Reserve Board (Fed). The central bank of the United States. It was created by Congress to provide the nation with a safer, more flexible, and more stable monetary and financial system. Its central agency conducts US monetary policy, and its 12 regional banks support and regulate commercial banks and thrifts.

Federal Housing Administration (FHA). One of the agencies of the federal government that insures first mortgage lenders against loss when a loan is made following FHA regulations. The FHA does not lend money; it only insures the loan.

Federal Law. A law of the United states that applies throughout the country. The **bankruptcy** law is an example of a federal law.

Federal National Mortgage Association (Fannie Mae) and Federal Home Mortgage Corporation (Freddie Mac). A high percentage of mortgages are now held by investors. The two largest investors that purchase mortgages on the secondary market are Fannie Mae and Freddie Mac. These "government sponsored enterprises" were created by Congress to provide liquidity or capital in the housing market by purchasing mortgages. This helps put money back into the hands of the originating lender so that new loans can be made. The originating lender must follow certain guidelines specified by Freddie Mac and Fannie Mae when qualifying the borrower for a loan, commonly called **underwriting** guidelines.

Fee. Any charge added to a loan.

Finance Charge. The amount of money a loan will cost you expressed as a dollar figure. The finance charge includes the interest together with certain other loan charges specified by the **Truth in Lending Act**. You will find the loan's finance charge on the **disclosure statement** given to you when you sign the loan papers.

Finance company. A company engaged in making loans to individuals or businesses. Unlike a bank, it does not receive deposits from the public.

Fixed-Rate Mortgage. A mortgage on which the interest rate is set for the term of the loan.

Flipping. The practice of refinancing a loan without providing a net benefit to the homeowner. Although some borrowers may receive cash as a result of flipped loans, the benefit of this compensation may be outweighed by the costs of losing equity or taking on unaffordable debt. See **property flipping**.

Force-Placed Insurance. The insurance policy your lender will "force" you to purchase if your insurance is cancelled or if your lender does not have proof of your insurance coverage. Force-placed insurance is very expensive.

Foreclosure. A legal process to terminate your ownership of real estate that is **collateral** for a debt, based on a **mortgage** or **deed of trust**. In some states, foreclosure involves a court proceeding ("judicial foreclosure"), while in others foreclosure occurs by creditor action alone ("non-judicial foreclosure").

Foreclosure Rescue Scam. This scam targets those who have fallen behind on their mortgage payments. A con artist promises to help consumers save their home but is actually intent on stealing the home or most of its accumulated equity.

Fraudulent Transfer. Giving away property to keep it out of the hands of creditors. The law allows **creditors** to sue to get the property back.

Freddie Mac. See **Federal Home Mortgage Corporation**.

Garnishment. A **creditor's** seizure, to satisfy a debt, of property belonging to the **debtor** that is in the possession of a third party. Usually a court has to authorize the seizure in advance. An example would be seizure of money in your bank account to repay a court judgment. Wages owed to you can also be garnished in many states.

Ginnie Mae. See **Government National Mortgage Association**.

Good Faith Estimate (GFE). An itemization of the estimated closing costs. Lenders or brokers must provide this list to the loan applicant for a mortgage loan within 3 business days after receipt of the application. The GFE is intended to assure that consumers have adequate information about closing costs early on to enable them to shop for those, as well as interest rates. This disclosure is required by the Real Estate Settlement Procedures Act.

Government National Mortgage Association (Ginnie Mae). It is a quasi-governmental agency that guarantees pools of Federal Housing Administration (FHA) and Veteran Administration (VA) insured-loans that had been securitized for investment purposes.

Guarantor. A person who agrees to pay another person's debt in the event that he or she does not pay. The term guarantor is often used interchangeably with **cosigner**, even though there are some minor legal distinctions in the collection process.

Government Mortgage Guarantors. There are special government programs that provide mortgage insurance or guarantees to lenders who make purchase-money mortgage loans to homebuyers who meet certain criteria. These programs are offered through the federal government (the Federal Housing Administration, part of the Department of Housing and Urban Development; the Rural Housing Service, part of the Department of Agriculture; and the Veterans Administration) or by a state housing finance agency. In addition to the insurance, these loans come with an obligation on the part of the insured lenders to work with homeowners to cure defaults.

Hazard Insurance. Insurance that covers property loss or damage, usually paid for by borrowers and required when obtaining a mortgage.

Holder. The mortgage holder "owns" the borrowers' mortgage. Since many mortgages are assigned by the originator to a purchaser on the secondary market, very often the mortgage holder will not be the bank or mortgage company who made the loan.

Home Equity Loan. Generally, this term is used to describe any mortgage loan that is not used to finance the purchase of the home.

Home Ownership and Equity Protection Act (HOEPA). This is a federal (national) law that provides special protection to homeowners when they obtain home mortgage loans at high interest rates or with high fees.

Homestead Exemption. The right, available in most states and in the **bankruptcy** process, to treat your residence as **exempt property** that can not be sold to satisfy the claims of **unsecured creditors**. In most states, the homestead exemption covers a certain dollar amount of your equity in your residence. A home can not normally be sold to pay claims of your creditors unless your equity in the home exceeds the amount of the exemption. A homestead exemption will not normally protect you from **foreclosure** when you have voluntarily pledged your home as **collateral**.

Index. A published rate often used to establish the interest rate charged on adjustable rate mortgages or to compare investment returns. Examples of commonly used indexes include Treasury bill rates, the prime rate, LIBOR (the London Interbank Offered Rate), and the 11th District cost-of-funds-index (issued by the San Francisco Federal Home Loan Bank).

Interest. Is the cost of borrowing money over time. Interest rates are expressed as a percentage.

Investor. A company that invests in mortgages that other companies have originated. They purchase the mortgage for a set amount and collect monthly payments, usually through a servicer.

Insolvent. A person or business that does not have sufficient assets to pay its debts.

Judgment. A determination by a court as to the outcome of a lawsuit, including any amounts owed.

Judgment Lien. A **lien** that attaches to property as the result of a **judgment**. For example, if you lose a collection lawsuit, the creditor normally has the right to an **attachment** on any real estate that you own.

Judgment-Proof. This term is applied to people or businesses with property of minimal value, which can be entirely protected by **exemptions**. If you are judgment-proof, it is difficult or sometimes impossible for any creditor to force you to pay a debt.

Kickback. Money paid by one of the settlement service providers, e.g., the lender, title company, or closing attorney, for referring a customer.

Lemon Law. This is a state law that gives you protection if you purchase an automobile that does not work properly and can not easily be fixed. Most lemon laws only apply to new cars, but some also apply to used cars.

Levy. A process, in some states, for **attachment** of a **judgment lien** and/or **execution** of that **lien**.

Lien. Also called a "security interest," it is a legal interest taken by creditors in your property to secure repayment of a debt. A lien can be created voluntarily in connection with a loan, such as when you pledge real estate by giving a creditor a **mortgage** or **deed of trust**. A lien can also be created without your consent by **attachment** based on a court order. A creditor with a lien is called a **secured creditor**.

Liquidation. Sale of property to pay creditors. The term is also used as a shorthand name for the chapter 7 bankruptcy process, even though property is not always sold in that bankruptcy process.

Lis Pendens. A notice, recorded in the chain of title to real property, required or permitted in some states to warn all persons that certain property is the subject of litigation and that any interests in the real property acquired during the pendency of the suit are subject to its outcome.

Loan Application. A standard form that creditors use to obtain personal and financial information from a borrower before deciding whether to make a loan.

Loan Term. The loan term is the length of time before the loan is due to be repaid in full. Most mortgage loans have 15 or 30-year terms. Many predatory consumer loans (payday loans, car title loans, refund anticipation loans) have very short loan terms, which increase the APR earned by the lender and/or pressure consumers into extending their loans at additional fees.

Loan to Value Ratio (LTV). The relationship, expressed as a percentage, between the loan amount and the value of the property securing the loan. The more equity in the property, the lower the percentage. Conversely, the less equity, the higher the percentage. A "high LTV loan" is one made with little or no equity in the property to secure the loan in the event of foreclosure. Conventional lenders require an LTV of, at most, 80%. **Subprime** lenders usually prefer a lower LTV, in the 70-75% range.

Lock. The **interest** rate selected by the borrower at a certain time during the loan process that is guaranteed by the lender for a specific number of days. This is called "locking" the rate. Once the rate is locked, neither the lender nor the borrower can change it.

Mandatory Arbitration. A clause in a loan contract that requires the borrower to use arbitration to resolve any legal disputes that arise from the loan. Mandatory arbitration typically means borrowers lose their right to pursue legal actions, including any appeals, in a court of law. Evidence indicates that arbitration is often costly for borrowers and may reduce their chances of receiving a fair outcome. Borrowers often are unaware that a mandatory arbitration agreement has been included in their home documents.

GLOSSARIES

Margin. The number added to the index to determine the interest rate on an adjustable rate mortgage. For example, if the index rate is 6%, and the current note rate is 8.75%, the margin is 2.75%.

Market Value. The highest price one would pay and the lowest price the seller would accept on a property. Market value may be different from the price a property could actually be sold for at a given time.

Mortgage. An agreement in which a property owner grants a **creditor** the right to satisfy a debt by selling the real property in the event of a **default**.

Mortgage-Backed Security. A type of investment backed by pools of mortgage loans, with payments on the underlying mortgages generating the return to investors. By selling mortgages in the secondary mortgage market, where they are collected and packaged as investments, lenders are able to generate more funds for future lending.

Mortgage Broker. An individual who offers to arrange financing for a homeowner. In theory, the broker operates as the agent for the homeowner, seeking the best product. States vary as to whether or not the brokers are regulated.

Mortgagee. The entity that obtains a security interest in the real property of another, usually the lender.

Mortgage Insurance. See **private mortgage insurance**.

Mortgage Servicer. A bank, mortgage company, or a similar business that communicates with property owners concerning their **mortgage** loans. The servicer usually works for another company that owns the mortgage. It may accept and record payments, negotiate **workouts**, and supervise the **foreclosure** process in the event of a **default**.

Mortgagor. The owner of real property who grants a **mortgage** to another, usually a lender.

Negative Amortization. Negative amortization occurs when your payments do not cover the amount of interest due for that payment period. For example, if you have a $50,000 loan at 10% interest for 15 years and make monthly payments of $400 a month, that loan will negatively amortize. At the end of the 15 years, even if you make all of your payments, you will still owe more than $50,000. Negative amortization is usually associated with a large **balloon payment** due in the last month of the loan.

Negative Equity. Negative **equity** arises when the value of an item of property you own is less than the total you owe on all the liens on that property. For example, if you own a home worth $100,000 and borrow $125,000 to consolidate debts, you have negative equity of $25,000.

Non-Purchase Money Security Interest. A non-purchase money security interest arises when you agree to give a lender collateral that was not purchased with money from that loan. For example, a finance company may insist that you give a lawn-mower or living room set as collateral for a loan you take out to pay for car repairs.

Non-Sufficient Funds (NSF). Fees are charged for non-sufficient funds (NSF) when a checking account is overdrawn. The threat of these charges contribute to the pressure payday borrowers are under to renew loans and pay repeated fees. NSF fees differ from overdraft fees, which are charged for the extension of a loan using bank funds to cover the amount you would have overdrawn.

Note. This term is commonly used as a name for a contract involving the loan of money.

Notice of Right to Cancel. This document explains your right to cancel a loan in some circumstances. You should receive such a notice in connection with most door-to-door sales and for **mortgage** loans that are not used to buy your residence.

Notice to Quit. In most states, this is a notice given by an owner of property (usually a landlord) demanding that a tenant leave within a specified period of time or face eviction proceedings.

Office of the Comptroller of the Currency (OCC). Charters, regulates and supervises all national banks. It also supervises all federal branches and agencies of foreign banks.

Office of Thrift Supervision (OTS). The successor thrift regulator to the Federal Home Loan Bank Board and a division within the Treasury Department. The OTS is responsible for the examination and regulation of federally chartered and state chartered savings associations.

Open-ended Loan. A loan without a definite term or end date.

Origination Fee. A fee paid to a lender for processing a loan application. It is stated as a percentage of the mortgage amount, or "points."

Originator. The lender who makes the loan and whose name is on the loan documents.

Overdraft Loan. Overdraft loans, also called bounce-check protection or courtesy overdraft protection, are a form of high-cost, short-term credit, wherein financial institutions cover their customers' overdrafts when they have a negative balance, and then charge them a fee. These loans have been exempted from interest rate disclosure requirements and can contribute to a devastating cycle of debt. See **bounce loan**.

Payday Loan. (Also called "cash advances," "deferred presentment," "deferred deposits" or "check loans.") Payday loan customers write the lender a post-dated check or sign an authorization for the lender to take money out of an account electronically for a certain amount. The amount on the check equals the amount borrowed plus a fee that is either a percentage of the full amount of the check or a flat dollar amount. The check (or debit agreement) is then held for up to a month, usually until the customer's next payday or receipt of a government check. At the end of the agreed time period, the customer must either pay back the full amount of the check (more than what the lender gave out), allow the check to be cashed, or pay another fee to extend the loan. Most payday borrowers get caught in a debt trap, unable to pay off the loan in the two-week term, and so are compelled to avoid default by paying repeated high fees for no new money.

Payment Option ARM (adjustable rate mortgage). A mortgage that allows a number of different payment options each month, including very minimal payments. The minimum payment option can be less than the interest accruing on the loan, resulting in negative amortization.

Payment Shock. An unmanageable rise in a consumer's monthly mortgage payment, typically the result of an increase in the interest rate on an ARM loan. For example, a 2% bump in a loan's interest rate can increase the consumer's monthly payment 24%.

Personal Property. Property other than real estate.

PITI. Principal + Interest + Taxes + Insurance. The total monthly mortgage expense.

Plaintiff. This is a person or business that begins a lawsuit.

Points/Loan Discount Points. A cost of the credit imposed by the lender. Points are prepaid in cash or financed as part of the loan principal. Each point is equal to 1% of the loan amount (e.g., two points on a $100,000 mortgage would cost $2,000). Generally in the conventional loan market and sometimes in the subprime market, points are paid to lower the loan's interest rate. In that event, the points are called discount points.

Power of Sale Clause. A provision in a mortgage or deed of trust permitting the **mortgagee** or trustee to sell the property without court authority if the payments are not made.

Predatory Lending. A term for a variety of lending practices that strip wealth or income from borrowers. Predatory loans typically are much more expensive than justified by the risk associated with the loan. Characteristics of predatory loans may include, but are not limited to, excessive or hidden fees, charges for unnecessary products, high interest rates, terms designed to trap borrowers in debt, fraud, and refinances that do not provide any net benefit to the borrower.

Preemption. A term used when one law or rule directly overrides an existing law or rule. Preemption provisions in a federal law generally displace state laws governing the same topic. In the area of predatory lending, federal preemption would nullify many state protections for homeowners and prevent states from addressing local predatory lending issues as they arise. Banks and other depository institutions claim broad preemption of state laws.

Prepayment. Paying off all or part of the loan balance before it is due.

Prepayment Penalty. A fee charged by a lender if the borrower pays the loan off early. The lender's rationale for imposing prepayment penalties is to cover the loss of costs advanced by the lender at the time of origination. Mortgage loans with prepayment penalties often include a yield spread premium payment by the lender to the broker.

Pre-Sale. Sale of property in anticipation of **foreclosure** or **repossession**, usually with the lender's consent. A pre-sale is likely to lead to a higher sale price than foreclosure or repossession.

Principal. The amount borrowed.

Private Mortgage Insurance (PMI). Insurance provided by non-government insurers that protects lenders against loss if a borrower defaults. This insurance is usually required when a borrower makes less than a 20% down payment. When the borrower's equity in the property equals 20%, she may request the insurance be canceled.

Processing Fee. A charge imposed by a creditor to process or handle a loan application.

Property Flipping. Property flipping scams typically involve speculators who buy dilapidated residential properties at low prices and resell them at huge markups to unsophisticated (and often first-time) homebuyers. Falsified **appraisals** are often the linchpin of property flipping scams.

Property Inspection Fee. A charge imposed by a servicer for inspections (usually drive-bys) to determine the physical condition or occupancy status of mortgaged property, often charged repeatedly once an account is placed in default status.

Pro Se. (Also called "pro per.") Representing yourself (without an attorney) in a legal case or bankruptcy proceeding.

Punitive Damages. Special damages that are sometimes awarded in court to punish a party which is responsible for serious misconduct.

Purchase Money Mortgage. The mortgage loan obtained to purchase a home.

Purchase Money Security Interest. A lien on property that arises when you agree to allow a lender to take as collateral the property you are purchasing with the loan.

Reaffirmation. An agreement in the **bankruptcy** process to pay back a debt that would otherwise be **discharged** in bankruptcy. Most reaffirmation agreements are a bad idea.

Real Estate Settlement Procedures Act (RESPA). The purpose of this **federal law** is to protect consumers from unnecessarily high settlement charges and certain abusive practices that have developed in the residential real estate market. The law requires disclosures before and at the **closing**, as well as periodically throughout the term of the **mortgage** loan. The disclosures address settlement costs, servicing transfers, and escrows. RESPA also prohibits kickbacks and fee-splitting between settlement servicer providers.

Reamortization. When a loan is reamortized, your payment is recalculated based on loan terms that are different from the original terms. For example, if you have paid for five years on a ten-year loan, your lender might consider starting the ten-year period again and recalculating your payments. This will lower your payments. Similarly, your **arrears** may be **capitalized** (included in the principal) and your loan reamortized to reflect the higher principal balance on which interest is accruing.

Redeem. Recovering **collateral** from a **creditor** by paying the entire amount you owe whether past due or not.

Redlining. In the mortgage lending context, the practice of denying the extension of credit to residents of a specific geographic area due to their race, ethnicity, age, or sex.

Refinancing. The process of paying off current debts by borrowing new money either from an existing **creditor** or a new creditor.

Refund Anticipation Loan. See **tax refund anticipation loans**.

Registry of Deeds. Also called Land Records or Recorder's Office. These offices are located in every county. Real property deeds, mortgages or deeds of trust, assignments, liens, and other documents affecting real property are filed in these offices.

Reinstatement. The process of remedying a **default** so that the lender will treat you as if you had never fallen behind. See **curing a default**.

Renewal. In some states, regulations limit the number of times a single payday loan can be extended or "rolled over." Payday lenders accomplish the same effect with loan renewals, also known as "back-to-back transactions." In a renewal transaction, the borrower pays off an existing payday loan in order to open another one (either immediately or after a cooling-off period). The borrower gets no new money, but pays another fee for the new loan.

Rent-to-Own. Rent-to-own companies "rent" merchandise to a consumer for a stated period, after which the consumer owns the merchandise. A consumer would pay over four times the value of the merchandise under a typical contract. The company is not required to disclose interest rates, although the transaction is much like a loan in that the company may levy unlimited finance charges for late payments, and may repossess the merchandise.

Reorganization (Chapter 13 Bankruptcy). This is a bankruptcy process to get relief from debts by making court-supervised payments over a period of time. The alternative is usually **liquidation** under chapter 7.

Replevin. The legal process in which a creditor seeks to recover **personal property** on which it claims a **lien**. Replevin is often threatened, but rarely occurs.

Repossession. (Often called "self-help repossession.") Seizure by the creditor of **collateral** after the debtor's **default**, usually without court supervision or permission. Repossession is most common in connection with car loans.

Rescission. This is a right under some laws to cancel a contract or loan. The most common example of rescission arises in home equity loan transactions. You have the right to rescind that loan within the first three business days after the loan is signed. In some cases, if the

creditor has violated the law, your right to rescind may continue after the three-day period is up.

Retaliatory Eviction. An **eviction** where a landlord seeks to punish a tenant for exercising his or her legal rights (such as complaining to the building inspector or forming a tenant's organization).

Reverse Mortgage. A **refinancing** option usually available only to older homeowners who have built up substantial equity in their property. In a reverse mortgage, money is drawn based on the value of the property without an immediate repayment obligation, because the lender expects repayment by sale of the property at some point in the future.

Reverse Redlining. The practice of extending credit on unfair terms to those in certain communities based upon race, ethnicity, sex, or age.

Rollover. Rollovers are common practice in payday lending. Payday loan terms are typically two weeks, but borrowers are flipped into rollovers: they pay another fee to keep the loan outstanding in an extension. Many borrowers pay a high fee every payday without ever paying down the principal or receiving new money, and end up paying many times the original loan amount in fees. See also **renewal**.

Sale/leaseback. An early form of payday lending circumvention, in which a payday lender avoids legal restrictions by claiming the loan they make is payment for an item the borrower owns, but pretends to "sell" to the lender, who then "leases" it back to the borrower for a fee. The "sale" proceeds are the loan, and the fee is the interest. Also commonly used in car title lending.

Satisfaction. This is a legal document that states that a debt has been fully paid or that partial payment has been accepted as payment in full. A satisfaction is a type of **discharge**.

Secondary Market. This term describes the phenomenon where originating lenders sell their loans to buyers (often called investors), usually in bulk. This enables mortgage companies specializing in home equity lending to operate with a small capital base. They can obtain a line of credit from a major bank, originate loans, and then obtain money to make new loans by selling them to investors. The secondary market includes "wholesale" lenders who buy loans from small lenders, and the securitization market, where mortgage loans are pooled and sold to investors.

Secured Credit Cards. A credit card for which the card issuer requires that the card holder place a certain amount of money in a bank account with the card issuer. If the debtor does not repay the credit card, the card issuer can seize the money in the bank account.

Secured Creditor. Any **creditor** that has **collateral** for a debt.

Secured Debt. A debt for which the **creditor** has **collateral** in the form of a **mortgage**, **lien**, or **security interest** in certain items of property. The creditor can seize the property (**collateral**) if the **debtor defaults** in repayment of the debt.

Securitization. It is the process of investing in and providing capital for the creation of mortgage loans. This process brings together a variety of entities to accomplish these goals. Loans are pooled and assigned to a trustee that supervises the servicer of the loans and distributes the monthly returns to the securities holders. The pools of loans are sometimes insured and they are rated by the various bond-rating agencies. An investment firm invites investors to buy certificates or mortgage-backed securities that pay an attractive interest rate over a specific term. Investors are compensated through interest payments that are often guaranteed by bond insurance companies. The borrower's monthly payments on the loan cover both the return to the investors and a profit to the lender. The risk of loss to the investors is negligible given insurance and recourse agreements between the trustee and the lender. Creating capital flow in this way for subprime lenders only took off following 1994.

Security Interest. See **lien**.

Self-Help Repossession. This is a process by which a **creditor** that has taken property as **collateral** can **repossess** the property without first getting court permission.

Servicer. See **mortgage servicer**.

Settlement. The closing of a mortgage loan. Also, the delivery of a loan or security to a buyer.

Settlement Statement ("the HUD-1"). The Real Estate Settlement Procedures Act requires lenders to give this disclosure at closing, or one day in advance of closing if the consumer requests it. It should be the final statement of settlement costs. The RESPA disclosure focuses on closing costs as a dollar amount.

Short-term credit. Payday lenders and purveyors of overdraft loans, car title loans and refund anticipation loans offer extremely short-term credit, typically a few days to one month, and charge interest rates in the triple digits. The excessive charges far outweigh the risks associated with these loans.

Short Sale. A type of **pre-sale** in which the **creditor** agrees to let you sell property (usually real estate) for less than the full amount owed and to accept the proceeds of the sale as full **satisfaction** of the debt.

State Law. A law passed by an individual state that only applies to transactions in that state.

Statute. Another word for a law passed by a state or federal legislative body. Laws enacted by local bodies, such as city councils, usually are called ordinances.

Steering. The practice of routing certain borrowers to lenders that charge higher fees or interest rates than the borrowers' credit histories warrant.

Subpoena. A document that is normally issued by a court in connection with a lawsuit, and that directs your attendance in a court or law office at a particular time. A subpoena may require production of documents related to the case.

Subprime Loan. A loan that is more expensive than a comparable prime loan. Subprime lending is generally defined as less than "A" (i.e. prime) lending. This type of lending is designed to provide credit to borrowers with no credit history or past credit problems at a higher cost than conventional "A" mortgage loans. Most of the predatory mortgage lending occurs in the subprime market.

Summons. (Also called "original notice" or "notice of suit.") This is a document that is provided at the beginning of the lawsuit to tell the **defendant** what is being requested and what must be done to respond to the **complaint**. The term "summons" is also sometimes used interchangeably with **subpoena** for other legal papers that direct a person to be at a particular place at a particular time.

Table-Funded Transaction. Is one where the nominal lender is actually originating the loan for another entity whose money is used to fund the loan. The loan will be transferred within a relatively short period of time after the **closing** to the lender who funded the loan.

Targeting. A practice in which lenders specifically market high-cost or predatory loans to potential customers based on factors such as race, ethnicity, or age. Targeting is a form of discrimination because it targets minorities and other populations and exploits them by offering loans with abusive terms and conditions.

Tax Refund Anticipation Loan. A loan to the **debtor** to be repaid out of the debtor's tax refund. The refund is often then sent directly to the lender. These loans can be very expensive.

Tax Service Fee. The fee charged by a lender for a report about whether the borrower is or has been delinquent on the payment of taxes.

Title. A legal document establishing the right of ownership.

Title Insurance. Insurance to protect the lender (lender's policy) or the buyer (buyer's policy) against loss arising from disputes over ownership or a property.

Title Search. A check of the title records to ensure that the seller is the legal owner of the property and that there are no outstanding liens or other claims on the property.

Triple-Digit Interest. Payday and overdraft loans typically carry triple digit interest rates. The annual percentage rate (APR) for payday and other predatory consumer loans generally exceeds 400%.

Trustee. A trustee is a person or business that is responsible for managing assets for others. In **bankruptcy**, the trustee is a person appointed to administer the bankruptcy case and its assets to maximize the recovery for unsecured creditors.

Truth in Lending Act (TILA). A federal (national) law that requires that most lenders, when they make a loan, provide standard form disclosures of the cost and payment terms of the loan.

Unsecured Creditor. A **creditor** that has no **collateral** for the debt owed.

Underwriting. The process of applying established lending criteria to the qualifications of a particular loan applicant.

Underwriting Fee. A fee charged by a creditor to perform **underwriting**.

Unsecured Creditor. A creditor that has no **collateral** for the debt owed.

Unsecured Debt. A debt that does not involve **collateral**.

Usury. The practice of lending money and charging the borrower interest, especially at an exorbitant or illegally high rate. Examples include **payday**, **overdraft**, and **auto title loans**. Payday loans typically carry an annual percentage rate (APR) of over 400%, sometimes exceeding 1000%. Societies and religions throughout history have banned or limited the charging of interest on loans. Click here to read about the History of Usury.

Variable Rate. Interest rate that changes periodically in relation to an index.

Variable-Rate Mortgage. This is a mortgage loan on which the interest rate can change over time. The changes can affect the amount of your monthly payments.

Wage Assignment. An agreement to have wages paid to a person other than yourself. For example, some people assign a portion of their wages to be paid directly to cover a credit union bill.

Wage Garnishment. Garnishment of the **debtor**'s wages from the debtor's employer.

Warranty. Goods or services you purchase contain explicit and/or implicit promises (called warranties) that the goods or services sold will meet certain standards. A seller's failure to live up to warranties often can be a **defense** to repayment of the debt.

Workout. This term covers a variety of negotiated agreements you might arrange with **creditors** to address a debt you are having trouble paying. Most commonly, the term is used with respect to agreements with a **mortgage** lender to restructure a loan to avoid **foreclosure**.

Yield Spread Premiums (YSP). A fee from a lender to a loan broker paid when the broker arranges a loan where the interest rate on the loan is inflated to an amount higher than the "par" rate. The par rate is the base rate at which the lender will make a loan to borrower on a given day.

Specialized Glossary of Mortgage Servicing Terms

The following is a glossary of terms related to the servicing of consumer mortgages. Advocates may find this glossary helpful in understanding mortgage escrow statements, loan histories, and other client account documents obtained through discovery or in response to a qualified written request under the Real Estate Settlement Procedures Act (RESPA). It includes abbreviations that commonly appear on account statements. However, these account documents often contain numerical codes and other cryptic notations used by servicers to designate particular account transactions. When possible, advocates should request that account histories and statements be provided in a complete and comprehensible format in which all codes are translated, or request that a separate explanation of all transaction codes used by the servicer be provided. The CD-Rom accompanying this handbook includes a list of transaction codes widely used in the mortgage servicing industry.

Acceleration. Action by lender/servicer to declare entire mortgage amount due before maturity date based on specific conditions listed in mortgage, such as payment default.

Accrued Interest. Interest earned for the period of time that has elapsed since interest was last paid.

Adjustment (Adj; Misc Adj). Change to prior account treatment of payment or expense, including reallocation of funds held in suspense account. Also may refer to change in loan terms.

Related terms: Late Charge Adjustment; Miscellaneous Adjustment; Miscellaneous Corporate Adjustments

Attorney Advance. Disbursement for attorney fees, often for collection and foreclosure services on account in default, to be recovered from borrower if permitted under mortgage.

Related terms: Corporate Advance

Bankruptcy (Bk; Bnkrpcy). Bankruptcy filed by borrower, often resulting in internal transfer of servicing to servicer's bankruptcy department or to default servicer.

Bankruptcy Fee. Fee charged to borrower by lender or servicer as a result of bankruptcy filing by borrower, often a flat fee included in amount owed listed on proof of claim filed by servicer in chapter 13 or added to account as recoverable expense or corporate advance without notice to borrower or bankruptcy court approval.

Related terms: Bankruptcy Monitoring Fee; Proof of Claim (POC) Fee

Broker's Price Opinion (BPO). Evaluation of property value typically based on drive-by exterior examination, public data sources, and recent comparable sales, obtained by servicer as alternative to full appraisal after loan is placed in default status or upon loan modification.

Capitalization. Addition of certain amounts to the outstanding principal balance, which may occur, for example, as part of loan modification.
Related terms: Modification

Corporate Advance (Corp Adv). Disbursement for servicing-related expenses (not escrow expenses) paid with servicer funds rather than escrow funds, to be recovered from borrower. May include foreclosure expenses, attorney fees, bankruptcy fees, force placed insurance, and so forth.
Related terms: Expense Advance; Corporate Recoverable Advances

Coupon Payment. Regularly scheduled mortgage payment made in amount reflected on payment coupon, typically sent by borrower to servicer's payment processing center.
Related terms: Lock Box Payment

Cushion. An additional sum of money required by lender to be paid into escrow account as part of monthly escrow payment to protect lender against increases in escrow expenses.
Related terms: Reserve

Daily Accrual Accounting. Method of calculating earned interest on a daily basis, if provided for in note and permitted by state law. Interest is computed at the contract rate on the unpaid balance on the account based on the number of days that lapse from the date prior payment received to the date current payment received.
Related terms: Simple Interest Loan

Default Servicer. Servicer of subprime, home equity, non-performing and other loans in which increased default-related activities are anticipated.
Related terms: Subservicer; Special Servicer

Deferred Charge (DFRD). Charge assessed to account but not initially collected, typically resulting from acceptance of installment payment that does not include, for example, amount for late charge or NSF fee.
Related terms: Deferred Late Charge; Late Charge Assessed; Deferred NSF Charge

Demand Letter. Letter notifying borrower of a delinquency or default, possibly a notice of intent to foreclose.
Related terms: Notice of Intent to Foreclose

Demand Letter Assessment. Fee for sending the demand letter or notice of intent to foreclose.

Disbursement (Disb). Use of funds to pay for servicing-related charges and expenses, including payments made out of escrow.
Related terms: Escrow Disbursement

Due Date. Date on which borrower's monthly installment of principal, interest, and escrow (if applicable) is due as stated in note.

Due Date of Last Paid Installment (DDLPI). Due date of the last fully paid monthly installment of principal, interest, and escrow (if applicable); not the date on which such payment was credited or date of next scheduled installment.

Escrow Account. Trust account into which a borrower's funds are deposited and held to pay taxes, insurance premiums, and other escrow expenses.
Related terms: Trust Account; Impound Account

Escrow Advance (Esc Adv). Disbursement for escrow expense paid with servicer funds at time when insufficient funds in borrower's escrow account, to be recovered from borrower as escrow shortage or deficiency.
Related terms: Expense Advance; Escrow Advance Repayment

Escrow Balance (Esc Bal). Amount of funds remaining in escrow account.

Escrow Deficiency. Amount of a negative balance in an escrow account at the time of an escrow analysis, resulting from escrow advances.

Escrow Payment. Portion of borrower's monthly mortgage payment held by the servicer in escrow account to pay for taxes, insurance premiums, or other escrow items as they become due.

Escrow Shortage. Amount by which current escrow account balance falls short of the projected target balance at the time of an escrow analysis.

Escrow Surplus. Amount by which current escrow account balance exceeds the projected target balance at the time of an escrow analysis.

Expense Advance (Exp Adv). May be either corporate advance or escrow advance (see definitions above).

Fee Code (Fee Cde; Tran). Numerical code used by servicer to designate type of account transaction.
Related terms: Transaction Code

Forbearance. Plan to cure default that may involve temporary suspension of payments or repayment plan based on modified payment amount (with portion paid towards past due amount), extending typically for 3 to 12 months.
Related terms: Loss Mitigation Option; Workout Plan

Force Placed Insurance. Hazard insurance purchased by servicer on borrower's home (covering only lender's interest) when policy purchased directly by borrower on non-escrow mortgage account has lapsed, when servicer contends that borrower has failed to provide proof of insurance coverage, or when account is in default.

Hazard Premium (Haz Ins). Premium for hazard insurance on borrower's home.

Interest on Escrow (Esc Int). Interest earned on funds held in escrow account paid either directly to borrower or credited to escrow account.

Interest Payment (Int). Portion of borrower payment applied to mortgage interest.

Interest Short (Int Sh; Int Arr; Bal). Earned interest remaining unpaid after application of mortgage payment, typically reflected on account history as negative balance. Frequently occurs on loans with negative amortization or when irregular payments made under daily accrual accounting method.
Related terms: Accrued but Unpaid Interest; Interest Shortfall

Irregular Payment. Mortgage payment made in amount or at time different than regularly scheduled payment under terms of note.
Related terms: Non-coupon Payment

Late Charge Assessed. Fee charged to borrower's account when payment made after due date (usually fifteen days after due date).
Related terms: Late Charge Adjustment; Deferred Late Charge

Loan Modification. Agreement to permanently change one or more terms of original mortgage (e.g., change in interest rate, payment amount, term, or capitalization of arrears over extended term) as means to resolve default or to settle litigation between parties.
Related terms: Loss Mitigation Option; Workout Plan

Lock Box Payment. Borrower payment sent to designated address (usually post office box) at the servicer's payment processing center (servicer may outsource service to third-party company who collects mail directed to post office box and deposits funds to servicer's bank account).
Related terms: Coupon Payment

Master Servicer. Servicer responsible for protecting interests of mortgage-backed securities' certificate holders and oversight of primary servicers.

Related terms: Primary Servicer

Mortgage Electronic Registration System (MERS). Electronic registry system for tracking ownership of individual mortgages, servicing rights, and security interests used by MERS members.

Mortgage Identification Number (MIN). Number assigned to a mortgage that is registered with MERS (see definition above) and used for identification and various other purposes for life of mortgage.

Mortgage Insurance Premium (MIP). Payment of private mortgage insurance (PMI) premium (see definition for PMI).

Partial Payment. Payment that is less than total amount due. Servicer will return to borrower or accept and either apply to account or hold as unapplied (typically in suspense account).

Related terms: Unapplied Payment; Payment Shortage

Partial Reinstatement. Change in account status from default to current based on borrower payment of less than total amount due and completion of repayment plan for remaining arrearage.

Related terms: Reinstatement; Full Reinstatement

Payment Amount (Pmt Amt). Regular installment payment amount, which includes principal, interest and, if applicable, escrow.

Pay-Off Fee. Fee charged to borrower for providing statement of amount required to pay off loan.

Related terms: Fax Fee

Primary Servicer. Servicer responsible for payment collection, cash management, escrow administration, and loan reporting to mortgage-backed securities' trustees and certificate holders. Some functions may be delegated to subservicer.

Related terms: Master Servicer

Principal (Prin). Sum of money outstanding on mortgage upon which interest is payable.

Principal Payment. Portion of borrower payment applied to mortgage principal.

Private Mortgage Insurance (PMI). Insurance to protect lender against loss if borrower defaults. Similar to insurance by government entities such as FHA, except issued by private mortgage insurance company. Premium is paid by borrower as part of monthly mortgage payment.

Property Inspection Fee (Insp). Fee charged to borrower for inspections (usually drive-by) to determine the physical condition or occupancy status of mortgage property, often imposed repeatedly once account is placed in default status.

Related terms: Property Preservation Fee

Property Preservation Disbursement. Disbursement by servicer for securing, winterizing, and repairing property that has been foreclosed (real estate owned). May also refer to fees for property inspections, broker price opinions, and foreclosure expenses.

Recovery. Distribution of borrower payment or funds to servicer as reimbursement of escrow, corporate, or other advances.

Related terms: Escrow Advance Recovery

Redistribution. Application of payment or other posting to two or more accounts.

Refund. Funds returned to borrower, often following escrow account analysis showing surplus.

Returned Check Fee (NSF Fee; NSF Chk Chg). Charge imposed for bounced check.

   Related terms: Non-sufficient Fund Fee; Deferred Charge

Real Estate Owned (REO). Property acquired by lender as a result of foreclosure or deed in lieu of foreclosure.

Reinstatement. Change in account status from default to current, typically upon acceptance of all payments due (full reinstatement).

   Related terms: Full Reinstatement; Partial Reinstatement

Repayment. Disbursement to servicer as recovery of corporate or escrow advance.

Reserve. An additional sum of money required by lender to be paid into escrow account as part of monthly escrow payment to protect lender against increases in escrow expenses.

   Related terms: Cushion

Reversal. Removal of previously imposed charge or reapplication of previously credited payment. Generally involves two-step accounting process in which item is reversed in one transaction and reapplied in another transaction.

   Related terms: NSF Reversal

Servicing Advances. Funds advanced by servicer under terms of agreement with lender to cover servicing costs and expenses as they occur.

Short Payment. Payment made in less than full monthly amount due under the loan payment schedule, often held in suspense account until full amount received.

   Related terms: Irregular Payment

SpeedPay Fee. Fee charged for making electronic payment.

Statutory Expense (Stat Exp). Any tax, special assessment, or other charge imposed by federal, state, or local taxing authority or other governmental entity. Generally does not refer to taxes paid through escrow account but rather corporate advances to cover such charges when account is in default or property facing tax sale, or following a foreclosure.

Suspense Account (Susp; Misc Susp). Catch-all account used as place to temporarily put funds that are in "suspense" until servicer makes decision on how to permanently allocate or apply, often used to hold less than full installment payments or payments received while account in default.

   Related terms: Corporate Suspense Account; Suspense Activity; Partial Payment; Unapplied Payment; Unapplied Funds

Suspense Balance (Susp Bal). Amount of funds held in suspense account.

   Related terms: Unapplied Funds

Tax Penalty. Interest, late charge, or other penalty imposed by taxing authority for late payment of taxes.

Transaction Date. Date reflected on payment or account history showing time when servicer completed account transaction or took other action.

Transaction Description. Notation on payment or account history often in code describing nature of, or reason for, application of payment, disbursement, or other servicer action.

Trustee Suspense Account. Suspense account used by servicer to hold payments received from chapter 13 bankruptcy trustee pursuant to borrower's chapter 13 plan providing for cure of pre-petition mortgage arrearages.

GLOSSARIES

Unapplied Payment. Payment that is less than total amount due. Servicer will return to borrower or hold as unapplied (typically in suspense account).

    Related terms: Partial Payment; Payment Shortage

Unapplied Funds. Portion of partial payment remaining after accepted by servicer and applied to one or more full installments, typically held in suspense account until enough funds received to make full installment.

    Related terms: Partial Payment

Index

NOTES

NOTES

NOTES

NOTES

NOTES

NOTES

NOTES

NOTES

ORDER FORM

☐ Foreclosure Prevention Counseling with CD-Rom .... $50.

☐ The NCLC Guide to Surviving Debt .... $20.

☐ The NCLC Guide to the Rights of Utility Consumers .... $15.

☐ The NCLC Guide to Consumer Rights for Domestic Violence Survivors .... $15.

☐ The NCLC Guide to Mobile Homes .... $12.

☐ Stop Predatory Lending with CD-Rom .... $60.

(orders before July 15, 2007—$50)

For Lawyers:

☐ Foreclosures: Defenses, Workouts and Mortgage Servicing with CD-Rom .... $90.

☐ Bankruptcy Basics (available after July 15, 2007) .... $70.

☐ Consumer Bankruptcy Law and Practice with CD-Rom .... $180.

Call for bulk discounts on orders of 5 or more of same title.

Prices include shipping and handling within the continental U.S.
Outside continental U.S., add $5 for each title.

Name _____

Organization _____

Street Address _____

City _____ State _____ Zip _____

Telephone _____

Fax _____

E-mail _____

Mail to: National Consumer Law Center
77 Summer Street, 10th Floor
Boston, MA 02110-1006

☐ Check or money order enclosed, payable
to the National Consumer Law Center

☐ MasterCard ☐ VISA ☐ AMERICAN EXPRESS Cards

3 Easy Ways to Order

📞 Call (617) 542-9595

📠 Fax (617) 542-8028

www Online
www.consumerlaw.org

Card# ☐☐☐☐☐☐☐☐☐☐☐☐☐☐☐☐

Exp. Date ☐☐☐☐ Signature _____

(card number, expiration date, and signature must accompany charge orders)

NATIONAL CONSUMER LAW CENTER

77 Summer Street, 10th Floor · Boston, MA 02110-1006

Tel. (617) 542-9595 · FAX (617) 542-8028 · publications@nclc.org

Order securely online at
www.consumerlaw.org

About the CD-Rom

This CD-Rom contains numerous consumer education brochures, handbooks, and many other documents to assist foreclosure prevention counselors and their clients. The documents are in Adobe PDF format, making them easy to print or view onscreen. The CD-Rom includes:

- Sample foreclosure prevention counseling forms;
- Consumer information, including information on credit card debt and an EITC brochure;
- Sample loan documents;
- Summaries of state foreclosure laws;
- Summaries of state real estate tax abatement laws;
- HUD handbooks and 18 mortgagee letters regarding FHA-insured loans;
- Handbooks and letters regarding Section 502 RHS-held loans;
- Handbooks regarding VA-guaranteed loans;
- Fannie Mae and Freddie Mac information;
- Schedule of standard attorney fees approved by HUD and investors;
- Bibliography and list of helpful websites; and
- PAD loan calculator.

Important Information Before Opening the CD-Rom Package

Before opening the CD-Rom package, please read this information. Opening the package constitutes acceptance of the following described terms. In addition, the <u>book</u> is not returnable once the seal to the <u>CD-Rom</u> has been broken.

The CD-Rom is copyrighted and all rights are reserved by the National Consumer Law Center, Inc. No copyright is claimed to the text of statutes, regulations, excerpts from court opinions, or any part of an original work prepared by a United States Government employee.

You may not commercially distribute the CD-Rom or otherwise reproduce, publish, distribute or use the disk in any manner that may infringe on any copyright or other proprietary right of the National Consumer Law Center. Nor may you otherwise transfer the disk or this agreement to any other party unless that party agrees to accept the terms and conditions of this agreement. You may use the disk on only one computer and by one user at a time.

The CD-Rom is warranted to be free of defects in materials and faulty workmanship under normal use for a period of ninety days after purchase. If a defect is discovered in the disk during this warranty period, a replacement disk can be obtained at no charge by sending the defective disk, postage prepaid, with information identifying the purchaser, to National Consumer Law Center, Publications Department, 77 Summer Street, 10th Floor, Boston, MA 02110. After the ninety-day period, a replacement will be available on the same terms, but will also require a $15 prepayment.

The National Consumer Law Center makes no other warranty or representation, either express or implied, with respect to this disk, its quality, performance, merchantability, or fitness for a particular purpose. In no event will the National Consumer Law Center be liable for direct, indirect, special, incidental, or consequential damages arising out of the use or inability to use the disk. The exclusion of implied warranties is not effective in some states, and thus this exclusion may not apply to you.

HOW TO USE THE CD-ROM

Use of this CD-Rom requires a Windows-based PC with a CD-Rom drive. (Mac users report success using NCLC CD-Roms, but the CD-Rom has only been tested with Windows-based PCs.) You must have Adobe Acrobat or Adobe Reader 5.0 or later to use this CD-Rom. An installation program for Adobe Reader 7 is included free on this CD-Rom in the Adobe_Reader_7 folder.

To use the CD-Rom, simply insert it into your CD-Rom drive, open your CD-Rom drive in My Computer, and double-click Start.pdf. Adobe Reader will start automatically and open the main menu. Click a button or bookmark to jump to a document. Click the START bookmark on the left or use Adobe Reader's Back button to return to the main menu.

PDF documents can be easily printed within Acrobat by clicking File→Print.

The sample foreclosure prevention counseling forms are also available in Microsoft Word format via a link on the main menu. If you do not have Microsoft Word, the files can be opened within WordPerfect by choosing File→Open and browsing the Word_files folder on the CD-Rom.

ABOUT THE CALCULATOR

The CD-Rom also includes a PAD loan calculator that can solve for the monthly payment amount, loan term, interest rate, or total amount due if you know the other three variables. It also allows you to recalculate any of these terms if a workout plan modifies one variable, but keeps two other variables constant.

The calculator is a spreadsheet that must be opened in Microsoft Excel (not included). To use it, find the file on the CD-Rom called PAD Loan Calculator.xls and double-click it to open it in Excel. Enter loan terms in the green boxes and press the Tab key to calculate the result.